Working with Discourse

2nd Edition

Working with Discourse
Meaning beyond the clause

J. R. Martin and David Rose

B L O O M S B U R Y

LONDON · NEW DELHI · NEW YORK · SYDNEY

Bloomsbury Academic
An imprint of Bloomsbury Publishing Plc

50 Bedford Square
London
WC1B 3DP
UK

1385 Broadway
New York
NY 10018
USA

www.bloomsbury.com

First published in 2003 by the Continuum International Publishing Group Ltd
This edition published 2007
Reprinted 2011, 2012
Reprinted by Bloomsbury Academic 2013

Acknowledgements
The authors are grateful to the following publishers for permission to reprint extracts:
Long Walk to Freedom, by Nelson Mandela. © Nelson Rolihlahla Mandela, 1994. By
permission of Little, Brown and Company (Inc.).
No Future without Forgiveness, by Desmond Tutu, published by Rider. Reprinted by
permission of The Random House Group Limited.

British Library Cataloguing-in-Publication Data
A catalogue record for this book is available from the British Library.

ISBN: HB: 978-0-8264-8849-7
PB: 978-0-8264-8850-3

Library of Congress Cataloging-in-Publication Data
Martin, J. R.
Working with discourse: meaning beyond the clause/J. R. Martin & David
Rose.
p. cm. — (Open linguistics series)
Includes bibliographical references and index.
ISBN 0-8264-5507-7 — ISBN 0-8264-5508-5 (pbk.)
1. Discourse analysis. I. Rose, David, 1955- II. Title. III. Series.
P302.M373 2002
401'.41–dc21
2002067099

Typeset by BookEns Ltd, Royston, Herts.

Contents

List of Figures

List of Tables

Preface to the Second Edition

In this edition of *Working with Discourse* we have expanded and refined the tools for discourse analysis offered in the first edition. The book takes Martin's 1992 book *English Text* as point of departure, and extends this work taking into account developments in the last decade or so, presenting it for a general audience interested in discourse analysis. The tools are informed by systemic functional linguistics, but we have endeavoured to keep them as accessible as possible for a broad readership. Our focus is on discourse semantics rather than grammar or social context because it seems to us that, while there is a lot of analysis at the levels of grammar and genre going on around the world, there is a growing need and expanding opportunities for work that bridges systematically between these levels. This book attempts to fill that gap with analyses of meanings beyond the clause that make contact with social context.

We are grateful to our functional linguistic colleagues around the world whose interest has given value to this work over the years, at meetings and over the Internet, and especially to readers of the first edition who have given us valuable feedback. Many of these work in the field of educational linguistics, where a lot of the analysis considered here has been deployed – especially in the context of Australia's distinctive genre-based literacy programmes across education sectors. Without this dialectic of theory and practice, the ideas in this book would never have evolved.

Our intellectual debt to Ruqaiya Hasan and Michael Halliday will be obvious to readers on every page. We respectfully dedicate the book to them, in gratitude for all the meanings they have given us to explore – meanings which have shaped our lives in so many many ways.

Sydney, September 2006

For Ruqaiya and Michael
whose meanings we're embroidering upon

Interpreting social discourse

1.1 An invitation

In this book we are concerned with interpreting discourse by analysing it. For us this means treating discourse as more than words in clauses; we want to focus on meaning beyond the clause, on semantic resources that lead us from one clause to another as a text unfolds. And it also means that we treat discourse as more than an incidental manifestation of social activity; we want to focus on the social as it is constructed through texts, on the constitutive role of meanings in social life. In a sense then this book is an invitation to grammarians to reconsider meaning in the clause from the perspective of meaning in texts; and it is also an invitation to social theorists to reconsider social activity as meaning we negotiate in discourse.

Our starting point then, for interpreting social discourse, is with texts in social contexts. Social discourse rarely consists of just single clauses, rather social contexts develop as sequences of meanings comprising texts. Since each text is produced interactively between speakers, and between writers and (potential) readers, we can use it to interpret the interaction it manifests. And since each interaction is an instance of the speakers' culture, we can also use the text to interpret aspects of the culture it manifests.

We should emphasize that although we can assign a name to each of these phenomena, a *clause*, a *text* or a *culture* are not 'things', but social processes that

clause
(Helena in time and place)

My story begins in my late
teenage years as a farm girl
in the Bethlehem district . . .

text
(Helena's story of injustice)

As an eighteen-year-old, I met a
young man in his twenties. He was
working in a top security structure.
It was the beginning of a beautiful
relationship. We even spoke about
marriage. A bubbly, vivacious man
who beamed out wild energy. Sharply
intelligent. Even if he was an Englishman, he was popular with all the
'Boer' Afrikaners. And all my girlfriends envied me. Then one day he
said he was going on a 'trip'. 'We
won't see each other again . . . maybe
never ever again.' I was torn to
pieces. So was he.

culture
(the struggle for justice in South Africa)

Figure 1.1 Clause–text–culture

unfold at different time scales. Culture unfolds through uncountable series of
situations, as our lives unfold through these situations as learners, speakers and
actors, producing texts that unfold as sequences of meanings. The relationship
between these phenomena is schematized in Figure 1.1, illustrating the scaling in
size and complexity from clause to text to culture.

Figure 1.1 shows one clause as an instance of the story of 'Helena', whose life
was caught up in the injustices of apartheid South Africa, as Helena's story is one
instance of the cultural changes that culminated with the release of Nelson Mandela
and the overthrow of apartheid. Helena's story is one of the texts we use to
interpret discourse throughout this book, and we will return to it often, examining
its sequences of meanings from different perspectives, to understand just how it
manifests the changing culture it is part of.

In order to keep our analyses manageable, we focus intensively in the book on a
small set of texts, all concerned with the processes of truth and reconciliation in
South Africa. We chose this context for two reasons: because we expect it will be
relatively familiar to many readers, and because we believe the reconciliation
process in post-apartheid South Africa is an inspiration for engaging with
difference in the post-colonial world. One text we focus on is Helena's story, which
is about the effects on herself and the men in her life of their violations of other

people's human rights; one is an argument by Desmond Tutu, about amnesty for such offenders, from his recent book *No Future without Forgiveness*; another is the Act of Parliament establishing the Truth and Reconciliation Commission; and the last is the film *Forgiveness*, the story of an ex-policeman asking forgiveness from the family of a resistance fighter he murdered in the apartheid years. These are complementary kinds of texts that allow us to explore a wide range of discourse meanings within a single field of social activity. As another strategy for keeping things manageable our primary focus is on written texts, but in this new edition we have included a new chapter on spoken discourse (see Eggins and Slade (1997) for excellent scaffolding for spoken discourse analysis). And we'll be sticking to English, although we know from our own work on two very different languages, Tagalog and Pitjantjatjara, and from the work of SFL researchers around the world, that comparable resources are found across languages (Caffarel *et al.* 2004, Rose 2001b, 2005a).

1.2 A framework for discussion

Any description or analysis involving language implies some theory of how language works, and we want to be explicit about the model we are using, rather than leaving it unsaid. The framework for our discussion is the model of language in social context that has been developed within the broad field of systemic functional linguistics (SFL). SFL researchers have been actively concerned for several generations with the semantics of discourse. However, we will not assume that readers are familiar with this theory, or with its grammatical descriptions of English and other languages. Rather we will introduce relevant aspects of theory and description as they are required, illustrating them with examples from our texts. In the process we will gradually introduce a shared language for talking about discourse – a metalanguage that includes both a model of language in context, and the terms we use for talking about it. We will use only those technical terms that we need to consolidate understandings and make them portable, so that they can be used easily for as wide a range of analytical tasks as possible. And portability is one aim of this book. We want to build up a tool kit for discourse analysis that readers can take away with them when they go. But we'll build up this metalinguistic tool kit the way people learn languages, by experiencing meaningful instances in actual texts.

SFL has been described as an 'extravagant' theory; its extravagance has evolved to manage the complexity of the phenomenon it describes. But despite the complexity of language in social contexts, the basic principles developed in SFL for managing it are relatively simple. To begin with we will briefly introduce two general perspectives for looking at the phenomena of discourse. These two perspectives are:

- [relevant] levels[1] of language: as grammar, as discourse, and as social context (known as the **strata** of language)
- three general functions of language in social contexts: to enact our relationships, to represent our experience, and to organize discourse as meaningful text (known as **metafunctions**).

Strata: grammar, discourse and social context

The focus of this book is on the analysis of discourse. In SFL, discourse analysis interfaces with the analysis of grammar and the analysis of social activity, somewhere between the work of grammarians on the one hand and social theorists on the other. This has partly to do with the size of what we're looking at; texts are bigger than a clause and smaller than a culture. Grammarians are particularly interested in types of clauses and their elements. But texts are usually bigger than single clauses, so a discourse analyst has more to worry about than a grammarian (expanded horizons). By the same token, cultures manifest themselves through a myriad of texts, and social theorists are more interested in how social contexts are related to one another than in how they are internally organized as texts (global horizons). Discourse analysis employs the tools of grammarians to identify the roles of wordings in passages of text, and employs the tools of social theorists to explain why they make the meanings they do. These two points of view on discourse are illustrated in Figure 1.2. Grammar, discourse and social activity are symbolized as a series of circles, in which discourse nestles within social activity and grammar nestles within discourse, suggesting three complementary perspectives on a single complex phenomenon. This type of diagram is often used in SFL to symbolize its evolving model of language in social context.

Realization: culture, meaning and wording

What is the relation between grammar, discourse and social context? Obviously cultures aren't just a combination of texts, and likewise texts aren't just a combination of clauses. Social activity, discourse and grammar are different kinds of phenomena, operating at different levels of abstraction: a culture is more abstract than a text, and the meanings that make up a text are in turn more abstract than the wordings that express them. The relation between these strata is described in SFL as **realization**; social contexts are realized as texts which are realized as sequences of clauses.

Realization is a kind of re-coding like the mapping of hardware through software to the images and words we see on the screen on our computers. Another

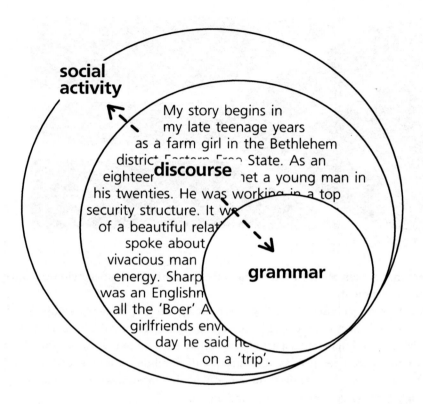

Figure 1.2 Points of view on discourse: from social activity and from grammar

way of thinking about this is symbolization. An example is the flag of the new democratic South Africa, reproduced in Figure 1.3 (and discussed in more detail in Chapter 9 below). The flag consists of a 'Y' shape converging from left to right, in six colours: red, white, blue, black, yellow and green. According to the South African government website (www.polity.org.za/html), the design:

> ... can be interpreted as the convergence of diverse elements within South African society, taking the road ahead in unity. The theme of convergence and unity ties in with the motto of the National Coat of Arms, 'Unity is Strength'.

The official interpretation cautions that 'individual colours, or colour combinations have different meanings for different people and therefore no universal symbolism should be attached to any of the colours'. But the new flag clearly does include historically significant symbols: red, white and blue were the colours of the South African flag of the pre-apartheid era (based on the British ensign), and black, green and yellow are the colours of the African National

Figure 1.3 New South African flag

Congress that Nelson Mandela led through the decades of anti-apartheid resistance and into government.

So we have the colours of the flag symbolizing 'diverse elements within South African society', and their convergence symbolizing 'the road ahead in unity'. Symbolizing is an important aspect of realization, since grammar both symbolizes and encodes discourse, just as discourse both symbolizes and encodes social activity. The concept of realization embodies the meanings of 'symbolizing', 'encoding', 'expressing', 'manifesting' and so on.

As the meaning of the South African flag is more than the sum of its shapes and colours, so too is discourse more than the sum of its wordings, and culture more than the sum of its texts. For example, here's part of the story we'll be working on later. The narrator, Helena, is talking about separating from her first love:

> Then one day he said he was going on a 'trip'. 'We won't see each other again...
> maybe never ever again.' I was torn to pieces.

The last clause here, *I was torn to pieces*, tells us how Helena felt; but because of the way meaning unfolds through the discourse phases of 'meeting', 'description' and 'leaving' it also tells us why she felt upset; there's an explanation going on which transcends the meaning of the individual clauses. Taken one by one, each clause describes what happened; taken together they explain it.

Similarly for text and culture. At the beginning of the argument we'll be working on below, Desmond Tutu asks a question and comments on its significance:

> So is amnesty being given at the cost of justice being done? This is not a frivolous
> question, but a very serious issue, one which challenges the integrity of the entire Truth
> and Reconciliation process.

He goes on to give reasons why he'd answer 'no'; and earlier he posed a similar question, which his exposition is just now getting round to answering:

Are the critics right: was the Truth and Reconciliation process immoral?

But there is more to his question than what precedes or follows in his book. The question strikes to the heart of the whole reconciliation process in South Africa and the role played in it by the Truth and Reconciliation Commission. A whole range of texts have posed the question, as a glance at Tutu's book or a visit to the Truth and Reconciliation website shows. The social processes round the issue are very complex, involving all kinds of discourse and a great range of interests. The social meaning transcends the meaning of the individual texts through which it is negotiated. What Tutu refers to as *the entire Truth and Reconciliation process* is a higher order meaning comprising just an aspect of the cultures we recognize as post-colonial episodes in our unfolding world.

Metafunctions: interpersonal, ideational and textual

The SFL model of language in social context recognizes three general social functions that we use language for: (i) to enact our social relationships; (ii) to represent our experience to each other; and (iii) to organize our enactments and representations as meaningful text. These are known as the **metafunctions** of language in social activity:

- the **interpersonal** metafunction to enact relationships
- the **ideational** metafunction to represent experience
- the **textual** metafunction to organize text.

As social discourse unfolds, these three functions are interwoven with each other, so that we can achieve all three social functions simultaneously. In other words we can look at any piece of discourse from any of these three perspectives, and identify different functions realized by different patterns of meaning.

In this book, each chapter considers sets of meanings serving one or another of these metafunctions. These sets of meanings are known as discourse systems. The name of each chapter is the name of the particular discourse system that it considers. These are grouped alongside their metafunction in Table 1.1. The table also gives a brief gloss of the overall function of each system.

Table 1.1 Chapters, discourse systems and metafunctions

Chapters	Discourse systems	Metafunction
Appraisal	'negotiating attitudes'	interpersonal
Ideation	'representing experience'	ideational
Conjunction	'connecting events'	ideational
Identification	'tracking people and things'	textual
Periodicity	'information flow'	textual
Negotiation	'enacting exchanges'	interpersonal

1.3 Genre

We use the term **genre** in this book to refer to different types of texts that enact various types of social contexts. As children, we learn to recognize and distinguish the typical genres of our culture, by attending to consistent patterns of meaning as we interact with others in various situations. Since patterns of meaning are relatively consistent for each genre, we can learn to predict how each situation is likely to unfold, and learn how to interact in it.

Such predictable patterns of meaning can vary from the relatively simple range of language resources we might use to greet our neighbours, or to buy goods in a shop, to the more complex meanings we might find in scientific reports or political debates. But even such complex meanings fall into consistent patterns that make it possible for us to recognize and predict how each genre is likely to unfold, and so manage new information, and interact appropriately and strategically.

The number of recognizably distinct genres in any culture may be quite large, but not unmanageably so. In contemporary western culture we could name many spoken genres whose patterns of meaning are more or less predictable, such as *greetings cards, service encounters, casual conversations, arguments, telephone enquiries, instructions, lectures, debates, plays, jokes, games* and so on; and within each of these general types, we could name many more specific genres. In this book we will mainly be exploring written genres that we will name and describe as we go.

For us a genre is a staged, goal-oriented social process. Social because we participate in genres with other people; goal-oriented because we use genres to get things done; staged because it usually takes us a few steps to reach our goals. In this book we're focusing on three families of genres – story, argument and legislation. We'll look briefly at their staging here so we can get a feel for the basic organization of these texts. As we develop our five strands of discourse analysis we'll look more and more closely at how they are organized.

First Helena's story. This story[2] is presented in Desmond Tutu's book *No Future without Forgiveness* to support his argument for amnesty for human rights violators, as part of South Africa's Truth and Reconciliation process. The narrator is introduced by Tutu, and Helena orients her story by setting it in time and place:

Orientation   My story begins in my late teenage years as a farm girl in the Bethlehem district of Eastern Free State.

Her tale then unfolds as a story genre known as an 'exemplum', a kind of moral tale related to fables, parables and gossip. Its social purpose is to present a problematic incident and then interpret it for the audience, commenting on the behaviour of the people involved. This story type contrasts with the 'narrative' story type that typically presents a problem which is then resolved by the lead characters. An exemplum consists of the basic stages Orientation, Incident and Interpretation.

Helena's story includes two Incident stages. The first Incident deals with her first love and the second Incident with her second love. Each Incident has basically the same organization, involving three phases. First Helena meets her love, he then starts working in secret police operations, and he and Helena then have to face the repercussions. This structure is summarized as follows, including the first clause of each phase:

Incident 1
'falling in love'   As an eighteen-year-old, I met a young man . . .
'operations'   Then one day he said he was going on a 'trip'.
'repercussions'   More than a year ago, I met my first love again . . .

Incident 2
'falling in love'   After my unsuccessful marriage, I met another policeman.
'operations'   Then he says: He and three of our friends have been promoted.
'repercussions'   After about three years with the special forces, our hell began.

Helena then goes on to interpret the significance of these events, and this Interpretation stage goes through three phases. The first phase outlines her new knowledge of the crimes committed by her man under orders from 'those at the top'; in the second she understands and identifies with the struggle of black South Africans; in the third she accuses the cowardly leaders of her own people:

Interpretation
'knowledge'   Today I know the answer to all my questions and heartache.
'black struggle'   I finally understand what the struggle was really about.
'white guilt'   What do we have? Our leaders are too holy and innocent.

Following her Interpretation, Helena ends her story with a Coda, quoting her 'wasted vulture's' perspective on his punishment:

Coda	*I end with a few lines that my wasted vulture said to me*

The stages of a genre are relatively stable components of its organization, that we can recognize in some form in instance after instance of the genre, such as the Orientation, Incident and Interpretation stages of an exemplum. These stages are some of the basic resources of the culture for organizing discourse at the level of the text; we use initial capitals to label them. But phases within each stage are much more variable; often, as in Helena's story, phases may be unique to the particular text, so we label them notionally, with quotation marks. Her story is presented below with its stages and phases indicated:

Orientation
My story begins in my late teenage years as a farm girl in the Bethlehem district of Eastern Free State.

Incident 1
'falling in love'
As an eighteen-year-old, I met a young man in his twenties. He was working in a top security structure. It was the beginning of a beautiful relationship. We even spoke about marriage. A bubbly, vivacious man who beamed out wild energy. Sharply intelligent. Even if he was an Englishman, he was popular with all the 'Boer' Afrikaners. And all my girlfriends envied me.

'operations'
Then one day he said he was going on a 'trip'. 'We won't see each other again. . . maybe never ever again.' I was torn to pieces. So was he. An extremely short marriage to someone else failed all because I married to forget.

'repercussions'
More than a year ago, I met my first love again through a good friend. I was to learn for the first time that he had been operating overseas and that he was going to ask for amnesty. I can't explain the pain and bitterness in me when I saw what was left of that beautiful, big, strong person. He had only one desire – that the truth must come out. Amnesty didn't matter. It was only a means to the truth.

Incident 2
'falling in love'
After my unsuccessful marriage, I met another policeman. Not quite my first love, but an exceptional person. Very special. Once again a bubbly, charming personality. Humorous, grumpy, everything in its time and place.

'operations'
Then he says: He and three of our friends have been promoted. 'We're moving to a special unit. Now, now my darling. We are real policemen now.' We were ecstatic. We even celebrated. He and his friends would visit regularly. They even stayed over for long

periods. Suddenly, at strange times, they would become restless. Abruptly mutter the feared word 'trip' and drive off. I . . . as a loved one . . . knew no other life than that of worry, sleeplessness, anxiety about his safety and where they could be. We simply had to be satisfied with: 'What you don't know, can't hurt you.' And all that we as loved ones knew. . .was what we saw with our own eyes.

'repercussions'
After about three years with the special forces, our hell began. He became very quiet. Withdrawn. Sometimes he would just press his face into his hands and shake uncontrollably. I realized he was drinking too much. Instead of resting at night, he would wander from window to window. He tried to hide his wild consuming fear, but I saw it. In the early hours of the morning between two and half-past-two, I jolt awake from his rushed breathing. Rolls this way, that side of the bed. He's pale. Ice cold in a sweltering night – sopping wet with sweat. Eyes bewildered, but dull like the dead. And the shakes. The terrible convulsions and blood-curdling shrieks of fear and pain from the bottom of his soul. Sometimes he sits motionless, just staring in front of him. I never understood. I never knew. Never realised what was being shoved down his throat during the 'trips'. I just went through hell. Praying, pleading: 'God, what's happening? What's wrong with him? Could he have changed so much? Is he going mad? I can't handle the man anymore! But, I can't get out. He's going to haunt me for the rest of my life if I leave him. Why, God?'

Interpretation
'knowledge'
Today I know the answer to all my questions and heartache. I know where everything began, the background. The role of 'those at the top', the 'cliques' and 'our men' who simply had to carry out their bloody orders. . . like 'vultures'. And today they all wash their hands in innocence and resist the realities of the Truth Commission. Yes, I stand by my murderer who let me and the old White South Africa sleep peacefully. Warmly, while 'those at the top' were again targeting the next 'permanent removal from society' for the vultures.

'black struggle'
I finally understand what the struggle was really about. I would have done the same had I been denied everything. If my life, that of my children and my parents was strangled with legislation. If I had to watch how white people became dissatisfied with the best and still wanted better and got it. I envy and respect the people of the struggle – at least their leaders have the guts to stand by their vultures, to recognise their sacrifices.

'white guilt'
What do we have? Our leaders are too holy and innocent. And faceless. I can understand if Mr F. W. de Klerk says he didn't know, but dammit, there must be a clique, there must have been someone out there who is still alive and who can give a face to 'the orders from above' for all the operations. Dammit! What else can this abnormal life be than a cruel human rights violation? Spiritual murder is more inhumane than a messy, physical murder. At least a murder victim rests. I wish I had the

power to make those poor wasted people whole again. I wish I could wipe the old South Africa out of everyone's past.

Coda

I end with a few lines that my wasted vulture said to me one night: 'They can give me amnesty a thousand times. Even if God and everyone else forgives me a thousand times – I have to live with this hell. The problem is in my head, my conscience. There is only one way to be free of it. Blow my brains out. Because that's where my hell is.' (Tutu 1999: 49–51)

Next the argument. Tutu's text belongs to the argument genre known as 'exposition'. An exposition consists of the basic stages Thesis and supporting Arguments. Its social purpose is to persuade an audience to the writer's point of view, the 'thesis'. Expositions contrast with the argument genre known as 'discussion', in which two or more points of view are presented and one argued for over the others.

In this exposition Tutu is debating whether giving amnesty is just. In the beginning, instead of stating his Thesis in the usual way, he poses the issue as a question:

Thesis   *So is amnesty being given at the cost of justice being done?*

He then develops three Arguments as to why his answer is 'No'. Each of these three Arguments has two phases. In the first phase Tutu gives the 'grounds' on which he is arguing, and in the second he reaches a 'conclusion' on the basis of this evidence. Tutu uses linkers *also* and *further* to guide us from one Argument to the next, and each conclusion is introduced with the linker *thus*. These linkers are underlined below:

Argument 1   *The Act required that where the offence is a gross violation*
'grounds'   *the application should be dealt with in a public hearing*
'conclusion'   *Thus there is the penalty of public exposure and humiliation*

Argument 2   *It is also not true that ... amnesty encourages impunity*
'grounds'   *because amnesty is only given to those who plead guilty*
'conclusion'   *Thus the process in fact encourages accountability*

Argument 3   *Further, retributive justice...is not the only form of justice*
'grounds'   *there is another kind of justice, restorative justice,*
'conclusion'   *Thus we would claim that... justice is being served*

In Tutu's original text, Helena's story follows the first Argument, supporting its conclusion, and the whole exposition is part of a longer debate (we'll come back to the ways genres fit together in discourse in Chapters 8 and 9):

Thesis

So is amnesty being given at the cost of justice being done? This is not a frivolous question, but a very serious issue, one which challenges the integrity of the entire Truth and Reconciliation process.

Argument 1

'grounds'

The Act required that where the offence is a gross violation of human rights – defined as an abduction, killing, torture or severe ill-treatment – the application should be dealt with in a public hearing unless such a hearing was likely to lead to a miscarriage of justice (for instance, where witnesses were too intimidated to testify in open session). In fact, virtually all the important applications to the Commission have been considered in public in the full glare of television lights.

'conclusion'

Thus there is the penalty of public exposure and humiliation for the perpetrator. Many of those in the security forces who have come forward had previously been regarded as respectable members of their communities. It was often the very first time that their communities and even sometimes their families heard that these people were, for instance, actually members of death squads or regular torturers of detainees in their custody. For some it has been so traumatic that marriages have broken up. That is quite a price to pay.

(The South Africa Broadcasting Corporation's radio team covering the Truth and Reconciliation Commission received a letter from a woman calling herself Helena (she wanted to remain anonymous for fear of reprisals) who lived in the eastern province of Mpumalanga. They broadcast substantial extracts.)

Argument 2

'grounds'

It is also not true that the granting of amnesty encourages impunity in the sense that perpetrators can escape completely the consequences of their actions, because amnesty is only given to those who plead guilty, who accept responsibility for what they have done. Amnesty is not given to innocent people or to those who claim to be innocent. It was on precisely this point that amnesty was refused to the police officers who applied for it for their part in the death of Steve Biko. They denied that they had committed a crime, claiming that they had assaulted him only in retaliation for his inexplicable conduct in attacking them.

'conclusion'

Thus the process in fact encourages accountability rather than the opposite. It supports the new culture of respect for human rights and acknowledgment of responsibility and accountability by which the new democracy wishes to be characterised. It is important to note too that the amnesty provision is an ad hoc arrangement meant for this specific purpose. This is not how justice is to be administered in South Africa for ever. It is for a limited and definite period and purpose.

Argument 3
'grounds'
Further, retributive justice – in which an impersonal state hands down punishment with little consideration for victims and hardly any for the perpetrator – is not the only form of justice. I contend that there is another kind of justice, restorative justice, which is characteristic of traditional African jurisprudence. Here the central concern is not retribution or punishment but, in the spirit of *ubuntu*, the healing of breaches, the redressing of imbalances, the restoration of broken relationships. This kind of justice seeks to rehabilitate both the victim and the perpetrator, who should be given the opportunity to be reintegrated into the community he or she has injured by his or her offence. This is a far more personal approach, which sees the offence as something that has happened to people and whose consequence is a rupture in relationships.

'conclusion'
Thus we would claim that justice, restorative justice, is being served when efforts are being made to work for healing, for forgiveness and for reconciliation. (Tutu 1999: 48–52)

Finally the legislation. Here we have chosen the Act of Parliament establishing the Truth and Reconciliation Commission. This is a much longer text including the following chapters:

1   Interpretation and application
2   Truth and Reconciliation Commission
3   Investigation of human rights violations
4   Amnesty mechanisms and procedures
5   Reparation and rehabilitation of victims
6   Investigations and hearings by Commission
7   General provisions.

These chapters are divided into smaller sections and sub-sections, which we'll pass over here. But before the chapters get going the Act outlines nine 'purposes'; and following this the Act reviews six constitutional 'motivations' for its enactment, each introduced with the causal linker *since*, foregrounded with capital letters. Here we will present just the purposes and motivations phases, leaving the chapters to the Appendix:

PROMOTION OF NATIONAL UNITY AND RECONCILIATION ACT, 1995.
It is hereby notified that the President has assented to the following Act which is hereby published for general information:–

'purposes'
To provide for the investigation and the establishment of as complete a picture as possible of the nature, causes and extent of gross violations of human rights...;
the granting of amnesty to persons who make full disclosure of all the relevant facts...;

affording victims an opportunity to relate the violations they suffered;

the taking of measures aimed at the granting of reparation. . . ;

reporting to the Nation about such violations and victims;

the making of recommendations aimed at the prevention of the commission of gross violations of human rights;

and for the said purposes to provide for the establishment of a Truth and Reconciliation Commission, a Committee on Human Rights Violations, a Committee on Amnesty and a Committee on Reparation and Rehabilitation;

and to confer certain powers on, assign certain functions to and impose certain duties upon that Commission and those Committees;

and to provide for matters connected therewith.

'motivations'

SINCE the Constitution of the Republic of South Africa, 1993 (Act No. 200 of 1993), provides a historic bridge between the past of a deeply divided society characterised by strife, conflict, untold suffering and injustice, and a future founded on the recognition of human rights, democracy and peaceful co-existence for all South Africans, irrespective of colour, race, class, belief or sex;

AND SINCE it is deemed necessary to establish the truth in relation to past events as well as the motives for and circumstances in which gross violations of human rights have occurred, and to make the findings known in order to prevent a repetition of such acts in future;

AND SINCE the Constitution states that the pursuit of national unity, the well-being of all South African citizens and peace require reconciliation between the people of South Africa and the reconstruction of society;

AND SINCE the Constitution states that there is a need for understanding but not for vengeance, a need for reparation but not for retaliation, a need for ubuntu but not for victimization;

AND SINCE the Constitution states that in order to advance such reconciliation and reconstruction amnesty shall be granted in respect of acts, omissions and offences associated with political objectives committed in the course of the conflicts of the past;

AND SINCE the Constitution provides that Parliament shall under the Constitution adopt a law which determines a firm cut-off date, which shall be a date after 8 October 1990 and before the cut-off date envisaged in the Constitution, and providing for the mechanisms, criteria and procedures, including tribunals, if any, through which such amnesty shall be dealt with;

BE IT THEREFORE ENACTED by the Parliament of the Republic of South Africa, as follows:. . . (Office of the President of South Africa 1995)

The chapters that follow spell out the 'provisions' of the Act, which can themselves be divided into 'definitions' and 'actual provisions'. The overall structure of the act is thus purpose, followed by motivation, followed by provisions, as follows. Since these may not be generalizable stages in this genre, we have labelled them with quotes.

'purpose'
'motivation'
'provisions'
    definitions
    actual provisions

1.4 Language, power and ideology

In our view ideology and power run through the whole ensemble of language and culture, positioning people within each social context with more or less power, and opening or narrowing their access to resources for meaning. Of course, up to a point all speakers of a language share an equal range of meaning-making resources, but there are also certain varieties of meanings that are not equally distributed. These include resources for engaging in the written discourses of contemporary social institutions, such as sciences, government and education. One important strand of work in SFL has been to provide access to these discourses through literacy pedagogies grounded in discourse analysis. Another strand has been to investigate the principles by which access to meaning is unequally distributed, along the lines of generation, gender, class, incapacity and ethnicity.

Until very recently, perhaps the most stark example of ideological divisions based on ethnicity was apartheid South Africa. After a long struggle, black South Africans finally overturned the apartheid regime, not with bullets but with words. They succeeded in persuading governments, multinational corporations, and eventually South Africa's white rulers themselves that apartheid was unacceptable and could not viably continue. Today they have embarked on a long-term programme to heal the deep rifts created by generations of state-sponsored racial hatred, large-scale violations of human rights, and impoverishment of the majority of the nation's people. This process has been institutionalized in part as the Truth and Reconciliation Commission, from which our texts are drawn.

Stated in these terms, the victory over apartheid seems like a simple one of right over wrong, good over evil. But of course social conflicts are rarely so simple, as all South Africans may attest. Rather there are usually multiple facets to any contested issue, and multiple positions by different groups. The voices of many groups are to be heard in the texts we analyse in this book, arguing, or being argued for or against, in many subtle ways. The discourse analyses we outline in each chapter enable these voices to emerge clearly, explicitly, from the patterns of meaning in which they are encoded. We'll return to the question of language and ideology in Chapter 9.

1.5 How this book is organized

The chapters of this book are organized around six key sets of resources for making meaning as text. These sets of resources are set out here in the order of the chapters in which they are discussed.

Appraisal is concerned with evaluation – the kinds of attitudes that are negotiated in a text, the strength of the feelings involved and the ways in which values are sourced and readers aligned. Appraisals are interpersonal kinds of meanings, which realize variations in the tenor of social interactions enacted in a text. We begin with appraisal in order to foreground the interactive nature of discourse, including written discourse.

Ideation focuses on the content of a discourse – what kinds of activities are undertaken, and how participants undertaking these activities are described and classified. These are ideational kinds of meaning, that realize the field of a text.

Conjunction looks at inter-connections between activities – reformulating them, adding to them, sequencing them, explaining them and so on. These are also ideational types of meanings, but of the subtype 'logical'. Logical meanings are used to form temporal, causal and other kinds of connectivity.

Identification is concerned with tracking participants – with introducing people, places and things into a discourse and keeping track of them once there. These are textual resources, concerned with how discourse makes sense to the reader by keeping track of identities.

Periodicity considers the rhythm of discourse – the layers of prediction that flag for readers what's to come, and the layers of consolidation that accumulate the meanings made. These are also textual kinds of meanings, concerned with organizing discourse as pulses of information.

Negotiation is concerned with interaction as an exchange between speakers – how speakers adopt roles and assign them to each other in dialogue, and how moves are organized in relation to one another.

Following the discussion of these discourse systems, we then apply them in Chapter 8 to the analysis of one significant text, the final chapter of Nelson Mandela's 1995 autobiography, *Long Road to Freedom*. And in Chapter 9 we then contextualize the discourse systems in models of the social contexts of discourse, including register and genre theory, and we make connections to multi-modal discourse analysis and critical discourse analysis.

We'll now illustrate each of the discourse systems very briefly, by way of flagging what's to come.

Appraisal (evaluation)

The focus here is on attitude – the feelings and values that are negotiated with readers. The key resources here have to do with evaluating things, people's character and their feelings. Helena for example records how she and her partner responded emotionally to his promotion:

> Then he says: He and three of our friends have been promoted. 'We're moving to a special unit. Now, now my darling. We are real policemen now.' We were **ecstatic**. We even **celebrated**.

Later, she judges its horrific consequences in moral terms:

> Dammit! What else can this **abnormal** life be than a cruel human rights violation? Spiritual murder is more **inhumane** than a messy, physical murder. At least a murder victim rests. I wish I had the power to make those poor **wasted** people **whole** again.

One important aspect of evaluation is the source of the opinions, which we would naturally attribute to Helena in the examples given above. But we need to be careful, since her story comes from a letter she sent to the South African Broadcasting Corporation's (SABC) radio team who broadcast extracts. Tutu introduces her story as follows:

> The South Africa Broadcasting Corporation's radio team covering the Truth and Reconciliation Commission received a letter from a woman calling herself Helena (she wanted to remain anonymous for fear of reprisals) who lived in the eastern province of Mpumalanga. They broadcast substantial extracts.

So in fact what we are looking at here is Tutu writing → that the SABC broadcast → that Helena wrote → that (for example) spiritual murder is more inhumane than physical murder. Each step in the reporting nuances the evaluation, and we need to be systematic about keeping track of the effects this has.

Ideation (the content of a discourse)

Here we're concerned with people and things, and the activities they're involved in. Since Helena's telling her story, there's lots of activity involved and it unfolds in sequences. There's a courtship sequence for example (woman meets man, they begin a relationship, they plan to marry):

> I met a young man in his twenties. . . It was the beginning of a beautiful relationship. We even spoke about marriage.

And a later sequence about consumption (people become dissatisfied, they want better, they get it):

> If I had to watch how white people became dissatisfied with the best and still wanted better and got it.

As well as sequences of activities, ideation is concerned with describing and classifying people and things. Helena's second love for example is classified (*policeman, man, murderer, vulture*), partitioned (*face, hands, eyes, throat, head, brains; personality, soul, conscience*) and variously described (*bubbly, charming, bewildered, dull like the dead, wasted* etc.).

Conjunction (inter-connections between processes)

Later in the narrative Helena comments on her understanding of the struggle against apartheid, outlining the conditions under which she herself would have joined the struggle:

> I finally understand what the struggle was really about. I would have done the same **had I** been denied everything. **If** my life, that of my children and my parents was strangled with legislation. **If** I had to watch how white people became dissatisfied with the best and still wanted better and got it.

To demonstrate her understanding she places herself in victims' shoes, outlining the conditions under which she would have done the same. The key resources here for establishing conditions are conditional conjunctions *If. . .*, *If. . .*, and the Subject–verb inversion *had I. . . .* These realizations serve to link Helena's intended action *I would have done the same*, with the conditions under which she would have done so, ***had I been. . .***, ***If my life. . .***, ***If I had to watch***:

I would have done the same

	discourse function	wording (grammar)
had I been denied everything	condition	Subject-verb inversion
If my life . . . was strangled with legislation.	condition	conjunction
If I had to watch how white people became dissatisfied . . .	condition	conjunction

Identification (concerned with tracking people and things)

Helena's narrative focuses on the two loves of her life and the way their violation of human rights destroyed their humanity. Her first love is introduced as *a young man*, and his identity is then kept track of using the pronouns *his* and *he*:

> As an eighteen-year-old, I met **a young man** in **his** twenties. **He** was working in a top security structure.

Years later Helena meets him once again, and he is reintroduced as *my first love*, to distinguish him from the other men in her life:

> More than a year ago, I met **my first love** again through a good friend.

The key English resources here are indefinite reference (*a*) to introduce the young man, pronouns to maintain his identity (*his*, *he*, *my*) and comparison (*first*) to distinguish him from Helena's second love:

	discourse functions	wording
A *young man*	presenting a participant	indefinite reference
his *twenties*	tracking a participant	pronoun
he	tracking a participant	pronoun
my first *love*	comparing participants	pronoun, ordinal number

Periodicity (the rhythm of discourse)

Here we're concerned with information flow: the way in which meanings are organized so that readers can process phases of meaning. Helena for example doesn't launch straight into her story by telling us she met a young man. To begin, she lets us know that she's going to tell a story about a teenage farm girl in Eastern Free State:

> My story begins in my late teenage years as a farm girl in the Bethlehem district of Eastern Free State.

And Tutu himself provided us with some more background to this story as he introduces it:

> The South Africa Broadcasting Corporation's radio team covering the Truth and Reconciliation Commission received a letter from a woman calling herself Helena (she wanted to remain anonymous for fear of reprisals) who lived in the eastern province of Mpumalanga. They broadcast substantial extracts.

This means that by the time Helena begins we know what to expect – which genre (a story), and something about where and when it took place and who was involved. This kind of predictability is absolutely critical for digesting information, and we need to look carefully at the ways in which texts tell us what's coming, alongside reminding us where we've been. Helena for example is just as clear about where her story ends:

> I end with a few lines that my wasted vulture said to me one night

Here she lets us know that the predictions that helped us through the story are closing down, and that a transition to something different is coming, in this case a big hop back to Tutu's argument. We use the term periodicity for these resources because they organize texts as waves of information; we surf the waves, taking a look back and forward on crests of informational prominence, so that we can glide smoothly through the troughs on the flow of meanings we expect.

Negotiation

The key resources here are for exchanging roles as an interaction unfolds, for example by asking a question and answering it, or demanding a service and complying with the command. Here one speaker demands information with a question, and the other responds with a statement:

| Sannie: | Are you leaving? |
| Coetzee: | – Of course I'm leaving. |

Next a father demands a service with a command, and his son complies:

| Hendrik: | Ernest, get those snoek [a kind of fish]. |
| Ernest: | – (Ernest proceeds to do so.) |

This is a new chapter in this edition, and we have left it till last because the examples we use to illustrate NEGOTIATION are from a film that recontextualizes, in the form of personal interactions, the issues of truth and reconciliation that we introduce through written texts in the preceding chapters.

1.6 How to use this book

The aim of the book is to enable discourse analysts to use the tools we offer for text analysis. Some applications will call for the full set of analytical tools presented in all chapters. Others may require analyses from just one or another of the chapters.

Each chapter starts with examples from our texts to give a simple outline of the relevant discourse system. The sections in each chapter then discuss resources in each part of the discourse system in turn. Again in each section we start with examples of discourse to illustrate the set of resources for meaning. The resources in each system are then summarized in tables, for easy reference, and also where appropriate in system diagrams to show how the whole system is organized.

Most chapters present more than one set of resources, within the overall system under focus. This means that texts may be analysed from more than one perspective. But we have endeavoured to set out each chapter and section as a clear set of steps that build on those that have gone before.

The text analyses and interpretations in each chapter are intended as models for the reader to apply to their own texts. The tables of resources are intended as references to assist the analyst to identify other examples in their texts, and the system diagrams help to distinguish between each type of meaning. If there is uncertainty about which category of meaning in a table applies to a particular instance in a text, the analyst can refer to the relevant discussion in the chapter.

In Chapter 8 we apply the tools we have built up to analyse the final chapter of Mandela's *Long Walk to Freedom*. This analysis is intended to illustrate how the discourse analysis tools can be used for a variety of purposes. We are particularly concerned in this chapter to show the discourse strategies that Mandela uses to evaluate his own and his country's transition from oppression to freedom, and to share his evaluations with readers.

Finally in Chapter 9 we outline connections between the discourse analysis tools we have discussed and other modes of analysis. These connections include firstly the model of social context we introduced briefly above, and assume throughout the following chapters. This model of register and genre is crucial for interpreting the roles of interpersonal, ideational and textual meanings in social discourse. Secondly we introduce a set of tools for analysing discourse in modes other than language, illustrated by re-interpreting Mandela's *Freedom* text in terms of its visual images. Thirdly we connect the tools for analysing discourse, register and genre to work in critical discourse analysis, extending our toolkit to build in a model of ideology and change in the development of texts, of speakers and of their cultures. And finally we briefly outline connections between our own work on discourse analysis and that of other functional linguists and SFL in general.

It needs to be emphasized that what we offer the reader here are only tools for discourse analysis. The tasks they can be applied to are many and varied, and each analyst will do so in their own way, depending on their needs. As with tools of any kind, skill is needed to use them with fluency and confidence, and this can only come with practice. What we have tried to do in this book is provide models that can guide the reader to develop such skills. What we hope is that readers will apply them as they choose, adapt them as they need, and develop them further.

Notes

1   We won't do more than touch on phonology and graphology in this volume, so will set aside this additional level of realization here.
2   For an alternative translation of this story, see Krog (1999), which also provides an extremely rich and harrowing contextualization of the South African contexts we survey here.

APPRAISAL: negotiating attitudes

2

Appraisal is concerned with evaluation – the kinds of attitudes that are negotiated in a text, the strength of the feelings involved and the ways in which values are sourced and readers aligned.

Following a general introduction in section 2.1, section 2.2 introduces the three main types of attitude – beginning with **affect**, then **judgement** and finally **appreciation**. Then in section 2.3 we consider the way in which attitudes can be amplified and hedged, developing **force** and **focus** as complementary dimensions of the system of **graduation**. Next in section 2.4 we turn to the source of attitudes and explore the ways in which quoting and reporting, modality and concession constitute an **engagement** system which can be used to introduce a range of voices into a text.

Having built up the system of appraisal in sections 2.2–2.4, in section 2.5 we look at how appraisal choices resonate **prosodically** through text, constructing the evaluative stance of an appraiser. Finally in section 2.6 we introduce a more detailed analysis of affect, judgement and appreciation – including tables of exemplary vocabulary realizing each type of feeling.

2.1 Negotiating attitudes

APPRAISAL is a system of interpersonal meanings. We use the resources of APPRAISAL for negotiating our social relationships, by telling our listeners or readers how we feel about things and people (in a word, what our attitudes are). We have chosen to begin with this chapter to foreground the interactive nature of discourse, whether spoken or written – as negotiation.

Attitudes have to do with evaluating things, people's character and their feelings. Such evaluations can be more or less intense, that is they may be more or less amplified. And the attitude may be the writer's own or it may be attributed to some other source. These are the three aspects of appraisal – attitudes, how they are amplified and their sources – that we will explore in this chapter. We will begin with a brief synopsis of each one, and then explore them in more detail.

Let's begin with kinds of attitudes. Helena's story is highly evaluative as she describes intense feelings and strong reactions to people and things. In the following passage she outlines her attitude to her first love's work and their relationship (things), his character (people), and the emotions of those involved (feelings):

> He was working in a **top** security structure. It was the beginning of a **beautiful** relationship. We even spoke about marriage. A **bubbly, vivacious** man who beamed out **wild energy**. **Sharply intelligent**. Even if he was an Englishman, he was **popular** with all the 'Boer' Afrikaners. And all my girlfriends **envied** me. Then one day he said he was going on a 'trip'. 'We won't see each other again. . . maybe never ever again.' I was **torn to pieces**. **So** was he.

She begins with the value of her love's work and their forthcoming relationship:

> a **top** security structure
> a **beautiful** relationship

She then turns to her love's character, which she holds in such high esteem:

> a **bubbly vivacious** man
> **wild energy**
> **sharply intelligent**
> **popular**

Next she describes her girlfriends' emotional response to their relationship, and her own and her lover's feelings on their separation:

> **envied**
> **torn to pieces**

So these evaluations can be divided into three basic kinds according to what is being appraised: (i) the value of things, (ii) people's character and (iii) people's feelings.

Next let's look at how attitudes are amplified. One thing that involves us in Helena's story is that her evaluations are highly charged. She judges her love for example not just as intelligent but as **sharply** intelligent, not just as energetic but as **wildly** so:

> **sharply** intelligent
> **wild** energy

And she wasn't just upset at their separation, but absolutely shattered:

> torn **to pieces**

So attitudes are gradable – their volume can be turned up and down depending on how intensely we feel. We can refer to the resources we use to show how strong our reactions are as amplification.

Finally let's look at the sources of attitudes. One thing we need to consider about attitudes is who they're coming from. Since it's a story, we assume that it's the narrator, Helena, who is evaluating, unless we're told otherwise. Helena does in fact suggest that the 'Boer' Afrikaners enjoyed her love's company, and that it was her girlfriends who envied her, although in each case we have to keep in mind that it's Helena who's telling us how they felt:

> he was **popular** with all the 'Boer' Afrikaners
> And all my girlfriends **envied** me.

One very common way to attribute feelings is of course to create another voice in the story, by using direct or indirect speech. Later in the story, for example, she quotes from her second love, who evaluates his life as a living hell:

> I end with a few lines that my wasted vulture said to me one night: '. . . I have to live with this **hell**.'

And as we noted in Chapter 1, Helena's story was itself quoted by Tutu, who is himself quoting from a broadcast by the SABC. So the immediate, intermediate and ultimate source of opinions in discourse is an important variable in discourse that we need to keep track of when analysing evaluations.

In simple terms then, what we see here are a range of resources for expressing attitudes, amplifying them and attributing them to sources. And there are three *affect*

main types of attitude: expressing emotion, judging character and valuing the worth of things. Technically we'll refer to resources for expressing feelings as **affect**, resources for judging character as **judgement** and resources for valuing the worth of things as **appreciation**. These basic resources are set out in Table 2.1 and then as a system network in Figure 2.1.

Table 2.1 Basic options for appraisal

attitude	affect	*envied*
		torn to pieces
	judgement	a *bubbly vivacious* man
		wild energy, sharply intelligent
	appreciation	a *top* security structure
		a *beautiful* relationship
amplification		*sharply* intelligent
		wild energy
source		he was *popular* with <u>all the 'Boer' Afrikaners</u>.
		And <u>all my girlfriends</u> *envied* me.

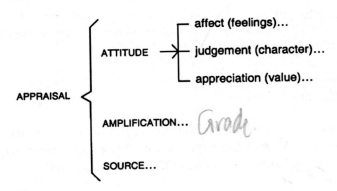

Figure 2.1 Basic system for appraisal

In Figure 2.1, the enclosing brackets on the left mean that the enclosed options for APPRAISAL are all selected <u>at the same time</u>, since when we express an attitude we also choose how amplified it is, and what its source is. Enclosing brackets in a system network like this means we select an attitude **and** its amplification **and** its source. By contrast the system shown on the right for ATTITUDE gives three <u>alternative options</u>. This means that, at this stage in our outline, we can express **either** affect **or** judgement **or** appreciation.

Next we will explore each of these options for APPRAISAL in more detail, beginning with kinds of attitudes.

2.2 Kinds of attitudes

In this section we look more closely at the three kinds of attitude we have identified: affect (people's feelings), judgement (people's character) and appreciation (the value of things).

Expressing our feelings: affect

As we explore how people express their feelings in discourse, we find that they vary in two general ways. Firstly, we can have good feelings or bad feelings, so affect can be **positive** or **negative**. Secondly people can express their feelings directly, or we can infer how people are feeling indirectly from their behaviour, so affect can be expressed **directly** or **implied**.

First let's look at positive and negative affect. More perhaps than any other family of genres, stories involve us in people's feelings. We empathize and sympathize with characters as they take part in extraordinary events. In her exemplum, Helena describes her own emotions as follows:

> I was **torn to pieces**
> I can't explain the **pain** and **bitterness** in me
> We were **ecstatic**
> We even **celebrated**
> Abruptly mutter the **feared** word 'trip'
> ... knew no other life than that of **worry**, sleeplessness, **anxiety** about his safety
> We simply had to be **satisfied** with
> Today I know the answer to all my questions and **heartache**
> I **envy** and **respect** the people of the struggle
> I **wish** I had the power
> those **poor** wasted people
> I **wish** I could wipe ...

And her second love's emotional states are even more fully elaborated:

> **Humorous, grumpy**, everything in its time and place
> We were **ecstatic**
> We even **celebrated**
> they would become **restless**
> Abruptly mutter the **feared** word 'trip'
> as a **loved** one

And all that we as **loved** ones knew
Withdrawn
Sometimes he would just **press his face into his hands** and **shake uncontrollably**
He tried to hide his **wild consuming fear**
I jolt awake from his **rushed breathing**
Eyes **bewildered**, but dull like the dead
And **the shakes**
The **terrible convulsions**
and **blood-curdling shrieks** of **fear** and **pain** from the bottom of his soul

It's not a happy story, as we can see. Most of the feelings are negative ones, things we'd rather not feel:

torn to pieces, pain, bitterness, feared, worry, anxiety, heartache, envy, grumpy, restless, feared, withdrawn, press his face into his hands, shake uncontrollably, wild consuming fear, rushed breathing, eyes bewildered, shakes, terrible convulsions, blood-curdling shrieks of fear and pain

Positive vibrations are few and far between:

ecstatic, celebrated, satisfied, respect, wish, humorous, loved

This contrast between good and bad vibes is a basic one as far as emotions and attitudes in general are concerned.

Next we'll look at **direct** and **implicit** expressions of feelings. From the lists above we can see Helena describes emotions in different ways. Often she refers directly to a mental state, using words that name specific emotions:

torn to pieces, pain, bitterness, ecstatic, feared, worry, anxiety, satisfied, heartache, envy, respect, wish, humorous, grumpy, loved, wild consuming fear, bewildered, blood-curdling, fear, pain

Alongside this, she refers at times to emotion physically, describing behaviour that also directly expresses emotion: uncontrollable shakes to express anxiety for example, or shrieks to express fear:

celebrated, restless, withdrawn, press his face into his hands, shake uncontrollably, rushed breathing, the shakes, terrible convulsions, shrieks

Related to this, and sometimes hard to distinguish from it, is her description of unusual behaviour which we read as an indirect sign of emotion:

very quiet; drinking too much; wander from window to window; rolls this way, that side of the bed; pale; ice cold in a sweltering night, sopping wet with sweat; sits motionless, just staring in front of him

Taken out of context, from this unusual behaviour we know something is wrong but we can't be quite so sure about the exact emotion being expressed; we need to use a bit of psychology perhaps. Read in context, however, we do know what Helena's on about, because these symptoms are surrounded by explicit references to emotions which tell us what the strange behaviour means. We can see the interplay in the text below, where physical symptoms are underlined and what we consider to be the more directly interpretable affect is in **bold**:

He became very quiet. **Withdrawn**. Sometimes he would just **press his face into his hands** and **shake uncontrollably**. I realized he was drinking too much. Instead of resting at night, he would wander from window to window. He tried to hide his **wild consuming fear**, but I saw it. In the early hours of the morning between two and half-past-two, I jolt awake from his **rushed breathing**. Rolls this way, that side of the bed. He's pale. Ice cold in a sweltering night – sopping wet with sweat. Eyes **bewildered**, but dull like the dead. And **the shakes**. The **terrible convulsions** and **blood-curdling shrieks** of **fear** and **pain** from the bottom of his soul. Sometimes he sits motionless, just staring in front of him.

We can also note here the role that metaphor plays in constructing emotion. Helena's love's eyes are dull like the dead, he's cold as ice, his fear and pain come from the bottom of his soul:

ice cold in a sweltering night
eyes bewildered, but dull like the dead
terrible convulsions and blood-curdling shrieks from the bottom of his soul

As we can see, Helena uses a range of resources to build up a picture of her second love's living hell, including direct expressions of emotional states and physical behaviour, and implicit expressions of emotion through extraordinary behaviour and metaphor.

In Helena's story these resources work together, reinforcing for example the desperation of her second love's emotional devastation, his spiritual murder as she describes it. This accumulative effect over a phase of text reflects the 'prosodic' nature of attitude, and of interpersonal meaning in general. Interpersonal meanings are often realized not just locally, but tend to sprawl out and colour a passage of discourse, forming a 'prosody' of attitude. By looking at phases of attitude, we can explore how readers are being aligned rhetorically as a text unfolds; we'll return to this issue of aligning the reader below.

Summing up then, we've seen that affect can be positive or negative, and that it can be realized directly or implicitly in text. And we've seen that direct and implicit realizations often work together to establish the mood of phases of discourse. These options for affect are set out in Table 2.2.

Table 2.2 Options for affect

positive		*We were ecstatic.*
		We even celebrated.
negative		*I was torn to pieces.*
		I can't explain the pain and bitterness in me...
direct	emotional state	*ecstatic*
		wild consuming fear
	physical	*Withdrawn*
	expression	*shake uncontrollably*
implicit	extraordinary	*wander from window to window*
	behaviour	*rolls this way, that side of the bed*
	metaphor	*ice cold in a sweltering night*
		eyes ... dull like the dead

Judging people's character

As with affect, judgements of people's character can be positive or negative, and they may be judged explicitly or implicitly. But unlike affect, we find that judgements differ between **personal** judgements of admiration or criticism and **moral** judgements of praise or condemnation.

We'll start with **personal** judgements – positive (admiring) and negative (criticizing). As we showed in Chapter 1, Helena's story is an exemplum. Exemplums relate an incident in order to comment on the behaviour of the people involved. This means that alongside telling how people feel emotionally, Helena judges them, she evaluates their character.

Helena's first love is at first characterized admiringly as *bubbly, vivacious, energetic, intelligent, popular* and later, retrospectively, as *beautiful, big* and *strong*. And he is also admired implicitly as *working in a top security structure*, i.e. an admirable role. Helena's second love is not quite so special, but described initially as *exceptional, special, bubbly* and *charming*. In both cases her lovers change, as a result of their security operations. Helena doesn't explicitly re-assess her first love, rather she implies criticism by telling us how she felt when she saw what was left of him:

> I can't explain the **pain** and **bitterness** in me when I saw what was left of that **beautiful, big, strong** person.

But she does <u>directly</u> criticize her second love as having something *wrong with him*, as maybe having *gone mad*, and as *wasted*. Their transformations from admiring judgements to critical ones are central to the impact of the two Incident stages of the story.

Next **moral** judgements: positive (praising) or negative (condemning). In the Interpretation stage of her story Helena judges South African leaders. She <u>condemns</u> her own leaders for their dishonesty:

> Our leaders are **too holy** and **innocent**. And **faceless**. I can understand if Mr (F. W.) de Klerk says he didn't know, but dammit, there must be a clique, there must have been someone out there who is still alive and who can give a face to 'the orders from above' for all the operations.

And for their inhumanity:

> Dammit! What else can this abnormal life be than a **cruel human rights violation**? Spiritual **murder** is more **inhumane** than a messy, physical **murder**. At least a **murder victim** rests.

But she <u>praises</u> the leaders of 'the people of the struggle' for having the courage to stand by their resistance forces and honour their activities:

> at least their leaders **have the guts** to stand by their vultures, to recognize their **sacrifices**

This shift in gears from Incident to Interpretation stages is significant. In the Incidents, Helena is not blaming anyone. At first she's full of admiration for her lovers, then worried sick about their problems. In the Interpretations, however, she both condemns and praises on moral grounds, as she deals with honesty and dishonesty, and with guilt and innocence in the face of the Truth and Reconciliation Commission. It's this shift to moral values in the later stages of the exemplum that drives home the point of the story and attracts Tutu to it by way of exemplifying one of his arguments about the cost of justice.

As with admiration and criticism, moral judgements can also be made directly or implied. When Helena says *I envy and respect the people of the struggle* for example, she's telling us how she's feeling emotionally; but both emotions <u>imply</u> something praiseworthy about the character of the people. Similarly, she morally condemns those at the top for bloody murder, without explicitly judging their character:

> while 'those at the top' were again targeting the next 'permanent removal from society' for the vultures

As with emotion, explicit judgements in the relevant phase of discourse tell us exactly how she wants us to judge the people targeted by accusations of this kind (i.e. as *murderers*):

> And today they all wash their hands in **innocence** and resist the **realities** of the Truth Commission. Yes, I stand by my **murderer** who let me and the old White South Africa sleep peacefully. Warmly, while 'those at the top' were again targeting the next 'permanent removal from society' for the vultures.

Metaphor also plays a role in judging character, as leaders wash the blood off their hands, operatives gnaw at carcasses and African families have the life choked out of them with legislation:

> And today they all **wash their hands** in innocence
> 'our men' who simply had to carry out their bloody orders... **like 'vultures'**
> If my life, that of my children and my parents was **strangled with legislation**

Perhaps the most powerful image in Helena's exemplum is that of 'spiritual murder', by way of capturing the immorality of 'those at the top' in relation to their *bloody orders*.

We can sum up the options for judgement that we've seen so far in Helena's story as Table 2.3.

Table 2.3 Examples of judgement of character (from Helena's story)

		direct	implied
personal	admire	*bubbly, vivacious, energetic, intelligent, popular*	*He was working in a top security structure.*
	criticize	*What's wrong with him? . . . I can't handle the man anymore!*	*I can't explain the pain and bitterness in me when I saw. . .*
moral	praise	*their leaders have the guts to stand by their vultures. . .*	*I envy and respect[1] the people of the struggle. . .*
	condemn	*Our leaders are too holy and innocent. And faceless.*	*. . . 'those at the top' were again targeting the next 'permanent removal from society' . . .*

Let's now turn to Desmond Tutu's exposition. Tutu is involved in a moral argument, an exposition dealing with the integrity of the Truth and Reconciliation process:

the cost of **justice**
the **integrity** of the entire Truth and Reconciliation process

● So we would naturally expect judgements of character to be foregrounded there. In fact we do find some emotion (*intimidated, humiliation, traumatic, fear, respect, wishes*), but this is indeed overwhelmed by the concern with moral issues.

Some of his judgements are like Helena's, everyday evaluations of character involving respectability, responsibility, accountability and veracity:

respectable members of their communities
who accept **responsibility**
encourages **accountability**
It is also not **true**

But many more of his judgements are judicial. They work as a kind of 'technicalized morality' that we associate with legal institutions. Note for example that he offers a definition of *a gross violation of human rights*, taken from the Promotion of National Unity and Reconciliation Act. Definitions are a sure sign that we are moving from common sense into uncommon sense knowledge:

a **gross violation of human rights** – defined as an abduction, killing, torture or severe ill-treatment

Here are some more examples of Tutu's judgmental legalese:

had committed a **crime**
sees the **offence**

the **perpetrator**
regular **torturers** of detainees
the **victim**

who plead **guilty**
innocent people
those who claim to be **innocent**

of **reprisals**
in **retaliation**
not **retribution** or **punishment**

encourages **impunity**
the granting of **amnesty**

a **miscarriage of justice**

For certain analytical purposes we might argue that these technical judgements should be left out of an appraisal analysis, since each in a sense refers to an ideational meaning that is precisely situated within legal institutions, rather than an interpersonal meaning like appraisal. But we're not sure their technicality totally robs them of their evaluative role. Most seem to us to carry with them some of their everyday attitudinal power, certainly for lay readers. By way of another example, when Robert Manne wrote that Australia's policy of removing Aboriginal children from their families by force was 'technically an act of genocide', we doubt that for most Australians its technicalization completely softened the moral blow:

> A national inquiry last year found that the government policy of forced removal was a gross violation of human rights and **technically an act of genocide** because it has the intention of destroying Australia's indigenous culture by forced assimilation. (Manne 1998)

Finally we can examine the Act of Parliament for its judgements. Like Tutu's exposition, the Act foregrounds judgement over affect and its judgements are mainly technical ones, as we'd expect from a legislative document. Some examples are highlighted below:

> To provide for the investigation and the establishment of as complete a picture as possible of the nature, causes and extent of **gross violations of human rights** committed during the period from 1 March 1960 to the cut-off date contemplated in the Constitution, within or outside the Republic, emanating from the conflicts of the past, and the fate or whereabouts of the **victims** of such **violations**
>
> the granting of **amnesty** to persons who make full disclosure of all the relevant facts relating to acts associated with a political objective committed in the course of the conflicts of the past during the said period
>
> affording **victims** an opportunity to relate the **violations** they suffered
>
> the taking of measures aimed at the granting of reparation to, and the rehabilitation and the restoration of the human and civil **dignity** of, victims of **violations of human rights**
>
> reporting to the Nation about such **violations** and **victims**
>
> the making of recommendations aimed at the prevention of the commission of gross **violations of human rights**
>
> and for the said purposes to provide for the establishment of a **Truth** and Reconciliation Commission, a Committee on **Human Rights Violations**, a Committee on **Amnesty** and a Committee on Reparation and Rehabilitation

Appreciating things

To this point we've looked at how people feel about people and the way they behave. What about things? Appreciation of things includes our attitudes about TV shows, films, books, CDs; about paintings, sculptures, homes, public buildings, parks; about plays, recitals, parades or spectacles and performances of any kind; feelings about nature for that matter – panoramas and glens, sunrises and sunsets, constellations, shooting stars and satellites on a starry night. As with affect and judgement, things can be appreciated positively or negatively.

Helena's narrative is more about people than things, and so foregrounds affect and judgement. But it does include evaluations of relationships:

> a **beautiful** relationship
> an **extremely short** marriage... **failed**
> my **unsuccessful** marriage

And of quality of life as well:

> **hell**
> **hell**
> this **abnormal** life
> **hell**
> **hell**

Relationships and qualities of life are abstract sorts of things, but can be evaluated as things nevertheless. Tutu's exposition, as we have seen, foregrounds judgement. But early on it does evaluate semiotic things, including a question, an issue and applications:

> a **frivolous** question
> a **very serious** issue
> virtually all the **important** applications to the Commission

And towards the end, Tutu does focus on relationships, by way of exploring the meaning of restorative justice:

> I contend that there is another kind of justice, **restorative justice**, which is characteristic of traditional African jurisprudence. Here the central concern is not retribution or punishment but, in the spirit of **ubuntu**, the **healing of breaches**, the **redressing of imbalances**, the **restoration of broken relationships**. This kind of justice seeks to **rehabilitate** both the victim and the perpetrator, who should be given the opportunity to be **reintegrated into the community** he or she has **injured** by his or her offence. This is a far more personal approach, which sees the offence as

something that has happened to people and whose consequence is a **rupture in relationships**. Thus we would claim that justice, **restorative justice**, is being served when efforts are being made to work for **healing**, for **forgiveness** and for **reconciliation**.

Tutu's use of the term justice in the context of *ubuntu* seems at first blush to indicate that he's judging behaviour here. But in fact he is more concerned with restoring the fabric of social relations than with western notions of retribution and punishment. On the positive evaluation side we have terms concerned with communal healing:

the **healing of breaches**
the **redressing of imbalances**
the **restoration** of broken relationships
rehabilitate both the victim and the perpetrator
the opportunity to be **reintegrated into the community**
restorative justice
healing
reconciliation

On the negative we have terms concerned with damage done:

broken relationships
the community he or she has **injured** by his or her offence
a **rupture** in relationships

We can summarize the positive and negative appreciations we've examined so far in Table 2.4.

Table 2.4 Examples of appreciation

positive	a *beautiful* relationship
	a *very serious* issue
	healing of breaches
	redressing of imbalances
	restoration of broken relationships
negative	my *unsuccessful* marriage
	a *frivolous* question
	broken relationships
	the community he or she has *injured*

In order to illustrate a prosody of positive appreciations, we'll switch fields for a moment and consider a review of the current CD edition of Stevie Ray Vaughan's album *Texas Flood* (courtesy of Amazon.com):

> This *legendary 1983 debut* by the fallen torchbearer of the '80s–'90s blues revival sounds *even more dramatic* in its remixed and expanded edition. Stevie Ray Vaughan's guitar and vocals are a *bit brighter* and *more present* on this 14-track CD. And the newly included bonus numbers (an *incendiary* studio version of the slow blues "Tin Pan Alley" that was left off the original release, and live takes of "Testify," "Mary Had a Little Lamb," and the instrumental "Wham!" from a 1983 Hollywood concert) illuminate the raw soul and passion that propelled his artistry even when he was under the spell of drug addiction. Texas Flood captures Vaughan as rockin' blues purist, paying tribute in his inspired six-string diction to his influences Larry Davis (who wrote the title track), Buddy Guy, Albert King, and Jimi Hendrix. His own *contemplative* "Lenny," a tribute to his wife at the time, also suggests a *jazz-fueled complexity* that would infuse his later work. (Drozdowski 2000)

This is a rave review from an in-house editor, designed to persuade Amazon's customers to purchase Vaughan's debut album. The album in general and certain tracks in particular are described in very positive terms:

legendary, even more dramatic, bit brighter, more present, incendiary, contemplative, jazz-fueled complexity

To these appraisals we might add some arguably experiential meanings with a positive value in the context of this new edition of *Texas Flood*:

remixed, expanded, bonus

The borderline of character and value

There are several instances of attitude in our texts that could perhaps be analysed as either judgement of character or appreciation of things. For example, closely related to the positive appreciation of Vaughan's album and its tracks are the evaluations of his performance:

raw soul and passion, artistry, inspired six-string diction

These bring us to the border of character and value (of judgement and appreciation). Because they directly value Vaughan's guitar playing rather than the man, we'll take them here as concerned with value rather than character. But they can also additionally be coded as tokens of Vaughan's enormous guitar playing abilities – as betokening one positive dimension of his character (as opposed to the negative dimension of drug addiction, also noted in the review). Even more borderline perhaps are the generalizations of these positive capacities when Vaughan is referred to as a torchbearer of the 1980s–1990s blues revival and a rockin' blues purist:

> torchbearer, rockin' blues purist

In the prosodic domain of this positive appreciation of the CD, these can arguably be included as positive appreciations; but just as strong a case might be made for reading items such as these as positive judgements of Vaughan's capacity as an artist, especially in contexts where character rather than performance is being evaluated. The context sensitivity of these borderline items underlines the importance of analysing appraisal in prosodic terms. So it is important to take co-text into account, rather than analysing simply item by item.

The key term for Tutu, judging from the title of his book, is forgiveness, which seems in this context to comprise aspects of both judgement and appreciation. Judgement in the sense that someone is generous enough to stop feeling angry and wanting to punish someone who has done something wrong to them; appreciation in the sense that peace is restored. It also seems that for Tutu, forgiveness involves a spiritual dimension, underpinned by his Christianity; the concept transcends ethical considerations towards a plane of peace and spiritual harmony. In appraisal terms what this means is that the politicized aesthetics of appreciation has recontextualized the moral passion plays of judgement.

If we take communal healing as one dimension of value analysis, then the Act can also be seen to be concerned with repairing social relations:

> SINCE the Constitution of the Republic of South Africa, 1993 (Act No. 200 of 1993), provides a historic bridge between the past of a *deeply divided society characterised by strife, conflict, untold suffering and injustice, and a future founded on the recognition of human rights, democracy and peaceful co-existence for all South Africans, irrespective of colour, race, class, belief or sex;*
> AND SINCE it is deemed necessary to establish the truth in relation to past events as well as the motives for and circumstances in which gross violations of human rights have occurred, and to make the findings known in order to prevent a repetition of such acts in future;
> AND SINCE the Constitution states that the pursuit of **national unity**, the well-being of all South African citizens and **peace** require **reconciliation** between the people of South Africa and the **reconstruction of society;**
> AND SINCE the Constitution states that there is a need for **understanding** but not for vengeance, a need for **reparation** but not for retaliation, a need for **ubuntu** but not for victimisation;
> AND SINCE the Constitution states that in order to advance such **reconciliation** and **reconstruction** amnesty shall be granted in respect of acts, omissions and offences associated with political objectives committed in the course of the **conflicts** of the past;

AND SINCE the Constitution provides that Parliament shall under the Constitution adopt a law which determines a firm cut-off date, which shall be a date after 8 October 1990 and before the cut-off date envisaged in the Constitution, and providing for the mechanisms, criteria and procedures, including tribunals, if any, through which such amnesty shall be dealt with

For this analysis we've concentrated on items that don't directly involve judgement. But the following paragraph gives us pause:

AND SINCE the Constitution states that there is a need for **understanding** but not for *vengeance*, a need for **reparation** but not for *retaliation*, a need for **ubuntu** but not for *victimisation*

Here the Act systematically opposes what we treated as appreciation above to terms which more explicitly involve ethical considerations, i.e. judgements about impropriety of people's behaviour:

appreciation (healing)	judgement (impropriety)
understanding	**vengeance**
reparation	**retaliation**
ubuntu	**victimisation**

Afro-Christian values are constructed as transcending western justice. Perhaps a better reading of the drift of feeling in the Act would be one that follows Tutu's comments on the meaning of ubuntu:

the spirit of **ubuntu**, the **healing** of **breaches**, the **redressing** of **imbalances**, the **restoration** of **broken** relationships

Here order subsumes disorder; peace breaks out. These are the values the Act wants people to align with in the new rainbow republic. Accordingly it might be wise to group judgement and appreciation together here, under the headings of order and disorder, by way of displaying the attitude to reconciliation the Act is designed to enact:

order
democracy, peaceful co-existence, national unity, peace, reconciliation, reconstruction of society, understanding, reparation, ubuntu, reconciliation, reconstruction; recognition of human rights, truth, well-being, amnesty, amnesty

disorder
deeply divided society, strife, conflict, conflicts; injustice, violations of human rights, vengeance, retaliation, victimisation, omissions, offences

It might be even wiser to pause for a moment and consider the extent to which our affect, judgement and appreciation framework represents a western construction of feeling. Tutu's Afro-Christian heritage might not factor attitude along these lines. We're not wise enough to gaze beyond our categories here. But we are confident that other cultures will take pause, and look at what we've done through different eyes.

2.3 Amplifying attitudes

One distinctive feature of attitudes is that they are gradable. This means that we can say how strongly we feel about someone or something. For example, Helena describes her first love as *sharply intelligent*. By doing so she places his intelligence on a scale and ranks it highly in relation to other choices she could have made:

extremely intelligent	↑	**high grading**
sharply intelligent		
really intelligent		
quite intelligent		
fairly intelligent		
somewhat intelligent	↓	**low grading**

As we can see, some choices turn the volume up (e.g. *extremely, sharply*) and others tone it down (e.g. *fairly, somewhat*). In English we seem to have more resources for turning the volume up than down, and use them more often.

In this section we will look at two kinds of resources for amplification. The first is for 'turning the volume up or down'. These include words that intensify meanings, such as *very/really/extremely*, and vocabulary items that include degrees of intensity, such as *happy/delighted/ecstatic*. We refer to this kind of amplifying as force. The second kind involves 'sharpening' or 'softening' categories of people and things, using words such as *about/exactly* or *real/sort of/kind of*. We refer to this kind of amplifying as focus.

Amplifying the force of attitudes

We can begin with words that amplify the force of attitudes, such as *very/really/ extremely*. These kinds of words are known as **intensifiers**. Helena for example intensifies how special her second love was, and how quiet he became, as well as how long her unsuccessful marriage lasted:

very special
very quiet
An **extremely** short marriage to someone else

Tutu also uses intensifying of this kind:

> a **very** serious issue
> **quite** a price to pay

Intensifiers make it possible for us to compare things – to say how strongly we feel about someone or something, by comparison to something else. Helena for example describes how white people had the best of everything and still wanted more:

> If I had to watch how white people became dissatisfied with the **best** and still wanted **better** and got it.

The *best* is implicitly compared with the *worst*, which is all the 'people of the struggle' had. And *best* is also compared with *better*, which is what white people wanted. These comparisons are possible because the worth of things is gradable:

> best/better/good/bad/worse/worst

Comparison is also found in Tutu's exposition and the Act:

> a **far more** personal approach
> **as complete** a picture **as possible**

His intensifiers belong to scales such as the following:

> slightly more/a little more/a lot more/far more
> less than/as much as/more than

Some comparison refers to an excess of feeling, as when Helena criticizes the lack of responsibility taken by the leaders of white South Africa and Tutu notes the problem of intimidation for some witnesses:

> **too** holy and innocent
> **too** intimidated to testify in open session

Too contrasts with *enough* in this region of meaning:

> not enough/enough/too much

We won't go into more detail about resources for intensifying feelings here. There is a useful discussion of 'amplifiers', 'downtoners' and 'emphasizers' in Quirk et al. (1985), and see also Hyland (1998) on 'hedging'. And there is a very useful outline of grading adverbs in Collins Cobuild (1998) which shows in particular that many intensifiers themselves involve attitude:

amazingly beautiful
unusually beautiful
dangerously beautiful
breathtakingly beautiful

There are also several other areas of meaning that involve grading for example quantity, manner and modality:

quantity	*all/several/some of my questions*
manner degree	*shake frantically/uncontrollably/excitedly*
modality	*there must/would/might have been someone out there*

A complete analysis of amplification would usefully include these kinds of meanings. We'll discuss modality further below under Sources, but here we'll restrict ourselves to graded feelings.

Next let's examine vocabulary items that include degrees of intensity, such as *happy/delighted/ecstatic*. These kinds of words are known as **attitudinal lexis**, i.e. 'lexis with attitude'. The intensifiers we have already looked at, like *better/best, all/several/some, must/would/might*, are grammatical items. That is their meaning depends on being combined with 'content words'. By contrast, 'content words' are referred to technically as lexical items, or simply lexis.

Attitudinal lexis plays a very important role in Helena's narrative, as it does in general across story genres. Helena for example says that she and her second love were *ecstatic* about his promotion, as opposed to say *happy, chuffed, delighted* or *elated*. These are all lexical items that refer to degrees of happiness. It's not always easy to arrange groups of words like these confidently along a scale, but there are obviously various degrees of feeling involved. With these items, amplification is fused into the words themselves, so that in the dictionary *chuffed* is defined as 'very pleased', with the amplification factored out as *very*.

Here are some more examples of attitudinal lexis from Helena's Incidents, with some suggested scales of intensity:

vivacious man	dull/placid/lively/vivacious
torn to pieces	saddened/grief stricken/torn to pieces
ecstatic	happy/chuffed/delighted/elated/ecstatic
bewildered	bemused/puzzled/confused/bewildered
blood-curdling **shrieks** of fear	whimper/groan/cry/screech/shriek
pleading	ask/request/pray/beseech/plead

With lexical resources like these, the line between categories can be hard to draw and it is not always clear just how many items to include as pushing up the volume in analysis. As a rule of thumb, the words recognized will be 'non-core vocabulary' (Carter 1987), i.e. lexical items other than those most commonly used in English, and they will tend to be defined in dictionaries with intensifiers like *very*.

Beyond this, we can also be guided by the prosody of feeling that colours a whole phase of discourse. In Helena's narrative for example attitudinal lexis is more a feature of her Incidents than her Orientation or Interpretations. And genre is also a factor. Tutu uses less of this resource in his exposition, but there are some examples:

> a **frivolous** question
> the full **glare** of television lights
> **humiliation** for the perpetrator
> **impunity**

On the other hand, the Act arguably uses no attitudinal lexis at all, just as it avoids intensifiers like *very*. So we can score various genres on how much amplification they are likely to display: narratives tend to amplify most, expositions less so, and administrative genres like the Act amplify very little.

Another feature of certain genres is that grading is erased when we technicalize attitude. For example, in common sense terms *gross* is at the extreme of scales such as *minor/unacceptable/gross* or *unpleasant/disturbing/gross*. But once we define *a gross violation of human rights* then *gross* doesn't scale how unacceptable or unpleasant the violation is any more. *Gross* simply becomes part of the name of the offence, classifying the type of offence, rather than intensifying it:

> a **gross** violation of human rights – defined as an abduction, killing, torture or severe ill-treatment

As well as the lexical items we've seen above, attitudinal lexis also includes metaphors and swearing. We've already considered Helena's metaphors in relation to affect, but we can note here that they also have an amplifying effect:

> **ice** cold in a sweltering night
> dull **like the dead**
> **blood-curdling** shrieks

These metaphors tell us how cold her second love was, how dull his eyes were, and how frightening his screams were.

As well as metaphors, Helena also uses swearing in her Interpretation to express her frustration with white South African leaders:

> Our leaders are too holy and innocent. And faceless. I can understand if Mr (F. W.) de Klerk says he didn't know, but **dammit**, there must be a clique, there must have been someone out there who is still alive and who can give a face to 'the orders from above' for all the operations. **Dammit!** What else can this abnormal life be than a cruel human rights violation?

Perhaps what we are looking at here is feeling which becomes so amplified it explodes – a kind of short-circuit which disengages amplification from what is being appraised (the leaders' character) and 'cuts loose' as a swear word. The role of swearing needs further exploration, including its relationship with 'interjections' (Quirk et al. 1985), such as *ugh, phew, gr-r-r-r, ow, whew, tut-tut* etc. Eggins and Slade (1997) and Allen and Burridge (2006) also have some relevant discussion.

Sharpening and softening focus

Now let's look briefly at the second dimension of graduation, **focus** – the sharpening and softening of experiential categories. What we've considered so far are resources for adjusting the volume of gradable items. By contrast, focus is about resources for making something that is inherently non-gradable gradable. For example, Helena introduces her second love as a *policeman*:

> After my unsuccessful marriage, I met another policeman.

Experientially, this sets him up as having one kind of job rather than another (tinker, tailor, soldier, spy etc.). Classifications of this kind are categorical distinctions – he was a policeman as opposed to something else. After his promotion, however, her second love describes himself as a *real* policeman, as if he hadn't quite been one before:

> We are **real** policemen now.

This in effect turns a categorical boundary between types of professions into a graded one, allowing for various degrees of 'policeman-hood'. It implies that when Helena met him he was less of a policeman than after his promotion:

> I met a **kind of** policeman
> I met a policeman **sort of**

Grading resources of this kind doesn't so much turn the volume up and down as sharpen and soften the boundaries between things. *Real policeman* sharpens the focus, *a sort of policeman* softens it. As well as things, we can also sharpen or soften types of qualities, such as *deep blue* or *bluish*. Even categorical concepts like numbers can be pushed around in this way:

After **about** three years with the special forces
vs
After **exactly** three years with the special forces

Here's another example of sharpened focus from Helena's story:

was what we saw with our **own** eyes

Here **own** sharpens the category 'our eyes', i.e. 'ours and no-one else's' – it's definitely not hearsay. And here's an example of softened focus:

not quite my first love

Tutu also sharpens focus a couple of times in his exposition, in order to be precise:

the **very** first time
precisely this point

However, as with force, the Act appears to avoid focus entirely, preferring categorical distinctions as a matter of legislation.

We won't pursue the full range of these resources for grading experiential boundaries in detail (Martin and White 2005 and Martin and Hood 2006 provide a fuller picture; for another very useful discussion of vague language of this kind, see Channel 1994). Here, however, are a few more examples from Stevie Ray Vaughan's admiring fans:

to what **real** blues sounds like
then you aren't a fan of **true**, god-blessed American music
two of the songs sound **exactly** alike
Whether you're a **hardcore** Stevie fan
Among Stevie was his brother, Dr. John, Angela Strehler (**or something**)
Here is an **authentic** blues artist
This video was the **epitome** of Stevie
It's **pure** perfection
Absolute intensity
If you're even a **part-time** blues fan

To sum up then, amplifying attitude involves a set of resources for adjusting how strongly we feel about people and things. Technically we refer to these resources as force. We use them to turn the volume up or down. Grading experiential boundaries involves resources that sharpen or blur apparently categorical distinctions. Technically these resources are referred to as focus. They make cut and dried distinctions negotiable. These options for amplification are set out in Table 2.5 and as a system in Figure 2.2. Technically these resources are referred to as **graduation.**

Table 2.5 Options for graduation

force	intensifiers	he still plays **great**
	attitudinal lexis	the second part is **fantastic** …
	metaphors	**ice** cold in a sweltering night
	swearing	**dammit**, there must be a clique
focus	sharpen	a **true** guitar legend
	soften	a **part-time** blues fan

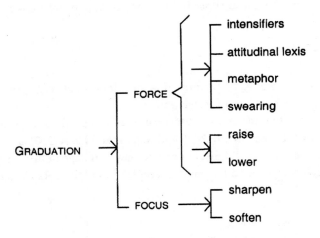

Figure 2.2 Options for graduation

2.4 Sources of attitudes

The final region of appraisal we need to consider has to do with the source of attitudes: who are the evaluations coming from?

We'll begin once again with Helena's narrative. On the face of it, we might argue that the evaluation in Helena's story comes from Helena. She's the narrator after all. So when she appreciates her relationship with her first love as *beautiful*, that's her opinion:

It was the beginning of **a beautiful relationship.**

And in a sense Helena is responsible for all of the evaluation since all of it is filtered through her narration. Helena does however explicitly give voice to other players by quoting or reporting what her first and second loves said:

> Then <u>he says</u>: He and three of our friends have been promoted. 'We're moving to a special unit. Now, now my darling. We are real policemen now.'

This potential for sourcing what is said was one of the factors that got the Russian linguist Bakhtin (1981) thinking about the dialogic nature of discourse, even in texts we traditionally think of as monologues. The French discourse analyst Kristeva introduced the term **heteroglossia** ('different voices') for this notion of multiple voicing in all kinds of discourse. Here we will use the term **heterogloss** where the source of an attitude is other than the writer, and **monogloss** ('single voice') where the source is simply the author.

Projecting sources

One thing we are able to do in discourse is quote or report what people say or think. Halliday and Matthiessen (2004) call this type of linguistic resource 'projection'. Projection is the relation between *he says* in the example above, and <u>what he said</u>: *He and three of our friends have been promoted. 'We're moving to a special unit. Now, now my darling. We are real policemen now.'* We can illustrate projection with a 'speech bubble' as in Figure 2.3.

Figure 2.3 Projection

Projections may <u>quote</u> the exact words that someone said, in which case 'speech marks' are usually used in writing:

> 'We're moving to a special unit. Now, now my darling. We are real policemen now.'

Or they may <u>report</u> the general meaning that was said, which normally doesn't require speech marks:

> He and three of our friends have been promoted.

As well as 'saying', it is also possible to quote or report what we think or feel:

> I realized he was drinking too much.
> I know where everything began, the background.
> I wish I could wipe the old South Africa out of everyone's past.

Through projection then we can introduce additional sources of evaluation. And because we can choose from projection over and over again, 'recursively', we can use it to explore the source of sources, and the source of the source of sources as Helena does when talking about what white South African leaders did and didn't know:

> I can understand if Mr (F. W.) de Klerk says he didn't know, but dammit, there must be a clique, there must have been someone out there who is still alive and who can give a face to 'the orders from above' for all the operations.

In this sentence, Helena chooses projection three times. Two projections are 'thinking' (*understand* and *know*), and one is 'saying' (*says*). We can present these recursive sources as a diagram, in Figure 2.4, in which thought bubbles and speech bubbles represent what is thought or said.

Figure 2.4 Recursive sources

In Helena's narrative, projection doesn't just happen within sentences, from 'saying' to 'what is said'. It can also happen across whole texts and text phases. For example Helena begins by presenting herself as narrator (*my story begins*):

> My story begins in my late teenage years as a farm girl in the Bethlehem district of Eastern Free State.

The rest of her story then is what she tells. And she closes her story by handing over to her second love (*a few lines...*):

I end with <u>a few lines that my wasted vulture said to me</u> one night

In both cases Helena's sentence 'projects' the sentences that follow, just as the SABC 'projected' Helena's story:

> <u>they broadcast substantial extracts</u>

And Tutu in turn projects the SABC broadcast:

> <u>The South Africa Broadcasting Corporation's radio team covering the Truth and Reconciliation Commission received a letter</u> from a woman calling herself Helena

So ultimately we have Tutu saying that the SABC said that Helena said that her second love said what he said. This is managed between sentences by naming 'speech acts', such as *my story, a few lines, a letter, substantial extracts*. This kind of projection between sentences is often associated with the beginning and end of texts.

Projections can also be found within clauses, where they explicitly assign responsibility for opinions to sources. Tutu uses this resource four times in relation to claims of innocence, the meaning of *ubuntu*, reputations and the values of the new South African democracy:

> Amnesty is not given to innocent people or to those who <u>claim to be</u> innocent.

> This is a far more personal approach, <u>which sees</u> the offence as something that has happened to people and whose consequence is a rupture in relationships.

> Many of those who have come forward had previously <u>been regarded as</u> respectable members of their communities

> the new culture of respect for human rights and acknowledgment of responsibility and accountability by which <u>the new democracy wishes to be characterised</u>

These projections within clauses include 'saying' *claim to be*, 'seeing' *sees, been regarded as* and 'feeling' *wishes to be*. The Act also uses projections within clauses in relation to claims of victimhood, and in relation to the powers of the Truth and Reconciliation Commission:

> . . . the gathering of information and the receiving of evidence from any person, including <u>persons claiming to be</u> victims of such violations or the representatives of such victims . . .

> . . . establish such offices as <u>it may deem</u> necessary for the performance of its functions

> . . . conduct any investigation or hold any hearing <u>it may deem</u> necessary and establish the investigating unit referred to in section 28

These are examples of 'saying' and 'thinking' (*claiming to be, may deem*).

Finally we need to consider cases where punctuation is used to signal that someone else's words are being used. Helena does this several times in her story:

> Even if he was an Englishman, he was popular with all the <u>'Boer'</u> Afrikaners. And all my girlfriends envied me. Then one day he said he was going on a <u>'trip'</u>.

> Abruptly mutter the feared word <u>'trip'</u> and drive off.

> The role of <u>'those at the top'</u>, the <u>'cliques'</u> and <u>'our men'</u> who simply had to carry out their bloody orders. . . like <u>'vultures'</u>. And today they all wash their hands in innocence and resist the realities of the Truth Commission. Yes, I stand by my murderer who let me and the old White South Africa sleep peacefully. Warmly, while <u>'those at the top'</u> were again targeting the next <u>'permanent removal from society'</u> for the vultures.

> . . . there must have been someone out there who is still alive and who can give a face to <u>'the orders from above'</u> for all the operations.

This device is sometimes referred to as 'scare quotes', and warns readers that these are not Helena's words but someone else's, for example the wording of her second love or white South African leaders. In spoken discourse speakers might use special intonation or voice quality to signal projection of this kind, and sometimes people use gesture to mimic quotation marks, acting out the special punctuation. The effect of this is to disown the evaluation embodied in the highlighted terms, attributing it to an alternative, unspecified, but usually recoverable source.

In sum we have seen four ways in which projection is used to attribute sources: as projecting clauses, as names for speech acts, as projecting within clauses, and as scare quotes. Examples of these are given in Table 2.6.

Table 2.6 Projecting sources

projecting clauses	Then *he <u>says</u>: He and three of our friends have been promoted.* *I <u>know</u> where everything began, the background.*
names for 'speech acts'	*I end with a few <u>lines</u> that my wasted vulture said to me* *they broadcast <u>substantial extracts</u>:*
projecting within clauses	*Many of those who have come forward had previously been regarded as respectable* *such offices as it may deem necessary*
scare quotes	*'those at the top', the 'cliques' and 'our men'*

Modality

Alongside projection, another way of introducing additional voices into a text is via modality, which we introduced above in relation to amplification. Halliday (1994) describes modality as a resource which sets up a semantic space between yes and no, a cline running between positive and negative poles. There are two general kinds of modality, one for negotiating services, and the other for negotiating information (see Chapter 7 below). Demands for a service can be negotiated as follows:

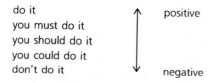

do it   ↑   positive
you must do it
you should do it
you could do it
don't do it   ↓   negative

On this scale we can say 'how obliged' you are to act. On the other hand, statements that give information can be negotiated as follows:

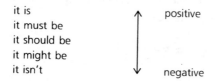

it is   ↑   positive
it must be
it should be
it might be
it isn't   ↓   negative

On this scale we can say 'how probable' a statement is. At each pole of these scales of modality is the choice of positive or negative polarity. As we've said, modality can be used as a resource for introducing additional voices into a text, and this includes polarity. To see how this works, let's start with polarity and the role of negation. Tutu begins his exposition with a question, which he follows up immediately with a negative clause:

> So is amnesty being given at the cost of justice being done? This is **not** a frivolous question, but a very serious issue, one which challenges the integrity of the entire Truth and Reconciliation process.

What Tutu is doing here is countering anyone who thinks that the cost of justice issue is a frivolous question (or perhaps anyone who says Tutu thinks it's frivolous). He uses a negative clause to pre-empt this position before it can cloud the discussion. Negation places his voice in relation to a potential opposing one; two voices are implicated. In this respect negative polarity is different from positive polarity; all things being equal, positive polarity invokes one voice whereas negative polarity invokes two. Here are some more examples from Tutu's exposition:

It is also **not true** that the granting of amnesty encourages impunity in the sense that perpetrators can escape completely the consequences of their actions, because amnesty is only given to those who plead guilty, who accept responsibility for what they have done. Amnesty is **not given** to innocent people or to those who claim to be innocent.

It is important to note too that the amnesty provision is an ad hoc arrangement meant for this specific purpose. This is **not how justice is to be administered** in South Africa for ever. It is for a limited and definite period and purpose.

Further, retributive justice – in which an impersonal state hands down punishment with little consideration for victims and hardly any for the perpetrator – is **not the only form of justice**.

Negation of this kind is a feature of persuasive writing where contesting positions need to be addressed and set aside. Tutu does not in fact allow his opposition to speak, as he would have to do if using projection to give them a voice; the position he gives them is that of a voice acknowledged but denied.

As we have seen, modality can be interpreted as a resource for grading polarity, for setting up degrees of positivity and negativity (an intermediate space between yes and no). Here are two more examples of these scales, beginning with positive at the top and sliding through to negative at the bottom:

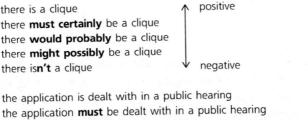

there is a clique   ↑ positive
there **must certainly** be a clique
there **would probably** be a clique
there **might possibly** be a clique
there is**n't** a clique   ↓ negative

the application is dealt with in a public hearing   ↑ positive
the application **must** be dealt with in a public hearing
the application **should** be dealt with in a public hearing
the application **could** be dealt with in a public hearing
the application is **not** dealt with in a public hearing   ↓ negative

Modality functions very much like negation when we look at it in terms of these scales (cf. Fuller 1998; Martin and White 2005). Arguing that something *must* be the case, for example, sounds assertive but in fact allows an element of doubt; it's stronger than saying something *would* be true, but not as strong as avoiding modality completely and arguing it *is* the case. So modality, like polarity, acknowledges alternative voices around a suggestion or claim. Unlike polarity, it doesn't take these voices on and deny them; rather it opens up a space for negotiation, in which different points of view can circulate around an issue, a space perhaps for mediation and possible reconciliation.

Tutu uses a range of modal resources in his exposition to acknowledge alternative positions, including usuality when he is generalizing about the effects of a public hearing:

> It was **often** the very first time that their communities and even **sometimes** their families heard that these people were, for instance, actually members of death squads or **regular** torturers of detainees in their custody.

Here the grading has to do with 'how often' something happened, along a scale like the following:

> it was the first time their families heard
> it was **always** the first time their families heard
> it was **often** the first time their families heard
> it was **sometimes** the first time their families heard
> it wasn't the first time their families heard

Helena uses modality even more often, across a range of modal meanings:

Negotiating information

| how usual | *He and his friends **would visit** regularly* |
| how probable | *there **must have been** someone out there who is still alive* |

Negotiating services

how obliged	*I **had to watch** how white people became dissatisfied with the best*
how inclined	*I **would have done** the same had I been denied everything*
how able	*who **can give** a face to 'the orders from above' for all the operations*

These examples show the five types of modality discussed by Halliday (1994): usuality, probability, obligation, inclination and ability.

The Act, because it is concerned with what should happen, is mainly concerned with obligation (how obliged people are to act):

> AND SINCE **it is deemed necessary** to establish the truth in relation to past events as well as the motives for and circumstances in which gross violations of human rights have occurred, and to make the findings known in order to prevent a repetition of such acts in future;
> AND SINCE the Constitution states that the pursuit of national unity, the well-being of all South African citizens and peace **require** reconciliation between the people of South Africa and the reconstruction of society;
> AND SINCE the Constitution states that there is **a need** for understanding but not for vengeance, **a need** for reparation but not for retaliation, **a need** for ubuntu but not for victimisation;
> AND SINCE the Constitution states that in order to advance such reconciliation and

> reconstruction amnesty **shall be** granted in respect of acts, omissions and offences associated with political objectives committed in the course of the conflicts of the past

The last example here makes use of what we might call 'legislative' *shall* to signal incontestable obligation. By Chapter 2 of the Act, this use of *shall* becomes dominant as the various processes around the establishment of the Truth and Reconciliation Commission are prescribed:

> (3) In order to achieve the objectives of the Commission –
> (a) the Committee on Human Rights Violations, as contemplated in Chapter 3, **shall deal**, among other things, with matters pertaining to investigations of gross violations of human rights;
> (b) the Committee on Amnesty, as contemplated in Chapter 4, **shall deal** with matters relating to amnesty;
> (c) the Committee on Reparation and Rehabilitation, as contemplated in Chapter 5, **shall deal** with matters referred to it relating to reparations;
> (d) the investigating unit referred to in section 5(d) **shall perform** the investigations contemplated in section 28(4)(a); and
> (e) the subcommittees **shall exercise, perform and carry out** the powers, functions and duties conferred upon, assigned to or imposed upon them by the Commission.

Some projections also include modality or polarity in their meaning, and so can be interpreted as heteroglossic with respect to both projection and modalization (Hyland 1998). Tutu uses three of these:

> They **denied** that they had committed a crime, **claiming** that they had assaulted him only in retaliation for his inexplicable conduct in attacking them.

> I **contend** that there is another kind of justice, restorative justice.

Denied includes the meaning of 'not true'; *claiming* allows for doubt; *contend* is less strong than *claim* (more 'should be' than 'must be true').

Concession

The third resource we need to consider, as far as heteroglossia in discourse is concerned, is known as 'counterexpectancy'. This is more a feature of Helena's narrative than the exposition or Act, and has to do with the way she tracks readers' expectations, adjusting them as her story unfolds. In her prayer for example, she tells God she can't handle her second love anymore, creating an expectation as she does so that she will try to leave. Then she counters this by saying that she can't leave.

> I can't handle the man anymore! **But**, I can't get out.

In this example Helena uses the conjunction *but* to signal that she is countering an expectation that she's created for the reader. At any point in a text, readers have an expectation about what is likely to follow, and Helena takes this into account as she counters it. In other words she is acknowledging voices in addition to her own, in this case those of her readers. Here are some more examples of this kind of monitoring from Helena's story:

> Not quite my first love, **but** an exceptional person.
> He tried to hide his wild consuming fear, **but** I saw it.
> Eyes bewildered, **but** dull like the dead.
> I can understand if . . . de Klerk says he didn't know, **but** dammit, there must be a clique

Conjunctions like *but*, that counter expectations, are termed **concessive**. Concessive conjunctions are discussed further in Chapter 4. Here we will review how they are used to monitor the reader's expectations.

But is the most common conjunction used to signal concession. But there are other possibilities, including *however* and *although*, and variations on the theme including *even if* and *even by*; *in fact, at least, indeed*; and *nevertheless, needless to say, of course, admittedly, in any case* etc:

> **Even if** God and everyone else forgives me a thousand times – I have to live with this hell.

Even if here means 'more than expected' – given the condition of forgiveness, his continued hell is unexpected.

> I envy and respect the people of the struggle – **at least** their leaders have the guts to stand by their vultures, to recognise their sacrifices.

> Spiritual murder is more inhumane than a messy, physical murder. **At least** a murder victim rests.

Monitoring expectancy is in fact a pervasive feature of conjunctions, realized as time, contrast and causes. In the next examples *suddenly* means 'sooner than expected' and *instead of resting at night* implies that 'resting at night' is what we'd normally expect:

> They even stayed over for long periods. **Suddenly**, at strange times, they would become restless.

> **Instead of** resting at night, he would wander from window to window.

Tutu also makes some use of concession in his exposition...

> Here the central concern is not retribution or punishment **but**, in the spirit of ubuntu, the healing of breaches, the redressing of imbalances, the restoration of broken relationships.

... including the 'internal' rhetorical sense of 'in spite of what I've led you to expect me to say' (as opposed to the 'external' meaning 'in spite of what you expect to happen'). Here Tutu means that although he's granted that public hearings weren't an absolute requirement, in fact virtually all important cases were heard that way:

> The Act required that where the offence is a gross violation of human rights – defined as an abduction, killing, torture or severe ill-treatment – the application should be dealt with in a public hearing unless such a hearing was likely to lead to a miscarriage of justice (for instance, where witnesses were too intimidated to testify in open session). **In fact**, virtually all the important applications to the Commission have been considered in public in the full glare of television lights.

The Act makes no use of this kind of expectancy monitoring at all.

Alongside conjunctions another important set of resources for adjusting expectations are **continuatives**. These are like conjunctions but they occur inside the clause, rather than at the beginning. They include words like *already, finally, still* and *only, just, even*. Continuatives that express time indicate that something happens sooner or later, or persists longer than one might expect. In the following example Helena comments on white peoples' greed as persisting longer than one might reasonably expect:

> If I had to watch how white people became dissatisfied with the best and **still** wanted better and got it.

Other continuatives indicate that there is more or less to a situation than has been implied:

> It was the beginning of a beautiful relationship. We **even** spoke about marriage.

> Amnesty didn't matter. It was **only** a means to the truth.

Tutu uses much less of this resource to adjust expectancy:

> They denied that they had committed a crime, claiming that they had assaulted him **only** in retaliation for his inexplicable conduct in attacking them.

Now that we have brought modality and concession into the picture, alongside projection, it is timely to introduce the technical term used to name this region of meaning, namely **engagement**.

Summing up, then, what we have are three main appraisal systems: attitude, amplification and source. Attitude comprises affect, judgement and appreciation: our three major regions of feeling. Amplification covers grading, including force and focus; force involves the choice to raise or lower the intensity of gradable items, focus the option of sharpening or softening an experiential boundary. Engagement covers resources that introduce additional voices into a discourse, via projection, modalization or concession; the key choice here is one voice (monogloss) or more than one voice (heterogloss). These key appraisal systems are outlined in Figure 2.5. In order to more accurately reflect the ways in which people combine different kinds of engagement, attitude and graduation in discourse, the network now contains three <u>simultaneous</u> systems for these regions of appraisal. That is we can choose from all of them at the same time.

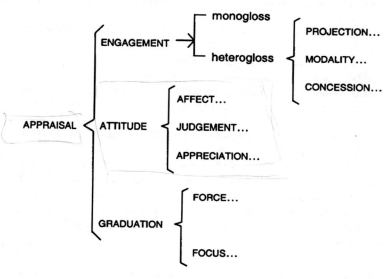

Figure 2.5 Appraisal systems: an overview

2.5 Prosody and genre

Appraisal resources are used to establish the tone or mood of a passage of discourse, as choices resonate with one another from one moment to another as a text unfolds. The pattern of choices is thus 'prosodic'. They form a prosody of attitude running through the text that swells and diminishes, in the manner of a musical prosody. The prosodic pattern of appraisal choices constructs the 'stance' or 'voice' of the appraiser, and this stance or voice defines the kind of community that is being set up around shared values. In everyday language, these stances are often discussed as ranging along a scale from more objective to more subjective.

As we have seen, among our genres the Act is well down towards the objective end of this scale, especially where it is defining terms:

CHAPTER 1
Interpretation and application
Definitions
1. (1) In this Act, unless the context otherwise indicates —

(i)   "act associated with a political objective" **has the meaning ascribed thereto** in section 20(2) and (3); (ii)

(ii) "article" **includes** any evidence, book, document, file, object, writing, recording or transcribed computer printout produced by any mechanical or electronic device or any device by means of which information is recorded, stored or transcribed; (xix)

(iii) "Commission" **means** the Truth and Reconciliation Commission established by section 2; (ix)

(iv) "commissioner" **means** a member of the Commission appointed in terms of section 7(2)(a); (viii)

(v)   "committee" **means** the Committee on Human Rights Violations, the Committee on Amnesty or the Committee on Reparation and Rehabilitation, as the case may be; (vii)

(vi) "Constitution" **means** the Constitution of the Republic of South Africa, 1993 (Act No. 200 of 1993); (iv)

(vii) "cut-off date" **means** the latest date allowed as the cut-off date in terms of the Constitution as set out under the heading "National Unity and Reconciliation"; (i)

(viii) "former state" **means** any state or territory which was established by an Act of Parliament or by proclamation in terms of such an Act prior to the commencement of the Constitution and the territory of which now forms part of the Republic; (xvii)

As far as appraisal resources are concerned, this kind of 'objectivity' appears to involve a range of factors, basically as little attitude, graduation and heteroglossia as possible. We might think of this as a kind of faceless stance. But the absence of feelings, intensification and alternative voices is itself a face, a cool excluding one perhaps, but it is a face. In the phase reproduced above, the Act is in fact taking pains to construct a very precise interpretation of the Truth and Reconciliation Commission. We could argue that the resources used to define terms (highlighted above) are in fact monoglossing resources designed to ensure that the Act speaks with one clear voice as far as its administrative goals are concerned. The absence of graduation helps to keep the definitions tight; the near absence of projection, modalization and concession works to reinforce the monovocal stance. This is not in other words a text to argue with – it's the law.

At the other end of the spectrum we have Helena's narrative, which uses a full range of attitudinal, graduation and engagement resources. Perhaps this is why we find narrative so enjoyable across a range of modalities (books, film, chat, TV, comics, radio and so on). There's all kinds of feelings to share; the volume pumps up and down to keep us interested and boundaries are squished to loosen or tighten things up; lots of voices are invoked and we get to be a part of things. It all hangs out.

Tutu's exposition is somewhere in between. It uses attitude, but not a full range. There is some, but not a lot of intensification; focus is used sparingly, to be precise, sharpening boundaries. Alternative voices are acknowledged, but mainly for rebuttal. Tutu is talking us round, persuading us. He makes the effort to argue for his position, unlike the Act which simply declares.

These kinds of differences between genres are reflected in differences between stages within genres. As noted above, Helena has more affect in her Incidents than her Interpretations, which tend in their turn to foreground judgement. Tutu's first and second arguments focus on judgement, but appreciation (around the concept of *ubuntu*) plays a major role in his third. The Act avoids appraisal almost completely in its definitions, but earlier projects the voice of the South African Constitution, including its modalization and reconciliation-oriented appreciations:

> AND SINCE the Constitution **states** that the pursuit of **national unity**, the **well-being** of all South African citizens and peace **require reconciliation** between the people of South Africa and the **reconstruction** of society;
> AND SINCE the Constitution **states** that there is a **need** for **understanding** but **not** for **vengeance**, a **need** for **reparation** but **not** for **retaliation**, a **need** for **ubuntu** but not for **victimisation**

In other words as texts unfold they try to move us in different ways, to form different kinds of relationship with us, to commune with us strategically. Appraisal is to rhetoric as conjunction is to logic we might say; it unfolds dynamically to engage us, to get us on side, not with one appeal, but through a spectrum of manoeuvres that work themselves out phase by phase.

We'll close this section with an example of stance shifting from one of Jim's papers where he tried to figure out what he found so moving about the final couple of pages of Nelson Mandela's autobiography *Long Walk to Freedom* (a text we'll return to in Chapter 7). He worked on this as a functional linguist and semiotician and organized his paper in six sections:

1. The text
2. Abstracting freedom
3. Enlightenment
4. Engagement

5.   Recontextualization
6.   Grace.

In order to get it published in a scholarly journal (*Discourse Studies*) he adopted a relatively objective stance (of the scholarly kind studied by Hunston (1994) and Myers (1989)), not completely faceless, but tending towards the monovocal and cool. By the end of this study however he was still feeling a little mystified about why the text he was analysing was so moving. His communion with Mandela, at such a distance in so many respects, seemed to transcend the sum of the analyses he had undertaken, however focused he tried to make them on what was going on. In exasperation, he decided to shift stance and wrote:

6. Grace

In this paper I have tried, from my own specific reading position, to analyse this instance of discourse in relation to the meanings I've been trained to decode. If allowed a reaction, the term that comes to mind is *grace*, in every meaning of the word. The gracefulness with which the recount unfolds, the charm of its rhetoric, the goodwill to all peoples... I can't help admiring the texture, and the Mandela it construes for me. And in this kind of reaction, I am not alone. Consider for example the evaluative terms used promotionally on the covers of Mandela 1995: *anger, sorrow, love, joy, grace, elegance, riveting, brilliantly, emotive, compelling, uplifting, exhilarating, epic, hardship, resilience, triumph, clarity, eloquence, burns with the luminosity of faith, invincible, hope, dignity, enthralling, great, indispensable, unique, truly stunning, extraordinary, vivid, unusual, courage, persistence, tolerance, forgiveness, extraordinary, well worth, greatness, struggle, idealism, inspired, cynicism, compulsory*. What is the appeal?

I suspect what we are examining here is Mandela's ability to naturalise radical values in terms that disarm rather than confront. Both the recount and its multimodal recontextualisation promote a politics of freedom that involves respecting and enhancing the freedom of others. Put into practice, this involves more than an end to apartheid and reconciliation with its perpetrators. Ultimately it involves the reconfiguration of a global economic order which distributes resources so unevenly that it has to be propped up by all manner of unbearable regimes. In a sense then, Mandela is promoting socialism in the name of freedom; he naturalises a comfortable reading position for those who might oppose his aims, and at the same time gives his sympathisers an inspirational shot in the arm. If discourse analysts are serious about wanting to use their work to enact social change, then they will have to broaden their coverage to include discourse of this kind – discourse that inspires, encourages, heartens; discourse we like, that cheers us along. We need, in other words, more positive discourse analysis (PDA?) alongside our critique; and this means dealing with texts we admire, alongside those we dislike and try to expose (Wodak 1996). (Martin 1999a: 51–2)

As the first paragraph indicates, Jim decided to change gears (invoking professorial privilege perhaps), to stop analysing the text for a moment and just react. He evaluates the text as graceful, he's charmed by it, he admires it and of course the man who wrote it. And he shows that in these reactions he's not alone, canvassing the range of attitudes used for promotional purposes on the covers of Mandela's book. Then quickly, before getting trounced by his editor (the ever exacting Teun van Dijk, no less), he pulls back in the following paragraph, gets cool, goes scholarly again and tries to figure out again, in academic terms, how Mandela manages to pull it off. He's wrestling with the sublime perhaps, but felt he got a little closer by changing gears than by plodding along. Allowing himself a reaction got him thinking about how Mandela finesses his radical politics, disarming people round the world into communities of admiring fans. And it allowed Jim to make a further point about the importance of focusing on heartening discourses of this kind instead of being so depressingly critical all the time by focusing solely on hegemony and all that's wrong with the world. Ultimately what the change of voices achieved perhaps was to bring a community of critical discourse analysts into contact with a community of political activists and supporters by way of saying 'c'mon guys, let's do something about this. These guys are heroes; let's see how they move the world along'. Two voices in tandem worked, where a single voice, the scholarly one, seemed to be kind of missing the point.

Just as we've been changing voices here; we'll pull back now, in case our scholarly credentials are wearing a little thin.

2.6 More detail on kinds of attitudes

Appraisal is a huge resource for constructing communities of feeling, and a great deal of it is realized through lexis as well as grammar, which makes it even more unwieldy to deploy than we've allowed for here. Lexis is the part of language after all that changes most quickly – it's flexi-language, designed to adjust quickly to changing times, new needs. There's a lot going on and it's hard to keep up. And a lot of attitude is specialized, used in some specific registers but not all. When Jim's 11-year-old son, a speaker of Marrickville English in Sydney Australia, says something 'rocks' you may know where he's coming from or you may not. Does it mean something is good or bad? Is *rocks* an evaluative item at all? So as a final step, we'll try and give you some more scaffolding for analysing attitude here. It won't be enough for all purposes, but it will get you going.

Affect

Affect can be realized in various grammatical niches. In Halliday's (1994) terms, these include 'qualities', 'processes' and 'comments' (grammatical functions for each type are given in the third column):

affect as 'quality'		
describing participants	a **happy** boy	Epithet
attributed to participants	the boy was **happy**	Attribute
manner of processes	the boy played **happily**	Circumstance
affect as 'process'[2]		
affective sensing	the present **pleased** the boy	Process (effective)
affective behaving	the boy **smiled**	Process (middle)
affect as 'comment'		
desiderative comment	**happily**, he had a long nap	Modal Adjunct

To classify affect, we can ask the following questions:

1. **are the feelings positive or negative**
2. **are the feelings a surge of emotion or an ongoing mental state**
3. **are the feelings reacting to some specific external agency or an ongoing mood**
4. **are the feelings as more or less intense**
5. **do the feelings involve intention rather than reaction**
6. **are the feelings to do with un/happiness, in/security or dis/satisfaction?**

Let's now examine these six questions in more detail.

(1) Are the feelings popularly construed by the culture as positive (good vibes that are enjoyable to experience) or negative ones (bad vibes that are better avoided)? We are not concerned here with the value that a particular psychological framework might place on one or another emotion (cf. 'It's probably productive that you're feeling sad because it's a sign that. . .').

positive affect	the boy was **happy**
negative affect	the boy was **sad**

(2) Are the feelings realized as a surge of emotion involving some kind of embodied paralinguistic or extralinguistic manifestation, or more prosodically experienced as a kind of predisposition or ongoing mental state? Grammatically this distinction is constructed as the opposition between behavioural (e.g. *She smiled at him*) vs mental (e.g. *She liked him*) or relational (e.g. *She felt happy with him*) processes.

behavioural surge	the boy **laughed**

mental disposition   *the boy **liked** the present/the boy felt **happy***

(3) Are the feelings construed as directed at or reacting to some specific external agency (typically conscious) or as a general ongoing mood for which one might pose the question 'Why are you feeling that way?' and get the answer 'I'm not sure.'

reaction to other   *the boy **liked** the teacher/the teacher **pleased** the boy*
undirected mood   *the boy was **happy***

(4) How are the feelings graded: towards the lower valued end of a scale of intensity, towards the higher valued end or somewhere in between? We don't wish at this stage to imply that low, median and high are discrete values (as with MODALITY, cf. Halliday 1994: 358–9), but expect that most emotions offer lexicalizations that grade along an evenly-clined scale.

low   *the boy **liked** the present*
'median'   *the boy **loved** the present*
high   *the boy **adored** the present*

(5) Do the feelings involve intention (rather than reaction), with respect to a stimulus that is irrealis (rather than realis).

realis   *the boy **liked** the present*
irrealis   *the boy **wanted** the present*

Irrealis affect seems always to be directed at some external agency, and so can be outlined as in Table 2.7 (setting aside parameter 3 above).

Table 2.7 Irrealis affect

DIS/INCLINATION	SURGE (of behaviour)	DISPOSITION
fear	tremble	wary
	shudder	fearful
	cower	terrorized
desire	suggest	incomplete (miss)
	request	lonely (long for)
	implore	bereft (yearn for)

(6) Finally we can group emotions into three major sets having to do with un/happiness, in/security and dis/satisfaction. For example:

in/security	the boy was **anxious/confident**
dis/satisfaction	the boy was **fed up/absorbed**
un/happiness	the boy was **sad/happy**

Feelings can be experienced as emotional <u>dispositions</u>, such as *sad* or *happy*, or they may appear as surges of behaviour, such as *crying* and *laughing*. Each group of emotions is set out in Table 2.8, including examples of both dispositions and surges. Each group includes both positive and negative feelings, with examples that express three degrees of intensity.

Table 2.8 Realis affect

UN/HAPPINESS	SURGE (of behaviour)	DISPOSITION	
unhappiness: misery [mood: 'in me']	*whimper* *cry* *wail*	*down* *sad* *miserable*	*[low]* *[median]* *[high]*
unhappiness: antipathy [directed feeling: 'at you']	*rubbish* *abuse* *revile*	*dislike* *hate* *abhor*	
happiness: cheer	*chuckle* *laugh* *rejoice*	*cheerful* *buoyant* *jubilant*	
happiness: affection	*shake hands* *hug* *cuddle*	*fond* *loving* *adoring*	

IN/SECURITY	SURGE (of behaviour)	DISPOSITION
insecurity: disquiet	*restless* *twitching* *shaking*	*uneasy* *anxious* *freaked out*
insecurity: surprise	*start* *cry out* *faint*	*taken aback* *surprised* *astonished*
security: confidence	*declare* *assert* *proclaim*	*confident* *assured* *boastful*
security: trust	*delegate* *commit* *entrust*	*comfortable with* *confident in/about* *trusting*

DIS/SATISFACTION	SURGE (of behaviour)	DISPOSITION
dissatisfaction: ennui	fidget yawn tune out	bored fed up exasperated
dissatisfaction: displeasure	caution scold castigate	cross angry furious
satisfaction: interest	attentive busy flat out	curious absorbed engrossed
satisfaction: admiration	pat on the back compliment reward	satisfied impressed proud

The framework for un/happiness, in/security and dis/satisfaction emerged from Jim's observations of his young sons, when they were in their first stages of socialization (up to about 2 years of age), and in particular of a cycle of demands structuring his elder son's temper tantrums over a period of several months. During these tantrums he would insist on having *baggy* (his blanket), and then when it was proffered and rejected his *bopple* (bottle), and then when this was proffered and rejected *Mummy* or *Daddy* (whichever was not present), and then baggy again, then bopple ... for up to an hour. If we take these primal screams as primitives, then a framework involving in/security (blanket), dis/satisfaction (bottle) and un/happiness (Mummy/Daddy) can be entertained. The in/security variable covers emotions concerned with ecosocial well-being – anxiety, fear, confidence and trust; the dis/satisfaction variable covers emotions concerned with telos (the pursuit of goals) – ennui, displeasure, curiosity, respect; the un/happiness variable covers emotions concerned with 'affairs of the heart' – sadness, anger, happiness and love. Unfortunately we have not been able to develop a more principled basis for classifying emotions in recent years and take little comfort from the array of divergent frameworks available elsewhere in the literature (including the evolving variations in Martin 1992 and 1996).

Judgement

Judgement can be thought of as the institutionalization of feeling, in the context of proposals (norms about how people should and shouldn't behave). Like affect, it has a positive and negative dimension corresponding to positive and negative judgements about behaviour. Media research reported in Iedema et al. (1994) has suggested dividing judgements into two major groups, social esteem and social sanction. Social esteem involves admiration and criticism, typically without legal implications; if you have difficulties in this area you may need a therapist. Social sanction on the other hand involves praise, and condemnation, often with legal implications; if you have problems in this area you may need a lawyer. Judgements of esteem have to do with normality (how unusual someone is), capacity (how capable they are) and tenacity (how resolute they are); judgements of sanction have to do with veracity (how truthful someone is) and propriety (how ethical someone is). Each of these varieties of judgements are exemplified in Table 2.9. For each set, examples are given that express various types of judgement (e.g. *lucky, normal, fashionable*), and different degrees of intensity within each type (e.g. *lucky, fortunate, charmed*).

Table 2.9 Types of judgement

SOCIAL ESTEEM 'venial'	positive [admire]	negative [criticize]
normality [fate] 'is s/he special?'	*lucky, fortunate, charmed...* *normal, average, everyday...* *in, fashionable, avant garde...*	*unfortunate, pitiful, tragic...* *odd, peculiar, eccentric...* *dated, daggy, retrograde...*
capacity 'is s/he capable?'	*powerful, vigorous, robust...* *insightful, clever, gifted...* *balanced, together, sane...*	*mild, weak, wimpy...* *slow, stupid, thick...* *flaky, neurotic, insane...*
tenacity [resolve] 'is s/he dependable?'	*plucky, brave, heroic...* *reliable, dependable...* *tireless, persevering, resolute...*	*rash, cowardly, despondent...* *unreliable, undependable...* *weak, distracted, dissolute...*
SOCIAL SANCTION 'moral'	positive [praise]	negative [condemn]
veracity [truth] 'is s/he honest?'	*truthful, honest, credible...* *sincere, genuine...* *frank, direct...*	*dishonest, deceitful...* *insincere, fake...* *deceptive, manipulative...*
propriety [ethics] 'is s/he beyond reproach?'	*good, moral, ethical...* *law-abiding, fair, just...* *sensitive, kind, caring...*	*bad, immoral, evil...* *corrupt, unfair, unjust...* *insensitive, mean, cruel...*

The kinds of judgement speakers take up is very sensitive to their institutional position. For example only journalists with responsibility for writing editorials and other comment have a full range of judgmental resources at their disposal; reporters writing hard news that is meant to sound objective have to avoid explicit judgements completely (Iedema *et al.* 1994; Martin and White 2005). The distinction between social esteem and social sanction in other words has important implications for the subjective or objective flavour of an appraiser's stance.

Appreciation

Appreciation can be thought of as the institutionalization of feeling, in the context of propositions (norms about how products and performances are valued). Like affect and judgement it has a positive and negative dimension corresponding to positive and negative evaluations of texts and processes (and natural phenomena). The system is organized around three variables: reaction, composition and valuation. Reaction has to do with attention (reaction: impact) and the emotional impact it has on us with the degree to which the text/process in question captures our

Table 2.10 Types of appreciation

	positive	negative
reaction: impact 'did it grab me?'	*arresting, captivating, involving, engaging, absorbing, imposing, stunning, striking, compelling, interesting...*	*dull, boring, tedious, staid...*
	fascinating, exciting, moving... remarkable, notable, sensational...	*dry, ascetic, uninviting... unremarkable, pedestrian ...*
	lively, dramatic, intense...	*flat, predictable, monotonous...*
reaction: quality 'did I like it?'	*lovely, beautiful, splendid... appealing, enchanting, pleasing, delightful, attractive, welcome...*	*plain, ugly... repulsive, off-putting, revolting, irritating, weird...*
composition: balance 'did it hang together?'	*balanced, harmonious, unified, symmetrical, proportional...*	*unbalanced, discordant, unfinished, incomplete...*
composition: complexity 'was it hard to follow?'	*simple, elegant...*	*ornamental, over-complicated, extravagant, puzzling...*
	intricate, rich, detailed, precise...	*monolithic, simplistic...*
valuation 'was it worthwhile?'	*challenging, significant, deep, profound, provocative, daring... experimental, innovative, original, unique, fruitful, illuminating... enduring, lasting...*	*shallow, insignificant, unsatisfying, sentimental... conservative, reactionary, generic... unmemorable, forgettable...*

attention (reaction: impact) and the emotional impact it has on us (reaction: quality). Composition has to do with our perceptions of proportionality (composition: balance) and detail (composition: complexity) in a text/process. Valuation has to do with our assessment of the social significance of the text/process. Examples of reaction, composition and valuation are shown in Table 2.10 above.

Of these dimensions, valuation is especially tied up with field, since the criteria for valuing a text/process are for the most part institutionally specific. But beyond this, since both judgement and appreciation are in a sense institutionalizations of feeling, all of the dimensions involved will prove sensitive to field. An example of this coupling of ideational and interpersonal meaning is presented in Table 2.11 for appreciations of research in the field of linguistics.

Table 2.11 Appreciation in a specialized field (linguistics)

linguistics	positive	negative
reaction: impact [notability]	*timely, long awaited, engaging, landmark...*	*untimely, unexpected, overdue, surprising, dated...*
reaction: quality [likeability]	*fascinating, exciting, interesting, stimulating, impressive, admirable...*	*dull, tedious, boring, pedantic, didactic, uninspired...*
composition [balance]	*consistent, balanced, thorough, considered, unified, logical, well argued, well presented...*	*fragmented, loose ended, disorganized, contradictory, sloppy...*
composition [complexity]	*simple, lucid, elegant, rich, detailed, exhaustive, clear, precise ...*	*simplistic, extravagant, complicated, Byzantine, labyrinthine, overly elaborate, narrow, vague, unclear, indulgent, esoteric, eclectic...*
valuation [field genesis]	*useful, penetrating, illuminating, challenging, significant, deep, profound, satisfying, fruitful...*	*shallow, ad hoc, reductive, unconvincing, unsupported, fanciful, tendentious, bizarre, counterintuitive, perplexing, arcane...*

Further complicating this issue is the implicit coupling of field with appreciation (the evocation variable noted above). As with affect and judgement, ideational meanings can be used to appraise, even though explicitly evaluative lexis is avoided. It perhaps should be stressed again here that appraisal analysts do need to declare their reading position, in particular since the evaluation one makes of evocations depends on the institutional position one is reading from. For example, according to reading position, formal and functional linguists will evaluate terms in the following sets of oppositions in complementary ways with firm convictions about what the good guys and the bad guys should celebrate:

rule/resource:: cognitive/social:: acquisition/development:: syntagmatic/paradigmatic:: form/function:: language/parole:: system/process:: psychology &philosophy/sociology&anthropology:: cognitive/social:: theory/description:: intuition/corpus:: knowledge/meaning:: syntax/discourse:: pragmatics/context:: parsimony/extravagance:: cognitive/critical:: technicist/humanist:: truth/social action:: performance/instantiation:: categorical/probabilistic:: contradictory/complementary:: proof/exemplification:: reductive/comprehensive:: arbitrary/natural:: modular/fractal:: syntax&lexicon/lexicogrammar. . .

NOTES

1   We're treating *envy and respect* as directly encoding affect here, and as indirectly implying judgement; see Martin and White (2005) for further discussion.

2   Affect as 'process' also includes relations such as *I'm pleased that ...*, *It's pleasing that ...*.

IDEATION: construing experience

3

Chapter Outline

Ideation is concerned with how our experience is construed in discourse. It focuses on sequences of activities, the people and things involved in them, and their associated places and qualities, and on how these elements are built up and related to each other as a text unfolds.

Following an introduction, this chapter has three main sections. Section 3.2 describes chains of relations between lexical elements in a text, such as repetition, synonymy and contrast. As they build up a picture of people and things as a text unfolds, these are known as **taxonomic relations**. Section 3.4 describes lexical relations between processes, people, things, places and qualities within each clause. As they are more or less central in the clause, these are known as **nuclear relations**. Section 3.5 describes relations between activities as a text unfolds. As they construe experience as unfolding in series of activities, these relations are known as **activity sequences**.

In section 3.2 a method is introduced for analysing taxonomic relations in a text, that allows us to see relations between lexical elements as a text unfolds, as well as the overall pictures of people and things that a text construes. Section 3.4 includes methods for analysing nuclear relations in a text, that display how people and things participate in activities, and how lexical elements are related across different parts of grammar. Section 3.5 concludes with a method for analysing activity sequences in a text that displays its phases of activities as well as its patterns of participation by people and things.

The final section 3.6 discusses what happens when lexical meanings are expressed by atypical wordings, such as realizing a process as a noun instead of a verb ('nominalization'). This is known as **grammatical metaphor**, and a method is described for unpacking grammatical metaphors to help analyse activity sequences.

3.1 Construing experience

The model of human experience at the heart of ideational meaning, in all languages, is of processes involving people, things, places and qualities. Halliday (1994: 106) proposes that this construal of experience lies behind the grammar of the clause:

> The clause ... embodies a general principle for modelling experience – namely the principle that reality is made up of PROCESSES. Our most powerful impression of experience is that it consists of goings on – happening, doing, sensing, meaning, being and becoming. All these goings-on are sorted out in the grammar of the clause.

The grammar of the clause organizes such 'goings on' as configurations of elements, such as a process, a person and a place:

> In this interpretation of what is going on, there is doing, a doer, and a location where the doing takes place. This tripartite interpretation ... is what lies behind the grammatical distinction of word classes into verbs, nouns and the rest, a pattern that in some form or other is probably universal among human languages. (*ibid.*: 108)

From a grammatical perspective, the clause is a structure of words and word groups, but from a discourse semantic perspective the clause construes an activity involving people and things. The core elements of such a figure are the process and the people and things that are directly involved in it, while other elements such as places and qualities may be more peripheral. This nuclear model of experience is diagrammed in Figure 3.1. The 'doer–doing' nucleus is represented as a revolving yin/yang complementarity, with 'place' and 'quality' in peripheral orbits.

Grammatical descriptions such as those in Halliday and Matthiessen (2004), and Caffarel *et al.* (2004), have richly elaborated this construal of experience within the clause, in various dimensions. They describe grammatical patterns that:

- distinguish types of processes – doing, happening, thinking, saying, being, having
- expand processes – in dimensions such as time, manner, cause
- differentiate roles of people and things participating in a process – for example as the Medium, Range or Agent of the process
- modify these participants – classifying, describing and counting them, their parts, possessions, facets and so on
- distinguish types of circumstances associated with activities – such as places, times and qualities.

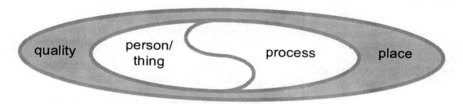

Figure 3.1 Nuclear model of experience as activity

As rich as these grammatical resources are for specifying aspects of experience, they still comprise only a part of the strategies that language provides us for construing experience. Two complementary sets of ideational patterns are equally necessary. One is the conjunctive relations that logically relate one clause to the next, so construing experience as unfolding series of activities. We outline these resources in Chapter 4 on CONJUNCTION. The other is lexical relations, that is semantic relations between the particular people, things, processes, places and qualities that build the field of a text. These relations between lexical elements comprise the system of IDEATION.

So fields of experience consist of sequences of activities involving people, things, places and qualities. These activities are realized by clauses and their elements. We are concerned in this chapter with lexical relations between these elements, within and beyond the clause. Our goal is to outline the patterns of lexical relations that can combine to construe a field.

We can identify three sets of lexical relations. The first is the chains of relations between elements as a text unfolds, from one clause to the next. These include relations such as repetition, synonymy and contrast, that build up a picture of people and things as the text progresses. For example, early in her story Helena begins to construct a picture of herself as a teenage girl: *late teenage years – farm girl – eighteen-year-old.* As they progressively construct taxonomies of people, things, places and their qualities, these are known as **taxonomic relations**.

The second is the configurations of elements within each clause. These include relations between people and things and the process they are involved in, and the places and qualities associated with the process, for example the configuration of two people and a process when Helena's romance starts: *Helena – meet – young man*. As they are more or less central to the unfolding of the process, as in Figure 3.1, these are known as **nuclear relations**.

The third is the sequence of activities construed by clauses as a text unfolds. These are the relations from one process to the next that imply a series of steps, such as *meeting – beginning relationship – marriage*. As they construe the field of a text as unfolding in series of activities, these relations are known as **activity sequences**. These three systems of IDEATION are summarised in Figure 3.2.

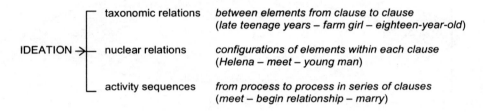

	taxonomic relations	between elements from clause to clause (late teenage years – farm girl – eighteen-year-old)
IDEATION →	nuclear relations	configurations of elements within each clause (Helena – meet – young man)
	activity sequences	from process to process in series of clauses (meet – begin relationship – marry)

Figure 3.2 IDEATION systems

3.2 Taxonomic relations

The first Incident of Helena's story principally concerns herself and her first love, who are seen from various perspectives as the events unfold. For example, she classifies her young self as *a farm girl*, and her lover as *a young man* and *an Englishman*, and contrasts this identity with *the 'Boer' Afrikaners*. Each mention of them is highlighted below in bold and bold italic.

> My story begins in **my late teenage years** as **a farm girl** in the Bethlehem district of Eastern Free State.
>
> As **an eighteen-year-old**, I met *a young man in his twenties*. He was working in a top security structure. It was the beginning of a beautiful relationship. We even spoke about marriage. A bubbly, vivacious man who beamed out wild energy. Sharply intelligent. Even if he was *an Englishman*, he was popular with *all the 'Boer' Afrikaners.* And all my girlfriends envied me.

If we extract these instances we can see more clearly how Helena and her lover are classified:

Helena	**her first love**	**others**
my late teenage years	a young man in his twenties	all the 'Boer' Afrikaners
a farm girl	an Englishman	
an eighteen-year-old		

Helena describes herself in terms of her youth and her origins, and her lover in terms of his youth and English ethnicity, and she then contrasts this with another ethnic group he was popular with. As he is the focus of the story, her description of him is far more developed, including many positive attributes, such as *bubbly, vivacious, beamed out wild energy, sharply intelligent, popular.* However, these inscribed judgements are dealt with as appraisals in Chapter 2, and we will set them aside in the discussion here, limiting ourselves to purely ideational categories.

Helena constructs an unfolding picture of herself and her lover as members of more general classes, such as age and ethnicity, that are not stated but are assumed by their instances in the text. We will refer to the relation between one instance of a class and the next as a **co-class** relation. In Table 3.1 we analyse each of these relationships as strings of lexical relations as the events unfold.

Table 3.1 Lexical strings of Helena and her first love

Helena's youth	**her lover**
late teenage years	*young man*
co-class	co-class
farm girl	*Englishman*
co-class	co-class
eighteen-year-old	*'Boer' Afrikaners*

Underlying these instances in the text are general social categories, including age, gender, ethnicity, capacity and class (see Chapter 9, section 9.3). Figure 3.3 shows some of their sub-categories, that are instantiated[1] in this phase of the story. Dotted lines show how people are cross-classified by multiple categories, such as *a farm girl* by her class, age and gender. (Triple dots represent unstated other sub-categories.)

If we pull back the focus from Helena and her first love, to the broader classes of people running through the story as a whole, we can make explicit the social world that she constructs in the story in Figure 3.4.

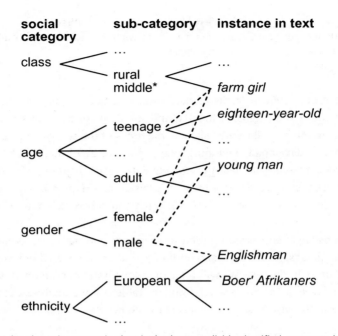

*Although Helena's socioeconomic class is the least explicitly classified category, in the context of apartheid South Africa we can perhaps assume that a European who writes about herself as a *farm girl* may be a daughter of small farmers, i.e. of the rural middle class.

Figure 3.3 Some social categories instantiated in Helena's story

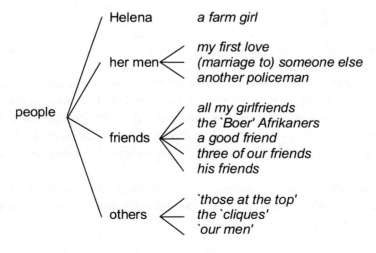

Figure 3.4 The social world in Helena's story

The taxonomy in Figure 3.4 displays Helena's construal of her social world in egocentric classes, from herself to the men in her life, her own and her lovers' friends, and finally those beyond her personal world, those in power and the men they turned into vultures. Note how the contrast between the personal world of friends and lovers and the others outside her world is emphasized by the 'scare quotes' surrounding the others. It is a world she has been told of but has no personal experience of, other than the damage it has done to her men.

Parts of wholes

In the 'repercussions' phase of the second Incident in her story, Helena construes her second love as a tortured organism composed of various parts, including his anatomy and physiology, and his soul, highlighted below.

> Sometimes he would just press **his face** into **his hands** and shake uncontrollably. I realized he was drinking too much. Instead of resting at night, he would wander from window to window. He tried to hide **his** wild consuming fear, but I saw it. In the early hours of the morning between two and half-past-two, I jolt awake from his rushed breathing. Rolls this way, that side of the bed. He's pale. Ice cold in a sweltering night – sopping wet with sweat. **Eyes** bewildered, but dull like the dead. And the shakes. The terrible convulsions and blood-curdling shrieks of fear and pain from **the bottom of his soul**. Sometimes he sits motionless, just staring in front of him. I never understood. I never knew. Never realised what was being shoved down **his throat** during the 'trips'. I just went through hell. Praying, pleading: 'God, what's happening? What's wrong with him? Could he have changed so much? Is he going mad? I can't handle **the man** anymore!

We will refer to the relation between one part of a whole and the next as a **co-part** relation. The parts of Helena's man are analysed as a lexical string in Table 3.2.

Table 3.2 Parts of Helena's second love

the man
part
his face
co-part
his hands
co-part
eyes
co-part
the bottom of his soul
co-part
his throat

In contrast to the **classifying taxonomy** in Figure 3.4 above, these parts of the man together make up a **compositional taxonomy**, consisting of wholes and their parts and sub-parts, which we can express as a tree diagram in Figure 3.5.

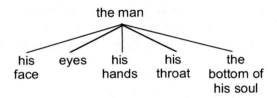

Figure 3.5 Parts of Helena's second love

Types of taxonomic relations

Relations between classes and members, and between parts and wholes, make up two types of taxonomies by which we construe fields of experience. People, things and places belong to more general classes of entities, and at the same time they are parts of larger wholes, and are composed of smaller parts. These are known as classifying and compositional taxonomies respectively. Both hierarchies may have many layers, particularly in technical fields, for example (classifying) *kingdom, phylum, class, order, family, genus, species, sub-species* and (composing) *ecosystem, food-chain, organism, organ system, organ, tissue, cell, organelle, metabolism...* Processes can also be viewed as instances of more general types, or as parts of larger activities, but their taxonomies are not as multi-layered as for people, things and places. Qualities may fall into more general classes, but they are not composed of parts.

These taxonomies give rise to several types of lexical relation in discourse, including class–member and co-class, whole–part and co-part. We can also include here **repetition**, in which the same lexical item is repeated, sometimes in different grammatical forms, such as *marry – married – marriage*. There is also **synonymy**, in which a similar experiential meaning is shared by a different lexical item, such as *marriage – wedding*.

Then of course there are contrasts between lexical items. The most familiar is perhaps **antonymy**, in which two lexical items have opposing meanings, such as *marriage – divorce*. But another type of opposition is **converse** roles, such as *wife – husband, parent – child, teacher – student, doctor – patient*, and so on. Although these are oppositional relations, they are not strictly speaking antonyms.

In addition to such oppositions, another type of contrast is series. These include **scales** such as *hot – warm – tepid – cold*, but also **cycles** such as days of the week *Sunday – Monday – Tuesday – Wednesday* and so on. This range of taxonomic relations is set out in Figure 3.6.

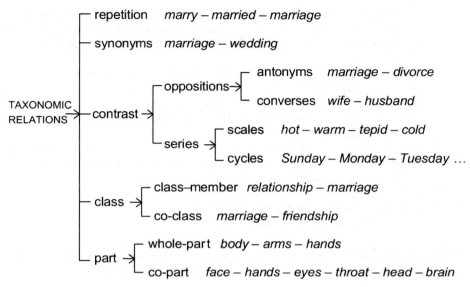

Figure 3.6 Taxonomic relations system

Each lexical item in a text expects further lexical items to follow that are related to it in one of these five general ways. A lexical item initiates or expands on the field of a text, and this field expects a predictable range of related lexical items to follow. Taxonomic relations between lexical items are interpreted in terms of the field, as the reader or listener understands it. For example, a reader who is familiar with South African history would recognize the co-class relation between *an Englishman* and *the 'Boer' Afrikaners*, and interpret it in terms of the historical conflict between these ethnic groups. It is with this expectation of ethnic conflict that the reader interprets as remarkable the popularity of Helena's English lover *even* with the *'Boer' Afrikaners*. So taxonomic relations help construe a field of experience as a text unfolds, by building on the expectancy opened up by each lexical item, or by countering such expectancy.

Repetition and synonymy

In Helena's story we have seen plenty of class and part relations, and some contrasts, but very little repetition and synonymy. Repetition and synonymy are particularly useful resources where the field of a text is very complex. They enable us to keep one or more lexical strings relatively simple, while complex lexical relations are constructed around them. For this reason, technical texts in many fields are common contexts to find repetition and synonymy. The Reconciliation Act is one such text. Its 'purposes' phase is presented below with some key lexical items highlighted.

To provide for the investigation and the establishment of as **complete a picture** as possible of the nature, causes and extent of **gross violations of human rights** ... ; the **granting of amnesty** to persons who make **full disclosure** of all the **relevant facts** ... ;

affording **victims** an opportunity to relate the **violations they suffered**;

the taking of measures aimed at the **granting of reparation** ... ;

reporting to the Nation about such **violations** and **victims**;

the making of recommendations aimed at the prevention of the commission of **gross violations of human rights**;

and for the said purposes to provide for the establishment of a **Truth and Reconciliation Commission**, a **Committee on Human Rights Violations**, a **Committee on Amnesty** and a **Committee on Reparation and Rehabilitation**;

and to confer certain powers on, assign certain functions to and impose certain duties upon that **Commission** and those **Committees**;

and to provide for matters connected therewith.

These lexical items are presented as lexical strings in Figure 3.7. The order in which they occur in the text is indicated by their position in the table.

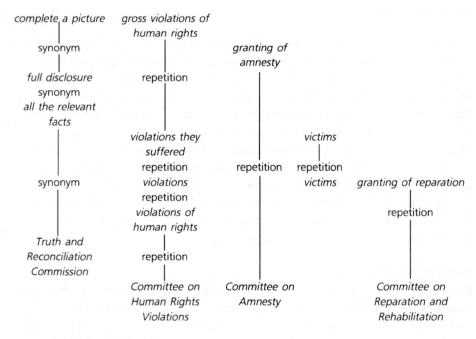

Figure 3.7 Lexical strings displaying repetition and synonymy

In building the purposes for the Commission and its three Committees, repetition and synonymy are used extensively to make quite clear which purpose is related to which Committee or Commission. This includes various synonyms for 'the whole truth', which is made explicit in the name of the Commission, and repetitions of *human rights violations, amnesty, victims* and *reparation*, which become the names of the Committees. At the same time there are other lexical relations between each of these simple strings. These include relations between *human rights violations* and *amnesty*, and between *victims* and *reparation*. However these lexical relations are less taxonomic than nuclear – human rights violators are to be granted amnesty, and victims are to be granted reparations. The simplicity of the taxonomic strings here enables the complexity of nuclear relations between their elements to be developed comprehensibly.

Taxonomic relations in abstract written discourse

Now let's turn to find how Tutu construes the field of Truth and Reconciliation through taxonomic relations. Institutional fields such as the law, government, education and so on consist largely of abstract things like *amnesty, justice, truth, reconciliation*. These abstractions often denote a large set of activities, which the reader is expected to recognize. Sometimes, however, the subordinate activities may be specified, particularly for pedagogic or legal purposes. For example, Tutu quotes the Act's definition of one type of offence as a set of more specific activities:

> The Act required that where the offence is a gross violation of human rights – defined as an abduction, killing, torture or severe ill-treatment . . .

This sentence explicitly instantiates a classifying taxonomy, as in Figure 3.8.

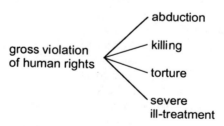

Figure 3.8 Instantial class

On the other hand, taxonomies are more often constructed implicitly as a text unfolds from clause to clause, as we saw for the people in Helena's story. A difference with technical fields, such as legal justice, is that the writer may deliberately construct a technical taxonomy as the text unfolds. In his third Argument stage, Tutu constructs a model of 'kinds of justice'. He does this by explicitly naming the superordinate class as *form of justice* or *kind of justice*, and explicitly contrasting sub-types, with *not the only form* and *another kind*:

Further, **retributive justice** – in which an **impersonal state** hands down **punishment with little consideration for victims and hardly any for the perpetrator** – is not the only **form of justice**. I contend that there is another **kind of justice, restorative justice**, which is characteristic of **traditional African jurisprudence**. Here the central concern is not **retribution** or **punishment** but, in the **spirit of** *ubuntu*, the **healing of breaches**, the **redressing of imbalances**, the **restoration of broken relationships**. This **kind of justice** seeks to **rehabilitate both the victim and the perpetrator**, who should be given the opportunity to be **reintegrated into the community** he or she has injured by his or her offence. This is a far more **personal approach**, which sees **the offence** as **something that has happened to people** and whose consequence is a **rupture in relationships**.

Thus we would claim that justice, **restorative justice**, is being served when efforts are being made to work for **healing**, for **forgiveness** and for **reconciliation**.

Tutu contrasts *retributive justice* with *restorative justice*, completing his case that justice is being done when amnesty is given. He explicitly states that *restorative justice* is part of *African jurisprudence*, so implying that *retributive justice* is non-African (i.e. Western). Table 3.3 gives the lexical strings in this stage.

Table 3.3 Kinds of justice

Western legal system	African legal system	offences
an impersonal state	traditional African jurisprudence	the offence
part	part	class
retributive justice	restorative justice	something that has
class	class	happened to people
punishment with little	the spirit of ubuntu	part
consideration for victims and	class	rupture in relationships
hardly any for the perpetrator	healing of breaches	
synonym	co-class	
retribution	redressing of imbalances	
synonym	co-class	
punishment	restoration of broken relationships	
	co-class	
	opportunity to be reintegrated into	
	the community (the perpetrator) has	
	injured by his or her offence	
	class	
	a far more personal approach	
	class	
	restorative justice	
	part	
	healing	
	co-part	
	forgiveness	
	co-part	
	reconciliation	

These relations construe two contrasting types of legal systems. In one an *impersonal state* hands down *retributive justice*; the other is *traditional African jurisprudence*, based on the pre-colonial *spirit of ubuntu*, and advocated by Tutu for contemporary *restorative justice*. Retributive justice includes the two attributes *retribution* and *punishment with little consideration for victims and hardly any for the perpetrator*. The three attributes of *the spirit of ubuntu* are *the healing of breaches, the redressing of imbalances* and *the restoration of broken relationships*. The four attributes of *restorative justice* are *healing, forgiveness, reconciliation* and *the opportunity to be reintegrated into the community*. These types of legal systems and their attributes are set out in Figure 3.9.

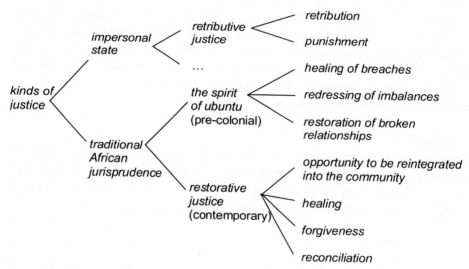

Figure 3.9 Types of legal systems and their components

By means of this classification Tutu advocates an approach to justice that draws on implicitly positive evaluations, which he contrasts with implicitly negative evaluations. As in the contrasting attributes of Helena's lovers, before and after their 'operations', taxonomic relations interact with resources of appraisal to categorize the world and evaluate the categories we construe. However, in Tutu's philosophical argument the categories are not people and their qualities, but institutional abstractions, including legal systems, principles of justice, and moral behaviours.

3.3 More on taxonomic relations

In our analyses above we have illustrated five types of taxonomic relations between elements: *repetitions, synonyms, contrasts, classes* and *parts*. This section provides some more detail about them.

Synonyms

Synonyms are different lexical items that share similar experiential meanings. For example Tutu uses the synonyms *public hearing* and *open session,* which denote the same kind of event. Synonyms are often used by writers to avoid repetition. The meanings of synonyms also usually differ in some way, such as the contexts in which they are typically used. For example *public hearing* may be used in a general context, and most of us will recognize the kind of event it denotes, whereas *open session* may refer to various kinds of events – not just court hearings. Furthermore synonyms may also differ in the <u>attitude</u> they express. So *public* and *open* are neutral in attitude, whereas other synonyms for these items that express a stronger attitude could be *exposed* or *naked.*

Contrasts

Contrasts are elements that differ significantly in meaning. They include elements that are <u>opposed</u> in meaning, such as *win–lose, happy–sad* or *married–single,* and <u>series</u> of differing meanings such as *hot–warm–tepid–cold.* Opposed elements include antonyms and converses. Antonyms come in pairs, e.g.:

    win – lose
    married – single
    quickly – slowly

Converses are associated with converse social roles or locations, e.g.:

    victim – perpetrator
    mother – son
    give – receive
    on top of – underneath
    before – after

Series include scales and cycles. Scales have outermost poles of meaning, e.g.:

    hot – warm – tepid – cold
    pass – credit – distinction – high distinction
    tutor – lecturer – senior lecturer – associate professor – professor

Cycles order items between two others, such as days of the week or years:

Sunday – Monday – Tuesday – Wednesday – Thursday – Friday – Saturday
2000 – 2001 – 2002 – 2003...

Contrasts are an important resource in many genres for constructing classifying taxonomies in which one class of phenomenon is distinguished from another. The following biology report first contrasts the **converse** roles of *producers* and *consumers*. Sub-types of consumers are then contrasted in a **series** as *primary, secondary* and *tertiary*:

> We have seen that organisms in an ecosystem are first classified as **producers** or as **consumers** of chemical energy. **Producers** in ecosystems are typically photosynthetic organisms, such as plants, algae and cyanobacteria. These organisms build organic matter (food from simple inorganic substances by photosynthesis). **Consumers** in an ecosystem obtain their energy in the form of chemical energy present in their 'food'. All consumers depend directly or indirectly on **producers** for their supply of chemical energy.
>
> Organisms that eat the organic matter of **producers** or their products (seeds, fruits) are called **primary consumers**, for example, leaf-eating koalas (Phascolarctos cinereus), and nectar-eating honey possums (Tarsipes rostratus). Organisms that eat **primary consumers** are known as **secondary consumers**. Wedge-tailed eagles that prey on wallabies are **secondary consumers**. Some organisms consume the organic matter of **secondary consumers** and are labelled **tertiary consumers**. Ghost bats (Macroderma gigas) capture a variety of prey, including small mammals. (Kinnear and Martin 2004: 38)

Contrasts are also an important resource for constructing arguments and interpretations, in which one position or set of behaviours and qualities is preferred over another. Helena used contrasts between her lovers' behaviour and qualities before and after their 'operations' to make her point about the damage that has been done to them. Tutu uses contrasts frequently to mount his argument for reconciliation over retribution. For example, he uses an antonym in his Thesis to emphasize the significance of the debate:

> So is amnesty being given at the cost of justice being done? This is not **a frivolous question**, but **a very serious issue**, one which challenges the integrity of the entire Truth and Reconciliation process.

And the contrast between innocence and guilt underlies his second Argument:

> It is also not true that the granting of amnesty encourages impunity in the sense that perpetrators can escape completely the consequences of their actions, because

> amnesty is only given to **those who plead guilty**, who accept responsibility for what they have done. Amnesty is not given to **innocent people** or to **those who claim to be innocent**. It was on precisely this point that amnesty was refused to the police officers who applied for it for their part in the death of Steve Biko. They denied that they had committed a crime, claiming that they had assaulted him only in retaliation for his inexplicable conduct in attacking them.

Here there is a double contrast implied, between the innocent and the guilty, and between those who confess their guilt and those who falsely claim innocence, thus compounding their crimes. Finally Tutu rests his case on the contrast between *retributive* and *restorative justice*. Interestingly he argues that both types treat the **converse** roles of *victim* and *perpetrator* in some ways similarly. Retributive justice gives *little consideration* to either, whereas restorative justice classifies both as *people*:

> Further, **retributive justice** – in which an impersonal state hands down punishment with little consideration for **victims** and hardly any for **the perpetrator** – is not the only form of justice. I contend that there is another kind of justice, **restorative justice**, which is characteristic of traditional African jurisprudence. Here the central concern is not retribution or punishment but, in the spirit of *ubuntu*, the healing of breaches, the redressing of imbalances, the restoration of broken relationships. This kind of justice seeks to rehabilitate both **the victim** and **the perpetrator**, who should be given the opportunity to be reintegrated into the community he or she has injured by his or her offence. This is a far more personal approach, which sees the offence as something that has happened to **people** and whose consequence is a rupture in relationships.

Many such antonyms are construed in the principles motivating the Reconciliation Act, with the contrast emphasized by negative polarity *not*, and the contrastive conjunction *but*:

> SINCE the Constitution states that there is a need for **understanding** but not for **vengeance**, a need for **reparation** but not for **retaliation**, a need for **ubuntu** but not for **victimization**;

In other genres, series are an important resource for interpreting things and events. Newspaper stories for example jump around in time, so that readers must be able to recover relations between times in order to construe the sequence of events. The following extract recounts the events surrounding the 2001 rescue of shipwrecked refugees trying to reach Australia by the Norwegian freighter *Tampa*, and the Australian government's shameful refusal to help them:

> DRIFTING 22km off Christmas Island and with food and supplies running low, Captain Arne Rinnan was **last night** trying to maintain order on his besieged ship after being turned away by Australia and warned off by Indonesia. The Norwegian captain of the

MS Tampa **last night** told The Daily Telegraph by satellite phone many of the 438 men, women and children on his ship were ill after **their 11th day at sea** ...

But Prime Minister John Howard said after a cabinet meeting **yesterday afternoon** that the ship would not be allowed to enter Australian waters ... **Hours later**, the Indonesian Government responded by saying the boat people – who are believed to be from Pakistan, Sri Lanka, Afghanistan and Indonesia – could not return to Indonesia.

Capt Rinnan told The Daily Telegraph he had not yet informed the boat people **last night** that Australia had refused them permission to land at Christmas Island. Asked if he was afraid of violence, he said: 'Not **at the moment**, but we were and we will be if they are turned away. They are starting to get frustrated.' ...

When he picked up the distress call **24 hours earlier**, he believed he would be carrying out a rescue operation, delivering the boat people to the nearest Indonesian port. After reaching the stricken 20m wooden vessel, KM Palapa 1, the crew helped the boat people on board. With the strong south-easterly winds which buffet the area at this time of year, it took the Tampa crew **three hours** to get them all on board ...

Capt Rinnan said the boat people had become distressed when told they might have to return to Indonesia **earlier in the day**, with some threatening to jump overboard. 'I said we are heading towards Indonesia and they said "No, you must head to Australia".' Capt Rinnan said they were 'just hanging around' **late yesterday**, waiting for Australian officials to come on board. (Tsavdaridis 2001: 1).

The potential complexity of tracking the events through the story is evident in the following list of times as they appear in the text:

last night
their 11th day at sea
yesterday afternoon
hours later
last night
at the moment
24 hours earlier
three hours
earlier in the day
late yesterday

As these times are out of sequence in such genres, time cycles are an essential lexical resource for recognizing a sequence of events.

Class to member

Relations of class to member are given various names in English, depending on the field, e.g. a _class_ of words, a _make_ of car, a _breed_ of dogs. Common examples include _class, kind, type, category, sort, variety, genre, style, form, make, breed, species, order, family, grade, brand, caste_. These can be used cohesively between messages, e.g. _Like my new car? Yes, what make is it?_ Technically, class–member relations are known as **hyponymy** (_hypo-_ from Greek 'under').

Wholes to parts

Likewise relationships of wholes to parts are also given various names in English, depending on the field, e.g. *part, content, ingredient, constituent, stratum, rank, plane, element, factor, fitting, member, component, faction, excerpt, extract, episode, chapter, selection, piece, segment, section, portion, measure.* In addition, facets name parts that are <u>locations</u> of wholes, e.g. *the <u>bottom</u> of his soul, top, inside, outside, side, edge, middle, perimeter, environs, start, finish, beginning, rest.* Measures name some <u>portion</u> of the whole, e.g. *a <u>cup</u> of coffee, glass, bottle, jug, can, barrel, loaf, mouthful, spoonful, ounce, pound, kilo, metre, acre.* Again part–whole relations can be used cohesively between messages:

parts	*The <u>chair's</u> broken. – Which <u>part</u>?*
facets	*Was it a good <u>marriage</u>? – Only at <u>the start</u>.*
measures	*How much is <u>petrol</u> today? – More than a dollar <u>a litre</u>.*

Technically whole–part relations are known as **meronymy** (*mero-* from Greek 'part').

In the past, studies of taxonomic relations have tended to focus on their roles in maintaining the cohesion of a text, through lexical ties between clauses (e.g. Halliday and Hasan 1976). The starting point in such cohesive models is with repetition, since the most explicit possible way of tying one item to the next is by repeating it. Next come synonymy and antonymy, which tie items to each other by similarity and contrast, with hyponymy and meronymy considered last. This is a grammar-based perspective, in which lexical relations are seen as serving textual functions, linking grammatical elements to each other in strings, similar to cohesive relations between reference items such as pronouns and articles: *a young man – this man – he* (see Chapter 5 below). In contrast the discourse semantic perspective we are taking here foregrounds the ideational function of lexical relations in building a field, so our starting point is with class and part relations: *a young man – my first love.* Synonymy draws on common class membership to identify items with each other, with repetition as the limiting case. Contrasts then function to distinguish categories. This is a metafunctional view on discourse semantics, in which taxonomic relations complement reference relations to build the field and maintain cohesion as a text unfolds.

3.4 Nuclear relations

As we flagged in the introduction to this chapter, the clause construes experience in terms of a process involving people and things, places and qualities. We have explored taxonomic relations between these elements, from one clause to the next as a text unfolds. In this section we will examine lexical relations between these elements within clauses. As they are more or less centrally involved in the process, lexical relations within the clause are known as nuclear relations.

Traditionally these kinds of lexical relations have been regarded as collocations, that is words that are commonly found together in the same structure, such as *tennis-ball* or *play-tennis*. What we will show in this section is how such collocations are dependent on the nuclear patterns of the clause, and again we will link lexical relations to the field construed in texts. The categories of nuclear relations presented in this section will then be applied to text analyses in the following section on activity sequences.

Nuclear relations within the clause

To set the scene for exploring nuclear relations, we first need to discuss a few of the semantic patterns within the clause described by Halliday (1994/2004). The essential experiential pattern is that people and things participate in a process. In Halliday's terms the core participant in the process is known as its **Medium**, 'without which there would be no process'. Here are some familiar examples:

he	was working
we	even spoke
I	never understood
what	's happening
Medium	**Process**

In addition to the Medium, one or two other participants may be involved in the process, including **Agent**, **Beneficiary** and various types of **Range**. An Agent instigates the process, which affects the Medium in some way:

he	's going to haunt	me
This question	challenges	the integrity of the entire Truth and Reconciliation process
Agent	**Process**	**Medium**

These effective clauses can be reversed in passive form, with the Agent as a 'by-phrase':

I	'm going to be	haunted by him
our integrity	is challenged	by this question
Medium	**Process**	**Agent**

Some effective processes can also be extended to a third participant, known as a **Beneficiary**:

The Commission	may grant	amnesty	to those who plead guilty
Agent	**Process**	**Medium**	**Beneficiary**
amnesty	is not granted	by the Commission	to innocent people
Medium	**Process**	**Agent**	**Beneficiary**
the police officers	were refused	amnesty	by the Commission
Beneficiary	**Process**	**Medium**	**Agent**

The Medium may be affected by the process, but the Agent is left implicit, as in *I'm going to be haunted, amnesty was refused*. As Agent and Beneficiary may be left out of the clause, they are relatively marginal in terms of nuclear relations.

How do these grammatical functions interact with the lexical elements that instantiate them in particular texts? In the grounds that Tutu gives for his second Argument, he names its field as *the granting of amnesty*. This field is expanded in the following clauses as processes of 'giving', 'not giving', 'refusing' and 'applying for'[2] (in italics below), of which *amnesty* is the Medium (in bold), with various Agents and Beneficiaries (underlined):

> It is also not true that THE GRANTING OF AMNESTY encourages impunity . . .
> because **amnesty** *is only given* <u>to those who plead guilty</u> . . .
> **Amnesty** *is not given* <u>to innocent people</u> or <u>to those who claim to be innocent</u>.
> It was on precisely this point that **amnesty** *was refused* <u>to the police officers</u>
> <u>who</u> *applied for* [**amnesty**] for their part in the death of Steve Biko.

Amnesty is construed here as a commodity that is given or refused to various recipients, by an implicit giver (*the Commission*), and is also demanded by potential recipients (*police officers*). The central elements in this construal are the processes of exchanging (*given, not given, refused, applied for*), the nuclear element is the commodity exchanged (*amnesty*), and the marginal elements are its givers and recipients. We can represent these nuclear relations in Figure 3.10.

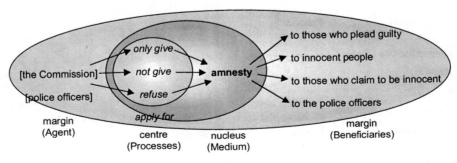

Figure 3.10 Nuclear relations of *granting amnesty*

We said earlier that a field consists of sequences of activities. The *granting of amnesty* is one activity within the *Truth and Reconciliation* field, that includes activities such as *applying for, giving* and *refusing.* This hierarchy of activities can be represented by a tree diagram, as in Figure 3.11.

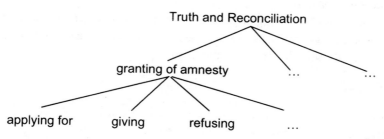

Figure 3.11 Activities of Truth and Reconciliation

Within the field of *granting amnesty,* people participate in each activity, as Medium, Agents or Beneficiaries, i.e. as nuclear or marginal elements of the activity. To show their lexical relations we can use:

- symbols for nuclear relations: '=' for central, '+' for nuclear, and '×' for marginal (following Halliday's 1994/2004 symbols for logical relations),
- lexical rendering of pronouns and implicit elements,
- '=' for relations between processes that are parts of a field, as follows:

		granting +	amnesty		
		=			
police officers	×	apply for +	amnesty		
		=			
the Commission	×	gives +	amnesty	×	to those who plead guilty
		=			
the Commission	×	gives +	amnesty	×	to innocent people
		=			
the Commission	×	not give +	amnesty	×	to those who claim to be innocent
		=			
the Commission	×	refused +	amnesty	×	to the police officers who ...

Lexical relations between the central elements of these activities are widely predictable across fields, i.e. the processes of exchanging (*applying for, granting, giving, refusing*). Relations between central and nuclear elements are predictable within the general field of *granting amnesty* (a common practice). But relations between these activities and more marginal elements are only predictable within the particular field of the Truth and Reconciliation Commission (e.g. who the Commission can and cannot grant amnesty to).

Other nuclear relations

A process may also be instigated by the Medium and extended to a second participant that is not affected by the process, known as a **Range**. The first type of Range is an **entity** that the process extends to:

all my girlfriends	envied	me
I	can't explain	the pain and bitterness
they	would mutter	the feared word
Medium	**Process**	**Range**

Another two kinds of Range are a **quality** or a **possession** of the Medium. In this case the process is one of 'being' or 'having', that relates the quality or a possession to the Medium:

quality	he	was	popular
	I	was	torn to pieces
	he	became	very quiet
	I	'm going	mad
possession	perpetrators	have	no excuse
	Helena	had	a new lover
	Medium	**Process**	**Range**

In addition there are three kinds of Range that are central to the Process, that we can call 'inner Ranges'. The first is where the lexical process is very general, such as *do, have, go, play* and so on, and the Range specifies the type of process, such as *do a dance, have a bath, play tennis*. Dancing, bathing and tennis are of course actually activities, but they can be realized as nouns that combine with general processes. These are known as **Range:process**.

The other two kinds of inner Range are a **class** or **part** of the Medium. Again the process is one of 'being' or 'having', that relates the class or part to the Medium:

class	he	was	an Englishman
	we	are	real policemen now
	these people	were	members of death squads
part	he	had	only one desire
	their leaders	have	the guts
	Medium	**Process**	**Range**

Finally, associated with a process are various kinds of **Circumstances** that vary in their degree of involvement in it. Circumstances of Place, Time and Cause do not participate in the activity, but are more peripherally associated with it:

place	he	was working	in a top security structure
	we're	moving	to a special unit
time	we	met	more than a year ago
	I	was to learn	for the first time
cause	I	jolt awake	from his rushed breathing
	Medium	**Process**	**Circumstance** (outer)

As they are peripheral to the process, we can call these 'outer Circumstances'. In contrast, Circumstances of Role, Means, Matter and Accompaniment are alternative ways of involving people and things involved in the activity. They are like participants and so are relatively nuclear:

role	my story	begins	as a farm girl
	we	knew	as loved ones
means	we	saw	with our own eyes
	he or she	has injured	by his or her offence
matter	we	even spoke	about marriage
	I	worried	about his safety
	Medium	**Process**	**Circumstance** (inner)

These inner Circumstances could be expressed as participants: *I was a farm girl, we loved ones knew, a few lines end my story, our own eyes saw, his offence injured the victims, we said marriage, his safety worried me.*

For our analyses of nuclear relations in clauses, we can distinguish four degrees of nuclearity: *centre, nucleus, margin* and *periphery*, schematized in Figure 3.12. The **centre** of the clause is occupied by the Process, and it may also include a Range:process, class or part, e.g. *do a dance, be an Englishman, have the guts.* The **nucleus** includes the Medium and any Range:entity, quality or possession. The **margin** includes Agents and Beneficiaries. And the **periphery** is occupied by Circumstances. These four degrees of nuclearity are then set out as a system in Figure 3.13.

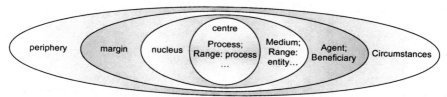

Figure 3.12 Nuclearity in the clause

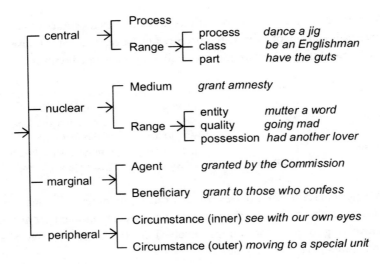

Figure 3.13 Nuclear relations in the clause

Nuclear relations below the clause

Below the clause, processes, participants and circumstances are themselves made up of groups of words, including lexical items. In Halliday's 1994/2004 model, *clause*, *group* and *word* are different **ranks** in the grammar; a *clause* is realized by a configuration of *word groups*, each of which is realized by a configuration of *words*. As with the clause, nuclear relations also pertain between lexical words in groups. To describe these relations, we need to distinguish two kinds of word groups – **nominal groups** that realize things and people, and **verbal groups** that realize processes.

Lexically, we are concerned with five functional elements of nominal groups. First, in Halliday's model, the central function of a nominal group is called the **Thing**. The lexical noun that realizes a Thing is a class of person or thing, such as *girl, man, window, bed*. Second, the Thing may be sub-classified by an item functioning as **Classifier**. Classifier and Thing together form a unified lexical element:

a	farm	girl
a top	security	structure
the	special	forces
the	'Boer'	Afrikaners
	restorative	justice
	Classifier	**Thing**

Third, people and things may also be described with qualities, that function in the nominal group as an **Epithet**:

my	late	teenage	years
a	young		man
an	extremely short		marriage
Epithet		**Classifier**	**Thing**

The Epithet is less central in a nominal group; structurally it is further from the Thing than the Classifier. Epithets may be intensified *very* late, *extremely* short, but Classifiers may not (*very teenage*).

Fourth, people and things may also be qualified, by circumstances or clauses that follow the Thing. These elements are known as **Qualifiers**. They are phrases or clauses that are 'downranked' and embedded as elements in the nominal group. In terms of nuclear relations, they are more peripheral still than Classifiers and Epithets:

a	young		man	in his twenties
an	extremely short		marriage	to someone else
	blood-curdling		shrieks	of fear and pain from the bottom of his soul
the		police	officers	who applied for amnesty
	Epithet	**Classifier**	**Thing**	**Qualifier**

Finally, we must also account for various 'of' structures in nominal groups. These include facets (*the side of the house*), measures (*a glass of beer*), types (*a make of car*), and so on. For simplicity we will label all these here as **Focus**. Like Classifier Thing structures, Focus Thing structures also comprise a single lexical element:

the bottom of	his soul
the early hours of	the morning
the only form of	justice
Focus	**Thing**

In verbal groups, we are concerned with just three functional elements. First, the lexical process in a verbal group is known as the **Event**, for example: *was **working**, won't **see**, was to **learn**, can't **explain***. A verbal group may include more than one Event, comprising separate lexical processes:

claim	to be
try	to resist
die	trying
Event	**Event**

Second, Events may be described with **Qualities** (manner adverbs in traditional grammar), that are more peripheral:

shake	uncontrollably
visit	regularly
mutter	abruptly
sits	motionless
Event	**Quality**

More central on the other hand are **Particles** in prepositional verbs, which comprise a single lexical item:

beam	out
look	out
look	up
scream	at
Event	**Particle**

These can often be paraphrased with a simple verb, e.g. *radiate, beware, research, abuse.* So at the rank of word group, the *centre* is occupied by the Thing and Classifier or Event and Particle, the *nucleus* by the Epithet or second Event, and the *periphery* by the Qualifier or Quality, schematized in Figure 3.14. These options in nuclearity in groups are then set out in Figure 3.15.

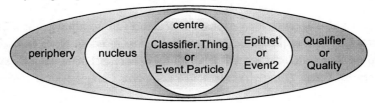

Figure 3.14 Nuclearity in nominal and verbal groups

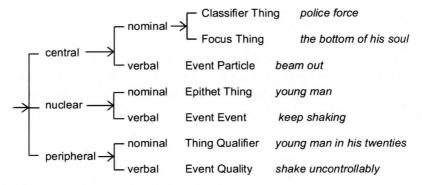

Figure 3.15 Nuclear relations below the clause

As we saw for *granting amnesty,* the predictability of nuclear relations in clauses and groups may correlate with the degree of nuclearity. Relations between central elements are often predictable across fields (*granting=refusing, police=force*), relations with nuclear elements may be predictable within general fields (*grant+amnesty, young+man*), while marginal/peripheral elements may only be predictable within specific sub-fields (*amnesty* × *those who plead guilty, shake* × *uncontrollably*).

Nuclear relations and taxonomic relations

Nuclear relations are particularly useful to inform analyses of activity sequences in texts, as we will show in the following section. On the other hand, for texts and text phases that are focused on entities rather than activities, nuclear relations can help to inform analyses of taxonomic relations between things and qualities. This is illustrated with the following descriptive report from school biology, describing the Australian class of reptiles known as *goannas*:

> Australia is home to 25 of the world's 30 monitor lizard species. In Australia, monitor lizards are called goannas.
>
> Goannas have flattish bodies, long tails and strong jaws. They are the only lizards with forked tongues, like a snake. Their necks are long and may have loose folds of skin beneath them. Their legs are long and strong, with sharp claws on their feet. Many goannas have stripes, spots and other markings that help to camouflage them. The largest species can grow to more than two metres in length.
>
> All goannas are daytime hunters. They run, climb and swim well. Goannas hunt small mammals, birds and other reptiles. They also eat dead animals. Smaller goannas eat insects, spiders and worms. Male goannas fight with each other in the breeding season. Females lay between two and twelve eggs. (Silkstone 1994)

The appearance phase of the report describes each part of the goanna in turn, with the sequence expected by the field of its anatomy, beginning with the body, tail and jaws, followed by the tongue, the neck, the legs, skin markings, and finally size. However the parts and their qualities are dispersed across various grammatical categories at clause and group rank. For example the part–whole relation is expressed as a process (**have flattish bodies**), or a preposition (**with forked tongues**), or a possessive (**their necks**). A nuclear relations analysis allows us to group these relations according to discourse semantic criteria.

In the analysis in Figure 3.16, there is one lexical string for goannas and other reptiles, and another string for their parts. In nuclear terms, classes and parts of things are *central*, qualities of things are *nuclear*, and locations are *peripheral*. So in addition to labelling taxonomic relations (vertically), we will label these nuclear relations (horizontally), using '=' for central, '+' for nuclear, and '×' for marginal/peripheral.

Including nuclear relations with the taxonomic relations analysis allows us to consistently track the relations of qualities and locations to each element in the lexical strings, despite their structural dispersal across various grammatical categories. A particularly complex example is the sentence *They are the only lizards*

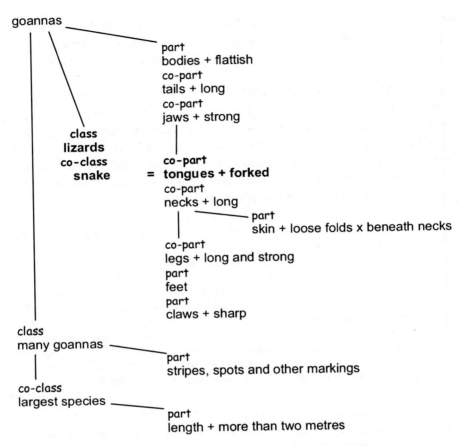

Figure 3.16 Taxonomic and nuclear relations in an entity focused text

with forked tongues, like a snake, which simultaneously classifies goannas as *lizards,* implicitly includes both *lizards* and *snakes* in a higher class (i.e. reptiles), assigns *forked tongues* as a part of both goannas and snakes, and excludes other lizards from having forked tongues. This configuration of relations is brought out very simply in the combined taxonomic and nuclear relations analysis, highlighted in Figure 3.16.

3.5 Activity sequences

We have shown how fields of experience are construed in discourse, from one perspective as taxonomies of people, things, processes, places and qualities, and from another perspective as configurations of these elements in clauses. Our third perspective on fields construed in texts is on sequences of such configurations. A field of human experience is composed of recurrent sequences of activities. Because they are recurrent, any sequence is to some extent predictable within a field, so that variations from such sequences are counterexpectant.

In other words, activity sequences are series of events that are expected by a field, as in *meeting – relationship – marriage*. The unmarked relation between events in such an expectant sequence is 'and', simply adding each event to the others in the series. So in oral personal recounts each clause commonly begins with 'and', illustrated in the following extract from testimony to the Australian *National Inquiry into the Separation of Aboriginal and Torres Strait Islander Children from Their Families*:

> The circumstances of my being taken, as I recollect, were that
> I went off to school in the morning
>
> **and** I was sitting in the classroom
>
> **and** there was only one room where all the children were assembled
>
> **and** there was a knock at the door, which the schoolmaster answered.
>
> After a conversation he had with somebody at the door,
>
> he came to get me.
>
> He took me by the hand
>
> **and** took me to the door.
>
> I was physically grabbed by a male person at the door,
>
> I was taken to a motor bike
>
> **and** held by the officer
>
> **and** driven to the airstrip
>
> **and** flown off the Island. (HREOC 1997: 99)

In this case the activity sequence is expected by the two fields of 'school in the morning' and 'abduction of Aboriginal children by the state'. Within each field the expectant activity sequence is constructed with simple addition, but the counterexpectant shift from one field to the next is signalled by the marked time Theme *After a conversation he had with somebody at the door* ... (see Chapter 6).

In science fields, by contrast, the unmarked relation between events in a sequence is typically assumed to be cause and effect, so that each succeeding effect is implied by the preceding cause. For this reason such event series are known as **implication sequences**. An example is the following explanation of cycles of bushfires and regeneration in the Australian *Mallee* woodland. The implication sequence is predicted by the opening sentence, and each step of cause and effect unfolds without any explicit markers:

> Regeneration of the Mallee depends on periodic fires.
> Old mallee produces a build-up of very dry litter and the branches themselves are often festooned with streamers of bark inviting a flame up to the canopy of leaves loaded with volatile eucalyptus oil.
> ^
> A dry electrical storm in summer is all that is needed to start a blaze,
> ^
> which, with a very hot northerly wind behind it will race unchecked through the bush.
> ^
> The next rains will bring an explosion of ground flora;
> ^
> the summer grasses and forbs not able to compete under a mallee canopy, will break out in a riot of colour.
> ^
> New shoots of mallee will spring from the lignotuber
> ^
> and another cycle of succession will begin. (Corrigan 1991: 100)

Few texts consist of continuous series of events, rather these are typically interspersed with phases of description, such as Helena's description of her first love, or by comments, reflections or reactions to the events. Even where a text is primarily concerned with series of events, these are typically organized into distinct phases. This is evident in the personal recount above, in which the second phase of events is counterexpectant to the first phase. It is also illustrated in the science explanation, in which one phase is concerned with fire and the next with regeneration, and the switch in field is signalled by the Theme *The next rains...*

For these reasons we need to analyse sequences in relation to the phases of a text. Types of phases are predicted by the text's genre, as activities within each phase are predicted by its field. For example, we would expect stories to include phases such as settings, episodes, descriptions, problems, reactions and so on, while phases in explanations may include causal steps, multiple factors, or multiple consequences (see Martin and Rose 2007b, Rose 2007 for more discussion).

Within each phase we would expect activities to be related, as members of a wider set of activities, or as sub-parts of larger activities. For example, the activities *meeting, relationship, marriage* belong to a wider set of social interactions, and activities such as *marriage* can be broken down into smaller components, such as *proposal, engagement, wedding, honeymoon* and so on. And *wedding* in turn can be broken down into smaller component activities.

Nuclear relations and activity sequences

Earlier we showed how nuclear relations can inform an analysis of taxonomic relations in an entity focused text. Here we combine analysis of activity sequences with nuclear relations, together with taxonomic relations between processes. Nuclear relations can show us the roles of people and things in activity sequences; taxonomic relations show how processes expect each other in an activity sequence, and how expectancy shifts from one phase to the next. Analysis of nuclear relations and activity sequences is illustrated here with a simple personal recount, a victim's statement from the Truth and Reconciliation Commission:

> On arriving back at Sandton Police Station, at what they call the Security Branch, the whole situation changed.
> ^
>
> I was screamed at, verbally abused,
> ^
>
> I was slapped around,
> ^
>
> I was punched,
> ^
>
> I was told to shut up,
> ^
>
> sit in a chair,
> ^
>
> then I was questioned.
> ^
>
> When I answered the questions
> ^
>
> I was told that I was lying.
> ^
>
> I was smacked again.
> ^
>
> And this carried on to an extent where I actually jumped up off the chair
> ^
>
> and started fighting back.
> ^
>
> Four, maybe five policemen viciously knocked me down,
> ^
>
> and they put me back on the chair
> ^

and handcuffed my hands through the chair,

which resulting that I could not get up.

I was then continuously smacked and punched ... (Testimony of Leonard Veenendal, Case No MR/146, 1996)

To prepare this text for analysis, we will:

- lexicalize pronouns and implicit participants,
- re-order the elements of clauses into consistent columns.

The **central** column in Table 3.4 includes Process and Quality, the **left-hand nuclear** column includes Agent of effective and Medium of non-effective clauses, the **right-hand nuclear** column includes Medium of effective and Range of non-effective clauses, and the **peripheral** column is for Circumstances. Taxonomic relations between processes are analysed, and these inform the division into **phases**, labelled to the right. Where a taxonomic relation between processes is separated by an intervening clause, the relation is indicated by a line.

Table 3.4 Nuclear relations and activity sequences: event focused text

nuclear	central	nuclear	peripheral	phases
	changed	the whole situation	at Sandton Police Station at the Security Branch	setting
policemen	screamed at co-class	Leonard		problem1 'abuse'
policemen	abused verbally co-class	Leonard		
policemen	slapped around co-class	Leonard		
policemen	punched	Leonard		
policemen	told	Leonard		problem2 'interrogation'
	sit co-class	Leonard	in a chair	
policemen	questioned co-class	Leonard		
Leonard	answered co-class	questions		
policemen	told co-class	Leonard		
Leonard	lying			

policemen	smacked again	Leonard		problem3 'abuse'
	jumped up co-class	Leonard	off the chair	reaction 'fighting back'
	started fighting back converse	Leonard		
four, maybe five policemen	knocked down viciously co-class	Leonard		effect 'constrained'
policemen	put back co-class	Leonard	on the chair	
policemen	handcuffed co-class	Leonard's hands	through the chair	
	not get up	Leonard		
policemen	smacked and punched continuously	Leonard		abuse continues

The analysis displays the following patterns:

- Taxonomic relations between processes organize the activity sequence into distinct phases. Two labels are assigned to each phase, the generic type of story phase – *setting, problem, reaction, effect* – and the specific field of the phase – 'abuse', 'interrogation', 'fighting back', 'constrained'. The latter denote a general activity that each process in the phase contributes to. Such taxonomic relations are the basis for expectancy between processes.
- Boundaries between phases are realized lexically, by a break in taxonomic relations between processes, or by a lexical contrast between processes, such as the converse relation between (Leonard) *started fighting back* and (policemen) *knocked down viciously*.
- Relative centrality, agency and 'voice' of people are explicitly displayed in the analysis. The narrator is the predominant Medium but never an Agent. The policemen act on and talk to Leonard, but his actions and locutions affect nobody.
- In the peripheral column, the chair stands out as the location of torture.

Some texts or text phases consist of activities but do not construe activity sequences; rather their primary function is classifying and describing. An example is the behaviour phase of the *Goannas* report above. A nuclear and activity analysis for this phase is displayed in Table 3.5. The **central** column includes both Process and Range:class/part. The nuclear column to the **left** includes both Agent in effective clauses and Medium in non-effective clauses, while the nuclear column to the **right** includes Range:entity/quality.

Table 3.5 Nuclear relations and activity sequences: entity focused text

nuclear	central	nuclear	peripheral
all goannas	daytime hunters		
	part		
they [goannas]	run, climb and swim well		
	part		
goannas	hunt	small mammals, birds and other reptiles	
	co-class		
they	eat	dead animals	
	repetition		
smaller goannas	eat	insects, spiders and worms	
	co-class		
male goannas	fight	with each other (male goannas)	in the breeding season
	co-class		
females	lay	between two and twelve eggs	

In this text, activities are taxonomically related by part or class; goannas are first classified as hunters, and the activities run, climb, swim are implicitly construed as components of hunting. But there is no implied series of events, rather the sequence is expected by the field of animal behaviours, and the descriptive report genre, so that feeding behaviours are expected by hunting behaviours, followed by breeding behaviours.

Unpacking grammatical metaphor in activity sequences

The testimonial recount above was relatively straightforward to analyse in terms of nuclear relations. Difficulties arise when processes are nominalized so that activities are coded as if they were things. An example is the nominal group *the beginning of a beautiful relationship*, in which the activity of two people relating to each other is nominalized as the Thing *relationship*, and so too is the phasing of this activity, as the Focus *the beginning of...* Halliday describes such patterns as **grammatical metaphors**, in which a semantic category such as a process is realized by an atypical grammatical class such as a noun, instead of a verb. In order to analyse such nominalizations in activity sequences, we can unpack them back to the processes from which they are derived, as follows:

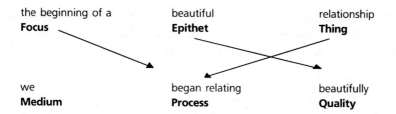

Nominalizations are a common form of grammatical metaphor. Reconstruing a process as a Thing has the twin advantage that i) Things can be classified and described with the rich resources of nominal group lexis, including many kinds of evaluation, and ii) the nominalized process and its qualities can be presented as the starting point or end point of the clause, as its Theme or New information (see Chapter 6).

The nominalized version also has certain connotations that our unpacking misses. The wording *a beautiful relationship* implies an object that can be contemplated and evaluated, and a whole set of activities that such a relationship involves, whereas *relating beautifully* has few such connotations. And a *relationship* is a general class which expects its sub-types, such as *marriage*, which is what Helena and her lover went on to talk about. On the other hand, unpacking a nominalization back to an activity reveals the people and things it involves ('we') that are elided by nominalizing.

As with metaphor in general, grammatical metaphors are read on two levels at once, a grammatical meaning and a discourse semantic meaning, and this double meaning may have several dimensions. Nevertheless, for the purpose of analysing activity sequences we will unpack grammatical metaphors wherever necessary. Other examples from Helena's story include nominalized processes and attitudinal qualities:

metaphorical	unpacked
wild energy	wildly energetic
extremely short marriage	married extremely briefly
pain and bitterness	hurt and bitter
only one desire	wanted only one thing
a means to the truth	how to tell the truth

In technical and institutional fields, grammatical metaphors become naturalized as technical terms. It may not be necessary to unpack these, unless we are trying for pedagogic purposes to relate technical terms to everyday meanings. For example, *amnesty* could be unpacked in commonsense terms as 'not punish for crimes'.

These unpacking strategies are used in the following analysis, Table 3.6. The macro-phases of Helena's story that we introduced in Chapter 1, 'meeting', 'operations', 'consequences', consist of smaller phases that are generic to all stories, *settings, descriptions, reactions, problems.* Inscribed attitudes are included here, to bring the appraisal into the ideational picture, distinguished from ideational lexis in italics.

Table 3.6 Nuclear relations and activity sequences: Helena's story

nuclear	central	nuclear	peripheral	phases
my story	begins	as a farm girl	in my late teenage years	'meeting' setting
Helena	met	as an eighteen-year-old a young man in his twenties		
young man	was working co-part		in a top security structure	
Helena + young man	began relating			
"	*beautifully* spoke co-part			
"	marrying			
young man		*bubbly, vivacious*		description
"		*wildly energetic*		
"		*sharply intelligent*		
"	was an Englishman			
"	was	*popular . . .*		
Helena's girlfriends	envied	Helena		
young man	said		one day	'operations' problem
"	going co-part		on a 'trip'	
Helena + young man	won't see	Helena + young man	again . . . maybe never ever again	
Helena + young man	was	*torn to pieces*		reaction1
Helena	married extremely briefly repetition	someone else		reaction2
"	married to forget			
Helena	met co-part	my first love through a good friend	again more than a year ago	'consequences' setting
"	learn	for the first time		

young man	operating		overseas	
"	going to ask			
	co-part			
"	not be punished		for his crimes	
Helena	can't explain			reaction
	co-class			
"	feels	*hurt and bitter*		
	co-class			
"	saw	what was left of that *beautiful*, big, strong person		
young man	*wanted*	only one thing		description
	co-class			
"	*wanted* to tell	truth		
	co-class			
"	*didn't care* not to be punished			
	co-class			
"	*only wanted* to tell	truth		

Relations between activities are as follows. First *meeting, beginning to relate* and *marrying* are parts of a 'romance' field that expect one another in a sequence. In the description phase, each of the young man's qualities is expected by the romantic field, and intensified by the girlfriends' *envying*. A problem is signalled by *then one day he said*, and then *going* and *won't see* are parts of 'leaving'. Helena's reactions include feelings (*torn to pieces*) and action (*married to forget*). The 'consequences' phase again begins with a setting, of which *learning for the first time* is expected by *meeting*. Then as parts of the Truth and Reconciliation field, *operating overseas* expects *not being punished*. This time Helena's reactions include saying (*can't explain*), feeling hurt and bitter, and seeing what was left. Finally *saw what was left* expects a description, in which we have unpacked *desire* as 'wanting', *must be told* as 'wanting to tell', *didn't matter* as 'didn't care', and *only a means to the truth* as 'only wanted to tell truth'. These are analysed as various processes of desire, which elaborate each other in this phase.

3.6 More on grammatical metaphor

Metaphor in general involves a transference of meaning in which a <u>lexical item</u> that normally means one thing comes to mean another. There are many examples of such lexical metaphors in Helena's story. For example she describes herself and her first love as *torn to pieces*, comparing the pain of separation with dismemberment. During her husband's 'trips' something dreadful was *shoved down his throat*, comparing the actions he was forced into with force-feeding. And as a consequence he and his colleagues acted *like 'vultures'*, meaning that they treated people like prey or carrion. Lexical metaphors of this kind are powerful resources for invoking evaluation.

Grammatical metaphors on the other hand involve a transference of meaning from one kind of <u>element</u> to another kind. A simple example in Helena's story is the <u>process</u> of *marrying*, which is reconstrued as a <u>quality</u> *married* and as a <u>thing</u> *marriage*. This kind of meaning transference seems so natural for readers with high levels of literacy that it hardly comes to our attention, except when it becomes hard to read in unfamiliar discourse. In modern written languages it is a powerful resource for expanding the set of meanings available for speakers and writers. Its development in English has accelerated over the past few centuries to enable expansion of the discourses of the sciences, humanities and bureaucracies that accompanied Europe's industrialization and colonial expansions.

In general the drift in meaning, by means of grammatical metaphor, has been from reality as processes involving people and concrete things, to reality as relations between abstract things, as with the transference from *marrying* as process to *marriage* as thing. Part of the reason for this shift has to do with the greater potential for expanding the meaning of things – numbering, describing, classifying and qualifying them. For example the process of *marrying* can be expanded with another process, such as *marrying <u>to forget</u>*, or a quality such as *marrying <u>well</u>*. But *marriage* as a thing can be expanded with a whole series of potentially evaluative qualities, classes and qualifiers, as in *an <u>extremely short</u> marriage <u>to someone else</u>*.

There is a set of regular principles for creating ideational metaphors – for re-construing one kind of element as another. The most common include:

(1) a process or quality can be reconstrued as if it was a thing
(2) a process, or a quality of a process, can be reconstrued as a quality of a thing

These are ideational metaphors of the <u>experiential</u> type, i.e. they are concerned with elements of figures. Ideational metaphors of the <u>logical</u> type are concerned with reconstruing a conjunction between figures as if it were a process or thing. We will look at the logical type in Chapter 4. For now we will exemplify each of these options for experiential metaphors.

Processes and qualities as things

One major advantage of presenting other elements as entities is that things can be described, classified and qualified in ways not available to other elements. This is illustrated in the following examples from our texts:

process ⟶	thing
begin	the **beginning**
relate	a beautiful **relationship**
marry	an extremely short **marriage**
travel	a **trip**
desiring	only one **desire**
reconcile	**Reconciliation**
apply	all the important **applications**
hear	a public **hearing**
violate	a gross **violation**
miscarry	a **miscarriage of justice**
penalize (punish)	the **penalty (punishment)**
expose and humiliate	public **exposure** and **humiliation**

quality ⟶	thing
painful and bitter	the pain and bitterness in me
true	Truth
just	justice
honest/just . . .	integrity

Reconstruing activities as things enables them to become participants and circumstances in other activities:

the application	should be dealt with	in a public hearing
Medium	**Process**	**Circumstance**

such a hearing	was likely to lead to[3]	a miscarriage of justice
Agent	**Process**	**Medium**

Processes and their qualities as qualities of things

Processes and qualities of processes (i.e. Qualities) can be reconstrued as qualities of things (Epithets and Classifiers), thus expanding the lexical potential of nominal groups:

process ⟶	quality of thing
secure an area	a top **security** structure
envying	an **enviable** relationship
closing the session	**closed** session
respecting the members	**respected** members

quality of process ⟶	**quality of thing**
operating overseas	**overseas** operations
relate beautifully	a **beautiful** relationship
marry very briefly	an **extremely short** marriage
violate grossly	a **gross** violation
expose publicly	**public** exposure
torture regularly	**regular** torturers

Things and people as parts of activities-as-things

When processes are reconstrued as things, the people that participate in the processes are often left out, which is one reason that abstract written discourse sometimes seems to be so alien to our everyday experience of things going on around us. However participants can be included when processes are reconstrued as things, by presenting them as <u>parts</u> of activities-as-things as possessions:

Helena got married ⟶ Helena's marriage ⟶ the marriage of Helena and her lover

victims were
    compensated ⟶ victims' compensation ⟶ compensation for victims

In the following example the processes of 'exposing' and 'humiliating' become things that qualify *the penalty*, and are themselves qualified by their participant *the perpetrator*:

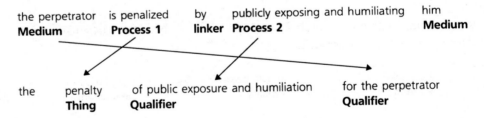

the perpetrator	is penalized	by	publicly exposing and humiliating	him
Medium	**Process 1**	**linker**	**Process 2**	**Medium**

the	penalty	of public exposure and humiliation	for the perpetrator
	Thing	**Qualifier**	**Qualifier**

Ideational metaphor tends to reconstrue our experience of reality as if it consisted of relations between institutional abstractions. These strategies have evolved to enable writers to generalize about social processes, and to describe, classify and evaluate them. One cost is that it may be hard to recover who is doing what to whom; another is that this type of discourse can be very hard to read and understand. Unpacking ideational metaphors as we have shown here can help to reveal how they construe reality and is one key strategy for teaching language learners how they work.

3.7 Seeing participants from the field: kinds of entities

As we have illustrated throughout this chapter, things and people are themselves classes of entities. Most generally we have distinguished between <u>concrete</u> entities, such as *man, girlfriends, face, hands*, and <u>abstract</u> entities, such as *amnesty, offence, applications, violation*. This distinction between concrete and abstract ways of meaning reflects a fundamental division in fields of activity in modern cultures – between the everyday activities of family and community, and the 'uncommonsense' fields of technical professions and social institutions such as law, medicine or education. Everyday fields are organized primarily by personal relations between interacting speakers, while uncommonsense fields are organized as much by written records.

We can distinguish kinds of entities in terms of more specific fields within the broad categories of concrete or abstract. To begin with there are many concrete types of things that belong less in everyday activities than in specialized occupations, including names for tools and machinery (e.g. *mattock, lathe, gearbox*). Although they are specialized, the meaning of these terms can be learnt, like everyday things, by pointing to them and using them. By contrast, the meanings of technical terms in professional occupations, such as economics, linguistics or biology (e.g. *inflation, metafunction, gene*), refer not to concrete objects but to abstract concepts, and can only be learnt through a long series of explanations in secondary and tertiary education. Although technical entities like genes, atoms or galaxies can potentially be pointed to and named through instruments, the only way to fully understand them is by getting involved in scientific explanations, typically in writing.

Other kinds of abstract things include those that are specialized to social institutions such as the law, many of which we find in Tutu's exposition (*offence, hearing, applications, violation, amnesty*). These are examples of administrative technicality. A third type includes abstractions that refer to semiotic entities – features of language (e.g. *question, issue, letter, extract*). Semiotic entities can be referred to in any field, but become more common in written discourses, and of course proliferate in fields like linguistics. A fourth type of abstraction names dimensions of meaning, such as the terms for classes and parts that we discussed under taxonomic relations above (e.g. *kind, class, part, colour, time, manner, way, cause*). We can refer to these as 'generic entities'; they feature in all kinds of fields, but specialized and technical fields tend to have their own sets of generic terms, such as the linguistics categories *word class, structure, function, genre* and many more.

In addition there is a third class of entities that are derived from ideational metaphor, including two general types of metaphoric entities – those derived from processes (e.g. *relationship, marriage, exposure, humiliation*), and those derived from qualities (e.g. *justice, truth, integrity, bitterness, security*). Kinds of concrete, abstract and metaphoric entities are summarized in Table 3.7.

Table 3.7 Kinds of entities

indefinite pronouns		*some/any/no thing/body/one*
concrete	everyday	*man, girlfriend, face, hands, apple, house, hill*
	specialized	*mattock, lathe, gearbox*
abstract	technical	*inflation, metafunction, gene*
	institutional	*offence, hearing, applications, violation, amnesty*
	semiotic	*question, issue, letter, extract*
	generic	*colour, time, manner, way, kind, class, part, cause*
metaphoric	process	*relationship, marriage, exposure, humiliation*
	quality	*justice, truth, integrity, bitterness, security*

Notes

1 The term 'instantiated' refers to instances of a semiotic system in a text.
2 We are treating 'applying for' here as a phrasal verb realizing an effective material process.
3 The process *likely to **lead to** a miscarriage of justice* is interpreted as 'cause a miscarriage'.

CONJUNCTION: logical connections

4

Conjunction looks at interconnections between processes – adding, comparing, sequencing, or explaining them. These are logical meanings that link activities and messages in sequences.

This chapter has six sections. Section 4.1 outlines four general dimensions of conjunction: the difference between conjunctions that relate activities and those that organize texts; the role of conjunctions in what we expect to happen in a text; the four main types of conjunction (adding, comparing, time and consequence); and three types of dependency between clauses (paratactic, hypotactic and cohesive). Section 4.2 describes conjunctions that are used to relate activities; as they construe a field beyond the text these are known as **external conjunctions**. Section 4.3 describes conjunctions that are used to organize texts; as this organization is internal to the text, these are known as **internal conjunctions**. Section 4.4 describes an additional small set of conjunctive resources known as **continuatives**. Section 4.5 presents a method for analysing conjunctive relations in a text, that displays how conjunction is used to relate activities in sequences and to organize arguments.

Finally section 4.6 discusses what happens when conjunctions are realized by other kinds of grammatical classes, such as verbs and nouns; this kind of

> grammatical metaphor is known as **logical metaphor**. A method is presented for unpacking logical metaphors to analyse activity sequences.

4.1 The logic of discourse

We showed an example of the work of CONJUNCTION in Chapter 1 (section 1.3), in which Helena gave the conditions under which she would have joined the anti-apartheid struggle:

> I finally understand what the struggle was really about.
> I would have done the same
> **had I** been denied everything.
> **If** my life, that of my children and my parents was strangled with legislation.
> **If** I had to watch how white people became dissatisfied with the best and still wanted better and got it.

We know these are conditions because of the conjunction *if*, which serves to link Helena's contemplated action *I would have done the same*, with the conditions under which she would have done so, *If my life was strangled... If I had to watch how white people became dissatisfied....* And the same conditional connection can also be realized by inversion of Subject and Finite, *had I been denied everything*. This kind of Subject–Finite inversion typically functions to ask a question (see Chapter 7, section 7.3 below), but in this instance its meaning is not 'question' but 'condition'.

This illustrates one reason why we need to set up CONJUNCTION as a discourse semantic system. The meanings of CONJUNCTION are realized through conjunctions such as *if* and *then*, but they are also realized by other kinds of wordings, and they are frequently left implicit, for the reader or listener to infer. Where grammar-based approaches such as Halliday and Hasan (1976) and Halliday and Matthiessen (2004) treat conjunctions as a grammatical resource for linking one clause to the next, the perspective we take here models CONJUNCTION as a set of meanings that organize activity sequences on the one hand, and text on the other.

External and internal conjunction

CONJUNCTION in other words has two faces. One side of the system interacts with IDEATION, construing experience as logically organized sequences of activities. The other side of the system interacts with PERIODICITY, presenting discourse as logically organized waves of information. Both systems use the same four general types of logical relations: **adding** units together, **comparing** them as similar or different, sequencing them in **time**, or relating them **causally** – as cause and effect, or evidence and conclusion. These four general types are known as **addition, comparison, time** and **consequence**. The units they relate range from simple clauses, to more complex sentences, to text phases, to stages of a genre.

For example, Tutu uses CONJUNCTION to organize his exposition as a series of three Arguments, each of which includes a 'grounds' phase and a 'conclusion' phase (see Chapter 1, section 1.3 above). He introduces the second and third Arguments with *also* and *further* to tell the reader that these are additional steps. And within each Argument he uses *Thus* to tell the reader that what follows is a conclusion. Here are the first lines of each phase:

Thesis	So is amnesty being given at the cost of justice being done?
Argument 1 'grounds'	The Act required that where the offence is a gross violation the application should be dealt with in a public hearing . . .
'conclusion'	**Thus** there is the penalty of public exposure and humiliation . . .
Argument 2 'grounds'	It is **also** not true that. . .amnesty encourages impunity because amnesty is only given to those who plead guilty . . .
'conclusion'	**Thus** the process in fact encourages accountability . . .
Argument 3 'grounds'	**Further**, retributive justice. . .is not the only form of justice. . .there is another kind of justice, restorative justice, . . .
'conclusion'	**Thus** we would claim that. . .justice is being served

Tutu uses addition (*also, further*) to add Arguments to support his Thesis. And he uses consequence (*thus*) to draw conclusions from each Argument. These items are not linking events in a field of experience beyond the text; rather they are used to link logical steps that are internal to the text itself. We refer to this system for logically organizing discourse as **internal conjunction**. And the system for linking events in an activity sequence is known as **external conjunction** (after Halliday and Hasan 1976).

Conjunction and expectancy

CONJUNCTION helps to manage what we expect to happen in a text. In an exposition, we expect a series of supporting Arguments, and Tutu confirms our expectations by explicitly adding each one. We also expect conclusions to be drawn from the arguments presented, and again Tutu meets our expectations by explicitly announcing each conclusion with *Thus*. In Chapter 3 (section 3.5) we saw that the unmarked relation in an activity sequence is simple addition, so that *and* is the most common conjunction in personal recounts, adding one event to another:

> The circumstances of my being taken, as I recollect, were that I went off to school in the morning **and** I was sitting in the classroom **and** there was only one room where all the children were assembled **and** there was a knock at the door, which the schoolmaster answered. After a conversation he had with somebody at the door, he came to get me. He took me by the hand **and** took me to the door. I was physically grabbed by a male person at the door, I was taken to a motor bike **and** held by the officer **and** driven to the airstrip **and** flown off the Island (HREOC 1997: 99).

Indeed sequence in time is so consistently expected by story genres that there is often no need to use any conjunctions:

> On arriving back at Sandton Police Station, at what they call the Security Branch
> the whole situation changed
> I was screamed at, verbally abused
> I was slapped around
> I was punched
> I was told to shut up
> sit in a chair
> **then** I was questioned
> **when** I answered the questions
> I was told that I was lying
> I was smacked again...

Conjunction between the first five activities in this sequence is left **implicit** – they just happen one after another – until the field shifts from physical and verbal abuse to interrogation, and this shift in field is signalled with the **explicit** conjunction *then*. We can now expect a different set of activities – concerned with questioning rather than beating. However the interrogators' response to their victim's answers was unexpected, at least to the victim, and this is again signalled with an explicit conjunction *when*.

This interplay of **explicit** and **implicit** conjunction to manage expectancy is well illustrated in the first Incident of Helena's story:

> As an eighteen-year-old, I met a young man in his twenties.
> He was working in a top security structure.
> It was the beginning of a beautiful relationship.
> We **even** spoke about marriage.
>
> A bubbly, vivacious man who beamed out wild energy.
> Sharply intelligent.

Even if he was an Englishman,
he was popular with all the 'Boer' Afrikaners.
And all my girlfriends envied me.

Then one day he said he was going on a 'trip'.
'We won't see each other again...maybe never ever again.'
I was torn to pieces.
So was he.
An extremely short marriage to someone else failed
all because I married to forget.

The first phase is sequenced in time, from *meeting* to *relationship* to *speaking about marriage*, but this sequence is expected by the field, as we discussed in Chapter 3 (section 3.5), so there is no need to make each step explicit with conjunctions. On the other hand, Helena uses *even* to make it explicit that speaking about marriage was more than we would normally expect at the beginning of a relationship. And in the description phase that follows, she uses *even if* in a similar way, to tell us that an Englishman being liked by the 'Boer' Afrikaners is counterexpectant (if they were expected to like him she might have said <u>*because*</u> *he was an Englishman*). In contrast, her girlfriends' reaction is explicitly added by starting a sentence with *And*, letting us know that their envy is entirely to be expected.

Then the next step from romance to tragedy is explicitly marked by *Then*, signalling that a new phase is beginning which is likely to be counterexpectant, and so probably bad news. After her reaction, *So was he* makes explicit that her lover's feelings about leaving were the same as hers, and that this was to be expected. And the failure of her subsequent marriage was also completely predictable, made explicit by the causal conjunction *all because*.

In sum the explicit conjunctions here realize our four types of conjunction: addition, comparison, time and consequence, and Helena uses them deftly to manage expectancy in the context of the events. They are set out in Table 4.1.

Like Tutu, Helena uses explicit conjunctions to signal the beginning of new phases in her story. But whereas Tutu uses them to organize his argument, Helena uses them to sequence the phases in time.

Table 4.1 Types of conjunction and expectancy

	expectant	counterexpectant
addition	**and** *all my girlfriends envied me*	
comparison	**so** *was he*	
time		**then** *one day he said he was going on a 'trip'**
consequence	**all because** *I married to forget*	**even if** *he was an Englishman*

*Note that *then* is not typically counterexpectant, but functions counterexpectantly in this context.

Incident 1 'meeting'	As an eighteen-year-old, I met a young man in his twenties. . . .
'operations'	**Then** one day he said he was going on a 'trip'. . . .
'consequences'	More than a year ago, I met my first love again . . . .
Incident 2 'meeting'	**After** my unsuccessful marriage, I met another policeman. . . .
'operations'	**Then** he says: He and three of our friends have been promoted. . . .
'consequences'	**After** about three years with the special forces, our hell began. . . .
Interpretation 'knowledge'	Today I know the answer to all my questions and heartache. . . .
'black struggle'	I **finally** understand what the struggle was really about. . . .
'white guilt'	I end with a few lines that my wasted vulture said to me one night:

Helena uses the time conjunctions *Then* and *After* to connect each phase to the immediately preceding events, but the scope of *finally* is the story as a whole. During all the preceding events Helena didn't understand the struggle, but now she *finally* does.

The other resources Helena uses here to sequence the story in time are Circumstances – *As an eighteen-year-old, one day, More than a year ago, After my unsuccessful marriage, After about three years with the special forces, Today*. These Circumstances set the events in an exact time period, while time conjunctions simply indicate the sequence.

Types of dependency

Before discussing each type of conjunction in more detail, we need to look briefly at three grammatical contexts in which they are realized, as different conjunctions are used in each context. The first type links a sequence of independent clauses:

I went off to school in the morning
and I was sitting in the classroom
and there was only one room where all the children were assembled
and there was a knock at the door

Each of the clauses beginning with *and* could stand independently. As each clause is potentially independent, the dependency relation between them is an equal one.

An equal dependency relation between two independent clauses is known as **paratactic** (from Greek *para* 'beside' and *taxis* 'arrange').

Another conjunction used in paratactic relations is *then*:

> I was told to shut up, sit in a chair
> **then** I was questioned

These two clauses cannot be reversed without reversing the logical relation between them. We cannot say, for example, **then I was questioned, I was told to shut up.* But the conjunction *when* does allow such a reversal:

> **when** I answered the questions
> I was told that I was lying
>
> I was told that I was lying
> **when** I answered the questions

The reason is that these two clauses are not equal in status. One is independent, and the other beginning with *when* is dependent on it. The *when* clause functions as the context in which the other takes place. In this respect its function is similar to a Circumstance of time such as <u>*after the questions*</u> *I was told that I was lying*, which can come at the start or end the clause. An unequal dependency relation between a dependent clause and an independent (dominant) clause is known as **hypotactic** (from Greek *hypo* 'under').

Third, two sentences can be logically related by a conjunction such as *Further* or *Thus*:

> It is also not true that the granting of amnesty encourages impunity. . .
> **Further**, retributive justice. . .is not the only form of justice.

> This is a far more personal approach, which sees the offence as something that has happened to people and whose consequence is a rupture in relationships.
> **Thus** we would claim that justice, restorative justice, is being served when efforts are being made to work for healing, for forgiveness and for reconciliation.

We will refer to these kinds of dependency relations between sentences as **cohesive** (following Halliday and Hasan 1976). As we go through each type of conjunction – addition, comparison, time, consequence – we will give examples as far as possible of the conjunctions used in each type of dependency relation – paratactic, hypotactic and cohesive.

Finally there is one other type of linker aside from conjunctions. These are known as continuity items or **continuatives**. Continuatives differ from conjunctions in two ways. More often than not, conjunctions occur at the beginning of a clause in English (although cohesive conjunctions can be positioned more flexibly). But continuatives primarily occur within a clause, rather than at the start. And their options for logical relations are far more restricted. Two that we have come across so far are *even* and *also*:

> We **even** spoke about marriage.
> It is **also** not true that the granting of amnesty encourages impunity.

To put *even* at the start of this clause completely changes its meaning – rather than *spoke about marriage* being unexpected, it is *we* that becomes unexpected. Also, placing *also* at the start of a clause is a marked option, as it more typically occurs within the clause.

4.2 External conjunction

External conjunction is concerned with logically organizing a field as sequences of activities. For each general type of external conjunction – addition, comparison, time, consequence – there are two or more sub-types, summarized in Table 4.2.

Table 4.2 Basic options for external conjunctions

addition	addition	*and, besides, in addition*
	alternation	*or, if not – then, alternatively*
comparison	similarity	*like, as if, similarly*
	contrast	*but, whereas, on the other hand*
time	successive	*then, after, subsequently; before, previously*
	simultaneous	*while, meanwhile, at the same time*
consequence	cause	*so, because, since, therefore*
	means	*by, thus, by this means*
	purpose	*so as, in order to; lest, for fear of*
	condition	*if, provided that; unless*

Each type is illustrated below for paratactic, hypotactic and cohesive relations.

External addition

We have seen that *and* can function to add clauses together in a paratactic sequence, one after another:

> . . . white people became dissatisfied with the best
> **and** still wanted better
> **and** got it

> Four, maybe five policemen viciously knocked me down,
> **and** they put me back on the chair
> **and** handcuffed my hands through the chair

However conjunctions such as *besides* or *as well as* add a dependent clause to a dominant clause in a hypotactic sequence that is reversible:

> **As well as** getting the best,
> they still wanted better.

> They still wanted better,
> **besides** getting the best.

The flipside of adding clauses together is to make a choice between them, using the conjunction *or*:

> If the individual is terminally ill, disabled, suffering a debilitating condition
> **or** will probably not survive the duration of the TRC...

This sentence gives us a series of alternative disabilities to choose from. The first option can be marked with *either*:

> **Either** the individual is terminally ill,
> (or is) disabled,
> (or is) suffering a debilitating condition
> **or** will probably not survive the duration of the TRC...

Only the last alternative choice
expressed implicitly by a comma
brackets – *or is*). This is identica

> If the individual is terminally
> (and is) disabled,
> (and is) suffering a debilitatin
> **and** will probably not survive

Other conjunctions that realize a

> dependent
> **If** they don't want restorativ
> **then** they could choose retri

> cohesive
> A witness may be terminally
> **Alternatively** she might be

As with lexical co
one meaning can be
These are all used in hyp

Instead of resting at night,
he would wander from windo

it is

As well as adding clauses together they can also be subtracted, with *neither* and *nor*:

> ...white people were **neither** dissatisfied with the best
> **nor** wanted better
> **nor** got it

In sum, options for external addition include **adding, subtracting** and **alternation**, set out in Figure 4.1.

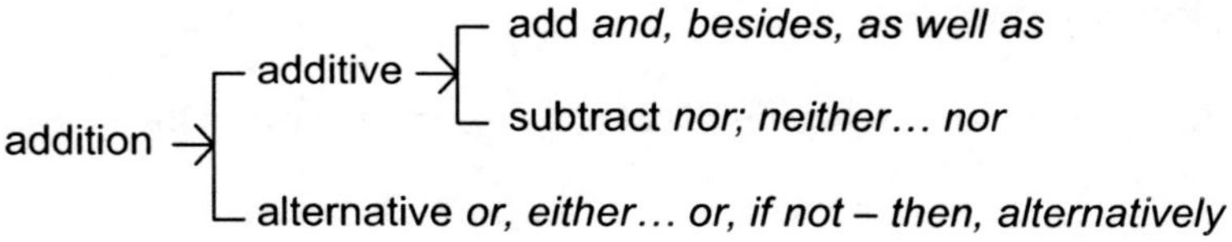

Figure 4.1 External addition

External comparison

The basic options for comparison are similarity versus difference. Perhaps the most common kind of comparison is to contrast two clauses as different, using *but*:

> This is not a frivolous question,
> **but** a very serious issue.

Here Tutu contrasts two abstract things, a *question* and an *issue*. There is a lexical contrast between their qualities – *frivolous* versus *very serious* – and this contrast is made explicit with *but*. The particular type of difference here is opposition: *frivolous* and *serious* realize **opposite** experiential meanings. *But* is used in paratactic relations, and opposition can also be realized in hypotactic relations with *whereas, while*:

> **Whereas** this is a simple question,
> a very serious issue.

trasts, there is more than one kind of logical difference. First, replaced by another using *instead of, in place of, rather than*. otactic relations:

w to window.

A third kind of difference is to make an **exception**, using *except that, other than, apart from*, which are again hypotactic:

> He wanted to rest at night
> **except that** he kept having nightmares.

> He used to rest at night
> **other than** when he had nightmares.

Conjunctions like *instead* and *rather* can also be used as cohesive:

> He should have slept at night.
> **Instead** he would wander from window to window.

Of course the flipside of contrast is **similarity**, using *like, as if*:

> The criminal and civil liability of the perpetrator are expunged
> **as if** the offence had never happened.

Here Tutu uses *as if* to suggest that *liability expunged* is in some way similar to *the offence never happened*. A cohesive conjunction that can express external similarity is *similarly*:

> Helena's first love worked in a top security structure.
> **Similarly** her second love worked for the special forces.

Similarity can also be expressed by the continuative *so*, with Subject–Finite inversion:

> I was torn to pieces.
> **So** was he.

In sum, options for external comparison include **similarity** or **difference: opposite, replacing** or **excepting**, set out in Figure 4.2.

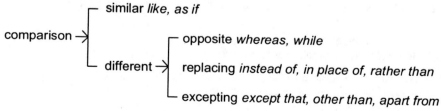

Figure 4.2 External comparison

External time

As we saw for Helena's story and Leonard Veenendal's testimony, time conjunctions like *then* tell us that events follow each other:

> It was the beginning of a beautiful relationship.
> We even spoke about marriage.
> **Then** one day he said he was going on a 'trip'.

> I was told to shut up, sit in a chair,
> **then** I was questioned.

This kind of time relation is **successive** – events happen one after another. Successive conjunctions used in hypotactic relations include *when, after, since, now that*:

> **when** I answered the questions
> I was told that I was lying

In these examples, succession in time is running forward – from the first events to the last. But conjunctions such as *before, prior to* allow us to run the succession backwards:

> **before** I was questioned
> I was slapped around

In none of these examples is it clear how much time has elapsed between the two events, they just happen **sometime** before or after. Other successive conjunctions indicate that an event happens **immediately** before or after, including *once, as soon as; until*:

> **as soon as** I answered
> I was slapped again

> I was slapped around
> **until** I started fighting back

Cohesive successive conjunctions include *subsequently, previously, at once*:

> I answered the questions.
> **Subsequently** I was told that I was lying.

> He said he was going on a 'trip'.
> **Previously** it had been a beautiful relationship.

> I started fighting back.
> **At once** four, maybe five policemen viciously knocked me down.

One example of *previously* in Tutu's exposition shows that cohesive conjunctions can be positioned relatively freely in a clause:

> ...there is the penalty of public exposure and humiliation for the perpetrator. Many of those in the security forces who have come forward had **previously** been regarded as respectable members of their communities.

As well as succeeding each other, events can happen at the same time. **Simultaneous** time is realized by *as, while, when*:

> My murderer let me and the old White South Africa sleep peacefully, **while** 'those at the top' were again targeting the next 'permanent removal from society'.

Cohesive simultaneous conjunctions include *meanwhile, simultaneously*:

> cohesive
> The old White South Africa slept peacefully.
> **Meanwhile** 'those at the top' were again targeting the next 'permanent removal from society'.

So options for external time include **successive: sometime** or **immediate** and **simultaneous,** set out in Figure 4.3.

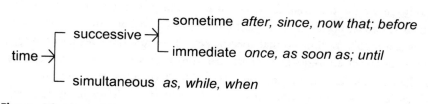

Figure 4.3 External time

External consequence

There are four general types of external consequence: cause, means, condition, purpose. Some basic options are shown in Table 4.3.

Table 4.3 Basic external consequence

cause	*because, so, therefore*
means	*by, thus*
condition	*if...then*
purpose	*so that, in order to*

Cause

When Helena's first marriage failed, she explained why it failed, using *all because*:

> An extremely short marriage to someone else failed
> **all because** I married to forget.

The conjunction *because* means that one event obligates another to happen, as cause and effect. By saying **all** *because*, Helena makes this obligatory relation even stronger, i.e. there was only one reason – *I married to forget.* In other words, cause modulates the relations between one event and the next, and like other such modal meanings (described in Chapter 2, section 2.2) it is gradable; for example, she could also have weakened the causal relation with *partly because*. This is an important principle, particularly in science writing, where the strength of causal relations is carefully evaluated.

Because functions in hypotactic relations; the corresponding paratactic conjunction is *so*, and cohesive conjunctions include *therefore, consequently*:

> I married to forget,
> **so** my first marriage failed.

> I married to forget.
> **Consequently** my first marriage failed.

In the introduction to this chapter we saw that ordinary conjunctions such as *then* can signal counterexpectancy in certain contexts. But for consequential conjunctions this is a regular option, so that specific sets of conjunctions realize each type of counterexpectant consequence. These are known as **concessive** conjunctions. (We looked at concession in Chapter 2 (section 2.3) in its role involving the reader's voice in appraisal.) Concessive cause is realized by *although, even though, even if, but, however.*

For example Helena's marriage failed *all because* she married for the wrong reasons, but it could have failed *even though* she married for the <u>right</u> reasons:

> An extremely short marriage to someone else failed
> **even though** I married for the right reasons.

Helena's first love was popular with the Afrikaners *even if* he was an Englishman; in a more tolerant South Africa he might have been popular *because* he was an Englishman:

> **Because** he was an Englishman,
> he was popular with all the 'Boer' Afrikaners.

But the most common realization of concessive cause is *but*:

> He tried to hide his wild consuming fear,
> **but** I saw it
>
> I can't handle the man anymore!
> **But** I can't get out

However *but* can also realize <u>comparison:difference</u>, which can be confusing. We can test whether the relation is concession by trying to substitute *but* with hypotactic or concessive conjunctions that we know realize consequential meanings, such as *although, however*:

> **Although** he tried to hide his wild consuming fear,
> I saw it.
>
> I can't handle the man anymore!
> **However** I can't get out.

If we substitute conjunctions that realize contrast, they don't make as much sense (**I can't handle the man anymore!* <u>*In contrast*</u> *I can't get out.* *<u>*Whereas*</u> *he tried to hide his wild consuming fear, I saw it*).

Means

While causes explain why an effect happens, the relation of means explains how something happens, typically with *by*:

> He expected to get amnesty
> **by** confessing.
>
> The objectives of the Commission shall be to promote national unity and reconciliation
> **by** establishing as complete a picture as possible of the causes, nature and extent of the gross violations of human rights.

Here the Commission intends to use *establishing as complete a picture as possible* as the means *to promote national unity and reconciliation*. Whereas cause <u>obligates</u> an effect to follow, the relevant meaning here is <u>ability</u>. Tutu's argument is that by establishing a complete picture, the Commission will be <u>able</u> to promote unity and reconciliation.

The hypotactic conjunction *by* is perhaps the most common way we express means. Other conjunctions of means include *thus, by this means*:

> He expected amnesty.
> **Thus** he confessed.

As complete a picture as possible of the causes, nature and extent of the gross violations of human rights will be established.
By this means the Commission will promote national unity and reconciliation.

With concessive means, one event is unable to happen, in spite of enough having been done to enable it:

Even by confessing
he didn't get amnesty

National unity and reconciliation may <u>still not</u> be promoted
even by establishing as complete a picture as possible of the causes, nature and extent of the gross violations of human rights.

And *but* can also be used for concessive means:

He confessed
but he didn't get amnesty.

Purpose

Purpose is concerned with actions and intended outcomes. A common conjunction for purpose is *in order to*:

The RRC committee will use the following two information instruments,
in order to make an informed recommendation.

Here the RRC committee's purpose is to make an informed recommendation. To achieve this, their action is to use two information instruments. Whereas cause <u>obligates</u> an effect to follow, with purpose the relevant modal meaning is <u>inclination</u>. We take an action because we desire an outcome.

As with *by* for expressing means, the hypotactic conjunction *to* is a common way of expressing purpose:

To make an informed recommendation,
the RRC committee will use the following two information instruments.

Other conjunctions that realize purpose include *so that, in case*:

The RRC committee will use the following two information instruments
so that it can make an informed recommendation,

These purpose conjunctions (*in order*) *to*, *so as*, indicate that the outcome is desired. But there is another kind of purpose where the outcome is <u>feared</u> – using *lest* or *for fear of*:

> The RRC committee will use the following two information instruments
> **lest** it make an uninformed recommendation.

With concessive desire, an action is performed *without* the effect occurring:

> The RRC committee used two information instruments,
> **without** being able to make an informed recommendation.

> The RRC committee used two information instruments,
> **even so** they could not make an informed recommendation.

As fear is already a negative option, there is no concessive alternative.

Condition

Condition is the relation between an outcome and the conditions under which it may occur, as we saw in Helena's story:

> I would have done the same
> **had I** been denied everything.
> **If** my life, that of my children and my parents was strangled with legislation.
> **If** I had to watch how white people became dissatisfied with the best and still wanted better and got it.

With condition the relevant modal meaning is <u>probability</u>. Helena considers it likely that she would join the struggle under sufficient conditions; and the more oppressive the conditions, the more likely she would have been to do the same.

Other conjunctions that realize condition include *if...then, provided that, so long as*:

> **If** my life, that of my children and my parents was strangled,
> **then** I would have done the same.

> I would have done the same
> **provided that** there was no risk to my relaxed and comfortable way of life.

These are all conditions under which an event may happen. On the other hand, *unless* introduces conditions that close off the possibility of an event happening:

> ... the application should be dealt with in a public hearing
> **unless** such a hearing was likely to lead to a miscarriage of justice

With concessive condition, an effect won't occur *even if* a condition is met:

> I would <u>not</u> have done the same
> **even if** I had known the truth

Options for external consequence, including expectant and concessive cause, means, purpose and condition, are shown in Figure 4.4.

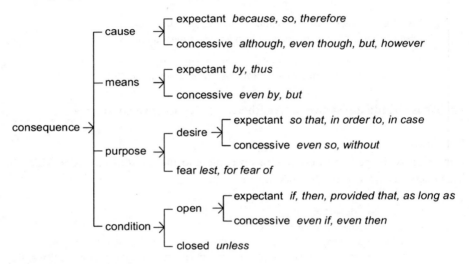

Figure 4.4 External consequence

The full system for external conjunction is displayed in Table 4.4.

Table 4.4 General options for external conjunction

Addition	additive	adding	*and, besides, both...and*
		subtracting	*nor, neither...nor*
	alternative		*or, either...or, if not...then*
Comparison	similar		*like, as if*
	different	opposite	*whereas, while*
		replacing	*instead of, in place of, rather than*
		excepting	*except that, other than, apart from*
Time	successive	sometime	*after, since, now that; before*
		immediate	*once, as soon as; until*
	simultaneous		*as, while, when*
Cause		expectant	*because, so, therefore*
		concessive	*although, even though, but, however*
Means		expectant	*by, thus*
		concessive	*even by, but*

Condition	open	expectant	*if, then, provided that, as long as*
		concessive	*even if, even then*
	closed		*unless*
Purpose	desire	expectant	*so that, in order to, in case*
		concessive	*even so, without*
	fear		*lest, for fear of*

4.3 Internal conjunction

The roles of internal conjunction in logically organizing discourse have become particularly elaborated in the written mode, building on older spoken ways of meaning. For this reason, internal conjunction includes the same four logical types as we have seen for external conjunctions. Furthermore many of the items that express internal relations are the same as external conjunctions, such as *also, thus,* but other internal conjunctions are quite different. The basic options are outlined in Table 4.5.

Table 4.5 Basic options for internal conjunctions

addition	additive	*further, in addition*
	alternative	*alternatively*
comparison	similar	*similarly, for instance*
	different	*on the other hand, in contrast*
time	successive	*firstly, finally*
	simultaneous	*at the same time*
consequence	concluding	*therefore, in conclusion, thus*
	countering	*admittedly, nevertheless*

Internal addition

We have already seen how internal addition can be used to add arguments in an exposition:

Argument 1	The Act required that where the offence is a gross violation the application should be dealt with in a public hearing
Argument 2	It is **also** not true that . . . amnesty encourages impunity because amnesty is only given to those who plead guilty
Argument 3	**Further**, retributive justice. . .is not the only form of justice. . .there is another kind of justice, restorative justice,

In the following spoken example (from the film *Forgiveness* – see Chapter 7), Sannie adds a judgement to her negative response:

Coetzee:	Won't your parents have any questions, you know, about what happened?
Sannie:	- No, **and** that's wrong.

Other conjunctions that express internal addition include *furthermore, moreover, in addition, as well, besides, additionally.*

As with external addition, we can also add alternative arguments, using the internal conjunction *alternatively*:

Retributive justice is one form of justice.
Alternatively there is another kind of justice, restorative justice.

There is also a set of conjunctions that are commonly used in spoken discourse to add new stages to what is being said – *now, well, alright, okay.* Here is an example from Chapter 7:

Luke:	You know I missed you two fuckers.
Llewelyn:	Sorry I can't say the same Luke.
Zuko:	Yeah me too.
Luke:	**Well** fuck you, man.

And there are other common items that are used to add a 'sidetrack' to the flow of discourse – *anyway, anyhow, incidentally, by the way.* Here's a couple of examples from an anecdote about language teaching and language knowledge:

A teacher was confused about which of *affect* and *effect* was the noun or verb (it's *affect* verb, *effect* noun **by the way**, except for one formal meaning of effect 'succeed in causing to happen'), or was perhaps unable to recognise the noun or verb in the sentence he was policing. He marked the student wrong, suggesting *affect* for *effect* or vice versa (I can't recall which). **Anyhow**, as it turned out, the student had been right; the teacher got it wrong. (Martin (2000), *Grammar meets Genre*).

Options for internal addition are summed up in Figure 4.5.

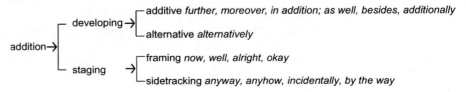

Figure 4.5 Options for internal addition

Internal comparison

Internal comparison provides a rich set of resources for written text, enabling writers to compare and contrast positions and evidence, rephrase, exemplify, generalize and specify.

One kind of internal similarity is to simply say that two ideas are the same in some way, using *similarly* or *again*:

> Relations of class to member can be used cohesively between messages
> . . .
> **Again** part–whole relations can be used cohesively between messages

> When Helena says *I envy and respect the people of the struggle* she implies something praiseworthy about the character of the people.
> **Similarly**, she morally condemns those at the top for bloody murder, without explicitly judging their character.

The similarity signalled by *Similarly* here is that Helena's praise and condemnation are both implicit. The conjunction makes it clear to the reader that we are focusing on two similar things.

As with addition, some conjunctions such as *similarly* can realize either external or internal comparison. We have to ask whether the clause introduced by the conjunction serves to compare events, things or qualities (external), or to compare one argument with another (internal).

However there are many other variations on internal similarity, including reformulating, exemplifying, generalizing and specifying. Ideas may be reformulated with *that is, i.e.* In this book we often state something in commonsense terms, and then reformulate it more technically:

> Attitudes have to do with evaluating things, people's character and their feelings.
> Such evaluations can be more or less intense,
> **that is** they may be more or less amplified.

Exemplification uses *for example, for instance, e.g.* to rework a general statement with a specific instance. Here Tutu gives an example of a condition under which an application would not be heard in public:

> The Act required that the application should be dealt with in a public hearing unless such a hearing was likely to lead to a miscarriage of justice
> (**for instance**, where witnesses were too intimidated to testify in open session).

But exemplifying is just one way of reworking a statement as more specific or more general. Other related conjunctions include *in general, in particular, in short.* Here are some examples from this book:

> Attitudinal lexis plays a very important role in Helena's narrative,
> as it does **in general** across story genres.

> Layers of New develop the point of a text,
> **in particular** they focus on expanding the ideational meanings around a text's field.

Expectancy may also be adjusted with *in fact, indeed, at least*. By repeatedly narrowing the conditions for a public hearing, Tutu leads us to expect that public hearings almost never occur. But he then counters this expectation by saying what happens *in fact*:

> The Act required that the application should be dealt with in a public hearing
> **where** the offence is a gross violation of human rights – defined as an abduction, killing, torture or severe ill-treatment –
> **unless** such a hearing was likely to lead to a miscarriage of justice
> (**for instance**, where witnesses were too intimidated to testify in open session).
> **In fact**, virtually all the important applications to the Commission have been considered in public in the full glare of television lights.

It is this strategy of leading us to expect one thing, and then countering it with 'reality', that enables Tutu to make his conclusion seem natural, simply by using *Thus*:

> **Thus** there is the penalty of public exposure and humiliation for the perpetrator.

We don't mean to imply that we think Tutu's conclusion is wrong. Rather he has argued it effectively by pre-empting any objections and countering them.

Likewise *indeed* means 'even more than expected', while *at least* means 'less than expected'. Tutu argues that losing the right to sue is a higher than expected price to pay:

> ... the victim loses the right to sue for civil damages in compensation from the perpetrator.
> That is **indeed** a high price to ask the victims to pay...

Helena claims that her men are victims of spiritual murder, and that being unable to rest is less than they should expect:

> Spiritual murder is more inhumane than a messy, physical murder.
> **At least** a murder victim rests.

An example from the spoken mode is the following (from *Forgiveness*), in which Zako counters Luke's expectant question:

Luke: You believe this shit?
Zako: **Actually** I do.

What of difference? As we saw for lexical contrasts in Chapter 3 (Section 3.2), differences are either oppositions or converses. We can oppose ideas using *rather, by contrast, on the other hand*:

> This is not a frivolous question,
> **rather** it is a very serious issue.

> To this point we have looked at clauses and their elements from the perspective of discourse. Grammarians, **on the other hand**, look at elements of clauses from the perspective of the grammar

Conversely is used to reverse two aspects of a message. In this example Malinowski interprets texts from the perspective of social contexts, whereas we suggest that contexts can only be interpreted as they are manifested in texts:

> Malinowski interpreted the social contexts of interaction as stratified into two levels, 'context of situation' and 'context of culture', and considered that a text (which he called an 'utterance') could be understood only in relation to both these levels. **Conversely**, we could say that speakers' cultures are manifested in each situation in which they interact, and that each interactional situation is manifested verbally as unfolding text.

Options for internal comparison are summed up in Figure 4.6.

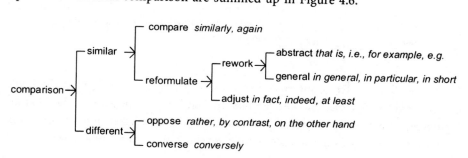

Figure 4.6 Internal comparison

Internal time

Internal time is a small set of resources for indicating that a new stage is beginning *firstly, second, next, finally, at the same time*. As such they can be used in similar ways to internal addition. So Tutu could have staged his argument as follows:

Argument 1	**Firstly** the Act required that where the offence is a gross violation the application should be dealt with in a public hearing...
Argument 2	**Secondly** it is not true that amnesty encourages impunity because amnesty is only given to those who plead guilty...
Argument 3	**Finally**, retributive justice...is not the only form of justice...there is another kind of justice, restorative justice...

In this book we also often use internal time like this to make the steps of our discourse clear to the reader:

> To begin with, the 'falling in love' phase can be divided into two parts – 'meeting' the young man, and then a 'description' of his qualities...
> **Secondly** we can divide the 'operations' phase into two parts – the 'news' about leaving, and the lovers' 'reaction' to the news...

We often use *next* in this way, to tell the reader we are starting a new stage:

> So evaluations can be divided into three basic kinds according to what is being appraised – (i) the value of things, (ii) people's character and (iii) people's feelings.
> **Next** let's look at how attitudes are amplified...

In the spoken mode, internal time may also be used to sequence arguments. In the following example (from *Forgiveness*), Llewelyn's first proposition is dismissed so he asks for a second:

Llewelyn:	I say maybe it was you who gave the cops Daniel's name.
Luke:	– Are you fucking berserk?
Llewelyn:	– **Then** who did?

These are all examples of internal succession – they order the steps in the text's internal logic as *first, second, next* and so on. But it is also possible to say that an argument, or piece of evidence, is **simultaneous** with another, using *still* or *at the same time*. The following example is from a report about our literacy work:

> Significant increases in student achievement have been measured...the average improvement in reading and writing was 2.5 levels...
> **At the same time**, teachers have noted a range of student learning outcomes that are more difficult to measure, like an increased level of student engagement in their learning.

Again, many conjunctions can realize either external or internal time – *first, next, finally, at the same time*... We have to ask whether the clause introduced by the conjunction serves to order the sequence of events (external), or to order the sequence of arguments in the discourse (internal).

Options for internal time are summed up in Figure 4.7.

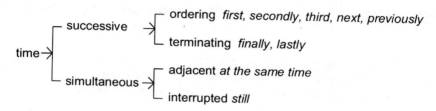

Figure 4.7 Internal time

Internal consequence

Internal consequence is concerned with drawing conclusions from arguments, and countering them. We have already seen how Tutu uses *Thus* to signal a conclusion for each of his Arguments:

> The Act required that the application should be dealt with in a public hearing …
> **Thus** there is the penalty of public exposure and humiliation
>
> …amnesty is only given to those who plead guilty …
> **Thus** the process in fact encourages accountability
>
> …there is another kind of justice, restorative justice,
> **Thus** we would claim that… justice, is being served

Conjunctions such as *thus, consequently, in conclusion* signal that a conclusion is being drawn. By this means the conclusion is construed as the expected outcome of the argument that has been presented.

In the spoken mode, *so* is commonly used for internal consequence:

Landlady:	**So**, you're off. (on entering room)
Coetzee:	– Yes.
Landlady:	– Well I hope you enjoyed your stay. Did you get what you wanted from the Grootbooms?
Coetzee:	– Yes.
Landlady:	– **So**, what is your connection with that family? Really?
Coetzee:	– Good-bye. Their son Daniel didn't die in a car hijacking. He was a freedom fighter and I killed him. At the time I was in the police force. But it was murder.

Another kind of internal consequence is to justify an argument, using *after all*:

> On the face of it, we might argue that the evaluation in Helena's story comes from Helena.
> She's the narrator **after all**.

In contrast, arguments may be dismissed with *anyway, anyhow, in any case, at any rate*:

> There have already been reports of taxis putting up 'out of service' signs and people changing seats on buses when confronted by dark-skinned people –
> as if changing your seat would save you if a bomb went off **anyway**

Arguments can also be conceded, with *admittedly, needless to say, of course*:

> Stated in these terms, the victory over apartheid seems like a simple one of right over wrong, good over evil.
> But **of course** social conflicts are rarely so simple

Or an argument may be countered as unexpected, with *nevertheless, nonetheless, still*:

> While the authors considered this two-component definition,
> they **nevertheless** favoured one component over the other one, behaving as if the two components could be taken separately

Internal counterexpectant consequence is known as **concessive**. In speech it is commonly realized by *but*:

> Coetzee: I told all this to the Commission.
> Ernest: – Yes,
> **but** now you're telling us.

Options for internal consequence are summed up in Figure 4.8.

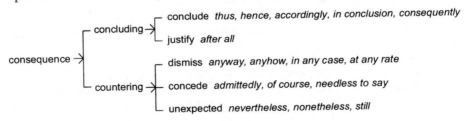

Figure 4.8 Internal consequence

The full system for internal conjunction is displayed as Table 4.6.

Table 4.6 General options for internal conjunction

Addition	developing	additive	further, furthermore, moreover, in addition, as well, besides, additionally
			alternative	alternatively
	staging	framing	now, well, alright, okay
		sidetracking	anyway, anyhow, incidentally, by the way
Comparison	similar	compare	similarly, again
		rework	that is, i.e., for example, for instance, e.g., in general, in particular, in short
		adjust	in fact, indeed, at least
	different	oppose	rather, by contrast, on the other hand
		converse	conversely
Time	successive	ordering	first, secondly, third, next, previously
		terminating	finally, lastly
	simultaneous	adjacent	at the same time
		interrupted	still
Consequence	concluding	conclude	thus, hence, accordingly, in conclusion, consequently
		justify	after all
	countering	dismiss	anyway, anyhow, in any case, at any rate
	(concessive)	concede	admittedly, of course, needless to say
		unexpected	but, however, nevertheless, nonetheless, still

4.4 Continuatives

As we predicted at the start of this chapter, we now need to mention a small set of linkers that are different from conjunctions. We'll refer to these here as continuatives. Logical relations realized by continuatives include addition, comparison and time:

addition	*too, also, as well*
comparison	*so (did he); only, just; even*
time	*already; finally, at last; still; again*

We have actually discussed several of these already, without explicitly distinguishing them from conjunctions. We met the continuative *also* in Tutu's exposition:

> The Act required that the application should be dealt with in a public hearing . . .
> It is **also** not true that the granting of amnesty encourages impunity . . .because amnesty is only given to those who plead guilty . . .

The kind of logical relation expressed by this continuative is addition. Other continuatives realize types of comparison *so (did he), even, only, just*:

> It was the beginning of a beautiful relationship.
> We **even** spoke about marriage.
>
> Amnesty didn't matter.
> It was **only** a means to the truth.

And other continuatives realize time:

> If I had to watch how white people became dissatisfied with the best
> and **still** wanted better and got it.
>
> I **finally** understand what the struggle was really about.
>
> 'those at the top' were **again** targeting the next 'permanent removal from society'.

Instead of coming at the beginning of the clause, continuatives typically occur next to the finite verb within the clause. Finite verbs are the ones that express tense or modality (see Chapter 7, section 7.3, below). They are underlined as follows: *is also, so was, even spoke, was only, still wanted, finally understand, were again...*

However, another perspective on continuatives is their role in managing expectancy. On this criterion we can group together *already, finally, still, yet, only, just, even*, since they all signal that an activity is in some way unexpected. This has already been touched on in Chapter 2 (section 2.4) in the discussion of concession as one kind of source for evaluations. For example, comparative continuatives indicate that there is more or less to a situation than might be expected. So it was <u>more</u> than we could expect of the relationship, to *even* speak about marriage:

> It was the beginning of a beautiful relationship.
> We **even** spoke about marriage.

But it was <u>less</u> than we might expect of amnesty, that it was *only* a means to the truth:

> Amnesty didn't matter.
> It was **only** a means to the truth.

Temporal continuatives indicate that something happens sooner or later, or persists longer, than one might expect. Helena is appalled at how white peoples' greed persists longer than might be reasonably expected:

> If I had to watch how white people became dissatisfied with the best and **still** wanted better and got it.

Helena also uses *finally* to signal that it took longer than expected to understand the struggle:

> I **finally** understand what the struggle was really about.

So we can classify continuatives both by the type of logical relations, and the type of expectancy they realize, as in Table 4.7.

Table 4.7 Continuatives

LOGICAL RELATION	EXPECTANCY	
addition	neutral	*too, also, as well*
comparison	neutral	*so (did he)*
	less than	*only, just*
	more than	*even*
time	sooner	*already*
	longer	*finally, at last*
	persistent	*still*
	repetitive	*again*

4.5 Displaying connections: conjunction an~~~~~

To this point we have illustrated how c~
discourse, and we have accumulated the
use for conjunction. We will now apply
organization of discourse, using diagran
need some simple labels for kinds of cor
   Second, we need to show connection
arrows. We can use these to indicate v
internal, by drawing lines on the right for
also useful as a check to insert conjunctio
are implicit. This is illustrated as follows:

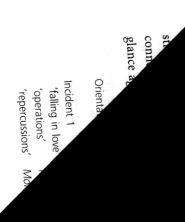

My story begins in my late teenage years as a farm girl . . .
(**that is**) As an eighteen-year-old, I met a young man in his twenties.
Then one day he said he was going on a 'trip'.

This type of diagram drawing connections between elements is known as a **reticulum**. In this example, *Then* explicitly signals succession between the second and third clauses. This is <u>external</u> succession of events in the story, so we have drawn the connection on the right. But there is also an <u>implicit</u> connection between the first and second clauses. The Orientation *My story begins in my late teenage years...* is elaborated by the first event *As an eighteen-year-old I met...*, so the logical relation between these clauses is one of similarity: reworking. To show this we have inserted an implicit conjunction in brackets (*that is*), and the connection is drawn on the left.

Table 4.8 Abbreviations for conjunction types

addition	additive	**add**
	alternative	**alt**
comparison	similar	**simil**
	different	**diff**
time	successive	**succ**
	simultaneous	**simul**
consequence	means	**means**
	consequence	**consq**
	condition	**cond**
	purpose	**purp**

This example shows how phases are connected within the first Incident of Helena's story. It is possible by these means to show all the logical connections in a text, but to simplify the presentation we can first show in one diagram how each generic stage and discourse phase is connected, and then show the connections within each stage in a separate diagram. This allows us to see a text's overall logical ~~stru~~cture, before examining more local connections. To begin with we'll show ~~conn~~ections between stages and phases in Helena's story, in Figure 4.9. First let's ~~look a~~gain at this structure of stages and phases:

~~Orienta~~tion   *My story begins in my late teenage years as a farm girl in the Bethlehem district of Eastern Free State.*

As an eighteen-year-old, I met a young man...
Then one day he said he was going on a 'trip'.
~~Mor~~e *than a year ago, I met my first love again...*

Incident 2

'falling in love' *After my unsuccessful marriage, I met another policeman.*
'operations' *Then he says: He and three of our friends have been promoted.*
'repercussions' *After about three years with the special forces, our hell began.*
Interpretation
'knowledge' *Today I know the answer to all my questions and heartache.*
'black struggle' *I finally understand what the struggle was really about.*
'white guilt' *What do we have? Our leaders are too holy and innocent.*
Coda *I end with a few lines that my wasted vulture said to me...*

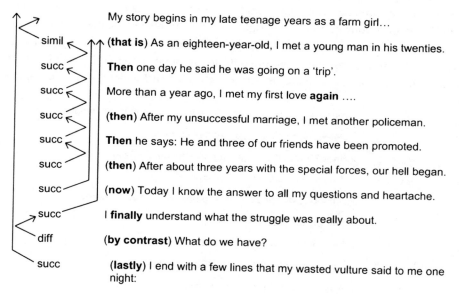

My story begins in my late teenage years as a farm girl...

simil (**that is**) As an eighteen-year-old, I met a young man in his twenties.

succ **Then** one day he said he was going on a 'trip'.

succ More than a year ago, I met my first love **again** ....

succ (**then**) After my unsuccessful marriage, I met another policeman.

succ **Then** he says: He and three of our friends have been promoted.

succ (**then**) After about three years with the special forces, our hell began.

succ (**now**) Today I know the answer to all my questions and heartache.

succ I **finally** understand what the struggle was really about.

diff (**by contrast**) What do we have?

succ (**lastly**) I end with a few lines that my wasted vulture said to me one night:

Figure 4.9 Conjunction between stages and phases in Helena's story

Note that in Figure 4.9 we have allowed at least one line between each connected figure, so that we can draw the connection. Most of the connections are external succession, as the story unfolds in time (drawn on the right). Some are realized explicitly by conjunction (*Then, again, Then, finally*), but others are realized by circumstances (*After my unsuccessful marriage, After about three years, Today*), so it is a simple matter to show this succession by inserting (*then*) in brackets.

Most of these successive connections are simply between phases as the story unfolds, but when we get to the Interpretation, their scope includes the whole story. They connect the Interpretation right back to the Orientation (*My story begins...*), spanning all the events between, as we have drawn. The same is also true of the internal connection between the Coda (*I end with a few lines...*) and the Orientation. This internal succession is realized lexically with *I end*, which we have rendered as the conjunction (*lastly*), and connected back to the start.

We have already discussed the implicit similarity between the Orientation and first Incident, rendered as (*that is*). There is also an implicit contrast between the two Interpretation phases of 'black struggle' and 'white guilt', which we have shown with (*by contrast*).

By these simple techniques we can show how a text unfolds logically, by conjunction between figures, phases and text stages. The relation may be implicit, but is apparent lexically as a circumstance (e.g. *After about three years*), a process (*I end*), or participants (*the people of the struggle* vs *our leaders*), and so can be rendered as a conjunction. We can simply show whether it is external or internal by drawing connections on the left or right, and we can also show their scope. Often more than one interpretation of implicit conjunction or scope of conjunction is possible. What is important is teasing out the discourse patterns they realize. Let's now turn to the discourse patterns within Helena's first Incident, shown in Figure 4.10.

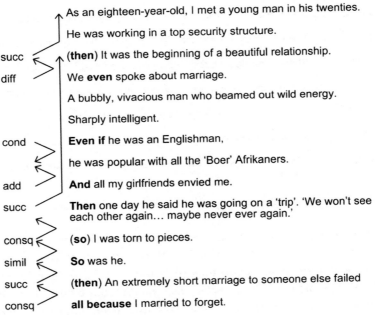

As an eighteen-year-old, I met a young man in his twenties.

He was working in a top security structure.

succ / diff — (**then**) It was the beginning of a beautiful relationship.

We **even** spoke about marriage.

A bubbly, vivacious man who beamed out wild energy.

Sharply intelligent.

cond — **Even if** he was an Englishman,

he was popular with all the 'Boer' Afrikaners.

add — **And** all my girlfriends envied me.

succ — **Then** one day he said he was going on a 'trip'. 'We won't see each other again... maybe never ever again.'

consq — (**so**) I was torn to pieces.

simil — **So** was he.

succ — (**then**) An extremely short marriage to someone else failed

consq — **all because** I married to forget.

Figure 4.10 Conjunction within one stage of Helena's story

Within this stage, connections are all external, as Helena recounts the events and describes her love. To begin with, succession is expressed lexically (*It was the beginning...*), and we have rendered it with (*then*), since the relationship implicitly follows the first meeting. Then unexpected contrasts are realized explicitly by *even* and *Even if*, but note that the direction of the latter connection is <u>forward</u> (to *he was popular...*) rather than back, like most connections. The addition of her girlfriends' reaction is also explicit (*And*), as is the succession of the 'operations' phase (*Then*). We have drawn the scope of this succession back to *the beginning of a beautiful relationship*. We have then rendered the connection between his leaving and Helena's reaction (*I was torn to pieces*) as consequence (*so*), and of course his reaction is the same (*So was he*). The next event in the succession is her short marriage, rendered with (*then*), and this is followed by its cause.

Let's now see how Tutu uses conjunction to organize his exposition, in Figure 4.11.

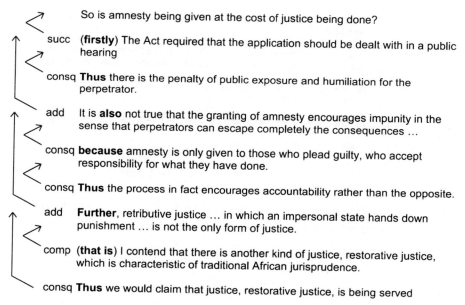

Figure 4.11 Conjunction between stages and phases in Tutu's exposition

In contrast to Helena's story, all the connections between stages and phases of the exposition are internal. We have rendered the relation between the Thesis and the first Argument as internal succession (*firstly*), and the following Arguments are explicitly added to each other (*also, Further*). Within each Argument, the grounds expect its conclusion (*Thus*). Now let's look at connections within one stage, in Figure 4.12.

In contrast to Helena's Incident, this Argument is organized primarily by internal conjunction. As we discussed earlier, the grounds for this Argument unfold as a series of conditions that we expect to negate Tutu's thesis, but are then countered with *In fact*. The scope of the conclusion (*Thus*) is the grounds as a whole. This is followed by the example, which we have rendered with (*e.g.*). This example unfolds as a sequence of consequences for the security force members, which we have rendered with (*so*). The last consequence is not another event, but

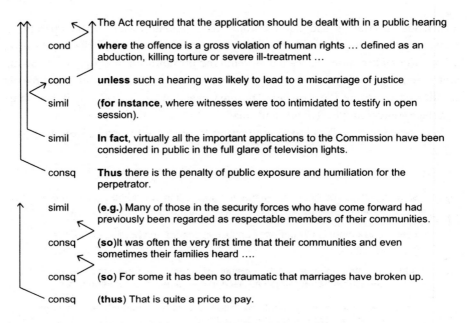

cond		The Act required that the application should be dealt with in a public hearing
cond		**where** the offence is a gross violation of human rights ... defined as an abduction, killing torture or severe ill-treatment ...
cond		**unless** such a hearing was likely to lead to a miscarriage of justice
simil		(**for instance**, where witnesses were too intimidated to testify in open session).
simil		**In fact**, virtually all the important applications to the Commission have been considered in public in the full glare of television lights.
consq		**Thus** there is the penalty of public exposure and humiliation for the perpetrator.
simil		(**e.g.**) Many of those in the security forces who have come forward had previously been regarded as respectable members of their communities.
consq		(**so**)It was often the very first time that their communities and even sometimes their families heard ....
consq		(**so**) For some it has been so traumatic that marriages have broken up.
consq		(**thus**) That is quite a price to pay.

Figure 4.12: Conjunction within one stage of Tutu's exposition

rather Tutu's conclusion about this penalty (*quite a price to pay*). Again the scope of this is the example as a whole, supporting the statement that *Thus there is a penalty...*

4.6 Logical metaphor

In Chapter 3 we introduced **ideational metaphor** and discussed the <u>experiential</u> type, in which elements of figures are reconstrued as if they were other kinds of elements, such as *process → thing* and *quality → thing*. Here we are going to look at how conjunctions are reconstrued as other kinds of elements, including processes, things, qualities and circumstances. This is the <u>logical</u> type of ideational metaphor, or **logical metaphor**. It is used to reconstrue logical relations between figures as if they were relations between elements within figures. Logical metaphor always involves experiential metaphor as well.

Conjunction as process
A common motif in abstract or technical writing is to present a consequential conjunction as a process:

such a hearing	*is likely to lead to*	*a miscarriage of justice*
Agent	**Process**	**Medium**

This strategy compresses a sequence of two activities into a single figure, by means of experiential and logical metaphors. Experientially, the Agent and Medium stand for activities ('hearing an application' and 'miscarrying justice') that are reconstrued as things (*a hearing, a miscarriage*). Logically, there is a relation of consequence between these activities ('if...then'), which is reconstrued as a process (*is likely to lead to*). We can unpack such a sequence as a sequence of two figures related by conjunctions:

> **if** such a hearing happens
> **then** justice will be miscarried.

However the logical metaphor of 'relation as process' incorporates more than simply consequence. For one thing, the probability of the result is graded as _likely to lead to_ (in contrast to high probability *will _certainly_ lead to* or low probability *will _possibly_ lead to*). And the necessity of the consequence is also graded lexically as _lead to_ (in contrast to the stronger _result in_ or weaker _associated with_).

So one of the reasons that writers use logical metaphors for conjunctions is that they can grade their evaluation of relations between events or arguments. This is a crucial resource for reasoning in fields such as science or politics, in which it is important not to overstate causal relations until sufficient evidence has been accumulated. This function of logical metaphors is oriented to engagement of the reader.

On the other hand, logical metaphors combine with experiential metaphors to package activity sequences as manageable chunks of information. This function of logical metaphor is oriented to periodicity. For example, this figure is one step in the argument that Tutu is advancing:

> The Act required that
> **the application** should be dealt with in **a public hearing**
> unless **such a hearing** was likely to lead to **a miscarriage of justice**
> (**for instance**, where witnesses were too intimidated to testify in open session).

In this sequence, Tutu first uses a passive clause to start the first message with *the application* and end with *a public hearing*. The *public hearing* is then the starting point for the next message (*such a hearing*), that ends with *a miscarriage of justice*. This is then exemplified in the next step. This sequencing of information is shown as follows:

> The Act required that the application should be dealt with in **a public hearing**
>
> unless **such a hearing** was likely to lead to **a miscarriage of justice**
>
> (**for instance**, where witnesses were too intimidated to testify in open session).

Such patterns of information flow are discussed further in Chapter 6 on periodicity. Here we can note that the logical metaphor (*is likely to lead to*) enables the sequence of cause (*such a hearing*) and effect (*a miscarriage of justice*) to be packaged as chunks of information within a single message.

Conjunction as circumstance

Another common motif in abstract or technical writing is to present a logical relation as a circumstance:

Is	amnesty	being given	at the cost of justice being done?
	Medium	**Process**	**Circumstance (accompaniment)**

The logical meaning of *at the cost of* is concessive purpose ('without'), giving the following sequence:

Is amnesty being given
without justice being done?

Again this strategy enables a sequence of two activities to be packaged as a single figure, with *amnesty* as one chunk of information and *justice being done* as another. But Tutu's rhetorical strategy here also includes other layers – the lexical metaphor *the cost of* implies a balance sheet, in which income (*amnesty*) is weighed against expenditure (*justice*). So reconstruing a sequence using this metaphor adds layers of meaning to the question.

Conjunctions as things and qualities

Conjunction can also be reconstrued as a thing or quality. Here are a few examples of conjunction as a thing:

conjunction ⟶	thing
before	the first time
then	sequel
so	reason, result, consequence
thus	conclusion
by	a means to
if	condition

The following are some examples of these conjunction-as-things in discourse, and their alternative realization as a sequence:

Time

Many of those in the security forces who have come forward had previously been regarded as respectable members of their communities.
It was often **the very first time** that their communities and even sometimes their families heard. . .

Before they came forward
their communities and even sometimes their families had not heard. . .

Consequence

Conjunctions have an important role in letting us know what to expect at each step of a discourse.
This is **one reason** they tend to come at or near the start of each sentence in English.

Conjunctions let us know what to expect
so they tend to come at or near the start of each sentence in English.

Means

Amnesty didn't matter.
It was only **a means** to the truth.

The truth would come out
by amnesty being given.

Condition

The only **conditions** for gaining amnesty were:
- The act for which amnesty was required should have happened between 1960. . . and 1994. . .
- The act must have been politically motivated. . .
- The applicant had to make a full disclosure . . .
- The rubric of proportionality had to be observed . . .

Amnesty is gained :
if the act happened between 1960 and 1994
if the act was politically motivated
if applicant made a full disclosure
if the rubric of proportionality was observed

In each case, the logical metaphor allows other meanings to be incorporated. Logical metaphor enables 'logical things' to be numbered, described, classified and qualified:

the **very first** time
one reason

only a means
the **only** conditions...1...2...3...4...

On the other hand, reconstruing conjunction as <u>qualities</u> means they can be used to modify things or processes:

conjunction ⟶	quality of thing (Epithet or Classifier) or process (Quality)
so	resulting action
by	enabling action
in fact	actual size
thus	conclusively proven
then	subsequently shown
before	previously regarded
if	conditionally approved

Here is an example of 'conjunction-as-quality' in Tutu's argument:

Many of those in the security forces who have come forward had **previously been regarded** ...as respectable members of their communities.

This could be unpacked as:

Many of those in the security forces who have come forward were regarded as respectable members of their communities **before** ...they came forward.

How much we choose to unpack ideational metaphors in our analyses will depend on our purposes. We have shown two advantages of unpacking experiential and logical metaphors. One is that by paraphrasing highly metaphorical discourse in a more spoken form, we can show learners how it means what it does, and also design a curriculum that leads from more spoken to more written modes. Another is that we can recover participant roles and logical arguments that tend to be rendered implicit by ideational metaphor. This can be a powerful tool for critical discourse analysis – revealing implicit nuclear relations such as agency and effect, and implicit logical relations such as cause and effect.

4.7 Conjunction resources in full

A full range of internal and external conjunction types is given in Tables 4.9 and 4.10, together with continuatives in Table 4.11, building in all the options we have discussed so far. These tables are intended as ready references to help with identifying the roles of conjunctions in text analysis.

Table 4.9 External conjunctions

Addition	additive	adding	*and, besides, both...and*
		subtracting	*nor, neither...nor*
	alternative		*or, either...or, if not...then*
Comparison	similar		*like, as if*
	different	opposite	*whereas, while*
		replacing	*instead of, in place of, rather than*
		excepting	*except that, other than, apart from*
Time	successive	sometime	*after, since, now that; before*
		immediate	*once, as soon as; until*
	simultaneous		*as, while, when*
Cause		expectant	*because, so, therefore*
		concessive	*although, even though, but, however*
Means		expectant	*by, thus*
		concessive	*even by, but*
Condition	open	expectant	*if, then, provided that, as long as*
		concessive	*even if, even then*
	closed		*unless*
Purpose	desire	expectant	*so that, in order to, in case*
		concessive	*even so, without*
	fear		*lest, for fear of*

Table 4.10 Internal conjunctions

Addition	additive	adding	*and, besides, both...and*
		subtracting	*nor, neither...nor*
	alternative		*or, either...or, if not...then*
Comparison	similar		*like, as if*
	different	opposite	*whereas, while*
		replacing	*instead of, in place of, rather than*
		excepting	*except that, other than, apart from*
Time	successive	sometime	*after, since, now that; before*
		immediate	*once, as soon as; until*
	simultaneous		*as, while, when*
Cause		expectant	*because, so, therefore*
		concessive	*although, even though, but, however*
Means		expectant	*by, thus*
		concessive	*even by, but*
Condition	open	expectant	*if, then, provided that, as long as*
		concessive	*even if, even then*
	closed		*unless*
Purpose	desire	expectant	*so that, in order to, in case*
		concessive	*even so, without*
	fear		*lest, for fear of*

Table 4.11 Continuatives

logical relation	expectancy	
addition	neutral	*too, also, as well*
comparison	neutral	*so (did he)*
	less than	*only, just*
	more than	*even*
time	sooner	*already*
	longer	*finally, at last*
	persistent	*still*
	repetitive	*again*

IDENTIFICATION: tracking participants

5

Chapter Outline

Identification is concerned with tracking participants – with introducing people and things into a discourse and keeping track of them once there. These are textual resources, concerned with how discourse makes sense to the reader by keeping track of identities.

Following a general introduction, section 5.2 considers resources for identifying people – through **presenting** reference if their identity is unknown, and **presuming** reference if it is recoverable. Section 5.3 looks at comparable patterns for things, including abstractions and meta-semiotic reference to surrounding text. In both sections the role of **comparative** reference between people and things is reviewed. Then in section 5.4 the different ways in which presumed identity can be recovered are introduced, including definitions of key terms such as **anaphora, cataphora, esphora, homophora, endophora** and **exophora**.

Having built up the system of identification in sections 5.2–5.4, in section 5.5 we consider the way in which tracking can vary in discourse depending on what we are presuming (people, things, abstractions or co-text) and the genre we are in (story, argument or legislation). Finally in section 5.6 we formalize our presentation of identification and tracking systems, and summarize the realization of these systems in **nominal group** structure.

5.1 Keeping track

In order to make sense of discourse, one thing we need is to be able to keep track of who or what is being talked about at any point. When we first start talking about somebody or something, we may name them, but then we often just identify them as *she, he* or *it*. By this means our listener/reader can keep track of exactly which person or thing we are talking about, i.e. which participant in the discourse. There are many other ways of introducing participants into a discourse, and keeping track of them as we go, that we will explore in this chapter.

For example, when Tutu first presents Helena's story, he introduces five participants: the SABC's radio team, the Truth and Reconciliation Commission, Helena, her letter and the reprisals that she fears:

> **The South Africa Broadcasting Corporation's radio team**
> covering **the Truth and Reconciliation Commission**
> received **a letter**
> from **a woman**
> calling **herself Helena**
> (**she** wanted to remain anonymous for fear of **reprisals**).

Helena, her letter and the feared reprisals are all introduced indefinitely, in expressions which don't assume that readers know what's being talked about:

> a letter
> a woman
> reprisals

But once she's been introduced as *a woman*, Helena is referred to by pronouns:

> herself
> she

These pronouns <u>do</u> assume that we know who's being referred to. And Tutu also names Helena with the pseudonym she's given to protect herself, a name that can be used to refer to her now we know who she is:

> **a woman** calling **herself Helena**

The other participants in Tutu's introduction are things referred to with 'the', which seems to assume we already know who he's talking about. Both these things are institutions that are mentioned right at the beginning of his book in the Acknowledgement section, so this assumption is certainly justified:

The South Africa Broadcasting Corporation's radio team
the Truth and Reconciliation Commission

In simple terms then, what we see here are a range of resources for introducing participants into a discourse and for keeping track of them once there. We can express this as a set of choices, first between introducing participants and tracking them; and second, within tracking, between pronouns, names, and entities with 'the'. These choices are shown in Figure 5.1. (Note that this is not drawn as a system network, as we need to expand the discussion before we're ready to draw the system for identification.) In this chapter we will explore these basic choices for identification as follows. We will look first at how people are introduced and tracked through texts; secondly at how things are introduced and tracked; thirdly at how we know who or what is being referred to; and fourthly at the different ways that people and things can be tracked through whole texts.

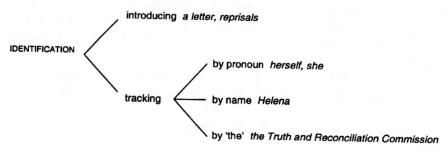

Figure 5.1 Basic choices in identification

5.2 Who's who?: identifying people

Let's begin by seeing how people are introduced and tracked through Helena's story. We'll start with resources for introducing people, and then look at how their identities are tracked.

Introducing people

Helena's story has three main characters: Helena and her first and second loves. Helena is introduced to us by Tutu:

> The South Africa Broadcasting Corporation's radio team covering the Truth and Reconciliation Commission received a letter from **a woman** calling herself Helena (she wanted to remain anonymous for fear of reprisals).

And Helena in turn introduces her two loves; her first love is introduced as follows:

> I met **a young man** in his twenties.

How are these people introduced? As we can see, the basic strategy here is to use 'a' to introduce **a** *woman* and **a** *young man*. The word 'a' tells us that this is someone whose identity we can't assume. When we can't assume an identity it is 'indefinite', so a participant with 'a' is traditionally known as 'indefinite'. On the other hand 'the' tells us that we <u>can</u> assume an identity, so a participant with 'the' is traditionally known as 'definite'.

Moving on to her second love, Helena introduces him as follows:

> I met **another policeman**.

Another identifies him in two ways. First *an* is indefinite like 'a', so we know we can't assume this identity; secondly *other* tells us that he is different from the first policeman. These two meanings (indefiniteness and difference) are fused together as *another*.

Helena also uses the same strategies for introducing minor characters. When she meets her first love again, it is through a friend, who is also indefinite:

> I met my first love again through **a good friend**.

A third man whom she briefly marries is introduced indefinitely as *someone*, i.e. nobody we know; and is also distinguished from her first love as *someone* <u>else</u>:

> An extremely short marriage to **someone else**

Tracking people

The minor players aren't mentioned again in the story; but Helena's first and second loves are. Her first love is tracked as follows:

> As an eighteen-year-old, I met **a young man** in **his** twenties.
> **He** was working in a top security structure.
> It was the beginning of a beautiful relationship.
> **We** even spoke about marriage.
> A bubbly, vivacious man who beamed out wild energy.
> Sharply intelligent.
> Even if **he** was an Englishman
> **he** was popular with all the 'Boer' Afrikaners.
> And all my girlfriends envied me.
> Then one day **he** said he was going on a 'trip'.

'**We** won't see each other again… maybe never ever again.'
I was torn to pieces.
So was **he**.
An extremely short marriage to someone else failed all because I married to forget.
More than a year ago, I met **my first love** again through a good friend.
I was to learn for the first time that **he** had been operating overseas
and that **he** was going to ask for amnesty.
I can't explain the pain and bitterness in me
when I saw what was left of **that beautiful, big, strong person**.
He had only one desire – that the truth must come out.

Once he is introduced as *a young man*, the main strategy for tracking his identity is with pronouns, which refer to him ten times on his own (*he* and *his*), and twice together with Helena (*we*). He's also identified twice as a kind of person: *my first love*, and *that beautiful, big, strong person*. We can re-present these resources as Table 5.1.

Table 5.1 Tracking Helena's first love

On his own	With Helena	As a kind of person
his (twenties)		
He		a young man
	we	
He		
He		
He		
He		
	we	
He		
		(my) first love
He		
He		
		that beautiful, big, strong person
He		
		(my) first love

Helena didn't name her first love, although she did make up a name for herself, as introduced by Tutu:

a woman calling herself **Helena**

The name gives us a useful way of referring to Helena, although in her story of course she relies on pronouns (*I, my; we, our*).

Another tracking resource is 'the', which Helena uses later to refer to her second love:

> I can't handle **the man** anymore!

Comparing people

We have seen that participants can be referred to as different from others, with *another* or *someone else*. These kinds of resources compare one participant with another, and so are known as **comparative** reference. Comparative reference may involve simple contrast, or numbers such as *first, second* and superlatives such as *best, better*:

> my **first** love
> someone **else**
> an**other** policeman

In English, unlike many languages, we tend to insist on signalling whether we are presenting or presuming every time a participant is mentioned. However comparison is optional; we just use it when we need to.

Possession

Another important resource for identifying participants is possessive pronouns. These pronouns (*my, your, her, his, its, our, their*) work like *a, some, the, this, that, these, those*, to tell us which participant we are talking about. In her story, Helena introduces her girlfriends, their police friends and the Africans' leaders in this way:

> all **my** girlfriends
> and three of **our** friends
> **their** leaders

As well as people, the possessions and parts of people can all be presented and presumed with this resource, for example, *his throat, my head*.

There are actually two identities in these expressions; one is realized by the possessive pronoun (e.g. *my*) and the other by the thing that is 'possessed' (e.g. *girlfriends*). The possessive pronoun always presumes an identity, but the thing that is 'possessed' may or may not have been previously mentioned.

The participant identification resources we've been looking at so far are summed up in Table 5.2, with ways of introducing participants on the left and ways of tracking them on the right.

So on the left we have resources that introduce us to people; and on the right we have resources which tell us who we already know. Technically, we can say that

Table 5.2 Basic resources for introducing and tracking people

Introducing (presenting)	Tracking (presuming)
a woman	**Helena**
another policeman	**his** twenties
someone else	**he**
	we
	my first love
	that . . . person
	the man

resources that introduce people are **presenting** reference, and those that track people are **presuming** reference. Words like *a, an* and *someone* are used for presenting reference. Words like *the, that, he, we* and names like *Helena* are used for presuming reference.

However, **comparative** reference and **possessive** reference are a little different, because they can be used in nominal groups which both present and presume. So *another policeman* and *someone else* both present a new person, at the same time as they presume the person they are compared with. The 'an' part of *another* presents a new person, but the 'other' part compares him with someone we already know. Likewise *someone* presents a new person, but *else* compares him with someone we already know. With possessive reference, *my first love* presumes someone we already know. However, *all my girlfriends* presents new people, even though *my* refers to someone we already know: the narrator, Helena.

Let's sum up the resources we've seen for identifying people, and add a few more in Table 5.3.

Table 5.3 Resources for identifying people

PRESENTING	a, an, one
	someone, anyone
PRESUMING	the
	this, that
	I, me, you, she, he, it; we, us, they, them
	Helena
POSSESSIVE	his (twenties)
	my (girlfriends)
	Helena's (friend)
COMPARATIVE	same, similar
	other, another, different, else

We can also now introduce a few basic terms for the words that English uses for identifying people and things. Of course words like *I, she, it, my, his* are **pronouns**. Words like *a* and *the* are known as **determiners**, since they 'determine' whether we can assume an identity or not; 'a' is an indefinite determiner, while 'the' is a definite determiner. Words like *this, that, these, those* are known as **demonstratives**, since they 'demonstrate' where to find an identity, 'near' with *this* or 'far' with *that*.

Instances that neither present nor presume participant identities

Usually, presenting reference is used when we first mention a person, and presuming reference is used for second or subsequent mentions. But in English this doesn't always hold. For example, what looks like presenting reference is used to describe Helena's first love, even after we know who he is:

> he was **an Englishman**

Similarly her second love is described indefinitely after he is introduced:

> (He was) Not quite my first love, but (he was) **an exceptional person**.

Helena even describes herself as a farm girl, after presuming her own identity twice with *my*:

> My story begins in my late teenage years as **a farm girl** . . .

The reason for these apparent anomalies is that these indefinite expressions are being used to describe or classify people, not to identify them. These kinds of expressions are discussed in more detail in Chapter 4. They include classifying figures:

> He was **an Englishman**
> It was only **a means to the truth**

And classifying roles:

> She lived **as a farm girl**.
> He worked **as a policeman**.

Since they don't actually identify people, we will set these expressions aside here as far as identification is concerned.

Another apparent anomaly is the use of what looks like presuming reference the first time a character is mentioned. Some examples of this include the use of 'the', and a proper name, for first mentions:

He was popular with all **the 'Boer' Afrikaners**.
I can understand if **Mr F. W. de Klerk** says

What's going on here is that Helena assumes that her readers will know who she's talking about. The identity of *the Boer Afrikaners* will obviously be known to a South African audience, and the same for the name of a former prime minister. The point here is that speakers/writers make assumptions on the go about what listeners/readers can and can't be expected to know. If someone's identity is as good as given then presuming reference is used, even where that character hasn't been mentioned before.

5.3 What's what?: identifying things

In Chapter 3 we looked at different kinds of entities that can participate in figures, including people, objects, institutions and abstractions, as well as figures that function like things. Each of these different kinds of entities can be identified in different ways.

Identifying objects

Concrete objects, that we can touch, taste, hear, see or feel, are identified pretty much like people. They are introduced indefinitely, and then tracked with determiners like *the* or pronouns like *it*:

We used **a yellow portable Robin generator** to send electric shocks through his body when we put **the generator** on his body was shocked stiff... [94]

they started to take **a plastic bag**
then one person held both my hands down and the other person put **it** on my head.
Then they sealed **it** so that I wouldn't be able to breathe
and kept **it** on for at least two minutes... [105]

There are a few ways of introducing plural participants (things or people). One way is to use the plural with no determiner:

In the upper abdomen were **twenty-five wounds**.
These wounds indicated that different weapons were used to stab him... [114]

For presenting participants, there is the plural of 'a', namely 'some':

they had **some** friends over
he had **some** milk for Helena

English uses the indefinite plural 'some' with things that can be counted like *friends*, and things that can't like *milk*. Things like milk are 'masses'. We can package them and then count the packages (*two bottles of milk*), but we can't count a 'mass' (**two milks*).

However with plural things or with masses we also have the option of presenting participants without 'a' or 'the':

> I put **garden shears** through his neck
> They were shot and massacred with **AK47s**
> they poured **acid** on his face.

Plural things are presented with the ending '-s', while plural masses are presented with neither an ending nor a determiner.

Institutions and abstractions

Less concrete things such as agencies (*special forces*) and abstractions (*price, marriage, amnesty*) are identified similarly to objects:

> We're moving to **a special unit**
> After about three years with **the special forces**, our hell began.
>
> Our freedom has been bought at **a very great price**.
> But to compute **that price** properly
>
> **An extremely short marriage** to someone else failed all because I married to forget
> After **my unsuccessful marriage**, I met another policeman.
>
> It was on precisely this point that **amnesty** was refused to the police officers who applied for **it** for their part in the death of Steve Biko.

Comparison can also be used to distinguish types of abstractions, for example *kinds of justice*:

> Further, **retributive justice** – in which an impersonal state hands down punishment with little consideration for victims and hardly any for the perpetrator – is not the only form of justice.
> I contend that there is **another kind of justice**, **restorative justice**, which is characteristic of traditional African jurisprudence

Identifying what people say: text reference

Beyond abstractions, it's possible to track things people say. Helena refers to her prayers for example as *all my questions and heartache*:

> 'God, what's happening? What's wrong with him? Could he have changed so much? Is

he going mad? I can't handle the man anymore! But, I can't get out. He's going to haunt me for the rest of my life if I leave him. Why, God?'
Today I know the answer to **all my questions and heartache**.

And Tutu refers to the question he's just asked as *this*:

So is amnesty being given at the cost of justice being done?
This is not a frivolous question, but a very serious issue

In abstract discourse such as Tutu's argument, this kind of reference to what was just said is very common to refer to a point that's just been made, possibly to evaluate it. What was said previously is typically tracked with demonstratives (*this*, *that*):

For some it has been so traumatic that **marriages have broken up**.
That is quite a price to pay.

Amnesty is not given to innocent people or to those who claim to be innocent.
It was on precisely **this point** that amnesty was refused to the police officers

Once amnesty is granted,
and **this** has to happen immediately

The advantage of this kind of tracking is that stretches of meaning can be packaged up to play a new role as the argument unfolds. In the following passage, for example, Tutu packages up the effect of amnesty in order to expand on its consequences for civil damages (*this means that...*). These consequences are in turn packaged up to be evaluated (*that is...*) and identified (*it is...*):

The effect of amnesty is as if the offence had never happened, since the perpetrator's court record relating to that offence becomes a tabula rasa, a blank page.
This means ... that the victim loses the right to sue for civil damages in compensation from the perpetrator.
That is indeed a high price to ask the victims to pay,
but **it** is the price those who negotiated our relatively peaceful transition from repression to democracy believed the nation had to ask of victims.

This kind of tracking of what was said is called **text reference**. As we've seen it is used to turn big meanings into smaller, more manageable ones, so that we can then make some more meanings with them. Meanings contract, in other words, so that new meanings can expand. The text is breathing, as the argument moves along.

Identifying things in legal and administrative discourse
In legal and administrative discourse quite a lot of pressure is put on identification resources in order to be precise. This includes some specialized features which we

can see in the Act which established the Truth and Reconciliation Commission. The word *said* for example is used alongside *the* to refer precisely to what has just been said, specifying dates:

> ... the nature, causes and extent of gross violations of human rights committed during **the period from 1 March 1960 to the cut-off date contemplated in the Constitution** ... acts associated with a political objective committed in the course of the conflicts of the past during **the said period**

And specifying purposes:

> **To provide for** the investigation and the establishment of as complete a picture as possible of the nature, causes and extent of gross violations of human rights committed and for **the said purposes** to provide for the establishment of a Truth and Reconciliation Commission, a Committee on Human Rights Violations, a Committee on Amnesty and a Committee on Reparation and Rehabilitation;

The words *said* or *aforesaid* are specialized versions of *the*, specifying that the identity presumed can be found in the preceding text. Another example of specialized reference is the tracking device *therewith*, which refers to a specific 'location' in the text. This is used to keep things open, to refer generally to the processes that have to be undertaken to establish the Commission and Committees and empower them:

> and for the said purposes to provide for the establishment of a Truth and Reconciliation Commission
> and to confer certain powers on, assign certain functions to and impose certain duties upon that Commission and those Committees
> and to provide for matters connected **therewith**.

Reference to location in space (*here, there*) and time (*now, then*) is also found in non-specialized discourse. It is used by Tutu to refer to restorative justice (*here*):

> I contend that there is **another kind of justice, restorative justice, which is characteristic of traditional African jurisprudence**.
> **Here** the central concern is not retribution or punishment but, in the spirit of *ubuntu*

As with *therewith* in the Act, identifying by location in space or time is a little more general than using a demonstrative. It treats discourse as a region of meaning that we can be oriented to, as opposed to a collection of people and things we pick out and name.

Another important aspect of the Act's specialized tracking resources is its elaborate naming system:

- sections 1, 2 , 3. . .49
- sub-section (1), (2), (3)
- paragraphs (a), (b), (c)
- sub-paragraphs (i), (ii), (iii)
- sub-sub-paragraphs (aa), (bb), (cc).

This allows the authors to refer exactly to certain paragraphs later (or earlier) in the document. So for example, section 3, subsection (3), paragraph (d) of Chapter 2 refers to sections 5(d) and 28(4)(a):

3 (3) (d) the investigating unit referred to in section **5(d)** shall perform the investigations contemplated in section **28(4)(a)**

Comparing things: comparative reference

Now that we've looked at how various things are identified (concrete objects, abstractions, institutions, and things that people say) we need to look at ways that these things can be compared. Helena uses several comparative references in some parts of her story:

I finally understand what **the struggle** was really about.
I would have done **the same** had I been denied everything.
If my life, that of my children and my parents was strangled with legislation.
If I had to watch how white people became dissatisfied with **the best**
and still wanted **better**
and got it.

She begins by presenting *the struggle* as though we all know what she means, and then refers to it as *the same*. Later she presents what white people already had as *the best*, and identifies what they still wanted as *better*. She doesn't need to say what is better, because words like *better* and *best* are resources for comparative reference, like *same, other, else*. So things can be identified by comparing the intensity of their qualities, with words like *better* and *best*. They can also be identified by comparing their quantity, with words like *most, more, fewer, less; so much, so little*:

Spiritual murder is **more** inhumane than a messy, physical murder.

What's wrong with him?
Could he have changed **so much**?

And they can be identified by comparing their order:

As an eighteen-year-old, I met **a young man** in his twenties.

An extremely short marriage to **someone else** failed all because I married to forget. More than a year ago, I met **my <u>first</u> love** again through a good friend.

Helena refers to him as her *first* love to distinguish him from someone else she later married. Other resources for identifying things by their order include *first, second, third; next, last; preceding, subsequent, former, latter.*

Tutu also uses comparison to identify things:

> the application should be dealt with in a public hearing
> unless **such a hearing** was likely to lead to a miscarriage of justice

Here *such a* refers to a particular <u>class</u> of hearing (a public one), and no other.

Let's now sum up the resources we've seen for identifying things and people, and add a few more, in Table 5.4.

Table 5.4 Resources for identifying things and people

type	resources
PRESENTING	*a, an, one; someone, anyone* *some, any; every, all* *AK-47s, acid*
PRESUMING	*the; this, that; these, those* *the said purposes* *each, both; neither, either* *I, me, you, she, he, it; we, us, they, them* *Helena; Section 5* *here, therewith*
POSSESSIVE	*his (twenties)* *my (girlfriends)* *Helena's (friend)*
COMPARATIVE	*same, similar, other, different, else...* *such inhumane, so inhumane, as inhumane as...* *first, second, third; next, last; preceding, subsequent, former, latter...* *more, fewer, less...* *better, best; more inhumane, most inhumane...*
TEXT REFERENCE	*this, that, it* *all my questions*

5.4 Where to look?

Whenever the identity of a participant is presumed, that identity has to be recovered. This can be done in various ways depending where the relevant information is.

Looking back or forward: anaphoric or cataphoric reference

In writing, the obvious place to look for a presumed identity is the surrounding text; usually we look back, like we did from *herself* to *a woman* in Tutu's introduction to Helena's story. But we may have to look forward, in order to find out what *it* means for example at the beginning of the Act, where *it* refers forward to the whole Act:

> BE *IT THEREFORE ENACTED* by the Parliament of the Republic of South Africa, as follows:-
> CHAPTER 1
> Interpretation and application
> Definitions
> 1. (1) In this Act, unless the context otherwise indicates –

At other times, the information assumed isn't actually in the text, but somewhere outside. If so, it might be sensible: something we can see, hear, touch, taste or smell, for example *Pass the salt*. Alternatively, it might be something virtually present, that we just all know about because of what we know, for example *You should tell the President*.

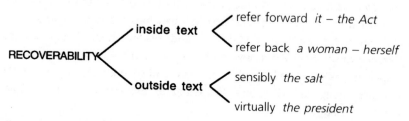

Figure 5.2 Recovering identities

As we noted in section 5.2, some tracking devices tell us where to look for presumed information. When we read *the said period* we look back in the preceding text to find the time referred to:

> gross violations of human rights committed during **the period from 1 March 1960 to the cut-off date contemplated in the Constitution**
> acts associated with a political objective committed in the course of the conflicts of the past during **the said** period

We may also be given instructions to look forward, although this is less common in most registers, except in legal and administrative discourse. For example, at the beginning of the Act **the following Act** refers forward to the Act itself that follows:

> It is hereby notified that the President has assented to **the following** Act which is hereby published for general information:
>
> **ACT**
> To provide for the investigation and the establishment of as complete a picture as possible of the nature, causes and extent of gross violations of human . . .

Legal and administrative discourse also depends quite a lot on its numbering system for forward reference. This allows specific connections to be made to following discourse:

> 1. (1) In this Act, unless the context otherwise indicates –
> (i) "act associated with a political objective" has the meaning ascribed thereto in section **20(2)** and **(3)**

The technical term for reference that points back is **anaphora**; and the term for reference that points forward is **cataphora**.

Looking outside: exophoric and homophoric reference

It may also be the case that presumed identities are to be found outside the verbal text. There are two main places to look for these identities: outside in the culture or outside in the situation of speaking. The first involves information which is to be found in the cultural knowledge that writer and reader share. Examples are Helena's reference to *the Boer Afrikaners* and *F. W. de Klerk*, who her readers are aware of. Proper names are usually used in this way, and so align a group of people who know who's being talked about, for example *Eastern Free State, God, Mpumalanga, Steve Biko*.

Definite reference can also be used in this way when the reference is obvious; Helena talks about *the* truth, '*those* at the top', '*the* cliques', *the* Truth Commission, *the* operations, *the* old White South Africa and *the* struggle in this way. The scare quotes around *those at the top* and *the cliques* indicate that she is addressing a special group of readers in the know. This communal reference, whether realized through names or definite nominal groups, is called **homophora**.

The second type of reference outside the text is harder to illustrate from our examples, because these written texts are so self-sufficient; the story, argument and act don't depend on accompanying images or action to make their meaning. So let's imagine that we are right now in Australia looking at an Aboriginal flag outside our window. If so, when we say *the black band, the red band* or *the yellow circle* in the following text, then we are referring outside what we are saying to something we can sense (see, hear, touch, taste or feel):

> **The black band** stands for Australian indigenous people (and for the night sky on which the Dreaming is written in the stars); **the red band** stands for the red Australian earth (and for the blood that Aboriginal people have shed struggling to share it with Europeans); and **the yellow circle** symbolizes the sun (and a new dawn for social justice for Aboriginal people).

Likewise, if Helena had read her story to us over the radio, then we could argue that her reference to herself is exophoric (from her words to the person speaking):

> **My** story begins in **my** late teenage years as a farm girl in the Bethlehem district of Eastern Free State.

The Act also refers to itself in a similar way, using both locative and demonstrative reference:

> It is **hereby** notified that the President has assented to the following Act which is hereby published for general information:
>
> 1. (1) In **this** Act, unless the context otherwise indicates

This kind of reference from language to outside the text is called **exophora**.

Referring indirectly: bridging reference

To this point, the resources we've looked at refer directly to the participant they identify. Less commonly, participants can be presumed indirectly. To illustrate we can use some examples from other stories in Tutu's book:

> Tshikalanga stabbed first . . . and he couldn't get **the knife** out of the chest of Mxenge [96]

In this story the identity of *the knife* is presumed even though it hasn't been directly introduced before; but it has been <u>indirectly</u> introduced, since the most likely thing for someone to stab with is a knife.

Similarly with *the plastic* in the following example; it hasn't been directly mentioned, but plastic bags are obviously made of plastic, and so its 'presence' is obvious:

> they started to take **a plastic bag** . . . then one person held both my hands down and the other person put it on my head. Then they sealed it so that I wouldn't be able to

> breathe and kept it on for at least two minutes, by which time **the plastic** was clinging to my eyelids [105]

This kind of inferred anaphoric reference is called **bridging**. Helena uses this kind of reference to presume *the bed* from her second love's sleeping habits in the following extract:

> Instead of **resting at night**, he would wander from window to window. He tried to hide his wild consuming fear, but I saw it.
> **In the early hours of the morning between two and half-past-two, I jolt awake** from his rushed breathing.
> Rolls this way, that side of **the bed**.

Self-identification: esphoric refence

Finally there is one resource that identifies participants without us having to look elsewhere in the text. This happens when one thing modifies another one and answers the question 'Which one?'. If for example Helena had referred simply to *the Bethlehem district, the realities, the people* or *the answer* we might have been entitled to ask 'Where's that?', 'Which realities?', 'Which people?', 'Which answer?' But Helena short-circuits the questions by expanding a thing with a qualifier which tells us <u>which</u> district, <u>which</u> realities, <u>which</u> people and <u>which</u> answer she means:

> the Bethlehem district <u>of Eastern Free State</u>
> the realities <u>of the Truth Commission</u>
> the people <u>of the struggle</u>
> the answer <u>to all my questions and heartache</u>

Facets of things work in the same way:

> the bottom <u>of</u> his soul
> the rest <u>of</u> my life
> the role <u>of</u> 'those at the top'

So the information presumed by *the* in these elements is resolved by the time we get to the end of them. When elements simply point into themselves like this it's called **esphora**.

Kinds of reference

The reference terms we have introduced above were nouns: *cataphora, anaphora, exophora,* etc. But each also has an adjective, which is more common than the noun, including *cataphoric, anaphoric, exophoric.* Here's a table summarizing what each term means. In Table 5.5, esphora is treated as a kind of pointing forward, and bridging as a type of pointing back. We can refer to the system as a whole as RECOVERABILITY.

Table 5.5 Types of reference

REFERENCE	where to look	example
anaphoric	backward	*a plastic bag – it*
bridging	indirectly backward	*a plastic bag – the plastic*
cataphoric	forward	*the following Act – Act*
esphoric	forward within same nominal group	*the people of the struggle*
homophoric	out to shared knowledge	*the Truth Commission*
exophoric	out to the situation	*(Look at) that view*

5.5 Tracking and genre

The way in which participants are identified is an important aspect of how a text unfolds. Of all genres, stories make by far the greatest use of reference resources to introduce and track participants through a discourse. In other genres, such as Tutu's exposition and the Act, general participants are presented and only briefly tracked. We've also already looked at the way in which reference helps construct the Act's staging, using pronouns and determiners to track information within sections but not between, relying on names to refer between sections. So we'll concentrate on Helena's story here.

Helena is in one sense the main character in her story. Tutu introduces us to her by name, and she uses this pseudonym to sign off at the end of her letter. In the story itself she appears more often than anyone else, always as pronouns (*I, my, we, our* and also *you* when she's quoting from her second love). Helena, however, is not so much telling us a story about herself as about her two loves, and the devastating effect their bloody work has had on them. Not surprisingly, the way in which these two key protagonists are tracked is more varied and more interesting than the steady pronominal reference to Helena. In addition other key participants are introduced and tracked through various phases, including her second husband's three friends, 'those at the top' and the people of the struggle.

Table 5.6 gives an overview of the resources used to introduce and track the main characters in Helena's story.

After Helena's name is presented by Tutu in his introduction to her letter, she is referred to with first and second person pronouns throughout the other stages.

Lexical resources are used to introduce her two loves (*a young man, another policeman*) and they are then tracked with pronouns until lexical resources are

Table 5.6 Identifying and story phases

	Helena	1st love	2nd love	3 friends	those at the top	the people
Orientation	my, I					
Incident 1	I, we, my, our, me*	a young man, his, he, we*, my first love, that beautiful big strong person				
Incident 2	I, my, our, you, me, we*	my first love	another policeman, he, our, we, my, his, they*	3 of our friends, we, we, his friends, they, they, they		
Interpretation 'knowledge'	I, my, me*		our men, my murderer		'those at the top', the 'cliques', their, they, their, 'those at the top'	
'black struggle'	I, my, our*					the people of the struggle, their, their, their
'white guilt'	we, I				Our leaders, Mr F. W. de Klerk, he	
Coda	I, my, me		my wasted vulture, me, I, my*			

* Types of pronominal tracking listed, but not all instances

needed again to evaluate them (*that beautiful big strong man* and *my murderer, my wasted vulture*). Incident 1 is about Helena's first love, and he is tracked through it and also mentioned once at the beginning of Incident 2. Her second love is then introduced and tracked through Incident 2 and also plays a role in two phases of the Interpretation.

The minor characters are more local. First the three friends are tracked through the early phases of Incident 2. The Interpretation introduces the other players in turn: *'those at the top'* when she discusses her new found 'knowledge', together with her second love who is re-presented as *my murderer*. Then *the people of the struggle* are introduced and tracked through her discussion of the 'black struggle'. In the 'white guilt' phase, 'those at the top' are re-presented as *our leaders* and *Mr F. W. de Klerk*. Finally she re-presents her second love as *my wasted vulture* in the Coda when he describes his mental torture.

Globally then such a table lets us survey the role in the development of the story by different characters, as they are presented and re-presented in each phase in turn. Locally, it lets us examine the way in which participants are introduced and tracked within each phase. This kind of display also lets us monitor the use of lexical resources instead of pronouns once a participant has been introduced, which as we've noted is connected with evaluation in Helena's narrative.

Now let's narrow the focus and have a look at how reference and lexical resources are used to introduce and track people through one phase of a story. We saw earlier how Helena's first love is tracked through Incident 1; these references to him are presented again in Table 5.7. Like Helena, he's tracked initially through a pronoun sequence: *he, his, we*. Then he's referred to as a kind of person, with a full nominal group: *my first love, that beautiful, big, strong person,* and finally as *my first love* again.

Table 5.7 References to Helena's first love

| PRESENTING | PREUSMING | | |
	pronoun	joint pronoun	lexical
a young man			
	his (twenties)		
	he		
		we (and Helena)	
	he		
	he		
	he		
	he		
		we (and Helena)	
	he		
			(my) first love
	he		
	he		
			that beautiful, big, strong person
	he		
			(my) first love

There are two points we can make here. The first is that referring to characters with names or full nominal groups, instead of pronouns, is associated with phases of storytelling. So we get Helena's name to introduce her story and sign off; and we get *a young man* to introduce the first love and *my first love* the last time he's mentioned; and *my first love* is also used when Helena meets him once again after many years. What we're looking at here is the use of pronouns to sustain reference within phases and nouns to <u>frame</u> phases in story telling.

The second point we need to make has to do with *that beautiful, big, strong person*. This reference is heavily evaluated, and harks back to the starry-eyed picture Helena paints of her first love at the beginning of the story (*young, bubbly, vivacious, wild energy, sharply intelligent, popular*). Her point is to contrast that man with what was left after his operations overseas. So another function of using full nominal groups to track participants is <u>evaluation</u>, as Helena shapes the point of the story for her readers.

We can see closely related functions (of framing phases and evaluating people) at work with Helena's second love. He's introduced as *another policeman*, referred to as *the man* when he becomes too much to handle, and as *my wasted vulture* the last time Helena mentions him:

> I met **another policeman**
> I can't handle **the man** anymore!
> I end with a few lines that **my wasted vulture** said to me one night

The second and third of these are also evaluative, referring to her second love as *the man* expresses the distance in their relationship, while *my wasted vulture* registers her sympathy with his living hell.

Tracking by possession

In relation to evaluation, the other tracking pattern we should look at is the frequent use of possessive reference connecting her second love to friends and relations and to his anguish and fear. Possessive reference is a key feature of the second Incident and Coda:

> 'operations'
> 'Now, now **my darling**. We are real policemen now.'
> He and **his friends** would visit regularly
> no other life than that of worry, sleeplessness, anxiety about **his safety**
> And all that we as loved ones knew. . .was what we saw with **our own eyes**

> 'repercussions'
> After about three years with the special forces, **our hell** began
> Sometimes he would just press **his face** into **his hands** and shake uncontrollably
> He tried to hide **his wild consuming fear**, but I saw it
> I jolt awake from **his rushed breathing**.

> The terrible convulsions and blood-curdling shrieks of fear and pain from the bottom of
> **his soul**
> I never knew. Never realised what was being shoved down **his throat** during the 'trips'
> He's going to haunt me for the rest of **my life** if I leave him
>
> Coda
> I end with a few lines that **my wasted vulture** said to me one night
> The problem is in **my head, my conscience**.
> There is only one way to be free of it. Blow **my brains** out. Because that's where **my
> hell** is.

The extensive use of possessive reference in these phases focuses on the interpersonal relations between Helena, her man and their friends, and on her man's relations to his body, his reactions and his consciousness.

Tracking in quoted speech

In quoted speech the pronouns used to track participants shift, from third person to first person for Helena's first and second loves:

> '**We** won't see each other again... maybe never ever again.'
> '**We**'re moving to a special unit. Now, now **my** darling. **We** are real policemen now.'
> 'What **you** don't know, can't hurt **you**.'
> 'They can give **me** amnesty a thousand times. Even if God and everyone else forgives
> **me** a thousand times – **I** have to live with this hell. The problem is in **my** head, **my**
> conscience. There is only one way to be free of it. Blow **my** brains out. Because that's
> where **my** hell is.'

So tracking resources have a role to play in setting up planes of narration, including what the narrator tells us directly alongside what she quotes from others. At one point in Helena's story we see a bit of tension between what the grammar tells us to expect and what in fact takes place. Helena seems about to quote (*Then he says* followed by a colon), but continues in the third person (*he and three of our friends*) without opening quotes:

> Then he says: **He and three of our friends** have been promoted.
> 'We're moving to a special unit. Now, now my darling. We are real policemen now.'

Within quotes she would have written '*Three of our friends and I ...*'. The tense of the verb (*have* not *had*) combines with the tracking to delay for one clause the actual move to the direct speech. The overall effect of this interaction between punctuation, grammar and discourse is to create a meaning somewhere between telling and quoting.

Another place where the story sends out mixed signals has to do with tracking Helena's second love and his special forces friends. In the passage below, we can't be completely sure whether *they* (in *they stayed over*) includes her second love or not. If her second love is living with her, presumably not; but if he's away living with his team, probably so. Helena hasn't made it clear whether moving to a special unit also meant moving away from home:

> Then he says: He and three of our friends have been promoted. 'We're moving to a special unit. Now, now my darling. We are real policemen now.' We were ecstatic. We even celebrated. He and his friends would visit regularly.
> **They** even stayed over for long periods.
> Suddenly, at strange times, **they** would become restless.

As the text unfolds it seems clear that *they* includes her second love, since he obviously takes off on trips with his team; and from this we might conclude that he has in fact moved away from home after promotion just like her first love:

> Then he says:
> **He and three of our friends** have been promoted.
> '**We**'re moving to a special unit. Now, now my darling.
> **We** are real policemen now.' We were ecstatic. We even celebrated.
> **He and his friends** would visit regularly.
> **They** even stayed over for long periods.
> Suddenly, at strange times,
> **they** would become restless.
> Ø Abruptly mutter the feared word 'trip'
> and Ø drive off.
> I . . . as a loved one. . .knew no other life than that of worry, sleeplessness, anxiety about his safety and where **they** could be.

So at one point we can't be sure; but looking back we feel more confident. This kind of tension shows us that participant tracking is a dynamic device that's very sensitive to just where we are as a discourse unfolds. In analysis it's important not to lose sight of indeterminacy that eventually gets resolved because we can look backwards, carefully, taking as much time as we like, and with hindsight weigh up the evidence and make sense of the meaning overall. The ways in which meaning accumulates in discourse is just as significant as what we finally decide a discourse meant. Reading opens; readings close.

Tracking identities implicitly

One part of the picture we haven't covered yet, but which is relevant here is the use of **ellipsis** as a tracking device. In the following example, Helena doesn't actually use a pronoun to tell us who abruptly muttered and who drove off, but we know perfectly well who she means because English can refer to participants by leaving them out:

> Suddenly, at strange times, **they** would become restless.
> Ø Abruptly mutter the feared word 'trip'
> and Ø drive off.

This kind of implicit reference is known as **ellipsis**. In many languages (e.g. Spanish, Japanese), ellipsis of this kind is far more common than pronouns; but English more often likes its pronouns there (for reasons outlined in Chapter 7, section 7.3). Once again here, Helena's punctuation isn't quite the norm for tracking by ellipsis of this kind; in English this would be more common <u>within</u> rather than between sentences.

Tracking abstractions

The things we've covered so far tell us most of what we need to know because identification is essentially a device for tracking people, who are after all the mainstays of storytelling and casual conversation. As we've seen, the same kinds of resources can be used for concrete things, and for abstract things and even discourse itself; but in general, with non-humans, there is much less tracking going on. As a rule of thumb, the more abstract a participant, the less likely it is to be presumed.

One important reason for this is that abstractions tend to occur in discourse which generalizes about things. Helena does make moves in this direction towards the end of her story as she spells out the point of her narrative. When she refers to *white people* for example, it's to white people in general; she doesn't have specific individuals in mind:

> If I had to watch how **white people** became dissatisfied with the best and still wanted better and got it.

Just as when she compares spiritual murder with physical murder she's talking about the concepts in general, not the spiritual murder of her second love or the physical murders he may have committed; similarly *a murder victim* refers to all members of this class of things:

> **Spiritual murder** is more inhumane than **a messy, physical murder**.
> At least **a murder victim** rests.

Because it refers to general classes of things, reference of this kind is called **generic** reference. As with the examples just considered, it involves much less tracking than specific reference to individuals.

In arguments this kind of reference is the norm. Tutu opens with a question about amnesty and justice in general, not amnesty or justice in relation to a specific case:

So is **amnesty** being given at the cost of **justice** being done?

Amnesty is referred to several times in the rest of the argument, but just once through a pronoun:

> the granting of **amnesty**
> **amnesty** is only given to those who plead
> **Amnesty** is not given to innocent
> that **amnesty** was refused to the police officers who applied for **it**
> Once **amnesty** is granted
> The effect of **amnesty** is as if the offence had never happened

And that pronoun *it* is in fact used to refer to the only specific reference to amnesty in Tutu's text – the specific refusal of amnesty in the case of the police officers who murdered Steve Biko:

> It was on precisely this point that **amnesty** was refused to the police officers who applied for **it** for their part in the death of Steve Biko.

These specific officers on the other hand are tracked pronominally, just like the characters in Helena's story.

> **to the police officers who applied for it**
> for **their** part in the death of Steve Biko
> **They** denied that
> **they** had committed a crime
> claiming that **they** had assaulted him only in retaliation
> for his inexplicable conduct in attacking **them**.

So whereas the examples in an argument identify specific participants like narratives do, the generalizations in an argument do not. The reason for this is that with generic reference there's not a lot of sorting out to do. If you know what *amnesty* means in English, you know what Tutu is talking about, because he's talking about amnesty in general. Helena on the other hand had to sort out several different men in her story: her first and second loves, her first husband, her second love's three friends, Mr de Klerk, 'those at the top' and so on. This puts a lot more pressure on the identification system to sort out who's who. For amnesty in general, a simple noun generally does the trick.

Where generic participants are presumed, it's often whole classes of people that are involved and the reference will tend to be local (within the same sentence) and not sustained (just 1 or 2 pronouns involved):

because amnesty is only given to **those who plead guilty**, who accept responsibility for what **they** have done

It is also not true that the granting of amnesty encourages impunity in the sense that **perpetrators** can escape completely the consequences of **their** actions

With text reference as well, tracking tends to be fairly local, with just one or two references back to what's been said. Here of course the reference is typically between sentences:

> **For some it has been so traumatic that marriages have broken up.**
> **That** is quite a price to pay.

> **It is important to note too that the amnesty provision is an ad hoc arrangement meant for this specific purpose.**
> **This** is not how justice is to be administered in South Africa for ever.
> **It** is for a limited and definite period and purpose.

Tracking in administrative discourse

With policy, almost everyone and everything mentioned is generic, since the provisions are designed to apply across the board. The exceptions to this are the specific agents and agencies set up by the provisions, and the provisions themselves. As noted above, the provisions are named section by section, paragraph by paragraph and so on as the text unfolds (using numbers and letters). And these names are used to refer forward and back in the document in almost every case such reference is required, very much more often than in narrative or argument because of legal pressures to be absolutely clear about how the parts of the text are tied together. The effect of this is a complex lattice of intratextual relations, as opposed to the chaining effect we see in narrative. Significantly, there is no text reference; naming does the work of distilling discourse so that it can play a role in another clause.

With other kinds of reference the general rule for policy is that participants can be tracked within but not between sentences. This holds true for generic classes of person and thing and for specific agents or agencies:

> (c) establishing and making known the fate or whereabouts of **victims** and by restoring the human and civil dignity of such victims by granting **them** an opportunity to relate **their** own accounts of the **violations** of which **they** are the victims, and by recommending reparation measures in respect of **them**;

> 4. The functions of **the Commission** shall be to achieve **its** objectives, and to that end the Commission shall

This local tracking rule also applies to demonstrative reference to provisions:

(c) The joint committee may at any time review any regulation made under **section 40** and request the President to amend certain regulations or to make further regulations in terms of **that section**.

41. (1) Subject to the provisions of subsection (2), **the State Liability Act, 1957 (Act No. 20 of 1957)**, shall apply, with the necessary changes, in respect of the Commission, a member of its staff and a commissioner, and in such application a reference in **that Act** to "the State" shall be construed as a reference to "the Commission", and a reference to "the Minister of the department concerned" shall be construed as a reference to the Chairperson of the Commission.

Comparative reference is similarly constrained:

(viii) "former state" means any state or territory which was established **by an Act of Parliament** or by proclamation in terms of **such an Act** prior to the commencement of the Constitution and the territory of which now forms part of the Republic;

(a) establishing as complete a picture as possible of the causes, nature and extent of the **gross violations of human rights which were committed during the period from 1 March 1960 to the cut-off date**, including the antecedents, circumstances, factors and context of **such violations**, as well as the perspectives of the victims and the motives and perspectives of the persons responsible for the commission of the violations, by conducting investigations and holding hearings

Overall, what this means is that unless we use a proper name to refer to something (e.g. *For the purposes of sections 10(1), (2) and (3) and 11 and Chapters 6 and 7...*), any information presumed must be available in the immediately preceding co-text. This kind of tracking has evolved, we presume, in order to avoid any ambiguities that might be exploited in a legal challenge. The result is a formally-partitioned text unfolding as short phases of proposals and definitions. We'll return to the significance of this kind of scaffolding in Chapter 6.

5.6 Identification systems in full

We're now in position to present a relatively technical summary of the identification system we've built up. We'll begin with identification resources in general, followed by resources for tracking, followed by the perspective from the grammar of nominal groups.

Identification systems

Identification systems involve two systems, shown in Figure 5.3: one for presenting (*a young man*) or presuming the identity of the participants in question, and another for optionally relating their identity to another identity through comparison (*another policeman*). Various resources are used to presume identity, divided into pronominal and nominal. Pronominal reference is usefully divided into speaker and addressee roles (1st and 2nd person) and other (3rd person); nominal reference involves either names (*Tutu*) or determined nouns, with determination split into the definite article (*the Commission*) and demonstratives (*this chapter*). Where the grammar allows, these options combine with the choice of comparative or not. This choice is shown by the simultaneous system with options of 'comparative' or not (shown by a dash '–').

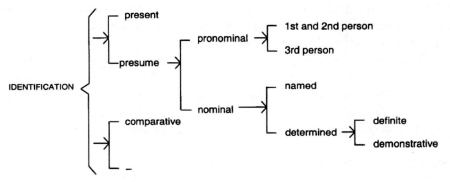

Figure 5.3 Identification systems

Tracking systems

As for tracking, presumed information can be recovered either on the basis of communal understandings (*the Truth Commission, Mandela*) or situational presence, as shown in Figure 5.4. Within a situation, information can be presumed from either verbal (endophora) or non-verbal modalities (exophoric). Reference to the co-text can point forward or back: if back, then direct reference can be

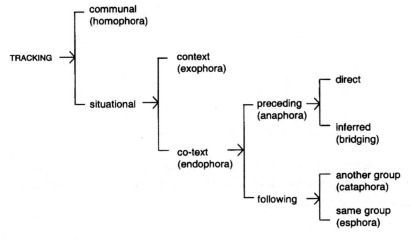

Figure 5.4 Tracking systems

distinguished from inference; if forward, then reference from a nominal group to something following that group can be distinguished from reference that's resolved within the same nominal group. Terminologically, we can refer to bridging as a type of anaphora; but forward reference within (esphora) is so much more common than forward reference beyond the nominal group that it's probably best to reserve the term cataphora for reference beyond.

Identification resources in the grammar of nominal groups

We introduced the grammatical perspective on participants in Chapter 3, in the structure of nominal groups that realize things and people. Each of the resources for identifying that we have discussed above are realized by one or another function in the nominal group. Deictic and Thing functions <u>identify</u> participants with a determiner or noun. Numerative and Epithet functions <u>compare</u> participants by their order (numbers) or qualities (adverbs). The Qualifier compares or locates the participant it qualifies. (The Classifier function is not involved in identifying.) These resources are set out in Table 5.8.

Table 5.8 Identification resources within nominal groups

Deictic	Numerative	Epithet	Classifier	Thing	Qualifier
'identify'	*'compare'*	*'compare'*	–	*'name'*	*'compare', 'locate'*
determiner	numeral	-er/-est adjective	noun	noun	clause/phrase
	adjective	submodified adjective			
presenting...					
a (certain), one					
some, any, Ø				*someone*	
every, all				*anyone*	
what				*everyone*	
presuming...					
the (said)	*first*	*such*		*Tim, Sue*	*else*
this, that	*next*	*better*		*section 3*	*here, there*
these, those	*fewer*	*best*			
each, both	*as much*	*as big*			
either, neither		*more lovely*			
which, whose					
my, your, her...				*I, you,*	
				she...	

Halliday also recognizes a Post-Deictic function in nominal groups. This is realized by an adjective which generally comes after the Deictic but before a Numerative. Several of these are comparative:

the **same** three..., a **similar** one..., the **other** two..., a **different** one..., someone **else**...

And just to complete our review of resources, there are also several locative expressions which presume information about time and space:

now, then; here, there; hereby, thereby; herewith, therewith

In 'little texts' such as headlines, telegrams, SMS messages on mobile phones, titles, labels, diagrams, billboards and so on, determiners are more often than not left out, so the distinction between presenting and presuming is neutralized. For example, 'the' is left out of the headings in the Act but included in the paragraphs.

CHAPTER 2
Ø Truth and Reconciliation Commission
Ø Establishment and **Ø seat** of **Ø Truth and Reconciliation Commission**
2. (1) There is for the purposes of sections 10(1), (2) and (3) and II and Chapters 6 and 7 hereby established a juristic person to be known as **the Truth and Reconciliation Commission**.
(2) **The seat** of **the Commission** shall be determined by the President.

We should also observe that various pronouns are commonly used in a generalized way that doesn't presume the identity of anyone in particular:

You don't know who your friends are 'til **you**'re down and out.
We just don't behave like that round here!
They're double parking both sides of the street again!
It's too damn hot!

Finally, there are various kinds of structural *it*, which presume information in the same grammatical configuration; these can be treated as text reference if desired. As with esphora, the discourse analysis doesn't really tell much that hasn't already been accounted for in grammatical analysis. Examples include:

It's **Tutu who forgave them**
It pleased me **he forgave them**
I like **it he forgave them**
It's good **he forgave them**
It's reported **he forgave them**
It appears **he forgave them**

PERIODICITY: information flow

Periodicity is concerned with information flow – with the way in which meanings are packaged to make it easier for us to take them in.

Following a general introduction, section 6.2 looks at information flow in clauses, introducing the concepts of **Theme** and **New**. Section 6.3 pushes this up a level to paragraphs, considering how information can be predicted by a **hyperTheme** (aka topic sentence) and summarized as **hyperNew**. Then in section 6.4 extensions of this patterning in longer carefully edited texts are explored (**macroTheme** and **macroNew**).

Having developed the concept of a **hierarchy of periodicity** in sections 6.2–6.4, section 6.5 goes on to compare hierarchical texts involving many layers of prediction and summary (waves within waves) with flatter texts which unfold serially from one section to the next. Then in sections 6.6 and 6.7 these ideas are used to explore two types of discourse which people often find hard to read, post-structuralist and legislative discourse, including a discussion of periodicity in relation to **headings**.

Finally in section 6.8 we concentrate on the interaction of discourse systems (appraisal, ideation, conjunction, identification and periodicity) as phases of discourse are consolidated to keep us on track or dissolved as we change gears.

6.1 Waves of information

Periodicity is concerned with information flow: with the way in which meanings are packaged to make it easier for us to take them in. People who were taught composition in school will remember something about 'topic sentences' and the 'Introduction – Body – Conclusion' organization recommended for essays; and people who learned some vestiges of rhetoric may recall the suggestion that 'You tell them what you're going to say, say it, and tell them what you've said'. These kinds of ideas are about information flow – giving readers some idea about what to expect, fulfilling those expectations, and then reviewing them.

We've already seen for example the way in which Helena's narrative was framed. Since Tutu is using it to exemplify one of his arguments, he carefully scaffolds the transition from his exposition:

> The South Africa Broadcasting Corporation's radio team covering the Truth and Reconciliation Commission received **a letter** from a woman calling herself Helena (she wanted to remain anonymous for fear of reprisals) who lived in the eastern province of Mpumalanga. They broadcast **substantial extracts**

Tutu uses names of discourse (*letter, extract*) to build the bridge. Then Helena takes over and names her genre (*my story begins*), setting up our expectations about the kind of letter we're about to read. And Helena explicitly brings her *story to a close, announcing she will **end** with a few **lines** from her wasted vulture.

The terms *letter, extract, story, lines* and *end* could be described as 'meta-discourse', since they refer to discourse as a thing (*letter, extract, story, line*), and as a process (*end*). Vocabulary of this kind is one important resource for packaging discourse. For Helena's narrative it frames the beginning and end of her story by naming them, and manages the relationship between her story and Tutu's exposition.

Halliday, Pike and others have used the metaphor of waves to describe this kind of information flow. Pike refers to meanings 'flowing together like ripples on the tide, merging into one another in the form of a hierarchy of little waves. . .on still bigger waves' (Pike 1982: 12–13).

Pike's notion of little waves on bigger ones is very important for understanding information flow since rhythm in discourse may have several layers. In the 'repercussions' phase of her second Incident, for example, Helena introduces her husband's agony with *our hell began* and then proceeds to spell out his suffering. In doing so she frames a layer of information inside one phase of her story; and as we've seen her story has been framed as a larger wave (*My story begins. . .* to *I end with a few lines. . .*) and beyond this her story in relation to Tutu's exposition is a still larger pulse. We can use indentation in the first instance to outline something of the relation of these larger waves of information to the smaller ones:

The South Africa Broadcasting Corporation's radio team covering the Truth and Reconciliation Commission received **a letter** from a woman calling herself Helena (she wanted to remain anonymous for fear of reprisals) who lived in the eastern province of Mpumalanga. They broadcast **substantial extracts**:

> My **story** begins in my late teenage years as a farm girl in the Bethlehem district of Eastern Free State. ...
>
> > After about three years with the special forces, **our hell began**.
> >
> > > He became very quiet. Withdrawn. Sometimes he would just press his face into his hands and shake uncontrollably. I realized he was drinking too much. Instead of resting at night , he would wander from window to window. He tried to hide his wild consuming fear, but I saw it. In the early hours of the morning between two and half-past-two, I jolt awake from his rushed breathing. Rolls this way, that side of the bed. He's pale. Ice cold in a sweltering night – sopping wet with sweat. Eyes bewildered, but dull like the dead. And the shakes. The terrible convulsions and blood-curdling shrieks of fear and pain from the bottom of his soul. Sometimes he sits motionless, just staring in front of him. I never understood. I never knew. Never realised what was being shoved down his throat during the 'trips'. I just went through hell. Praying, pleading: 'God, what's happening? What's wrong with him? Could he have changed so much? Is he going mad? I can't handle the man anymore! But, I can't get out. He's going to haunt me for the rest of my life if I leave him. Why, God?' ...
>
> **I end with a few lines** that my wasted vulture said to me one night: 'They can give me amnesty a thousand times. Even if God and everyone else forgives me a thousand times – I have to live with this hell. The problem is in my head, my conscience. There is only one way to be free of it. Blow my brains out. Because that's where my hell is.'

The term 'wave' is used to capture the sense in which moments of framing represent a peak of textual prominence, followed by a trough of lesser prominence. So discourse creates expectations by flagging forward and consolidates them by summarizing back. These expectations are presented as crests of information, and the meanings fulfilling these expectations can be seen as relative diminuendos, from the point of view of information flow. The term **periodicity** is used to capture the regularity of information flow: the tendency for crests to form a regular pattern, and for the hierarchy of waves to form a predictable rhythm. Discourse, in other words, has a beat; and without this rhythm, it would be very hard to understand.

6.2 Little waves: Themes and News

The notion of waves of information has been an important part of functional linguistics, in the work for example of the Prague school on communicative dynamism, in the 1930s, and in SFL since the 1960s. Halliday treats the clause itself, from the point of view of textual meaning, as a wave of information. The peak of prominence at the beginning of the clause is referred to as its **Theme**.

Analysing Themes

To do a Theme analysis we take a phase of discourse and divide it into clauses; let's use Helena's description of her husband's agony as an example here.

Since we're working on discourse, we need to fill in the participants that have been ellipsed, as their identities are part of the listener/reader's expectations. We'll show these ellipsed participants in square brackets, together with the ellipsed verbal elements they are associated with:

> He became very quiet.
> [He became] Withdrawn.
> Sometimes he would just press his face into his hands
> and [he would] shake uncontrollably.
> I realized
> he was drinking too much.
> Instead of resting at night, he would wander from window to window.
> He tried to hide his wild consuming fear,
> but I saw it.
> In the early hours of the morning between two and half-past-two, I jolt awake from his rushed breathing.
> [He] Rolls this way, that side of the bed.
> He's pale.
> [He's] Ice cold in a sweltering night
> [He's] – sopping wet with sweat.
> [His] Eyes [are] bewildered,
> but [his eyes are] dull like the dead.
> And [he had] the shakes.
> [He had] The terrible convulsions and blood-curdling shrieks of fear and pain from the bottom of his soul.
> Sometimes he sits motionless,
> just staring in front of him

It's sometimes difficult to know how much to fill in; we've given a pretty rich reading above, filling all the 'holes' except the one in the last non-finite clause (*just staring in front of him*).[1] Filling in gives us a richer text to work with from the point of view of Theme analysis.

The next step is to highlight Themes – which in writing is basically everything up to and including the participant that functions as the Subject of the clause. The Subject of a clause in English is the participant whose identity is picked up in a tag question:

> **He** tried to hide his wild consuming fear, didn't **he**?
> But **I** saw it, didn't **I**?

So the most common choice for the Theme of a clause is the Subject. Ideational meaning that comes before the Subject is referred to as **marked Theme**, and has a different discourse function from the ordinary Subject/Theme, which we'll look at in a moment. All the Themes are highlighted, and the marked Themes underlined below:

> **He** became very quiet.
> [**He** became] Withdrawn.
> **Sometimes he** would just press his face into his hands
> **and** [he would] shake uncontrollably.
> **I** realized
> **he** was drinking too much.
> <u>**Instead of resting at night,**</u> **he** would wander from window to window.
> **He** tried to hide his wild consuming fear,
> **but I** saw it.
> <u>**In the early hours of the morning between two and half-past-two,**</u> **I** jolt awake from his rushed breathing.
> [**He**] Rolls this way, that side of the bed.
> **He**'s pale.
> [**He**'s] Ice cold in a sweltering night
> [**He**'s] – sopping wet with sweat.
> [**His**] Eyes [are] bewildered,
> **but** [his eyes are] dull like the dead.
> **And** [he had] the shakes.
> [**He** had] The terrible convulsions and blood-curdling shrieks of fear and pain from the bottom of his soul.
> **Sometimes he** sits motionless,
> just staring in front of him . . .

The main recurrent choice for Subject/Theme in this phase is Helena's husband, realized as *he*. This identity gives us our basic orientation to the field for this phase of discourse; Helena's husband is the hook round which she spins the new information she gives us in each figure. As the Theme of each clause, he is our recurrent point of departure, our angle on the field in each figure. These kinds of Subject/Themes give continuity to a phase of discourse. Because they are the most frequent kind of Theme in discourse, listeners/readers perceive them as 'unmarked' Themes; they are mildly prominent in the flow of discourse, because they are the point of departure for each clause, but because they are typical they are not especially prominent.

Marked Themes
Themes that are not Subject have a different effect; they are more prominent because they are atypical, so we refer to them as 'marked' Themes. Marked Themes

can include circumstantial elements, such as places or times, or they may be participants that are not the Subject of the clause. Marked Themes are often used to signal new phases in a discourse: a new setting in time, or a shift in major participants; that is they function to scaffold <u>discontinuity</u>.

In Helena's story, marked Themes play an important role in moving us from one phase of the story to the next. The story's key marked Themes are outlined below. We can see the role they play in moving us from Incident to Incident and from Incidents to Interpretation; and the role they play within Incidents to frame the meeting, operations and repercussions phases. These are underlined below:

Incident 1
<u>As an eighteen-year-old</u>, I met a young man in his twenties
Then <u>one day</u> he said he was going on a 'trip'
<u>More than a year ago</u>, I met my first love again through a good friend

Incident 2
<u>After my unsuccessful marriage</u>, I met another policeman
[Then he says: He and three of our friends have been promoted]
<u>After about three years with the special forces</u>, our hell began

Interpretation
<u>Today</u> I know the answer to all my questions and heartache

New information

At the other end of the clause in writing we typically have what Halliday calls **New**. This is a different kind of textual prominence having to do with the information we are expanding upon as text unfolds. In the phase of discourse we are concentrating on here, the News have to do with how Helena's husband felt and so the dominant pattern has to do with negative appraisal (depressed mental states and strange behaviour). Note how the choices for New are much more varied than the choices for unmarked Theme. They elaborate with human interest, whereas choices for unmarked Theme tend to fix our gaze.

An outline of information flow at this level of analysis is provided in Table 6.1. For Halliday there are two overlapping waves involved: a thematic wave with a crest at the beginning of the clause, and a news wave with a crest at the end (where the main pitch movement would be if the clause were read aloud). In this phase, participant identification links the unmarked Themes together, and patterns of negative appraisal link up the choices for New. Recurrent choices for Theme and related choices for New work together to package discourse as phases of information.

Table 6.1 Information flow in the description of Helena's husband

Marked Theme	Subject/Theme	New
after about three years with the special forces	our hell	**began**
	he	became **very quiet**
	[he]	[became] **withdrawn**
	(sometimes) he	would just press his face **into his hands**
	(and) [he]	[would] shake **uncontrollably**
	{I realized}	
	he	was drinking **too much**
instead of resting at night	he	would wander **from window to window**
	he	tried to hide **his wild consuming fear**
	(but) I	**saw** it
in the early hours of the morning between two and half-past-two	I	jolt awake **from his rushed breathing**
	[he]	rolls **this way, that side of the bed**
	he	**'s pale**
	[he]	['s] ice cold **in a sweltering night –**
	[he]	['s] **sopping with sweat**
	[his] eyes	**bewildered**
	(but) [eyes]	**dull like the dead**
	[he]	[had] **the shakes**
	[he]	[had] **the terrible convulsions and blood-curdling shrieks of fear and pain from the bottom of his soul**
	(sometimes) he	sits **motionless**
	–	just staring **in front of him**

6.3 Bigger waves: hyperThemes and hyperNews

The packaging of discourse as choices of Theme and New, that we have seen in each clause, is reflected by larger scale patterning of phases of discourse. These patterns predict what will happen in each phase of discourse, and distil the new information that each phase presents.

Predicting phases of discourse

As noted at the beginning of this chapter Helena introduces the phase of discourse we've just been considering as 'living hell', and she does so with a marked Theme:

> <u>After about three years with the special forces</u>, **our hell began**.

Her evaluation of their life as *our hell* functions as a kind of 'topic sentence' for the events which follow as she spells out what hell is. From a linguistic perspective we can treat this 'topic sentence' as a kind of higher level Theme: a **hyperTheme**. In doing so we're saying that its relation to the text which follows is like the relation of a clause Theme to the rest of its clause. In both contexts the Theme gives us an orientation to what is to come: our frame of reference as it were. Beyond this, the hyperTheme is predictive; it establishes expectations about how the text will unfold.

In many registers, hyperThemes tend to involve evaluation, so that the following text justifies the appraisal, at the same time as it gives us more detail about the field of the hyperTheme (its 'topic'). This can be used in storytelling to build momentum as we move from one phase to the next, as in the following extract from *Nathaniel's Nutmeg*, by Milton (1999). Evaluation in the hyperThemes is in bold, and the discourse they predict is indented below:

> This was **only the beginning of his misfortune**.
>> When all the Englishmen in the town had been captured, including Nathaniel Courthope, they were herded together and clapped in irons; 'my selfe and seven more were chained by the neckes all together: others by their feete, others by their hands.' When this was done, the soldiers left them in the company of two heavily armed guards who 'had compassion for us and eased us of our bonds, for the most of us had our hands so straite bound behind us that the blood was readie to burst out at our fingers' end, with pain unsufferable'.

> Middleton still had no idea why he had been attacked, but he was soon to learn **the scale of the Aga's treachery**.
>> Not only had eight of his men been killed in the 'bloudie massacre' and fourteen severely injured, he now heard that a band of one hundred and fifty Turks had put to sea 'in three great boats' with the intention of taking the **Darling** – now anchored off Mocha – by force.

> The attack caught the Darling's crew **completely unawares**.
>> Knowing nothing of the treachery ashore they first realised something was amiss when dozens of Turks were seen boarding the ship, their swords unsheathed. The situation quickly became desperate; three Englishmen were killed outright while the rest of the company rushed below deck to gather their weapons. By the time they had armed themselves the ship was almost lost. 'The Turkes were standing very thicke in the waist [of the ship], hollowing and clanging their swords upon the decke.'

It was a **quick thinking** crew member who saved the day.

Realising their plight was helpless he gathered his strength and rolled a huge barrel of gunpowder towards the Turkish attackers, then hurled a firebrand in the same direction. The effect was as dramatic as it was devastating. A large number of Turks were killed instantly while the rest retired to the half-deck in order to regroup. This hesitation cost them their lives for the English had by now loaded their weapons which they 'set off with musket shot, and entertayned [the Turks] with another trayne of powder which put them in such feare that they leaped into the sea, hanging by the ship's side, desiring mercy, which was not there to be found, for that our men killed all they could finde, and the rest were drowned, only one man who was saved who hid himselfe till the furie was passed, who yielded and was received to mercie'.

The Darling had been saved but Middleton's situation was now **even more precarious** . . . (Milton 1999)

Distilling new information

While hyperThemes predict what each phase of discourse will be about, new information accumulates in each clause as the phase unfolds. In written texts in particular, this accumulation of new information is often distilled in a final sentence, that thus functions as a **hyperNew** to the phase. HyperThemes tell us where we're going in a phase; hyperNews tell us where we've been.

As a general rule, writing looks forward more often than it looks back. So hyperThemes are more common than hyperNews; there's more 'prospect' than 'retrospect'. But examples of higher level News are not hard to find. Here are two examples from Mandela's summary of his life at the end of his autobiography *Long Walk to Freedom* (we'll return to this text in Chapter 8). Both examples include a hyperTheme, complementing the consolidating hyperNew (in bold):

But then I slowly saw that not only was I not free, but my brothers and sisters were not free. I saw that it was not just my freedom that was curtailed, but the freedom of everyone who looked like I did.

That is when I joined the African National Congress, and that is when the hunger for my own freedom became the greater hunger for the freedom of my people. It was this desire for the freedom of my people to live their lives with dignity and self-respect that animated my life, that transformed a frightened young man into a bold one, that drove a law-abiding attorney to become a criminal, that turned a family-loving husband into a man without a home, that forced a life-loving man to live like a monk. I am no more virtuous or self-sacrificing than the next man, but I found that I could not even enjoy the poor and limited freedoms I was allowed when I knew my people were not free.

Freedom is indivisible; the chains on any one of my people were the chains on all of them, the chains on all of my people were the chains on me.

When I walked out of prison, that was my mission, to liberate the oppressed and the oppressor both. Some say that has now been achieved. But I know that this is not the case.

The truth is that we are not yet free; we have merely achieved the freedom to be free, the right not to be oppressed. We have not taken the final step of our journey, but the first step on a longer and even more difficult road. For to be free is not merely to cast off one's chains, but to live in a way that respects and enhances the freedom of others.

The true test of our devotion to freedom is just beginning.

In general terms, the hyperTheme is paraphrased by the body of the paragraph, which is in turn paraphrased by the hyperNew. But the hyperNew is never an exact paraphrase of the hyperTheme, nor is it simply a summary of the wave's trough; it takes the text to a new point, which we could only get to by surfing through the waves.

The following examples of history writing display a similar kind of sandwich structure, with hyperThemes predicting what's to come, and hyperNews distilling what's been said (the 'you tell them what you're going to say, say it, and tell them what you've said' rhetoric noted above). For both of these texts note just how precisely the hyperTheme predicts the pattern of Themes which follow (underlined), and the hyperNew consolidates the pattern of News which precede it:

The Second World War further encouraged the restructuring of the Australian economy towards a manufacturing basis.

Between 1937 and 1945 the value of industrial production almost doubled. This increase was faster than otherwise would have occurred. The momentum was maintained in the post-war years and by 1954–5 the value of manufacturing output was three times that of 1944–5. The enlargement of Australia's steel-making capacity, and of chemicals, rubber, metal goods and motor vehicles all owed something to the demands of war.

The war had acted as something of a hot-house for technological progress and economic change.

For one thousand years, whales have been of commercial interest for meat, oil, meal and whalebone.

About 1000 A.D., whaling started with the Basques using sailing vessels and row boats. They concentrated on the slow-moving Right whales. As whaling spread to other countries, whaling shifted to Humpbacks, Grays, Sperms and Bowheads. By 1500, they were whaling off Greenland; by the 1700s, off Atlantic America; and by the 1800s, in the south Pacific, Antarctic and Bering Sea. Early in this century, the Norwegians introduced explosive harpoons, fired from guns on catcher boats, and whaling shifted to the larger and faster baleen whales. The introduction of factory ships by Japan and the USSR intensified whaling still further.

The global picture, then, was a mining operation moving progressively with increasing efficiency to new species and new areas. Whaling reached a peak during the present century.

Both hyperNews include evaluative metaphors, a not untypical feature of higher level News in writing of this kind. Patterns of clause Themes have been described as constructing a text's 'method of development'; patterns of News establish its 'point' (Fries 1981).

6.4 Tidal waves: macroThemes, macroNews, and beyond

In many written texts, waves of Theme and New extend well beyond clauses and paragraphs to much larger phases of discourse. We have already introduced the higher level Theme and New introducing and closing Helena's narrative, and the still higher level Theme linking Tutu's exposition to her story. Beyond this we know that Tutu's exposition was itself introduced with an even higher level Theme: his question about the cost of justice. So Helena's description of her husband's anguish is just a wave of ripples in a more expansive hierarchy:

> So is amnesty being given at the cost of justice being done? **This is not a frivolous question, but a very serious issue, one which** challenges the integrity of the entire Truth and Reconciliation process.
>
> The Act required that where the offence is a gross violation of human rights – defined as an abduction, killing, torture or severe ill-treatment – the application should be dealt with in a public hearing...
>
> Thus there is the penalty of public exposure and humiliation for the perpetrator... It was often the very first time that their communities and even sometimes their families heard that these people were, for instance, actually members of death squads of regular torturers of detainees in their custody. For some it has been so traumatic that marriages have broken up. That is quite a price to pay.
>
> The South Africa Broadcasting Corporation's radio team covering the Truth and Reconciliation Commission received **a letter** from a woman calling herself Helena (she wanted to remain anonymous for fear of reprisals) who lived in the eastern province of Mpumalanga. They broadcast **substantial extracts**:
>
>> **My story begins** in my late teenage years as a farm girl in the Bethlehem district of Eastern Free State. ...
>>
>> After about three years with the special forces, **our hell began.**
>>
>> He became very quiet. Withdrawn...
>>
>> **I end with a few lines** that my wasted vulture said to me one night: 'They can give me amnesty a thousand times. Even if God and everyone else forgives me a thousand times – I have to live with this hell. The problem is in my head, my conscience. There is only one way to be free of it. Blow my brains out. Because that's where my hell is.'

We can refer to higher level Themes predicting hyperThemes as macro-Themes, and higher level News distilling hyperNews as macroNews. Beyond this it would be unwieldy to give a new term for every layer, since the layering can go on indefinitely depending on the complexity of the phasing of information in the text. It's easier to keep track of things by simply numbering the higher level Themes and News, ascending from the smaller waves as we've done for Tutu's exposition below.

To this description we have added the title of Tutu's Chapter 4, *What about justice?*, as an even higher level macroTheme (beyond this of course are the Table of Contents for his chapters, his acknowledgments, the title of the book as a whole, and the comments on the jacket cover – all higher level Themes, and the Postscript and Index of the book as its culminating higher level News):

macroTheme[iv]
What about justice? . . .

macroTheme[iii]
So is amnesty being given at the cost of justice being done? This is not a frivolous question, but a very serious issue, one which challenges the integrity of the entire Truth and Reconciliation process.
The Act required that where the offence is a gross violation of human rights – defined as an abduction, killing, torture or severe ill-treatment – the application should be dealt with in a public hearing. . .
Thus there is the penalty of public exposure and humiliation for the perpetrator.

macroTheme[ii]
The South Africa Broadcasting Corporation's radio team covering the Truth and Reconciliation Commission received a letter from a woman calling herself Helena. . .

macroTheme[i]
My story begins in my late teenage years as a farm girl in the Bethlehem district of Eastern Free State. . . .

hyperTheme
After about three years with the special forces, our hell began.
He became very quiet. Withdrawn. . .

macroNew
I end with a few lines that my wasted vulture said to me one night. . .

Figure 6.1 summarizes the wave patterns we've been reviewing here. The diagram suggests that layers of Theme construct the method of development of a text, and that this development is particularly sensitive to the staging of the genre in question. Layers of New on the other hand develop the point of a text, focusing in particular on expanding the ideational meanings around a text's field.

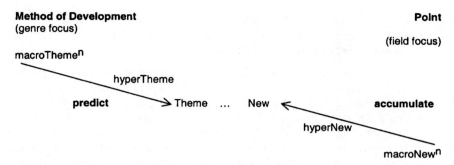

Figure 6.1 Layers of Themes and News in discourse

6.5 How texts grow: hierarchies and series

As analysts, we tend to treat texts as objects, and reify the structure that in fact unfolds as spoken or written discourse is produced. So it is important to keep in mind that the periodicity we are discussing here is an unfolding process, not a rigid structure linking parts to wholes.

The strategy of predicting phases of discourse with macroThemes and hyperThemes constructs a 'hierarchy' of periodicity of smaller units of discourse 'scaffolded' within larger units. But there are alternative ways of constructing unfolding discourse so it is sensible to the reader. One way to highlight this is to compare hierarchy with an alternative strategy for expanding text, which is the strategy Tutu uses to build up his argument. We can call this 'serial expansion'.

Serial expansion of discourse

Serial expansion is more of a chaining strategy than is periodicity, in the sense that discourse is added on to what went before without being predicted by a higher level Theme. Tutu, for example, begins his Chapter *What about justice?* with the issue he is arguing about:

> **What about justice?**
> Can it ever be right for someone who has committed the most gruesome atrocities to be allowed to get off scot-free, simply by confessing what he or she has done? Are the critics right: was the Truth and Reconciliation process immoral?

But instead of tackling this right away as he does in the argument proper, he takes a moment to develop some background information about the Promotion of National Unity and Reconciliation Act which he feels he needs before he starts arguing. So before we get to the exposition, we have a report outlining the conditions for gaining amnesty:

The Promotion of National Unity and Reconciliation Act, which established the Commission, did not even require an applicant to express any contrition or remorse. The only conditions for gaining amnesty were:

- The act for which amnesty was required should have happened between 1960, the year of the Sharpeville massacre, and 1994, when President Mandela was inaugurated as the first democratically-elected South African head of State.
- The act must have been politically motivated. Perpetrators did not qualify for amnesty if they killed because of personal greed, but they did qualify if they committed the act in response to an order by, or on behalf of, a political organisation such as the former apartheid state and its satellite Bantustan homelands, or a recognised liberation movement such as the ANC or PAC.
- The applicant had to make a full disclosure of all the relevant facts related to the offence for which amnesty was being sought.
- The rubric of proportionality had to be observed – that the means were proportional to the objective.

If those conditions were met, the law said that amnesty 'shall' be granted. Victims had the right to oppose applications for amnesty by trying to demonstrate that conditions had not been met, but they had no right of veto over amnesty.

Later we realised that the legislature had been a great deal wiser than we had at first thought in not making remorse a requirement for amnesty. If there had been such a requirement, an applicant who made a big fuss about being sorry and repentant would probably have been judged to be insincere, and someone whose manner was formal and abrupt would have been accused of being callous and uncaring and not really repentant. It would have been a no-win situation. In fact, most applicants have expressed remorse and asked for forgiveness from their victims. Whether their requests have stemmed from genuine contrition is obviously a moot point. (Tutu 1999: 47–8)

Then, having built up this common ground, he restates the issue and moves into his exposition. Tutu's transition from issue to report and from report to exposition is not scaffolded with higher level Themes, nor distilled in higher level News. He does not actually tell us before the report that he has to build some background first before discussing the issue; nor does he sum up at the end of the report what it is we needed to know. At both points he just moves on, expanding the issue with the report and then expanding the report with an exposition.

This is a serial movement from one moment in the discourse to another. We are simply expected to follow along, without the careful scaffolding of phases we get once his exposition is underway. And following his exposition the chapter expands along similar lines (some serial expansion, some hierarchy of periodicity), a kind of tandem act during which we're sometimes warned where we're going and reminded where we've been, and other times we just keep reading and find out as we go.

The important point here is that both serial expansion and hierarchy of periodicity are dynamic resources through which a text unfolds as a process. The meanings don't emerge by crystallizing. A text isn't like an image downloading from the web, taking on detail and shape and focus here and there before our very eyes. Rather meanings flow, as texts unfold. The text materializes through time, however thing-like our written records of this dynamic misrepresent a text to be.

Interplay of periodicity with serial expansion

We can see the same combination of serial expansion and hierarchy of periodicity operating towards the end of Mandela's autobiography. As an autobiographical recount, his story moves through time. And so there is a tremendous amount of serial expansion, from one setting in time to the next, and lots of sequential development within each of these. The final chapter of his book, for example, begins with a recount of Inauguration Day, May 10, 1994. Skipping a line in the paragraphing, Mandela then expands on this by reflecting on the unimaginable sacrifices of his people, and his own personal failures at the expense of his family. Then, skipping another line, Mandela moves on serially again to the recount that sums up his life, some of which we've already seen.

Here's the whole text, analysed for its generic staging. This is a story genre known as a **recount**, with the typical recount stages:

orientation ˆ record of events ˆ reorientation

We can also show how recount is organized with layers of hyperThemes and hyperNews (in bold):

orientation
I was not born with a hunger to be free.

> I was born free – free in every way that I could know. Free to run in the fields near my mother's hut, free to swim in the clear stream that ran through my village, free to roast mealies under the stars and ride the broad backs of slow-moving bulls. As long as I obeyed my father and abided by the customs of my tribe, I was not troubled by the laws of man or God.

record of events
It was only when I began to learn that my boyhood freedom was an illusion, when I discovered as a young man that my freedom had already been taken from me, that I began to hunger for it.

> At first, as a student, I wanted freedom only for myself, the transitory freedoms of being able to stay out at night, read what I pleased and go where I chose. Later, as a young man in Johannesburg, I yearned for the basic and honourable freedoms of achieving my potential, of earning my keep, of marrying and having a family – the freedom not to be obstructed in a lawful life.

But then I slowly saw that not only was I not free, but my brothers and sisters were not free.

> I saw that it was not just my freedom that was curtailed, but the freedom of everyone who looked like I did. That is when I joined the African National Congress, and that is when the hunger for my own freedom became the greater hunger for the freedom of my people. It was this desire for the freedom of my people to live their lives with dignity and self-respect that animated my life, that transformed a frightened young man into a bold one, that drove a law-abiding attorney to become a criminal, that turned a family-loving husband into a man without a home, that forced a life-loving man to live like a monk. I am no more virtuous or self-sacrificing than the next man, but I found that I could not even enjoy the poor and limited freedoms I was allowed when I knew my people were not free.

Freedom is indivisible; the chains on any one of my people were the chains on all of them, the chains on all of my people were the chains on me.

It was during those long and lonely years that my hunger for the freedom of my own people became a hunger for the freedom of all people, white and black.

> I knew as well as I knew anything that the oppressor must be liberated just as surely as the oppressed. A man who takes away another man's freedom is a prisoner of hatred, he is locked behind the bars of prejudice and narrow-mindedness. I am not truly free if I am taking away someone else's freedom, just as surely as I am not free when my freedom is taken from me.

The oppressed and the oppressor alike are robbed of their humanity.

When I walked out of prison, that was my mission, to liberate the oppressed and the oppressor both.

> Some say that has now been achieved. But I know that this is not the case. The truth is that we are not yet free; we have merely achieved the freedom to be free, the right not to be oppressed. We have not taken the final step of our journey, but the first step on a longer and even more difficult road. For to be free is not merely to cast off one's chains, but to live in a way that respects and enhances the freedom of others.

The true test of our devotion to freedom is just beginning.

reorientation

I have walked that long road to freedom. I have tried not to falter; I have made missteps along the way. But I have discovered the secret that after climbing a great hill, one only finds that there are many more hills to climb. I have taken a moment here to rest, to steal a view of the glorious vista that surrounds me, to look back on the distance I have come. But I can only rest for a moment, for with freedom come responsibilities, and I dare not linger, for my long walk is not yet ended. (Mandela 1995: 750–1)

There are five hyperThemes here that organize Mandela's recount of his growing desire for freedom (its 'method of development'). We'll use an '=' sign to indicate the way in which the higher level Themes and News paraphrase the information they predict or distil. Halliday 1994 refers to these kinds of relation as elaboration:

1 I was not born with a hunger to be free

= ...

2 It was only when I began to learn that my boyhood freedom was an illusion... that I began to hunger for it.

= ...

3 But then I slowly saw that not only was I not free, but my brothers and sisters were not free.

= ...

4 It was during those long and lonely years that my hunger for the freedom of my own people became a hunger for the freedom of all people, white and black.

= ...

5 When I walked out of prison, that was my mission, to liberate the oppressed and the oppressor both

= ...

And three hyperNews that distil his conclusions about the struggle for freedom (its 'point'):

3 ... = Freedom is indivisible; the chains on any one of my people were the chains on all of them, the chains on all of my people were the chains on me.

4 ... = The oppressed and the oppressor alike are robbed of their humanity.

5 ... = The true test of our devotion to freedom is just beginning.

Beyond the hyperThemes and hyperNews in each phase, the Orientation functions as its macroTheme and its Reorientation as its macroNew. And with respect to Mandela's book as a whole, this recount functions as a higher level macroNew, both summarizing his journey and distilling the meaning of his life. The key point here is that texts expand, and that this expansion may or may not be explicitly scaffolded by layers of Themes and News. In most texts we find a mix of scaffolding through periodicity, and serial expansion that is not so clearly scaffolded, since these are simply two complementary strategies through which texts grow.

6.6 Hard reading

Some texts are hard to read, no matter how interested we happen to be in what they're trying to say. Figuring out the hierarchy of periodicity in abstract discourse can be a big help in digesting them, and so we'll look briefly at one example of hard reading here.

Interplay of periodicity with other resources

The following text is a paragraph from Rafael's post-colonial discourse on translation and Christian conversion in the Philippines, *Contracting Colonialism*. Let's begin to dig into this by drawing on some of the tools we've built up for conjunction (in bold) and periodicity:

> There is a sense, **then**, in which the demand for a total recollection of sins results in the unlimited extensions of discourse purporting to extract and convey one's successes and failures in accounting for past acts and desires.
>> Accounting **thus** allows confession to become a self-sustaining machine for the reproduction not only of God's gifts of mercy but of "sin" as well. **For** God's continued patronage – the signs of His mercy – requires a narrative of sins to act upon. The confessor who sits in lieu of an absent Father needs the penitent's stories, without which there can be no possibility of asserting and reasserting the economy of divine mercy. Without the lure of sin, the structure of authority implicit in this economy would never emerge. Confession was crucial **because** it produced a divided subject who was **then** made to internalise the Law's language. The penitent became "the speaking subject who is also the subject of the statement" (Foucault 1980: 1:61). **But** confession was **also** important **because** it made for the ceaseless multiplication of narratives of sin through their ever-faulty accounting. **In** introducing the category of "sin", confession converted the past into a discourse that was bound to the Law and its agents.
> **In this way** the accounting and recounting of the past generated the complicitous movement between sin and grace. (Rafael 1988: 103)

The function of confession is previewed in the hyperTheme, then expanded upon, and finally distilled as *the complicitous movement between sin and grace* as hyperNew. However, the argument is constructed by an interplay with other resources. How does Rafael employ ideation, conjunction, and identification to achieve this?

Firstly, a glance at ideation shows several taxonomic strings – foregrounding both religion (the topic of the book) and discourse (the post-structuralist stance Rafael adopts):

> narrative–stories–narratives–accounting–accounting–recounting
> demand–asserting–reasserting–speaking

sins–successes–failures–mercy–sin–mercy–sins–mercy–sin–sin–sin–sin–grace
God–God–confessor–Father–penitent–penitent
etc.

Secondly we find conjunction doing lots of work across sentence boundaries, and within sentences as well, to construct the logic of Rafael's argument:

There is a sense, **then**, in which the demand for a total recollection of sins
Accounting **thus** allows confession to become a self-sustaining machine
For God's continued patronage . . . requires a narrative of sins to act upon.
Confession was crucial **because** it produced a divided subject who was **then** made to internalise
But confession was **also** important **because** it made for the ceaseless multiplication . . .
In introducing the category of "sin", confession converted
In this way the accounting and recounting of the past generated the complicitous movement

Thirdly, although the text is a very abstract one, that generalizes across classes of participant, we do find that some participants are tracked:

God's–God's–His mercy
Confession–it
confession–it
narratives of sin–their ever-faulty accounting
the Law–its agents

Significantly, conjunctions and reference chains interact at both the beginning and end of the text. At the end, the identity of _the accounting and recounting of the past_ specifies the scope of _this_, in the linker _in this way_; the presumed information appears to be the deconstruction of accounting and recounting in the preceding paragraph.

But at the beginning of the paragraph, we need to resolve the identity of _the demand for a total recollection of sins_ and the scope of the linker _then_, which on its own simply tells us that what preceded is causally connected to what follows. To do this we need to connect _the demand_ to _the Spanish demand_ referred to by Rafael earlier on. And to retrieve this we need to put the paragraph in context, within the hierarchy of periodicity of Rafael's text:

This internalisation of an exterior hierarchy consists of two interrelated procedures: the accounting of past events and the reproduction of the discourse of interrogation contained in the confession manuals.

First, the process of accounting. All confession manuals contain the unconditional demand that all sins be revealed . . .

> **The Spanish demand** is that nothing be held back in confession.
> One is to expend all that memory can hold in a discourse that will bring together both the self that recalls and that which is recalled. The present self that confronts the priest in confession is thus expected to have managed to control his or her past – to reduce it, as it were, to discursive submission. Whereas the examination of conscience requires the division of the self into one that knows the Law and seeks out the other self that deviates from it, a "good confession" insists on the presentation of a self in total control of its past.
> It is in this sense that confessional discourse imposes on the individual penitent what Roland Barthes called a "totalitarian economy" involving the complete recuperation and submission of the past to the present, and by extension of the penitent to the priest (Barthes 1976: 39–75).
>
> Yet insofar as the ideal of a perfect accounting of sins also necessitated their recounting in a narrative, it was condemned to become a potentially infinite task. Given the limitations of memory, accounting "engenders its own errors." And the errors created by faulty accounting become further sins that have to be added to the original list. The very possibility of a correct accounting engenders an erroneous accounting, just as remembering one's sins would make no sense unless there existed the possibility of forgetting them. It is thus the guarantee of a faulty accounting of sins that makes conceivable the imperative for total recall. Barthes puts it more succinctly: "Accountancy has a mechanical advantage: for being the language of a language, it is able to support an infinite circularity of errors and of their accounting" (Barthes 1976: 70).
>
> There is a sense, then, in which **the demand** for a total recollection of sins results in the unlimited extensions of discourse purporting to extract and convey one's successes and failures in accounting for past acts and desires. ... In this way the accounting and recounting of the past generated the complicitous movement between sin and grace.
>
> These considerations bring us to the second moment in the interiorisation of hierarchy prescribed by confession: the reproduction of the discourse of interrogation (Rafael 1988: 101–3)

This longer phase opens with a transition from what preceded (*This internalisation of an exterior hierarchy*), to what ensues (*two interrelated procedures*). These 'procedures' are scaffolded as they appear by the linker *first*, and the comparative identification *second*. And they are finally resolved through the identity of <u>the process of accounting</u> and <u>the reproduction of the discourse of interrogation</u>. How Rafael scaffolds these two 'procedures' is brought out in the following summary of his hierarchy of periodicity:

> macroTheme[ii]
> This internalisation of an exterior hierarchy consists of **two** interrelated procedures: **the accounting of past events** and **the reproduction of the discourse of interrogation** contained in the confession manuals.

macroTheme[i]
FIRST, the process of accounting. All confession manuals contain the unconditional demand that all sins be revealed. . .

> hyperTheme
> There is a sense, then, in which the demand for a total recollection of sins results in the unlimited extensions of discourse purporting to extract and convey one's successes and failures in accounting for past acts and desires. . . .

> hyperNew
> In this way the accounting and recounting of the past generated the complicitous movement between sin and grace.

macroTheme[i]
These considerations bring us to the second moment in the interiorisation of hierarchy prescribed by confession: **the reproduction of the discourse of interrogation**

Ideational metaphor and periodicity

We wouldn't suggest that scaffolding of this kind solves all our problems. The text is also chock full of ideational metaphors alongside the occasional concrete participant (i.e. *manuals, the priest, the penitent*):

> This **internalisation** of an exterior hierarchy consists of two **interrelated procedures**: the **accounting** of past events and the **reproduction** of the discourse of **interrogation** contained in the **confession** manuals.
> First, the **process** of **accounting**. All **confession** manuals contain the **unconditional demand** that all sins be revealed

In terms of abstraction, discourse of this kind is probably the most metaphorical to have evolved in the history of writing in the world. Each sentence packs a lot of information into dense strings of abstract terms that derive from ideational metaphors, such as *internal → internalize → internalization*.

In this kind of discourse, higher level Themes and News have more information to predict and distil than lower level ones. This puts even more pressure on them to deploy grammatical metaphors that pack in the information they predict and distil. Ironically then, the very things we need to steer us round the text can be among the things that are hardest to understand.

Beyond this, the abstract discourse both includes and enables a great deal of specialized lexis. Since we're talking about Catholicism, there's a representation of religion, including the focus of discussion, *confession*:

> [confession] & sins, priest, penitent, penitent, priest, sins, sins, sins, sins, sins, God's

> gifts of mercy, "sin", God's, His mercy, sins, Father, penitent's, divine mercy, lure of
> sin, penitent, sin, "sin", sin, grace

And since the church as a colonizing institution is at issue here, there's administrative lexis as well:

> exterior hierarchy, two interrelated procedures, unconditional, manuals, process,
> manuals, submission, the Law's, Law, individual, "totalitarian economy", submission,
> guarantee, original list, patronage, structure of authority, Law, agents, hierarchy,
> prescribed

And intriguingly (thanks to Lacan), there's a sizeable list of terms we might refer to as psychoanalytic:

> internalisation, memory, the self, the present self, recalls, recalled, conscience, the
> division of the self, the other self, a self in total control, the limitations of memory,
> remembering, forgetting, conceivable, total recall, total recollection, desires, a divided
> subject, internalise, "the subject who is also the subject of the ...", interiorisation

And there is a much longer list of terms having to do with discourse (thanks to Barthes and Foucault); and we might well have included *confession* in this list too:

> accounting, discourse, interrogation, accounting, demand, revealed, demand,
> discourse, discursive, discourse, accounting, recounting, narrative, accounting,
> accounting, accounting, accounting, accounting, imperative, account-ancy, language,
> language, accounting, demand, discourse, accounting, accounting, signs, narrative,
> stories, asserting, reasserting, language, speaking, statement, narratives, accounting,
> introducing, discourse, accounting, recounting, considerations, discourse, interroga-
> tion, & [confession]

If we're not sure about these specialized terms, or not used to them being used in conjunction with one another as they are here, then of course it will be difficult to recognize scaffolding even when it's there. Take the second macroTheme at level 1 for example:

> These considerations bring us to the second moment in the interiorisation of hierarchy
> prescribed by confession

The specialized lexis of psychoanalysis, administration and religion are each represented here (*interiorisation, hierarchy prescribed* and *confession* respectively). *These considerations* names and points back to the first internalization procedure, as *the second moment* names and points forward to the next, explicitly fulfilling the text's higher level macroTheme (...*two interrelated procedures...*). And the scaffolding is highly metaphorical, with 'thoughts' bringing readers to another time, meaning 'now that we have considered the first procedure, we can move on to the second'. But without some grip on the scaffolding, we'd get lost in the argument, excluded from the discourse. And that's not Rafael's intention in a book designed to give us some new ways to think about the Church and colonization in the Philippines. His discourse has evolved to denaturalize modernity, not exclude us; but that doesn't make it any easier to read.

Perhaps what we can learn from discourse of this kind is the significance of interaction among discourse systems. Conjunction, identification, ideation and periodicity are all interfacing in various ways to scaffold the argument and grammatical metaphor is catalysing this symbiosis at every turn. For most of us, a little discourse analysis wouldn't hurt, when first learning to access texture of this kind.

6.7 A note on headings

We have already had a look at the overall structure of the Act in Chapter 1, in relation to its generic structure. And in our work on identification we looked at the Act's elaborate numerical and alphabetical labelling system for sections and their parts:

- sections 1, 2 , 3...49
- sub-section (1), (2), (3)
- paragraphs (a), (b), (c)
- sub-paragraphs (i), (ii), (iii)
- sub-sub-paragraphs (aa), (bb), (cc).

In addition sections are grouped into chapters:

1	Interpretation and application	[1]
2	Truth and Reconciliation Commission	[2–11]
3	Investigation of human rights violations	[12–15]
4	Amnesty mechanisms and procedures	[16–22]
5	Reparation and rehabilitation of victims	[23–27]
6	Investigations and hearings by Commission	[28–35]
7	General provisions	[36–49]

And chapters and sections have titles as well as numbers, but these titles are never used to refer to parts of the document. Here, for example, are the headings for Chapters 3 and 4 and their sections:

Another point we made in the identification chapter was that information is presumed within sentences, but never between unless a numerical/alphabetical name is used. This intra-sentential constraint is the key to understanding how information is packaged in the Act.

The basic strategy the Act uses to phase information is to make grammar do as much work as possible, that is to use the grammar within sentences to do work that would normally be done by discourse strategies in texts. In fact the whole Act is actually one sentence, beginning...

> It is hereby notified that the President has assented to the following Act which is hereby published for general information:

... which the rest of the Act expands upon. Following a statement of the purposes of the Act, we have another such sentence beginning:

> BE IT THEREFORE ENACTED by the Parliament of the Republic of South Africa, as follows:

This is in fact the end of a long sentence, which includes six preceding justifications:

> SINCE the Constitution of the Republic of South Africa, 1993 (Act No. 200 of 1993), provides a historic bridge between the past of a deeply divided society characterized by strife, conflict, untold suffering and injustice, and a future founded on the recognition of human rights, democracy and peaceful co-existence for all South Africans, irrespective of colour, race, class, belief or sex;
> AND SINCE it is deemed necessary to establish the truth in relation to past events as well as the motives for and circumstances in which gross violations of human rights have occurred, and to make the findings known in order to prevent a repetition of such acts in future;

AND SINCE the Constitution states that the pursuit of national unity, the well-being of all South African citizens and peace require reconciliation between the people of South Africa and the reconstruction of society;

AND SINCE the Constitution states that there is a need for understanding but not for vengeance, a need for reparation but not for retaliation, a need for ubuntu but not for victimization;

AND SINCE the Constitution states that in order to advance such reconciliation and reconstruction amnesty shall be granted in respect of acts, omissions and offences associated with political objectives committed in the course of the conflicts of the past;

AND SINCE the Constitution provides that Parliament shall under the Constitution adopt a law which determines a firm cut-off date, which shall be a date after 8 October 1990 and before the cut-off date envisaged in the Constitution, and providing for the mechanisms, criteria and procedures, including tribunals, if any, through which such amnesty shall be dealt with;

BE IT THEREFORE ENACTED by the Parliament of the Republic of South Africa, as follows

Similar patterns are found throughout the text. In a sense what we are looking at here is an exploration of the limits of grammar: how far can we push grammar before it runs out of steam and discourse semantics takes over. A peculiar kind of grammarian's dream, or legislative nightmare, depending on our attitude to discourse of this kind.

As far as hierarchy of periodicity is concerned, this push to grammar has a particular effect. Take the following phase of Chapter 1 for example, which is concerned with defining terms:

(xix) "victims" includes –
    (a) persons who, individually or together with one or more persons, suffered harm in the form of physical or mental injury, emotional suffering, pecuniary loss or a substantial impairment of human rights –
        (i) as a result of a gross violation of human rights; or
        (ii) as a result of an act associated with a political objective for which amnesty has been granted

We could of course rewrite this as a paragraph, reducing the complexity of the complex of clauses as follows:

There are two kinds of victim. There are persons who, individually or together with one or more persons, suffered harm in the form of physical or mental injury, emotional suffering, pecuniary loss or a substantial impairment of human rights as a result of a gross violation of human rights. And there are those who suffered as a result of an act associated with a political objective for which amnesty has been granted.

As we do this we establish a familiar hyperTheme and trough structure, in place of the clause complex:

There are two kinds of victim.
> There are persons who, individually or together with one or more persons, suffered harm in the form of physical or mental injury, emotional suffering, pecuniary loss or a substantial impairment of human rights as a result of a gross violation of human rights. And there are those who suffered as a result of an act associated with a political objective for which amnesty has been granted.

Discourse semantics, hierarchy of periodicity to be precise, takes over from grammar as the packaging device for this bundle of information.

Similarly in Chapter 2, section 3, we find grammatical organization of the following kind:

> 3. (1) The objectives of the Commission shall be to promote national unity and reconciliation in a spirit of understanding which transcends the conflicts and divisions of the past by –
>
> (a) establishing as complete a picture as possible of the causes, nature and extent of the gross violations of human rights which were committed during the period from I March 1960 to the cut-off date, including the antecedents, circumstances, factors and context of such violations, as well as the perspectives of the victims and the motives and perspectives of the persons responsible for the commission of the violations, by conducting investigations and holding hearings;
>
> (b) facilitating the granting of amnesty to persons who make full disclosure of all the relevant facts relating to acts associated with a political objective and comply with the requirements of this Act;
>
> (c) establishing and making known the fate or whereabouts of victims and by restoring the human and civil dignity of such victims by granting them an opportunity to relate their own accounts of the violations of which they are the victims, and by recommending reparation measures in respect of them;
>
> (d) compiling a report providing as comprehensive an account as possible of the Activities and findings of the Commission contemplated in paragraphs (a), (b) and (c), and which contains recommendations of measures to prevent the future violations of human rights.
>
> (2) The provisions of subsection (1) shall not be interpreted as limiting the power of the Commission to investigate or make recommendation concerning any matter with a view to promoting or achieving national unity and reconciliation within the context of this Act.
>
> (3) In order to achieve the objectives of the Commission –
>
> (a) the Committee on Human Rights Violations, as contemplated in Chapter 3, shall deal, among other things, with matters pertaining to investigations of gross violations of human rights;
>
> (b) the Committee on Amnesty, as contemplated in Chapter 4, shall deal with matters relating to amnesty;
>
> (c) the Committee on Reparation and Rehabilitation, as contemplated in Chapter 5, shall deal with matters referred to it relating to reparations;
>
> (d) the investigating unit referred to in section 5(d) shall perform the investigations contemplated in section 28(4)(a); and

(e) the subcommittees shall exercise, perform and carry out the powers, functions and duties conferred upon, assigned to or imposed upon them by the Commission.

Subsections 3(1) and 3(3) could both be rewritten along the lines exemplified above. Here's our reworking of 3(1); we'll leave 3(3) for you:

> The objectives of the Commission shall be to promote national unity and reconciliation in a spirit of understanding which transcends the conflicts and divisions of the past. It will accomplish this in four ways.
>
>> First, it will establish as complete a picture as possible of the causes, nature and extent of the gross violations of human rights which were committed during the period from 1 March 1960 to the cut-off date, including the antecedents, circumstances, factors and context of such violations, as well as the perspectives of the victims and the motives and perspectives of the persons responsible for the commission of the violations, by conducting investigations and holding hearings.
>>
>> In addition it will facilitate the granting of amnesty to persons who make full disclosure of all the relevant facts relating to acts associated with a political objective and comply with the requirements of this Act.
>> Next it will establish and make known the fate or whereabouts of victims and by restoring the human and civil dignity of such victims by granting them an opportunity to relate their own accounts of the violations of which they are the victims, and by recommending reparation measures in respect of them.
>>
>> Finally it will compile a report providing as comprehensive an account as possible of the Activities and findings of the Commission contemplated above, and which contains recommendations of measures to prevent the future violations of human rights.

If that's not challenging enough, consider Chapter 2, section 4. Another layer of depth to the hierarchy of periodicity is required here. We've flagged potential higher level Themes on the text below:

macroTheme potential
4. The functions of the Commission shall be to achieve its objectives, and to that end the Commission shall —

hyperTheme potential
(a) facilitate, and where necessary initiate or coordinate, inquiries into —
(i) gross violations of human rights, including violations which were part of a systematic pattern of abuse;
(ii) the nature, causes and extent of gross violations of human rights, including the antecedents, circumstances, factors, context, motives and perspectives which led to such violations;
(iii) the identity of all persons, authorities, institutions and organisations involved in such violations;

     (iv) the question whether such violations were the result of deliberate planning on the part of the State or a former state or any of their organs, or of any political organisation, liberation movement or other group or individual; and

     (v) accountability, political or otherwise, for any such violation;

(b) facilitate, and initiate or coordinate, the gathering of information and the receiving of evidence from any person, including persons claiming to be victims of such violations or the representatives of such victims, which establish the identity of victims of such violations, their fate or present whereabouts and the nature and extent of the harm suffered by such victims;

(c) facilitate and promote the granting of amnesty in respect of acts associated with political objectives, by receiving from persons desiring to make a full disclosure of all the relevant facts relating to such acts, applications for the granting of amnesty in respect of such acts, and transmitting such applications to the Committee on Amnesty for its decision, and by publishing decisions granting amnesty, in the Gazette;

(d) determine what articles have been destroyed by any person in order to conceal violations of human rights or acts associated with a political objective;

(e) prepare a comprehensive report which sets out its activities and findings, based on factual and objective information and evidence collected or received by it or placed at its disposal;

hyperTheme potential
(f) make recommendations to the President with regard to –

     (i) the policy which should be followed or measures which should be taken with regard to the granting of reparation to victims or the taking of other measures aimed at rehabilitating and restoring the human and civil dignity of victims;

     (ii) measures which should be taken to grant urgent interim reparation to victims;

(g) make recommendations to the Minister with regard to the development of a limited witness protection programme for the purposes of this Act;

(h) make recommendations to the President with regard to the creation of institutions conducive to a stable and fair society and the institutional, administrative and legislative measures which should be taken or introduced in order to prevent the commission of violations of human rights.

In summary then, where hierarchy of periodicity is used across many registers to orchestrate information flow, in the Act this packaging is as far as possible grammaticalized. The Act uses complex sentences where other registers would use introductions, topic sentences and paragraphs.

At the same time there seems to be some concern that this localization of discourse organization might make it difficult for people to actually find their way around in the Act. So alongside the number and letter labelling used to refer to sections and their parts, each section is given a heading, and the sections are grouped into Chapters, which have headings of their own. The headings make it possible for us to find our way round in the Act at a global level. They function as a surrogate hierarchy of periodicity for layreaders, alongside the local grammatical organization which the legislators themselves use to package information. The Act is thus an interesting genre in which the scaffolding needs of readers are in tension with the legislative needs of writers. As ever in language, resources are deployed until a compromise is reached. The graphological resources of headings and punctuation are the key to reconciliation here.

6.8 Texture: phasing discourse systems

As we've seen, discourse gets packaged in various ways. Explicit scaffolding involves the erection of a hierarchy of periodicity beyond the clause, with layers of Theme and News telling us where we're coming from and where we're going to. With serial expansion there's a change of gears from one discourse phase to the next, without any explicit scaffolding of the change. In some kinds of discourse, such as legislation, explicitness is in a sense pushed to its limits by (i) grammaticalizing as much hierarchy as possible within very complex sentences and/or (ii) naming sections of the text numerically and/or alphabetically, and/or providing them with headings. Many texts involve some combination of all these resources for phasing information into digestible chunks.

This variation in explicitness is possible because the interaction of discourse systems in a text tells us a lot about what's continuing and what's changing, from one phase to the next. So to round off the chapter let's look for a moment at how this interaction works. We'll refer to meanings that continue as 'continuity', and meanings that change as 'discontinuity'.

To do this, we'll take the 'repercussions' phase of Helena's second Incident. This time round we're asking how it holds together as a phase, and how it shifts from one perspective on 'our hell' to another. Here's the text again, with its hyperTheme set off from its trough, which has been divided into two sub-phases. We can label these two sub-phases as 'his hell' and 'her hell':

After about three years with the special forces, our hell began.

'his hell'
He became very quiet. Withdrawn. Sometimes he would just press his face into his hands and shake uncontrollably. I realized he was drinking too much. Instead of resting at night, he would wander from window to window. He tried to hide his wild consuming fear, but I saw it. In the early hours of the morning between two and half-past-two, I jolt awake from his rushed breathing. Rolls this way, that side of the bed. He's pale. Ice cold in a sweltering night – sopping wet with sweat. Eyes bewildered, but dull like the dead. And the shakes. The terrible convulsions and

blood-curdling shrieks of fear and pain from the bottom of his soul. Sometimes he sits motionless, just staring in front of him.

'her hell'
I never understood. I never knew. Never realized what was being shoved down his throat during the 'trips'. I just went through hell. Praying, pleading: 'God, what's happening? What's wrong with him? Could he have changed so much? Is he going mad? I can't handle the man anymore! But, I can't get out. He's going to haunt me for the rest of my life if I leave him. Why, God?'

As far as conjunction is concerned the two sub-phases exhibit <u>continuity</u> since there are very few conjunctions to signal changes:

'his hell':   instead of, but
'her hell':   but, if

Basically this is a series of descriptions, with the text expanding as a list.

With identification on the other hand there is both continuity and discontinuity. The main identity chain in 'his hell' is Helena's husband, with Helena playing a minor role:

he, he, his, his, he, he, he, his, his, he, his, he, him; I, I, I; fear-it

In 'her hell' on the other hand, Helena and her husband both get in on the act:

I, I, I, I, I, me, my, I; his, him, he, he, the man, he; God, God

With ideation, taxonomic relations in 'his hell' feature parts of her husband's body, and restlessness:

face, hands, eyes; resting, jolt awake, sits motionless, staring

On the other hand 'her hell' features processes of cognition, supplication, departure and madness:

understood, knew, realised; praying, pleading; get out, leave; wrong, changed, going mad

As far as expectancy is concerned, 'his hell' develops around a break-down, while 'her hell' develops around her growing awareness and need to escape.

Appraisal involves some very striking differences across the sub-phases. 'His hell' foregrounds affect, and a great deal of amplification, while modality is concerned with occasional and habitual behaviour (*sometimes, would*):

attitude
very quiet, withdrawn, wild consuming fear, bewildered, blood-curdling, fear, pain, press his face into his hands, shake uncontrollably, drinking too much, instead of resting, wander from window to window, his rushed breathing, rolls this way, that side of the bed, pale, ice cold in a sweltering night, sopping wet with sweat, the shakes, the terrible convulsions, shrieks, sits motionless, staring in front of him

force
dull like the dead, very quiet, shake uncontrollably, too much, wild consuming fear, ice cold, sweltering night, sopping wet, terrible convulsions, blood curdling shrieks. . .from the bottom of his soul

modality
sometimes, would, sometimes

'Her hell' is much less explicit about inscribing Helena's feelings (*can't handle, haunt*) and uses some appreciation (*went through hell*) and judgement (*mad, wrong*) while modality is absolute (*never, can't*). And from the perspective of engagement, 'her hell' is much more dialogic than 'his hell', explicitly invoking God's voice to answer Helena's desperate queries:

attitude
went through hell, wrong, mad, can't handle, haunt

force
hell, pleading, so much, the rest of my life

modality
never, never, never, can't, can't

mood variation
[declarative, interrogative: polar & wh]

With periodicity, little waves foreground some of these differences as recurrent selections for Theme and New. In 'his hell', the method of development is Helena's husband, established through Subject/Themes:

he, he, he, he, he, I, I, he, eyes

In 'her hell', we have more of a trinocular perspective: Helena, her husband and the things she can't understand:

I, I, what, I, what, what, he he, I, I, he, I, why

As far as News is concerned, the point of 'his hell' is Helena's husband's feelings:

> began, very quiet, withdrawn, into his hands, uncontrollably, too much, from window to window, his wild consuming fear, from his rushed breathing, this way, that side of the bed, pale, in a sweltering night, sopping with sweat, bewildered, dull like the dead, the shakes, the terrible convulsions and blood-curdling shrieks of fear and pain from the bottom of his soul

Again the point of 'her hell' is more varied: Helena's confusion, her supplication, her husband's madness, her escape:

> understood, knew, realised, during the 'trips', hell, praying, pleading, happening, wrong with him, so much, mad, anymore, get out, the rest of my life, leave him

In general terms then the transition is from effects on him to effects on her. But as far as certain discourse patterns are concerned, 'her hell' overlaps with 'his hell' and this gives continuity to the phase as a whole, while developing distinctive patterns as well (sub-phasing).

The key point here is that co-patterning of this kind is all we need to recognize a distinct discourse phase. The generic stages of an exemplum (Orientation, Incident, Interpretation) are recurrent enough in the culture to be highly predictable. They are predicted by the genre itself. But phases within such generic stages, such as the 'repercussions' phase here, are much more variable. It is the co-patterning of discourse features that enables us to recognize a distinct phase. While Helena has used explicit scaffolding to frame the phase as a whole, the hyperTheme *our hell began*, she hasn't needed it to shift her gaze within the phase. We shift perspective with her; the ripples within clauses and connections between them are more than enough to do the job.

NOTE

1   Non-finite clauses are omitted from a Theme analysis because one reason they're non-finite is to take them out of the mainstream of information flow in a phase of discourse.

NEGOTIATION: interacting in dialogue

7

Chapter Outline

Negotiation is concerned with interaction as an exchange between speakers: how speakers adopt and assign roles to each other in dialogue, and how moves are organized in relation to one another.

Following a general introduction, section 7.2 builds up the basic types of **speech function**, section 7.3 relates these to their grammatical realization in **mood**, and section 7.4 considers the **responses** they entail.

Then in section 7.5 we look at how these choices are sequenced as **moves** in **exchanges**, turning in section 7.6 to additional interrupting moves which **track** ideation or **challenge** the development of an exchange. In section 7.7 the analysis is extended to handle more complicated dialogue involving **move complexes** and **exchange complexes**.

Finally in section 7.8 we formalize mood, speech function and negotiation in system networks and touch on the interaction of negotiation with appraisal, identification and conjunction in conversation.

7.1 Interacting in dialogue

The three principal texts we have used in the book up to now were essentially monologues. At certain points however both Helena and Tutu became more conversational. Helena, for example, talks to God, asking a series of questions about her husband's disintegration and exclaiming about how she feels:

> 'God, what's happening? What's wrong with him? Could he have changed so much? Is he going mad? I can't handle the man anymore! But I can't get out. He's going to haunt me for the rest of my life if I leave him. Why, God?'

And Tutu addresses his readers with questions about the integrity of the Truth Commission:

> Can it ever be right for someone who had committed the most gruesome atrocities to be allowed to get off scot-free, simply by confessing what he or she has done? Are the critics right: was the Truth and Reconciliation process immoral? . . . So is amnesty being given at the cost of justice being done?

Helena doesn't get an answer from God, and Tutu has to answer his own questions in the argument that follows. So a conversation never really develops. But in spoken discourse, both the feelings we discussed in Chapter 2 and the ideational meanings we presented in Chapter 3 are indeed negotiated between speakers. The system of resources that enables this to-and-fro of dialogue is called NEGOTIATION.

In order to explore NEGOTIATION we have to set up a spoken context, which we'll base on the South African film *Forgiveness*, directed by Ian Gabriel (2004). *Forgiveness* tells the story of someone very like Helena's second husband, a white former policeman named Tertius Coetzee, who arrives in Paternoster, a poor fishing village on the Atlantic coast of South Africa. Ten years earlier, while working in the police force under the former apartheid regime, Coetzee had shot dead a political activist, Daniel Grootboom, whom he and his colleagues were torturing for information about a planned attack on a nuclear reactor. Like Helena's husband, Coetzee has testified before the Truth Commission and been given amnesty, but is tormented by his past. Seeking absolution, he visits Daniel's family (whose ethnicity is known in South Africa as 'Coloured'). Daniel's parents, Hendrik and Magda, are prepared to give Coetzee a chance, but his sister Sannie and his younger brother Ernest refuse to forgive him. Sannie contacts Daniel's former comrades, Llewelyn, Luke and Zako, who set off on a long trip by car to Paternoster, to seek revenge. A priest, Father Dalton, acts as a go-between for Coetzee and the Grootboom family. Here are the relevant cast:

Tertius Coetzee	ex-policeman (Daniel's killer)
Hendrik Grootboom	Daniel's father (Paternoster fisherman)
Magda Grootboom	Daniel's mother
Sannie Grootboom	Daniel's sister (young woman)
Ernest Grootboom	Daniel's brother (adolescent)
Daniel Grootboom	elder brother (deceased)
Llewelyn	Daniel's coloured comrade
Luke	Daniel's white comrade
Zako	Daniel's African comrade
Father Dalton	Paternoster priest

It's a gripping film and we won't give any more away here. Our examples are adapted from its script, which involves code switching between English and Afrikaans – especially by the Grootboom family, who speak Afrikaans as their mother tongue. (In spite of his Afrikaans name, the white Coetzee speaks English throughout the film, one of the many complex ironies in this tale.) We've relied on the film's subtitles for the dialogue taken from the Afrikaans.

NEGOTIATION provides resources for taking up speech roles in conversation – making statements, asking questions, offering services and demanding goods. Below, Sannie gives Coetzee information about how the family feels, and demands information about his plans:

Sannie:	We're not so worried about your past.
Coetzee:	– No of course not.

Sannie:	Are you leaving?
Coetzee:	– Of course I'm leaving.

Turning to the realm of behaviour, when Coetzee arrives with Father Dalton for dinner at the Grootboom's, Hendrik offers a seat to his guests:

Hendrik:	So, shall we take a seat?
all:	– (Coetzee, Grootboom family and Father Dalton sit down.)

In another scene after a successful fishing trip, Hendrik instructs his son Ernest to bring the fish for cleaning:

Hendrik:	Ernest, get those snoek [a kind of fish].
Ernest:	– (Ernest proceeds to do so.)

As we can see, each statement, question, offer and command positions people to respond – by acknowledging, answering, accepting and complying. So the moves in conversation tend to come in pairs – 'adjacency pairs' as conversation analysts have called them. In practice, of course, we know that longer sequences are possible. Invited with his family to a hotel restaurant by Coetzee, Hendrik orders wine:

Hendrik:	Could I have a bottle of your best dry red?
Waitress:	– Yes.
Hendrik:	– Thank you.

And we know that people don't always respond as positioned. Sometimes they may not have caught the drift of what was said, and need to check it out. Here Llewelyn asks Sannie for clarification when she telephones him with the news of Coetzee's arrival:

Sannie:	He's here.
Llewelyn:	– What?
Sannie:	– Coetzee.
	He's in Paternoster.

At other times they won't readily co-operate. For example, Magda is not keen to accept Coetzee's invitation:

Coetzee:	Would you consider having dinner with me tonight at the hotel please?
Magda:	– I can't go.
Coetzee:	–Please Mrs Grootboom.
Sannie:	– It'll be fine Ma.
	Thanks Mr Coetzee, we'll be there.
Coetzee:	– Good.

So responses may be compliant or they may not. Summing up, there are three dimensions we need to consider in dialogue – the kind of moves that speakers make, how they are sequenced, and what happens when things don't work out as smoothly as planned. We'll begin with our model of kinds of moves, focusing initially on statements, questions, offers and commands and compliant responses to them, as set out in Table 7.1.

We'll then move on to consider exchange structure, which deals with longer sequences of moves.

Table 7.1 Basic speech functions

	initiating	responding
giving information	**statement**	**acknowledgement**
demanding information	**question**	**answer**
giving goods-and-services	**offer**	**acceptance**
demanding goods-and-services	**command**	**compliance**

7.2 Exchanging roles: SPEECH FUNCTION

Based on the examples introduced above we can extract three basic parameters of negotiation – what it is we are negotiating, whether we are giving or demanding it, and whether a move initiates the exchange or responds. First, there is the question of what we are negotiating – information or goods-and-services. Note, as illustrated below, that when negotiating information we expect a verbal response (or gesture), whereas when negotiating goods-and-services we expect action.

negotiating **information:**

| **initiating** | Hendrik: | Everything OK? |
| **responding** | Coetzee: | – Yes. |

negotiating **goods-and-services**:

| **initiating** | Coetzee: | Shall we go inside? |
| **responding** | Grootbooms: | – (family turns and proceeds to enter the hotel) |

These examples also illustrate a second parameter – the complementarity of initiating and responding moves in dialogue. Compliant responding moves may be quite elliptical, since the content being negotiated is easily recovered from the initiating move; and with goods-and-services transactions, language is in any case an optional accompaniment to behaviour (unless we are promising future action).

The third parameter to consider is that of giving vs demanding. This opposes **statements** to **questions** as far as information is concerned, and **offers** to **commands** for goods-and-services:

giving information (**statement**):

| Llewelyn: | They took my cell phone. (when the comrades' car was robbed at a service station) |
| Luke: | – Did they? |

giving goods-and-services (**offer**):

Magda:	Some tea, father?
Father Dalton:	– Yes please.

demanding information (**question**):

Hendrik:	How do you know Daniel was involved?
Coetzee:	– We found explosives in his room at university... drawings and maps of the Nuclear Power Plant.

demanding goods-and-services (**command**):

Hendrik:	We have to gut and salt.
Sannie:	– OK.

These three oppositions are summarized and exemplified in Table 7.2. They give rise to eight speech acts, which form the heart of the discourse semantic system we'll refer to as SPEECH FUNCTION.

Table 7.2 Basic speech functions exemplified

giving information	**statement**	**acknowledgement**
	They took my phone	*– Did they?*
demanding information	**question**	**answer**
	Everything OK?	*– Yes.*
giving goods-and-services	**offer**	**acceptance**
	Some tea, Father?	*– Yes, please.*
demanding goods-and-services	**command**	**compliance**
	We have to gut and salt	*– OK*

Minimally, we need five more speech acts to complete the picture. Two are concerned with greeting and leave-taking (the *hellos* and *good-byes* framing conversations as people come and go, phone up and sign off). We can refer to these as **greeting** and **response to greeting** moves. Here Llewelyn greets Sannie (as his peer):

Llewelyn:	Hello.
Sannie:	– Hello.

And he greets Sannie's parents (as his elders who respond to him as a junior):

Llewelyn:	Mrs Grootboom. Mr Grootboom.
Magda:	– Llewelyn.

Then there is the question of getting people's attention once they are there – **call** and **response to call**. Here Hendrik calls Sannie's attention, to check on Coetzee, who has been injured by Ernest:

Hendrik:	Sannie.
Sannie:	– What?
[Hendrik:	– Go with Father Dalton. Make sure that man's OK.]

Finally we need to consider outbursts of appraisal, such as Helena's *Dammit!* in the Interpretation stage of her exemplum. Luke mutters a couple of these expressing his exasperation as he joins Father Dalton, Coetzee and the Grootboom family at Daniel's grave:

| Luke: | Bullshit; bullshit. |

These **exclamations** may also function as emotional responses to speech acts of other kinds, for example Ernest's move when Sannie tells her brother that his behaviour has driven Coetzee away:

| Sannie: | He'll leave now. |
| Ernest: | – **Hallelujah**! |

Luke engages in some verbal jousting with his former comrades in a similar way:

Luke:	You know I missed you two fuckers.
Llewelyn:	– Sorry I can't say the same Luke.
Zuko:	– Yeah me too.
Luke:	– **Well fuck you, man**.
	Fuck both of you.
All:	– (laughter as Luke realizes his mates were teasing)

As explosions of personal affect, exclamations are not really negotiable – so we very seldom need to recognize a responding move.

This account gives us a speech function system comprising the basic options displayed in Figure 7.1.

Moves may contain names which specify who is expected to respond (vocatives). For analysis purposes we recommend not treating vocatives as distinct moves when they simply accompany a speech act, addressing its receiver. This would mean treating Ernest's move addressing Coetzee below as a statement including the vocative *you white piece of shit*, and his father's move as a command including the vocative *Ernest*:

Ernest:	You understand nothing, **you white piece of shit**.
	(Ernest throws his notebook at Coetzee)
Hendrik:	– **Ernest**, enough.

So vocatives are only taken as separate speech acts when they function as a move on their own, in greeting or calling sequences, as illustrated above (i.e. *Mrs Grootboom. Mr. Grootboom. – Llewelyn*, and *Sannie. – What?*).

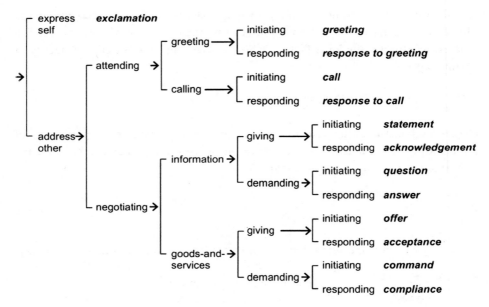

Figure 7.1 An outline of speech functions

Moves may also end with tag 'questions' (*don't you?, isn't he?*, etc.) oriented to the addressee. These tags do not function as separate moves, but are better treated as explicit invitations to a listener to respond. Both of Sannie's speech acts below would thus be treated as tagged statements (not as statements followed by questions). There is after all only one proposition being negotiated, not two:

tagged statements:

Sannie:	You think you can just buy forgiveness, **don't you**?
Coetzee:	– No.

Sannie:	You could have killed the man, **you know**?
Ernest:	– I wish I had.

7.3 Speech function and mood

In the previous section we proposed an inventory of 13 basic speech acts; we now need to think about how to distinguish them from one another when analysing conversation. One useful set of markers includes *please, kindly, ta, thanks, thank-you, OK, alright, no worries, you're welcome, not a problem*, which normally indicate moves concerning goods-and-services. Here Ernest pleads with Coetzee to stay and talk to his parents (until the comrades can get there to kill him):

Ernest:	**Please** Mr Coetzee, I need you to talk to them. **Please**.
Coetzee:	– **OK**, I'll be there.

And Hendrick orders wine for dinner with Coetzee and his family:

Hendrik:	Could I have a bottle of your best dry red?
waitress:	– Yes.
Hendrik	– **Thank you**.

Where such markers are not present, we can check to see if they could have been (adding for example *please* to Hendrik's command and *alright* to verbalize Sannie's response to her father below):

Hendrik:	Don't stay up too late.
Sannie:	– (nods)

What these examples additionally reveal however is that different grammatical structures can be used to realize the same speech function. Ernest's *I need you to talk to them* and Hendrik's *Could I have a bottle of your best dry red* and *Don't stay up too late* are all arguably commands; that's how they function in the conversation. But from a grammarian's perspective, *I need you to talk to them* is declarative, *Could I have a bottle of your best dry red* is interrogative and *Don't stay up too late* is imperative. This kind of variation, outlined in Table 7.3, is an important variable in discourse analysis. Accordingly we'll introduce some basic grammar here, so we can pin this down.

Table 7.3 Alternative grammatical realizations of commands

	speech function	grammatical mood
I need you to talk to them.	**command**	**declarative**
Could I have a bottle of your best dry red?	**command**	**interrogative**
Don't stay up too late.	**command**	**imperative**

Let's begin with the following exchange in which Ernest challenges Coetzee:

Coetzee: I understand how you feel.
Ernest: – **You don't** understand how I feel.

Ernest uses *You don't* to counter the polarity of Coetzee's statement; had Ernest included a tag, it is precisely these two elements that would have been picked up, in reverse order.

Ernest: **You don't** understand how I feel, **do you**?

In Halliday's functional grammar of English these two repeatable clause functions are referred to as Subject (*you*) and Finite (*don't*). The Finite is that part of a verbal group that realizes tense (past, present, future), modality (probability, usuality, obligation, inclination, ability) and polarity (positive, negative). In declarative clauses Subject comes before Finite, whereas in most interrogatives Finite comes before Subject:

declarative
    You don't understand how I feel.

interrogative
    Don't you understand how I feel?

The way to find the Subject and Finite elements of structure then is either to add a tag to the clause, or change its mood between declarative and interrogative. The tag repeats the Subject and Finite (*you don't...do you?*), and a change in mood reverses their sequence (*you don't/don't you*).

In English imperatives, we usually leave the Subject and the Finite out:

imperative
    Understand how I feel.

However Subject and Finite do pop up in tags – *Understand how I feel, won't you?* and in commands that are inclusive (*let's go*), negative (*don't go*), explicitly second person (*you go*) and 'emphatic' (*do go*).

What these examples show is that in English it is the presence or absence of Subject and Finite, and their sequence, which determines mood. This means that Subject and Finite are all we may need to negotiate speech function in responses. Below, Sannie's statement implies that Coetzee's visit revitalized their luck with fishing, but Ernest refuses to accept Coetzee as Subject (i.e. as modally responsible):

Sannie:	You know who brought the fish back.
Ernest:	– **The sea did**.

The addressee Subject *you* in a question, can become the speaker Subject *I* in the response:

Sannie:	Are you leaving?
Coetzee:	– Of course **I am**.

Where Subject and Finite are implicit in a command, the response can make them explicit:

Ernest:	Go.
Sannie:	– **I won't**.

All things being equal, English speakers use declaratives to make statements, interrogatives to ask questions and imperatives to give commands. But as we illustrated for commands above, sometimes contextual considerations mean that an alternative grammatical realization will be more effective – when we're pleading for example, or when trying to be urbanely polite in a hotel dining room that was once for whites only:

command realized by declarative
    Please Mr Coetzee, **I do** need you to talk to them. Please.

command realized by interrogative
    Could I have a bottle of your best dry red?

The effect of realizing a command by an imperative is quite different to realizing it through an alternative mood. The 'indirect speech acts', as they have been called, in some sense combine the discourse semantic meaning of command with the grammatical meaning of declarative (i.e. 'giving information') or interrogative (i.e. 'demanding information'). The resulting meaning is more than the sum of its parts, because the discourse semantics and grammar are in tension with one another. A command positions the addressee as the one to carry out the service, as the servant of the speaker, but interrogative mood positions the addressee as the one who knows the answer, the authority in the situation. Realizing a command as an interrogative thus masks the inequality in status implied by the command (*Could I have a bottle...?*). But an interrogative is still a demand, if only for information, so an even more indirect way to realize a command is with declarative mood, which is not even a demand, but appears to give information (*I need you to talk to them*); and notice that the speaker is Subject in these examples, rather than the addresee.

We can illustrate the same phenomenon for other speech functions, such as questions. All things being equal, the natural way to ask for someone's name in English is to use a wh-question – that is, an interrogative beginning with a wh-phrase specifying the kind of information you are seeking, *who, what, when, where, how, why...*

> question realized by wh- interrogative
> **What**'s your name?
> – Coetzee.

This could be asked less directly with a polar interrogative, which apparently gives the option of refusing:

> question realized by polar interrogative
> **Could you tell me** your name?
> – Coetzee.

But assuming a position of more authority, we can also ask for the information using an imperative (i.e. commanding someone to give it) or an incomplete declarative (getting someone to complete our statement for us):

> question realized by imperative
> Tell me your name.
> – Coetzee.

> question realized by declarative
> And your name is...?
> – Coetzee

From one point of view, in each case the result is the same: the person asking gets the information they want. At the same time, each interaction is different, constructing a different kind of social relationship between speakers, opening up more possibilities for negotiating status.

Following Halliday (e.g. Halliday and Matthiessen 2004), we can refer to the 'all things being equal' realizations as congruent, and the indirect ones as metaphorical – since what we are looking at here is one dimension of what they call grammatical metaphor, in particular interpersonal metaphor. This picture is outlined in Table 7.4. Interpersonal metaphors open up a huge potential for finely grading meanings such as obligation in commands. Of the four major speech functions introduced earlier, offers are the odd one out since they don't have a congruent grammatical realization of their own; interrogatives with Finite *shall* are their most distinctive form (but this form is fairly British in provenance). We won't deal further with the possibility of metaphorical offers here.

Table 7.4 Congruent and metaphorical realizations of speech function

	congruent realization	sample metaphorical possibility
statement	This abnormal life is a cruel human rights violation.	What else can this abnormal life be than a cruel human rights violation?
question	Who is this?	And this is. . .?
command	Do it tomorrow!	You've got to/ought to/could do it tomorrow.
offer	Shall we sit down?	—

7.4 Responding

As noted above, statements, questions, offers and commands position the person we are conversing with to respond. Compliant responses accept the terms of the negotiation established by the Subject–Finite structure of the initiating move. This may involve a full clause, or just the Subject and Finite, eliding the rest of the clause, or perhaps merely a signal of polarity (e.g. *Yes, No, OK*) with the content of the preceding move completely presumed. When Llewelyn asked for his old comrade, Zako's brother could have responded in several ways:

> Llewelyn: Does Zako live here?
> Zako's brother: – He lives here.

> Llewelyn: Does Zako live here?
> Zako's brother: – He does.

> Llewelyn: Does Zako live here?
> Zako's brother: – Yeah. . .

The same kind of pattern is found even when we don't accept the polarity of the initiating move:

> Coetzee: I understand how you feel.
> Ernest: – You don't understand how I feel.

> Coetzee: I understand how you feel.
> Ernest: – You don't.

> Coetzee: I understand how you feel.
> Ernest: – No.

For wh-questions, compliant responses offer the information being sought, in isolation or as part of a complete clause. Hendrik interrogates Coetzee about the cover-up of his eldest son's murder as follows:

| Hendrik: | Whose idea was it to make it look like a car hijack? |
| Coetzee: | – Mine. |

And asking his daughter for his other son's whereabouts:

| Hendrik: | – Where's Ernest? |
| Sannie: | – At home. |

And a fisherman asks Hendrik why everyone is so excited:

| Fisherman: | What's happening? |
| Hendrik: | – The snoek are running boys! |

Meanings closely associated with the meaning of Finite verbs, such as time and modality, are also regularly involved in responses, although they may shift the terms of the argument slightly. Modal adverbs are sometimes included (*maybe, probably, surely, seldom, usually, never*, etc.). The conspirators are discussing Coetzee in the next example:

| Llewelyn: | He's not buried, not yet. |
| Luke: | – **Perhaps** not. |

Temporal adverbs (e.g. *still, already, finally*) can also be found. Hendrik is still worried about Ernest:

| Hendrik: | Is Ernest back yet? |
| Sannie: | – Not **yet**. |

We can thus define a response as a move which:

(1) takes as given the experiential content of its initiating pair part and

(2) accepts the general terms of its argument established by its Subject–Finite structure (i.e. its polarity/modality/temporality).

This definition allows for changes in polarity, modality and temporality. For example, Coetzee and Ernest adjust the polarity and modality of Sannie's statements as follows:

| Sannie: | You probably even lied to the Truth Commission. |
| Coetzee: | – No, I didn't. |

| Sannie: | You could have killed the man, you know? |
| Ernest: | – I wish I had. |

But a response does not allow for changes to the nub of the argument (its Subject), or to the content of what is being argued about in the rest of the clause. By definition, any move making changes of this kind would not be considered a response but a new initiating move. Reasoning along these lines, Coetzee is responding here to the first of Sannie's moves about her brother that Coetzee killed (*it's his own fault*), not to her second move (*is **that** what you're saying?*):

Sannie:	So **it**'s his own fault he's dead.
	Is **that** what you're saying?
Coetzee:	– No, **it**'s my fault.

And Sannie's first move below (*I'm not*) responds to Ernest's accusation about her feelings for Coetzee, but the second (*Ma is*) is a fresh initiation:

Ernest:	Don't you be getting soft on him.
Sannie:	– **I**'m not getting soft on him;
	Ma is.

Similarly, Ernest's first move below (*Yes*) would be treated as a response to Coetzee's statement. But his second is a new initiating proposition (*but now you're telling us*) since it changes who Coetzee is confessing to (shifting from the Truth Commission to the Grootbooms):

Coetzee:	I told all this to **the Commission**.
Ernest:	– Yes,
	but now you're telling **us**.

This strict definition of a response makes it easier to decide what is a response and what isn't, in our analyses. Otherwise we run into the problem of deciding how much change we allow before a move stops being a response. It does mean however that we have to show the relationship between two initiating moves in other ways, drawing on the ideational analyses in Chapter 3 below, and the possibility of challenging moves in exchange structure, which we'll develop in the next section.

Two borderline cases where we might stretch the point and allow for a response which doesn't negotiate the same Subject and Finite elements involve i) text reference (see Chapter 6 below) and ii) certain exclamations. With text reference, the pronoun *it* or a demonstrative (usually *that*) is used to refer directly to the previous speech act, enabling a 'meta' comment upon it. Hendrik's wife is not reassured by his promise of protection:

Hendrik:	No harm will come to you if I am with you.
Magda:	– ? I wish **it** was true.

Sannie judges her parents' lack of curiosity about their son's murder:

Coetzee:	Won't your parents have any questions, you know, about what happened?
Sannie:	– No,
	– ? and **that**'s wrong.

And many exclamations directly evaluate a preceding move, scoping attitudinally over it. Ernest objects to his mother implying his guilt for his brother's death:

Magda:	That is where you must ask forgiveness, from Daniel.
Ernest:	– ? **Jesus** Ma!

If moves of this kind are included as responses, then both Coetzee and Ernest below can be analysed as negotiating and disagreeing with each other about Sannie's interpretation of Coetzee's motive for visiting them:

Sannie:	He passes here for the sympathy.
Coetzee:	– ? I don't think that's true.
Ernest:	– ? Bullshit, man.

The key role played by Subject and Finite in conversation can also be used to define what counts as an independent statement, question, command or offer in dialogue. The simplest way to put this is to say that a move is a unit that can be tagged:

Sannie:	You know who brought the fish back (**don't you?**).
Ernest:	– The sea did (**didn't it?**).
Magda:	God brought the fish back (**didn't he?**).
Coetzee:	I told all this to the Commission (**didn't I?**).
Ernest:	– Yes (you did, **didn't you?**),
	but now you're telling us (**aren't you?**).

Technically speaking, what we are saying is that a move is a ranking clause, including any clauses embedded in it, and in addition any clauses dependent on it. So we can tag the main clauses in the examples below; they are negotiable. Coetzee makes others responsible for the torture facility, not his role in it:

Coetzee:	They had a facility outside Capetown <u>that we used to farm for information</u> (**didn't they?** not *****didn't we?**).

And Sannie makes the village gossipmongers responsible, not her family:

> Sannie: They'll say <u>we're selling the house</u> (**won't they?** not ***aren't we?**).

The underlined clauses are not directly negotiable; to make them so would require an additional initiating move in which they are promoted from a subordinate to an arguable position. One variation on this principle to watch out for involves certain mental process clauses in first or second person present tense (*I think...*, *I suppose...*, *do you reckon...*, *don't you suppose*, etc.). These are actually modalities involving grammatical metaphor (Halliday and Matthiessen 2004). In these cases it is the dependent clause, not the main clause, which is being negotiated, as the tag shows:

> Hendrik: I think **we've** heard enough (**haven't we?** not ***don't I?**).
> Coetzee: – I know **this must** be very difficult for you (**isn't it?** not ***don't I?**).

So both of Sannie's moves below respond to Coetzee's statement; Sannie's not negotiating what she thinks but rather what her parents should and shouldn't do:

> Coetzee: They don't want to talk to me.
> Sannie: – No,
>   but I think they should.

Exclamations, and call and greeting sequences, tend to be realized by words and phrases instead of clauses and so 'tag-ability' isn't relevant as a guide for recognizing moves. As a rule of thumb we can include expletives and vocatives in other moves where possible, and treat them as independent moves only when there is nothing to append them to. So *Sannie* would be a vocative in the following command by her father:

> Hendrik: Sannie, go with Father Dalton.
> Sannie: – (goes)

But in the movie version of this exchange, Coetzee has been attacked and injured by Ernest, and in the ensuing chaos Hendrik has to first get Sannie's attention before negotiating his demand for service:

> Hendrik: Sannie.
> Sannie: – What?
>
> Hendrik: Go with Father Dalton.
> Sannie: – (goes)

7.5 Sequencing moves: EXCHANGE STRUCTURE

So far we've looked at snatches of dialogue from the point of view of how moves may or may not pair off. But as we forecast above, it may take more than two moves to negotiate information or goods-and-services – and it might take less. Having taken Hendrik's wine order at the family's dinner with Coetzee, the waitress might return later for example and simply pour a glass without first offering to do so or being instructed to:

Waitress:	Your wine, sir (pouring).

This would count as a complete negotiation, with the service having been performed.

Alternatively Hendrik could initiate a comparable exchange by requesting wine, followed by the waitress's promise to comply:

Hendrik:	Could I have a bottle of your best dry red?
Waitress:	– Yes.

Since actually fetching the goods will take a minute or two, the promise stands in for the behaviour to ensue.

Alternatively, the negotiation could have begun with the waitress offering wine:

Waitress:	Wine?
Hendrik:	– Could I have a bottle of your best dry red?
Waitress:	– Yes.

And any of these three exchanges might have been extended with Hendrik thanking the waitress.

Waitress:	Wine?
Hendrik:	– Could I have a bottle of your best dry red?
Waitress:	– Yes.
Hendrik:	– Thank you.

And she could have extended this quartet of moves by politely diminishing the 'cost' of her service:

Waitress:	Wine?
Hendrik:	– Could I have a bottle of your best dry red?
Waitress:	– Yes.
Hendrik:	– Thank you.
Waitress:	– Not a problem.

From these variations we can see that an exchange of goods-and-services can involve one, two, three, four or five moves. This depends on who actually initiates the exchange – Hendrik or the waitress – and on whether or not they follow up when the waitress pours the wine or promises to get some.

We can find the same kind of patterning with exchanges of information. On ringing Llewelyn, Sannie might simply have announced that Coetzee had arrived:

Sannie: Coetzee's here.

Alternatively Llewelyn might have elicited this information with a question:

Llewelyn: Who's there?
Sannie: – Coetzee.

Alternatively, Sannie might have alerted Llewelyn that she has some news before actually imparting it:

Sannie: You'll never guess who's here.
Llewelyn: – Who?
Sannie: – Coetzee.

However this exchange begins, once the information is transmitted Llewelyn can follow up, explicitly acknowledging what he has heard:

Sannie: You'll never guess who's here.
Llewelyn: – Who?
Sannie: – Coetzee.
Llewelyn: – Is he?

And this opens the way for Sannie to confirm:

Sannie: You'll never guess who's here.
Llewelyn: – Who?
Sannie: – Coetzee.
Llewelyn: – Is he?
Sannie: – Yeah.

We can interpret what is going on here as follows, drawing on work by Ventola (1987), who was in turn building on work by Berry (e.g. 1981). Minimally speaking, exchanges consist of one obligatory move. When negotiating goods-and-services, this is the move that proffers the goods or performs the service; when negotiating information, this is the move that authoritatively establishes the facts of the matter.

Berry refers to goods-and-services negotiations as action exchanges, and information exchanges as knowledge ones. And she refers to the person responsible for
proffering goods or performing a service as the primary actor, and the person who
has the authority to adjudicate information as the primary knower. On this basis, the
waitress's move below is nuclear A1 move, and Sannie's is K1:

| Waitress: | A1 | – Your wine, sir (pouring). |
| Sannie: | K1 | – Coetzee's here. |

Berry refers to the dialogue partner for primary actors as a secondary actor, who is
the person who receives the goods or has the service performed for them; the
secondary knower is the person who receives the information professed by the
primary knower. Where exchanges are initiated by the secondary actor (requesting
goods-and-services) or the secondary knower (requesting information), we find
canonical two-part exchanges like the following:

Hendrik:	A2	Could I have a bottle of your best dry red?
Waitress:	A1	– Yes.
Llewelyn:	K2	Who's there?
Sannie:	K1	– Coetzee.

A third possibility is for exchanges to be initiated by primary actors and knowers
who anticipate proffering goods or performing a service by offering first to do so,
or anticipate professing information by first alerting their addressee that it is
coming. These anticipatory moves in a sense delay the exchange of goods-and-
services and information, and so are referred to by Berry as dA1 and dK1 moves
(with 'd' standing for 'delay'):

Waitress:	dA1	Wine?
Hendrik:	A2	– Could I have a bottle of your best dry red?
Waitress:	A1	– Yes.
Sannie:	dK1	You'll never guess who's here.
Llewelyn:	K2	– Who?
Sannie:	K1	– Coetzee.

These dK1^K2^K1 sequences can be used in conversation to re-affirm a
proposition that needs to be foregrounded, for example as part of an argument
amongst Daniel's comrades about who betrayed him to the authorities.

Luke:	dK1	Who hid the AK47s, Zako?
Zako:	K2	– You did.
Luke:	K1	– Damn right I did.

This is also a favourite exchange sequence for quiz shows, where the quiz master adjudicates answers, and for classrooms, where teachers ask students questions about what teachers already know:

Quizmaster:	dK1	Now, for $64,000, where was Mandela imprisoned?
Contestant:	K2	– Robben Island.
Quizmaster:	K1	– Correct!
Teacher:	dK1	Who headed the Truth Commission?
Student:	K2	– Archbishop Tutu.
Teacher:	K1	– Right.

In both these contexts, the exchange is not complete until the quizmaster and teacher play their obligatory K1 moves.

To complete the picture we can now allow for the possibility of follow-up moves by the secondary actor or knower (with 'f' standing for 'follow up'):

Waitress:	dA1	Wine?
Hendrik:	A2	– Could I have a bottle of your best dry red?
Waitress:	A1	– Yes.
Hendrik:	A2f	– Thank you.
Sannie:	dK1	You'll never guess who's here.
Llewelyn:	K2	– Who?
Sannie:	K1	– Coetzee.
Llewelyn:	K2f	– Is he?

And if they do follow up, then there is the possibility of a further follow-up move by the primary actor or knower:

Waitress:	dA1	Wine?
Hendrik:	A2	– Could I have a bottle of your best dry red?
Waitress:	A1	– Yes.
Hendrik:	A2f	– Thank you.
Waitress:	A1f	– Not a problem.
Sannie:	dK1	You'll never guess who's here.
Llewelyn:	K2	– Who?
Sannie:	K1	– Coetzee.
Llewelyn:	K2f	– Is he?
Sannie:	K1f	– Yeah.

We can sum up the various possibilities reviewed here using parentheses for optional moves. The structure potential for action exchanges is thus:

$$((dA1) \char`\^ A2) \char`\^ A1 \char`\^ (A2f \char`\^ (A2f))$$

And for information exchanges, we find the same possibilities:

((dK1) ˆ K2) ˆ K1 ˆ (K2f ˆ (K2f))

Expressed as a network of choices, we have a resource with three intersecting systems. One system is concerned with how the exchange is initiated – by the primary actor/knower or the secondary one, and if by the primary actor/knower, whether the nuclear A1/K1 move is anticipated or directly enacted. Another system distinguishes between action and knowledge exchanges, and for action exchanges allows for negotiations in which goods can be proffered or services enacted immediately (in which case verbalizing the A1 move is optional, and in a sense redundant) and negotiations in which some time will pass before the goods are proffered or the service enacted (in which case verbalizing the A1 move as a promise is obligatory, and actually acting to fulfil the promise may not eventuate). Finally there is a system allowing for follow-up moves, first for the secondary actor/knower, and then, if they do make a move, for the primary actor/knower. These options are set out in Figure 7.2.

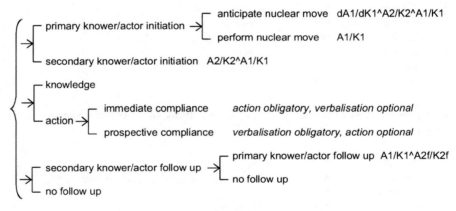

Figure 7.2 System of NEGOTIATION for exchange structure

7.6 Interrupting exchanges: tracking and challenging

In the previous section we looked at exchanges in which the negotiation unfolds smoothly. The interlocutors were clear about what they were negotiating and happy with the terms of the argument. Sometimes, however, one party may not be clear about what is being discussed, and won't make the move predicted by the structure potentials outlined above until they get things sorted out. Below, for example,

Coetzee mentions the farm where they tortured and murdered Daniel; but Hendrik has never heard of this farm and so interrupts for clarification. Once this is received he acknowledges Coetzee's information with a nod:

Coetzee:	K1	We took him to the farm.
Hendrik:		– What farm?
Coetzee:		– We had a facility outside Capetown that we used.
Hendrik:	K2f	– (nods)

We'll refer to dependent moves of this kind which clarify in some way the ideational content of what is being negotiated as **tracking** moves, and label them **tr** (for track) and **rtr** (for response to track) as required.

In other cases one party may not be happy about the way they are being positioned in the exchange and resist until they find a more comfortable position. Below, Sannie invites Coetzee to tea, so that Coetzee will stick around long enough for Daniel's comrades to come and kill him. Relations with the Grootboom family have been so unpleasant to this point that Coetzee can't be sure the invitation is genuine. He checks to make sure before agreeing to come:

Sannie:	A2	You can come tomorrow, for tea.
Coetzee:		– Are you sure about this?
Sannie:		– I wouldn't be here if I wasn't sure.
Coetzee	A1	– OK, I'll come.

We'll refer to dependent moves of this kind which resist in some way the interpersonal thrust of an exchange as **challenging** moves, and label them **ch** (for challenge) and **rch** (for response to challenge) as required.

With tracking moves, all or part of the content of a preceding move may be in doubt. Sometimes a complete repetition of the move is needed:

Sannie:	K1	Coetzee's here.
Llewelyn:	tr	– Pardon?
Sannie:	rtr	– Coetzee's here.
Llewelyn:	K2f	– Really?

If only part of the preceding move needs clarification it can be probed with the appropriate wh- phrase:

Sannie:	K1	Coetzee's here.
Llewelyn:	tr	– Who?
Sannie:	rtr	– Coetzee.
Llewelyn:	K2f	– Really?

Wh-questions with a tracking function are often referred to as 'echo questions'. Grammatically speaking they are declarative rather than interrogative, with Subject preceding Finite and the wh-phrase in the place we'd normally expect to find the information we're probing:

Coetzee:	K1	We had a facility outside Capetown that we used.
Hendrik:	tr	– You had a facility **where**?
Coetzee:	rtr	– Outside Capetown.
Hendrik:	K2f	– Right.

Where speakers think they have heard what is being negotiated but need to check, repetitions rather than wh-phrases can be used:

Coetzee:	K1	We had a facility outside Capetown that we used.
Hendrik:	tr	– Outside Capetown?
Coetzee:	rtr	– Yeah.
Hendrik:	K2f	– Right.

Tracking moves involving partial repetition and K2f moves realized by *Mm, Mm hm, Uh huh* and the like are very common in telephone conversations, where they serve to reassure listeners that the channel is open and information is being received. These 'feedback' moves are spoken on a falling intonation to signal that clarification is not required:

Sannie:	K1	Coetzee's here.
Llewelyn:	tr	– Coetzee
Sannie:	K1	He came in yesterday by car.
Llewelyn:	K2f	– Mm hm.
Sannie:	K1	It really upset Ma.
Llewelyn:	K2f	– Uh huh.

Because challenges involve uncooperative behaviour, they are sensitive to where speakers find themselves in either a knowledge or an action exchange. Below, Luke positions Llewelyn as a primary knower with a K2 move – a position Llewelyn can't accommodate because he doesn't know the answer:

| Luke: | K2 | How's she gonna keep him there? |
| Llewelyn: | ch | – I don't know. |

In the following exchange Ernest challenges Coetzee's sincerity, by rejecting his authority as primary knower about his own feelings:

Coetzee:	K1	I didn't pass here for sympathy.
Ernest:	ch	– Bullshit man.

And dK1 moves can invite listeners' interest in the information to come, or give them the opportunity of expressing disinterest:

Sannie:	dK1	You'll never guess who's here.
Llewelyn:	ch	– I don't want to know.

Challenges to dA1 moves centre on reluctance by the listener to oblige the primary actor to perform. Father Dalton does not want to impose on Magda:

Magda:	dA1	Some tea father?
Dalton:	ch	– No, I can see you have a lot of work to do.

With A2 moves, primary actors may be unwilling or unable to comply. Here Sannie refuses all of Ernest's three commands:

Ernest:	A2	Call the Ahoy B&B
	A2	and tell him not to come.
	A2	Go.
Sannie:	ch	– I won't go.

For A1 moves, secondary actors have to act quickly to nip things in the bud:

Waitress:	A1	Some more wine (starting to pour)?
Magda:	ch	– Not for me thanks.

In both knowledge and action exchanges, perhaps the most effective way to challenge is to change the terms of the argument. Incensed by Llewelyn's accusation of betrayal, Luke doesn't simply deny the charge. Rather he shifts the argument twice, challenging Llewelyn's sanity, and then his credibility:

Llewelyn:	K1	I say maybe it was you who gave the cops Daniel's name.
Luke:	ch	– Are you fucking berserk?
	ch	– You believe this shit?

Similarly, Hendrik doesn't directly refuse Coetzee's invitation to dinner, but shifts ground by explaining that coloured people are not really welcome in Paternoster's hotel:

| Coetzee: | A2 | Mr Grootboom, would you and the family consider having dinner with me tonight at the hotel please? |
| Hendrik: | ch | – Mr Coetzee, hotels are not the place for people like us. |

Sannie then retorts 'Apartheid is long gone, Pa', dismissing her father's challenge. In doing so, however, she has allowed Hendrik to sidestep the invitation for a moment, as an information exchange about discrimination delays the resolution of the goods-and-services exchange about dinner.

7.7 Extended exchanges: MOVE and EXCHANGE complexes

At this point we'll shift context again, moving from Paternoster to a school in the township of Sobantu, in the city of Pietermaritzburg in Kwazulu-Natal province. Dialogue based on film isn't continuous enough for us to illustrate the analysis we've built up, so we need some extended interactive discourse. We'll join David in a secondary history classroom there, where he is teaching African students to read academic prose. His students speak Zulu as their first language, and English as a second, mainly spoken, language. The text he is working on concerns the uprisings in South African townships in the mid-1980s, in protest against the apartheid regime.

Revolutionary days: The 1984 to 1986 uprising

In the mid-1980s South African politics erupted in a rebellion in black townships throughout the country. The government's policies of repression had bred anger and fear. Its policies of reform had given rise to expectations amongst black people of changes which the government had been unable to meet. The various forces of resistance, which we outlined in the previous section, now combined to create a major challenge for the government.

The townships became war zones, and in 1985 the ANC called on its supporters among the youth to make these areas 'ungovernable'. The army occupied militant township areas. The conflict was highly complex and violent; it involved not only clashes between the security forces and the resisters, but violence between competing political organizations, between elders and youth, and between people who lived in shantytowns and those who lived in formal townships. (Nuttal *et al.* 1998: 117).

As we join the class, David is working on what he calls *Detailed Reading*, which involves taking students carefully through the wording of the text line by line. We'll look at his detailed preparation for the text's first sentence here.

To begin, David prepares the class to read the first sentence by telling them what it means, paraphrasing it in terms they can all understand, and then reads it to them. He then prepares the students to identify one element of the sentence, its initial temporal circumstance, by giving them its transitivity category 'when' and telling them exactly where to find it ('that sentence starts by telling us...'). The logical relation between the sentence and the two preparations is **elaboration** (Halliday and Matthiessen 2004). Following Ventola (1987) we can treat this semantic triplet as a **move complex**, filling a single slot in exchange structure – two statements in other words functioning together as a K1 move. We'll highlight these move complexes by putting '=' as a superscript before elaborating moves, and using dependency lines on the left, to group them with one another:

TURN	EXCHANGE	
		Prepare sentence
Teacher	K1	Now the first sentence tells us that the trouble blew up in the townships, and that the people were rebelling against the government.
Teacher and Students	=K1	– In the mid-1980s South African politics erupted in a rebellion in black townships throughout the country. [teachers reads aloud, students along silently]
		Prepare element
Teacher	=K1	Now that sentence starts by telling us *when* they were rebelling.

David then plays a dK1 move to get them to focus on the words in the text and identify the element. A student identifies the element correctly with a K2 move, but before confirming this and so closing the exchange with the obligatory K1 move, David initiates a tracking sequence to involve the whole class in the identification and celebrate their success. Here we use dependency arrows on the right to group tracking moves:

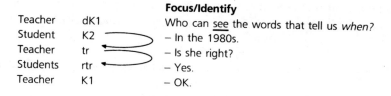

		Focus/Identify
Teacher	dK1	Who can <u>see</u> the words that tell us *when*?
Student	K2	– In the 1980s.
Teacher	tr	– Is she right?
Students	rtr	– Yes.
Teacher	K1	– OK.

Next David switches to an action exchange, using an inclusive imperative (*let's*), to get everyone to highlight the temporal circumstance with their highlighter pens, and the students comply, non-verbally, with his suggestion:

		Highlight
Teacher	A2	Let's all do *mid-1980s*.
Students	A1[nv]	– (students highlight)

David now moves on to what happened in the mid-1980s. He first prepares the next wording in the written text, by paraphrasing it with a K1 move. He then uses a dK1 move complex that repeats this paraphrase and helps them focus on the wording, by giving its exact position in the sentence. A student identifies the process *erupted* (K2), David concurs by excitedly repeating *erupted* (K1) and then initiates another tracking sequence to involve the whole class in identifying and affirming:

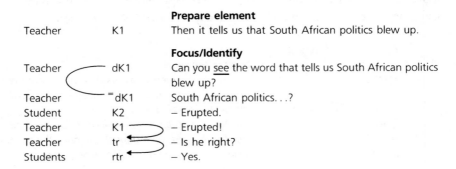

		Prepare element
Teacher	K1	Then it tells us that South African politics blew up.
		Focus/Identify
Teacher	dK1	Can you <u>see</u> the word that tells us South African politics blew up?
Teacher	=dK1	South African politics. . .?
Student	K2	– Erupted.
Teacher	K1	– Erupted!
Teacher	tr	– Is he right?
Students	rtr	– Yes.

He then asks a genuine question (K2) to make sure everyone is with him and, satisfied that they are on track, initiates the highlighting service exchange:

		Highlight/Focus
Teacher	K2	Can you see the word that says erupted?
Students	K1	– Yes.
Teacher	A2	– Lets do that one, *erupted*.
Student	A1	– (students highlight)

At this point David takes some time to explain the metaphorical use of the term *erupted* in the context of rebellion. He unpacks the first layer of the metaphor (K1), and checks whether they've heard about volcanoes erupting (K2^K1^tr^rtr):

		Extend
Teacher	K1	The reason they use the word erupted is because that's what volcanoes do.
Teacher	K2	– Have you heard that before?
Students	K1	– Yes.
Teacher	tr	– A volcano erupts?
Students	rtr	– Yes.

He then switches back to teacher questions to get the students to recognize the analogy themselves, in a dK1 move complex, and then confirms the students' response with a K1 complex. Finally, he builds on the students' recognition by explaining the second layer of analogy in the metaphor with a paraphrasing K1:

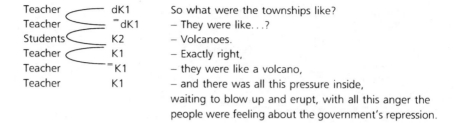

Teacher	dK1	So what were the townships like?
Teacher	⁼dK1	– They were like…?
Students	K2	– Volcanoes.
Teacher	K1	– Exactly right,
Teacher	⁼K1	– they were like a volcano,
Teacher	K1	– and there was all this pressure inside, waiting to blow up and erupt, with all this anger the people were feeling about the government's repression.

David next turns to the nominalization *rebellion*, which he paraphrases in a K1 move as 'people were rebelling'. Again he asks them to focus and identify this wording with a dK1 move complex, and once again culminates the exchange with a celebratory tracking sequence. This is again followed by a highlighting action exchange:

Prepare

Teacher	K1	OK, South African politics erupted, and then it tells us that people were rebelling.

Focus/Identify

Teacher	dK1	Can you <u>see</u> the word that means people were rebelling?
Teacher	⁼dK1	– South African politics erupted in a…?
Students	K2	– Rebellion.
Teacher	K1	– Rebellion!
Teacher	tr	– Is he right?
Students	rtr	– Yes.

Highlight

Teacher	A2	OK, everybody do *rebellion*.
Students	A1 [nv]	– (students highlight)

The next phase of *Detailed Reading* for this sentence is an interesting one. By now the identification routine is so well established that as David gives a K1 preparation, the students preempt his dK1 move, by jumping in and identifying <u>where</u> the rebellion took place. This emphasizes the sense in which dialogue is an on-going process of negotiation in which speakers can reconstrue preceding moves for their own purposes. By this time the students know where to find the information his questions demand, and can preempt which elements of a sentence his 'wh' cues refer to (people, things, processes, places, times):

Prepare/Identify

Teacher	K1/dK1	Then it tells us where that rebellion happened.
Students	K2	– In townships.
Teacher	K1	– Exactly right.
Teacher	dK1	– Which townships did it happen in?

Student	K2	– In black townships.
Teacher	K1	– OK.

Highlight

Teacher	A2	Let's all do *black townships*.
Students	A1 [nv]	– (students highlight)

Extend

Teacher	K1	So it happened in townships like Sobantu...
Teacher	⁼K1	– So it was your parents that were involved in this.

Teacher	K2	– Is that right?
Students	K1	– Yes.

Teacher	K2	– Have they told you about that time?
Students	K1	– Yes.

Here David accepts the students' preemptive move into identification, and then adjusts their reading with another dK1 exchange. This is followed by highlighting (A2^A1) and an extension phase in which David relates the text to the personal experience of his students, asking a couple of genuine questions about their parents' lives, so these are K2 moves, in contrast to dK1 moves.

As we have seen, teacher and students put a lot of work into just one sentence. This degree of detail is intended by David to ensure that all students learn to read abstract written discourse of this kind (Martin 2006, Martin and Rose 2005, Rose 2004a, 2005a, in press). It is a pedagogic routine that is based on the cycles of ordinary classroom discourse, often known as 'triadic dialogue' or 'Initiate-Respond-Feedback' (IRF) (Sinclair and Coulthard 1975, Wells 1999). But in the *Detailed Reading* pedagogy, the cycles are carefully redesigned to enable all students to read a text with complete understanding. The various phases of this cycle were labelled as *Prepare, Focus, Identify, Highlight* and *Extend* in the examples above.

Of these phases, the nucleus is *Identify*, where the students actively do the reading for themselves. Sandwiching this reading there are two elaborating phases, one initial (*Prepare*) and one final (*Extend*), whose job it is to shunt to and fro between the written text and the spoken discourse that the students can more readily understand. In addition there are two inter-modal phases, surrounding the nucleus and connecting the spoken discourse of the classroom to the writing – *Focus* which ensures students attend perceptually to the text, and *Highlight* which amplifies this by instructing them to physically highlight the words or phrases under scrutiny:

Identify	nuclear IRF exchange ('reading')
Prepare	prospective elaboration
Extend	retrospective elaboration

| Focus | perceive text |
| Highlight | modify image |

The interdependencies among these phases are outlined in Figure 7.3. In effect what we have is a sandwich structure in which the reading task itself is bracketed by phases which get the student to act perceptually and physically on the text, and this in turn is bracketed by phases which paraphrase the meaning of the text so that students can understand it and relate the uncommon sense knowledge and the discourse of its expression to their own personal experience.

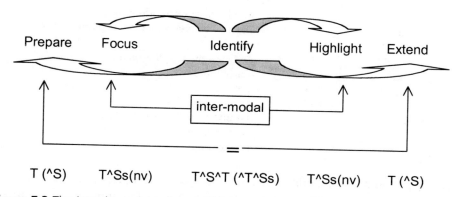

Figure 7.3 The interdependent phases of Rose's *Detailed Reading Cycle*

In pedagogic terms what we are looking at here is scaffolding which has been carefully designed to ensure teachers support students as they move into academic discourse of this order. From the point of view of exchange structure what we are looking at is exchange complexing. Each exchange is designed to realize the goals of its Prepare, Focus, Identify, Highlight or Extend phase; and they are sequenced in relation to one another according to the *Detailed Reading Cycle* just outlined (see Figure 7.3).

Not all registers of dialogue have exchange complexing of this kind. But as a rule of thumb we can expect that the more institutionalized the discourse, the more likely it is to display exchange routines of this order. In some contexts these routines may be so conventionalized that we treat them as stages of a genre – as with Ventola's work on service encounters for example (or Sinclair and Coulthard's 1975 work on classroom discourse for that matter).

The more 'chatty' a conversation on the other hand, the less likely we are to find higher order exchange complexing of this kind, and the more likely we are in fact to find series of exchanges consisting of just single moves. Below, friends in their early 20s are discussing an old friend David Allenby and his sister Jill at a dinner party (Eggins and Slade 1997: 151). Aside from Nick tracking the drugs Allenby was taking, the conversation is basically a series of K1 moves. What holds the conversation together is not exchange structure, but appraisal, as the friends evaluate Jill's intelligence and Allenby's precocious but naughty ways (in bold below):

David	K1	Jill's **very bright** actually.
	K1	– She's **very good**.
Fay	K1	– She's **extremely bright**.
David	K1	– Academ – academically she's probably **brighter** than David.
David	K1	– David's always **precocious** with his. . .
David	K1	– The only **sixteen-year-old superstar** (?) arrives in Sydney to (?)
David	K1	– And **straight into the mandies**.
Nick	tr	– Straight into what?
Fay	rtr	– Mandies. [laughs]
David	K1	– He was a **good boy**,
David	K1	– But **just no tolerance for alcohol**.
David	K1	– I've pulled him out of **so many fights**.
David	K1	– It's **ridiculous**.

As Eggins and Slade point out, at dinner parties it's important to keep the conversation flowing; silence is embarrassing. And re-initiating exchanges in an ever expanding series of K1 moves is a good way to keep things going. Discourse of this kind is the special concern of Eggins and Slade (1997), which we've illustrated with a small fragment of their data here. The complementarity of more and less institutionalized talk is explored in Martin (2000).

The exchange negotiated by David, Nick and Fay about the 'mandies' above illustrates the way in which exchanges may involve more than two parties. Similarly, Sannie's K1 move dismissing Coetzee's motives below is negotiated by both Coetzee and Ernest, with Coetzee disagreeing with Sannie, and Ernest challenging his retort:

Sannie:	K1	He passes here for the sympathy.
Coetzee:	K2f	– I don't think that's true.
Ernest	ch	– Bullshit, man.

Similarly, Coetzee, Magda and Ernest each play a role in the following three-party action exchange, highlighting Magda's sympathy and Ernest's antagonism:

Coetzee:	A2	Do you have headache pills for me please. Mrs H. . .
Magda:	A1	– Yes there (turns to get some)
Ernest:	ch	(interrupting) – We don't have anything for him.

Alongside multi-party exchanges we occasionally run across multi-party moves. In the dinner conversation introduced above, just before the exchanges we reviewed, Nick makes a positive comment about Allenby, which he seems then about to counter with a negative one; but he never in fact finishes this move which is in fact completed by Fay:

Nick:	K1	Oh, I like David a lot.
Nick:	K1	Still, but...
Fay:		(completing) ...he has a very short fuse with alcohol.

That said, overwhelmingly speakers initiate exchanges in the expectation i) that they will complete their move, ii) that the person they're addressing will respond (as specified by a vocative and explicitly invited with a tag where necessary), iii) that the addressee will hear what they say, and iv) that they will negotiate compliantly – accepting both the nub of the argument (its Subject) and the terms of the argument (its Finite and related modality and polarity) – thereby culminating the telos of the exchange. But the path towards this culmination may be a crooked one, as we have seen; and where successful challenges are mounted, the negotiation may never be consummated at all.

7.8 Negotiation and beyond

In this chapter we've developed two systems for analysing dialogue. The first, SPEECH FUNCTION, was designed to explore the relationship between moves and their realization in grammar (technically speaking their MOOD). The relevant network of choices is consolidated in Figure 7.4, and allows for the 13 basic speech acts presented above. Further delicacy is of course possible; we could for example distinguish questions asking for missing content from those exploring the modality and polarity of a given clause (i.e. *Who betrayed Daniel?* vs *Did one of his friends betray Daniel?*). This kind of specificity is much further developed in Eggins and Slade (1997) and in the work of Hasan and her colleagues (e.g. Hasan 1996).

As far as the realization of SPEECH FUNCTION in MOOD is concerned, we noted the important role played by indirect speech acts (Halliday's mood metaphors) as far as expanding the meaning potential available for speakers to negotiate within dialogue. The major MOOD options for the English clause are outlined in Figure 7.5. Technically speaking, speech function is a discourse semantic system realized through the grammar of mood (including vocation, tagging, modality and polarity which are not included in Figure 7.5).

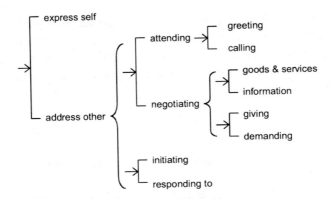

Figure 7.4 Consolidated SPEECH FUNCTION network

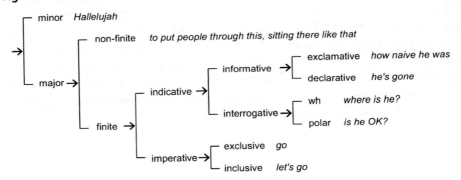

Figure 7.5 Basic MOOD options

Above SPEECH FUNCTION, in the discourse semantics, we have the system of NEGOTIATION, which sequences moves. The basic system allows for exchanges consisting of between one and five moves, as outlined in Figure 7.6. In addition there are tracking and challenging options which have not been included in the network. Either can increase the number of moves an exchange works through before establishing its obligatory K1 or A1 move; and in many cases challenges abort an exchange completely by refusing to comply and perhaps leading the negotiation off in another direction (by initiating a new exchange).

The different roles of dK1, K2, K1, K2f, K1f, dA1, A2, A1, A2f, A1f and tracking or challenging moves can be shown in analysis by modelling the former as constituency to the left of the move labels, and the latter as dependency to the right:

Coetzee	K1	We took him to the farm.
Hendrik:	tr	– What farm?
Coetzee:	rtr	– We had a facility outside Capetown, for farming information.
Hendrik:	K2f	– Right.

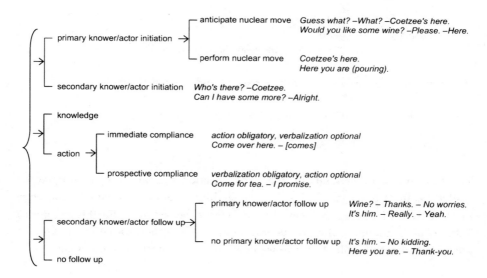

Figure 7.6 Basic NEGOTIATION options for exchange structure

MOOD, SPEECH FUNCTION and NEGOTIATION are of course only part of the picture of how a conversation unfolds. APPRAISAL resources can be used to scope prosodically over several moves, as in Luke's reaction to his comrades teasing:

Luke:	You know I missed you two fuckers.
Llewelyn:	– Sorry I can't say the same Luke.
Zako:	– Yeah me too.
Luke:	– Well **fuck you** man.
	Fuck both of you.
All:	(laughter)

With respect to IDENTIFICATION, using a pronoun or demonstrative to refer to a preceding move (technically text reference) can be treated as providing an additional criterion for treating something as a responding move (even though the nub and at times the terms of the argument have changed):

Sannie:	My parents didn't want the ANC at the funeral.
Hendrik:	– **That** isn't the reason.
Sannie:	– **It**'s one of them.

For its part, CONJUNCTION often plays an important role in relation to contradictions and challenges by introducing justification. Sannie, for example, might have avoided a confrontation with Ernest by giving reasons for her refusal:

Ernest:	Give me Llewlyn's number. I'll call him.
Sannie:	– No.
	(I'm refusing **because**) I'll call him myself.

In the movie, she chose not to give a reason, and is challenged:

Ernest:	Give me Llewlyn's number. I'll call him.
Sannie:	– No.
Ernest:	– Why not?

These and many other kinds of inter-move relation can be brought into play by readers, as these other kinds of interpersonal, ideational and textual relations were introduced in Chapters 3–5. Meanwhile we'll leave the last move for this chapter to Tutu, as he is quoted in the production notes to *Forgiveness* on DVD, the kind of gracious and memorable A2 move we have come to expect from this man:

| Tutu: | Having looked the beast of the past in the eyes, having asked and received forgiveness... let us shut the door on the past – not to forget it, but to allow it not to imprison us. |

Tackling a text

This chapter illustrates how the discourse systems described in the preceding chapters can be used to analyse a text. The text we use is the final chapter of Nelson Mandela's *Long Walk to Freedom*, that includes three sections: a recount of his Presidential Inauguration Day, a report about the cost paid by himself and his comrades for their courage in the struggle against apartheid, and a condensed autobiographical recount that summarizes his growing understanding of the meaning of freedom.

We begin this chapter by presenting these texts, and some general principles for getting started with analysis; these include identifying the genres, and then using the the text's formatting and periodicity to help identify how its field unfolds in phases. Each subsequent section then analyses a section of Mandela's chapter.

In section 8.2 we show how the Inauguration Day recount is organized in phases of activities that shift back and forth in time, as Mandela evaluates the past, present and future. In section 8.3 we analyse how he uses contrasts extensively in the report on the cost of courage, to emphasize values such as courage, freedom, rights, mercy, generosity and obligations to one's family and people. In section 8.4 we find that his autobiography uses strategies such as negation and concession, to anticipate what the reader may assume about his life, and about the meaning of freedom, and counter this with events and insights that may be unexpected. Although his story begins congruently as recollections of childhood, we show how abstraction is gradually introduced to interpret his life, and build more complex conceptions of freedom and responsibility.

8.1 Getting going

In order to get going with discourse analysis we need to settle on something to analyse, and this is not as easy as it seems. The advice we usually give our students is to start with whole texts just a page or two long, and to choose something they really like or can't stand. In theoretical terms what we are saying is that register, genre and ideology all matter. From the angle of field, we want to analyse texts whose subject matter interests us, or at least is relevant to the topic we are studying or researching; from tenor, we are interested in how speakers in oral interactions negotiate their relationships, and in how written texts engage their readers, or position us to accept their authors' point of view; and from mode we are interested in the interplay between spoken and written ways of meaning, and in their relation to other modalities of communication (e.g. image, sound, activity). The concept of genre then gives us the kind of handle on discourse that the clause gives us for grammar – a genre is a recurrent configuration of meaning that matters in the culture, just as a clause is the recurrent configuration of meaning that matters for discourse. And from an ideological perspective there's no point in analysing something that isn't compelling, because analysis is a considerable investment in time and mental labour, so it has to be worth our while. It's for these reasons that we have based this book on a field that fascinates us and is surely one of the key topics of our time, the overthrow of the world's last regime of constitutional racism. We focused on three genres (exemplum, exposition and act) and chose texts that exemplified this field in relation to personal experience, public discourse and institutional law, texts that could motivate us no matter how long we analysed them, and which convey an ideological message that we consider worth promoting.

In this chapter we are going to illustrate a few of many possible approaches to analysing a text, using the tools we have laid out in the book. The text we have chosen is in the same field, but this time it is a canonical text in the field, by its central protagonist, the final chapter of Nelson Mandela's autobiography *Long Walk to Freedom*. The chapter includes three sections that are divided from each other by spacing in the book. The first is a recount of the events on the day of Mandela's inauguration as President of the new South Africa, including an extract of his inaugural speech, in which he pledges to 'Let freedom reign'. The second describes the transformation from 'one of the harshest, most inhumane, societies the world has ever known' to 'one that recognized the rights and freedoms of all peoples regardless of the colour of their skin', as Mandela reflects on the significance of the day's events and the tragic cost that so many of his countrymen, including himself and his family, have paid for their courage. The third we have already met in Chapter 6, the synopsis of his life's story that concludes the book, in which the stages of his life project an inner narrative of his growing conception of freedom.

To begin our analysis, we'll name these three sections *Inauguration Day*, *Cost of Courage*, and *Meaning of Freedom*, and use these titles to present the chapter as follows:

Chapter 115 Freedom

Inauguration Day

10 May dawned bright and clear. For the past few days I had been pleasantly besieged by dignitaries and world leaders who were coming to pay their respects before the inauguration. The inauguration would be the largest gathering ever of international leaders on South African soil.

The ceremonies took place in the lovely sandstone amphitheatre formed by the Union Buildings in Pretoria. For decades this had been the seat of white supremacy, and now it was the site of a rainbow gathering of different colours and nations for the installation of South Africa's first democratic, non-racial government.

On that lovely autumn day I was accompanied by my daughter Zenani. On the podium, Mr de Klerk was first sworn in as second deputy president. Then Thabo Mbeki was sworn in as first deputy president. When it was my turn, I pledged to obey and uphold the constitution and to devote myself to the well-being of the republic and its people. To the assembled guests and the watching world, I said:

Today, all of us do, by our presence here ... confer glory and hope to newborn liberty. Out of the experience of an extraordinary human disaster that lasted too long, must be born a society of which all humanity will be proud.

... We, who were outlaws not so long ago, have today been given the rare privilege to be host to the nations of the world on our own soil. We thank all of our distinguished international guests for having come to take possession with the people of our country of what is, after all, a common victory for justice, for peace, for human dignity.

We have, at last, achieved our political emancipation. We pledge ourselves to liberate all our people from the continuing bondage of poverty, deprivation, suffering, gender and other discrimination.

Never, never, and never again shall it be that this beautiful land will again experience the oppression of one by another. ... The sun shall never set on so glorious a human achievement.

Let freedom reign. God bless Africa!

A few moments later we all lifted our eyes in awe as a spectacular array of South African jets, helicopters and troop carriers roared in perfect formation over the Union Buildings. It was not only a display of pinpoint precision and military force, but a demonstration of the military's loyalty to democracy, to a new government that had been freely and fairly elected. Only moments before, the highest generals of the South African Defence Force and police, their chests bedecked with ribbons and medals from days gone by, saluted me and pledged their loyalty. I was not unmindful of the fact that not so many years before they would not have saluted but arrested me. Finally a chevron of Impala jets left a smoke trail of the black, red, green, blue and gold of the new South African flag.

The day was symbolized for me by the playing of our two national anthems, and the vision of whites singing 'Nkosi Sikelel' iAfrika' and blacks singing 'Die Stem', the old anthem of the republic. Although that day neither group knew the lyrics of the anthem they once despised, they would soon know the words by heart.

Cost of Courage

On the day of the inauguration, I was overwhelmed with a sense of history. In the first decade of the twentieth century, a few years after the bitter Anglo-Boer war and before my own birth, the white-skinned peoples of South Africa patched up their differences and erected a system of racial domination against the dark-skinned peoples of their own land. The structure they created formed the basis of one of the harshest, most inhumane, societies the world has ever known. Now, in the last decade of the twentieth century, and my own eighth decade as a man, this system has been overturned forever and replaced by one that recognized the rights and freedoms of all peoples regardless of the colour of their skin.

That day had come about through the unimaginable sacrifices of thousands of my people, people whose suffering and courage can never be counted or repaid. I felt that day, as I have on so many other days, that I was simply the sum of all those African patriots who had gone before me. That long and noble line ended and now began again with me. I was pained that I was not able to thank them and that they were not able to see what their sacrifices had wrought.

The policy of apartheid created a deep and lasting wound in my country and my people. All of us will spend many years, if not generations, recovering from that profound hurt. But the decades of oppression and brutality had another, unintended, effect, and that was that it produced the Oliver Tambos, the Walter Sisulus, the Chief Luthulis, the Yusuf Dadoos, the Bram Fischers, the Robert Sobukwes of our time – men of such extraordinary courage, wisdom and generosity that their like may never be known again. Perhaps it requires such depths of oppression to acquire such heights of character. My country is rich in the minerals and gems that lie beneath its soil, but I have always known that its greatest wealth is its people, finer and truer than the purest diamonds.

It is from these comrades in the struggle that I have learned the meaning of courage. Time and again, I have seen men and women risk and give their lives for an idea. I have seen men stand up to attacks and torture without breaking, showing a strength and resilience that defies the imagination. I learned that courage was not the absence of fear, but the triumph over it. I felt fear myself more times than I can remember, but I hid it behind a mask of boldness. The brave man is not he who does not feel afraid, but he who conquers that fear.

I never lost hope that the great transformation would occur. Not only because of the great heroes I have already cited, but because of the courage of the ordinary men and women of my country. I always knew that deep down in every human heart, there was mercy and generosity. No one is born hating another person because of the colour of his skin, or his background, or his religion. People must learn to hate, and if they can learn to hate, they can be taught to love, for love comes more naturally to the human heart than its opposite. Even in the grimmest times in prison, when my colleagues and I were pushed to our limits, I would see a glimmer of humanity in one of the guards, perhaps just for a second, but it was enough to reassure me and keep me going. Man's goodness is a flame that can be hidden but never extinguished.

We took up the struggle with our eyes wide open, under no illusion that the path would be an easy one. As a young man, when I joined the African National Congress, I saw the price my comrades paid for their beliefs, and it was high. For myself, I have never regretted my commitment to the struggle, and I was always prepared to face the hardships that affected me personally. But my family paid a terrible price, perhaps too dear a price, for my commitment.

In life, every man has twin obligations – obligations to his family, to his parents, to his wife and children; and he has an obligation to his people, his community, his country. In a civil and humane society, each man is able to fulfil those obligations according to his own inclinations and abilities. But in a country like South Africa, it was almost impossible for a man of my birth and colour to fulfil both of those obligations. In South Africa, a man of colour who attempted to live as a human being was punished and isolated. In South Africa, a man who tried to fulfil his duty to his people was inevitably ripped from his family and his home and was forced to live a life apart, a twilight existence of secrecy and rebellion. I did not in the beginning choose to place my people above my family, but in attempting to serve my people, I found that I was prevented from fulfilling my obligations as a son, a brother, a father and a husband.

In that way, my commitment to my people, to the millions of South Africans I would never know or meet, was at the expense of the people I knew best and loved most. It was as simple and yet as incomprehensible as the moment a small child asks her father, 'Why can you not be with us?' And the father must utter the terrible words: 'There are other children like you, a great many of them...' and then one's voice trails off.

Meaning of Freedom

I was not born with a hunger to be free. I was born free – free in every way that I could know. Free to run in the fields near my mother's hut, free to swim in the clear stream that ran through my village, free to roast mealies under the stars and ride the broad backs of slow-moving bulls. As long as I obeyed my father and abided by the customs of my tribe, I was not troubled by the laws of man or God.

It was only when I began to learn that my boyhood freedom was an illusion, when I discovered as a young man that my freedom had already been taken from me, that I began to hunger for it.

At first, as a student, I wanted freedom only for myself, the transitory freedoms of being able to stay out at night, read what I pleased and go where I chose. Later, as a young man in Johannesburg, I yearned for the basic and honourable freedoms of achieving my potential, of earning my keep, of marrying and having a family – the freedom not to be obstructed in a lawful life.

But then I slowly saw that not only was I not free, but my brothers and sisters were not free.

I saw that it was not just my freedom that was curtailed, but the freedom of everyone who looked like I did. That is when I joined the African National Congress, and that is when the hunger for my own freedom became the greater hunger for the freedom of my people. It was this desire for the freedom of my people to live their lives with dignity and self-respect that animated my life, that transformed a frightened young man into a bold one, that drove a law-abiding attorney to become a criminal, that turned a family-loving husband into a man without a home, that forced a life-loving man to live like a monk. I am no more virtuous or self-sacrificing than the next man, but I found that I could not even enjoy the poor and limited freedoms I was allowed when I knew my people were not free.

Freedom is indivisible; the chains on any one of my people were the chains on all of them, the chains on all of my people were the chains on me.

It was during those long and lonely years that my hunger for the freedom of my own people became a hunger for the freedom of all people, white and black.

I knew as well as I knew anything that the oppressor must be liberated just as surely as the oppressed. A man who takes away another man's freedom is a prisoner of hatred, he is locked behind the bars of prejudice and narrow-mindedness. I am not truly free if I am taking away someone else's freedom, just as surely as I am not free when my freedom is taken from me.

The oppressed and the oppressor alike are robbed of their humanity.

When I walked out of prison, that was my mission, to liberate the oppressed and the oppressor both.

Some say that has now been achieved. But I know that this is not the case. The truth is that we are not yet free; we have merely achieved the freedom to be free, the right not to be oppressed. We have not taken the final step of our journey, but the first step on a longer and even more difficult road. For to be free is not merely to cast off one's chains, but to live in a way that respects and enhances the freedom of others.

The true test of our devotion to freedom is just beginning.

I have walked that long road to freedom. I have tried not to falter; I have made missteps along the way. But I have discovered the secret that after climbing a great hill, one only finds that there are many more hills to climb. I have taken a moment here to rest, to steal a view of the glorious vista that surrounds me, to look back on the distance I have come. But I can only rest for a moment, for with freedom come responsibilities, and I dare not linger, for my long walk is not yet ended.

(Mandela 1995: 746–51)

The formatting of the chapter thus gives us three main units of discourse to work with (although we need to keep in mind that formatting reflects but does not determine discourse structure). Generically speaking, *Inauguration Day* is a recount, a genre that chronicles an episode of experience, *Cost of Courage* is a report, a genre for making generalized descriptions, and *Meaning of Freedom* is an autobiographical recount, a genre for chronicling the significant stages of the author's life.

We can be confident that these are the genres we are looking at by asking a few probing questions. First is the global structure one of activities unfolding in time, or of phenomena described out of time? This criterion distinguishes the first and third sections, which are sequenced in time, from the second section, which describes and reflects on the struggle and its protagonists, but is not sequenced in time. Secondly, is the sequence of activities about specific people and events or about generic participants? This distinguishes stories from explanations and histories in the natural and social sciences. Thirdly is the story structured around a major disruption to the course of events or does it simply recount a series of events? This distinguishes narratives, anecdotes and exemplums (which involve a significant disruption) from recounts (whose series of events may or may not be problematic). And finally is it a recount of events in an episode of experience, as in the first recount, or of stages in a person's life, as in the last? These and other generic criteria are discussed in detail in Martin and Rose (2007).

Crucially all texts have more than one purpose, and for this reason they will include elements that we would expect to find in other genres. But all texts also have a global defining purpose, and it is this global purpose that predicts the stages the text will go through to achieve this goal, i.e. its genre. Its additional purposes are realized below the level of generic stages, in the variable phases of meaning within each stage, and within the messages that make up each phase. Identifying the genre of a text sometimes involves some shunting up and down, from identifying its global purpose, to analysing its stages and phases, and back up again to its purpose. As with other features of language, a first glance is often not sufficient to identify a genre. A useful guide is the table of genres, their purposes and stages, presented as an Appendix to this book.

Technically then Chapter 115 is a **macro-genre**, comprising three genres – a recount extended by a report, extended in turn by another recount. Within this overall structure, the first recount projects a pledge by quoting Mandela's inauguration speech, which is marked in the formatting by indenting. So within macro-genres (such as books and chapters), genres are interdependent – extending, elaborating or projecting each other, as illustrated in Figure 8.1.

Genre and field

Having established the genres we are working with, our next step in analysis is to interpret how the field unfolds through each genre. One reason we start with the field is that the steps in which it unfolds are readily accessible to conscious reflection. This can be illustrated by asking people to retell a text they have heard or read; they will rarely repeat its language features, but will typically summarize its sequence of phases. As analysts, the things we are interested in include the ideational language resources that construe the unfolding field, the interpersonal resources which evaluate it from phase to phase, and the textual resources that present each phase as a pulse of information. First identifying phases from the

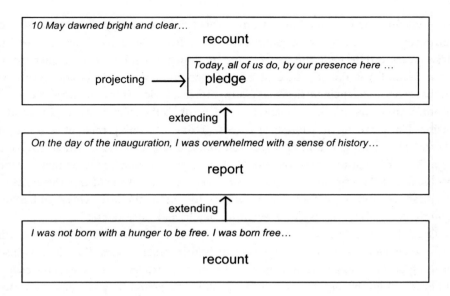

Figure 8.1 Genre interdependency in Chapter 115 'Freedom'

perspective of genre and field can provide a useful scaffold for us to identify other less obvious discourse patterns.

As we introduced in Chapter 1, text phases are sensitive to both genre and field: while the stages of a genre unfold in a highly predictable sequence, the phases within each stage are partly predictable from the genre, and partly from its construal of a particular field of activities and entities. Stories, for example, unfold through phases such as settings, problems, people's reactions, descriptions, solutions to problems, author's comments and participants' reflections on the significance of the events. Orators and authors use such phases in highly variable combinations, as the basic building blocks of stories, as we saw for Helena's story. The phases of recounts are often a series of episodes, and in biographical recounts these episodes correspond to the person's life stages. In argument genres, phases may include grounds and conclusions, as we saw for Tutu's exposition, as well as evidence, examples and so on. In the Act we found phases such as purposes, motivations, provisions and definitions. In reports, each phase will tend to describe an element or aspect of the phenomenon under focus. These may include phases such as appearance, behaviour, location, types, parts and so on, depending on the particular type of report and its particular field. We have not attempted an exhaustive study of phase types in this book, as genres are not our primary focus (but see Martin and Rose 2007, and Rose 2007 for discussion of phases in various genres). It is an area of considerable variation that is wide open to further research; the tools we present here will help the analyst to develop this research.

Phases and paragraphing

As with larger segments in written texts discussed above, formatting can be a useful starting point, but now it is the paragraphing that can help to indicate the phases in which the field unfolds. As paragraphing tends to coincide with the hierarchy of periodicity, we can adjust and expand the information that paragraphing gives us by looking at what is presented as hyperThemes and hyperNews. For example, what is presented first in each paragraph of the *Inauguration Day* recount are **times** that scaffold the activity sequence of the day's events and of Mandela's speech:

> **10 May** dawned bright and clear. . .
> **On that lovely autumn day** I was accompanied by my daughter Zenani. . .
> **Today**, all of us do, by our presence here confer glory and hope. . .
> We, who were outlaws **not so long ago**, have today been given the rare privilege. . .
> We have, **at last**, achieved our political emancipation. . .
> **Never, never, and never again** shall it be. . .
> **A few moments later** we all lifted our eyes in awe. . .

The day's activity sequence is concluded in the hyperNew of the second last paragraph, with *Finally. . .*, and is then reoriented in the last paragraph, beginning with *The day. . .*

> **Finally** a chevron of Impala jets left a smoke trail. . .
> **The day** was symbolized for me. . .

The global scaffolding resource here is sequence in time, expressed as external conjunctions and temporal circumstances. In contrast, the *Cost of Courage* report is organized around the people that struggled against apartheid, who are identified at the beginning of each paragraph, from *the policy of apartheid* to *the comrades in the struggle*, to *I* (Mandela), to *we*, to *every man*:

> **The policy of apartheid** created a deep and lasting wound. . .
> It is from **these comrades in the struggle** that I have learned the meaning of courage. . .
> **I** never lost hope. . .
> **We** took up the struggle with our eyes wide open. . .
> In life, **every man** has twin obligations. . .

The last paragraph then begins *In that way. . .*, to culminate Mandela's explanation of the price his family paid for his commitment to the struggle:

> **In that way**, my commitment to my people, to the millions of South Africans I would never know or meet, was at the expense of the people I knew best and loved most...

The global scaffolding resource operating here is identification – initially of people, and finally text reference in a circumstance of manner. Expressions of this kind are closely related to internal conjunction in their global text orchestrating function, as we could see by substituting the manner conjunction *thus* for *in that way*.

   The organization of paragraphs supports this scaffolding in different ways. Here are two examples from *Cost of Courage*, in which the first sentence serves as hyperTheme, and the rest of the paragraph expands on it:

> On the day of the inauguration, I was overwhelmed with a sense of history.
> In the first decade of the twentieth century...the white-skinned peoples of South Africa patched up their differences and erected a system of racial domination... Now, in the last decade of the twentieth century, and my own eighth decade as a man, this system has been overturned forever ...

> It is from these comrades in the struggle that I have learned the meaning of courage. Time and again, I have seen men and women risk and give their lives for an idea... The brave man is not he who does not feel afraid, but he who conquers that fear...

Similarly hyperNews are regularly included in the paragraph they distil. Here the last sentence distils the paragraph with a metaphor:

> ...I always knew that deep down in every human heart, there was mercy and generosity... Even in the grimmest times in prison, when my colleagues and I were pushed to our limits, I would see a glimmer of humanity in one of the guards, perhaps just for a second, but it was enough to reassure me and keep me going. Man's goodness is a flame that can be hidden but never extinguished.

However the relationship between paragraphs and hierarchy of periodicity is a variable one: hyperThemes tend to function as the 'topic sentence' of paragraphs which elaborate them, but we need to be cautious about correlating paragraphs with discourse phases. For example in the culminating phase of *Cost of Courage*, the hyperNew is treated as a new paragraph, which has the effect of foregrounding it. The hyperTheme on the other hand is the last sentence in the preceding paragraph:

> We took up the struggle with our eyes wide open ... For myself, I have never regretted my commitment to the struggle, and I was always prepared to face the hardships that affected me personally. [**hyperTheme**] But my family paid a terrible price, perhaps too dear a price, for my commitment.
> In life, every man has twin obligations – obligations to his family, to his parents, to his wife and children; and he has an obligation to his people, his community, his

country. . . . in attempting to serve my people, I found that I was prevented from fulfilling my obligations as a son, a brother, a father and a husband.
[**hyperNew**] In that way, my commitment to my people, to the millions of South Africans I would never know or meet, was at the expense of the people I knew best and loved most. . .

Finally macroThemes and macroNews tend to be accorded a paragraph of their own, especially where they are developed over more than one sentence – as in the final summary paragraph of the Freedom recount:

[preceding recount]
I have walked that long road to freedom. I have tried not to falter; I have made missteps along the way. But I have discovered the secret that after climbing a great hill, one only finds that there are many more hills to climb. I have taken a moment here to rest, to steal a view of the glorious vista that surrounds me, to look back on the distance I have come. But I can only rest for a moment, for with freedom come responsibilities, and I dare not linger, for my long walk is not yet ended.

8.2 Inauguration Day: from outlaw to president

Let's start our analysis of the chapter with the episodes through which *Inauguration Day* recounts the key events of the day. From the perspective of genre, the typical stages of a recount include Orientation, Record of Events and (optionally) Reorientation. In this text, the first two paragraphs frame its Orientation stage, including two setting phases: the first presenting its time (*10 May*) and some key protagonists (*dignitaries and world leaders*), and the second presenting its location (*the lovely sandstone amphitheatre*). Mandela uses both settings to comment: first on the people: *the largest gathering ever of international leaders on South African soil*; and then on the location: *the seat of white supremacy...now it was the site of a rainbow gathering*. This pattern of recounting, describing and then commenting is a major motif throughout the chapter. A related pattern, that we will also return to repeatedly, is the contrasts that Mandela continually draws between the past and the future in the making.

Following these two settings, the first episode is the 'swearing in' of de Klerk, Mbeki and Mandela, including his quoted pledge, in which the paragraphing also distinguishes four phases: first an 'appeal' for *a society of which all humanity will be proud*, then 'thanks' to the *distinguished international guests*, including them in the *common victory*, thirdly a 'pledge' to *liberate all our people*, and finally a 'prophecy' that oppression will never return to South Africa.

The second episode is then the 'military display', which Mandela interprets as a *demonstration of the military's loyalty to democracy*, emphasizing the institutionalization of the new ideals in state power, where once *they would not have saluted but arrested me*. The last episode is the 'singing', which he introduces as symbolically significant (*The day was symbolized for me by the playing of our two national anthems...*), and he then uses it to reorient the recount towards the future, in which black and white South Africans *would soon know the words by heart*.

While the global structuring of the recount is a series of episodes unfolding one after another, there is a continual shifting back and forth in time within this generic framework. Before and as the events unfold, Mandela uses the activities and setting to reflect on the past, its transformation into a new present, and the certainty of a better future.

Field and patterns of discourse

We now turn to the discourse patterns in which this to-ing and fro-ing in time is managed. This brings us to the central challenge of micro-analysis – the immense complexity of discourse. In one sense the problem is simply one of scale. Texts are very dense phenomena, because they derive from social semiotic systems, which are the most complex systems we know of. So we have to be selective. But how do we decide which analyses to undertake – avoiding both the problem of doing too much and getting overwhelmed, and the problem of doing too little and not getting to the point?

A first step in deciding which analyses to undertake is to look for patterns that are revealed by the field unfolding through the text phases, as we have done above. The next step is to ask how these patterns are managed by discourse systems. To answer this question, the key things to look for are **foregrounding** and **co-articulation.**

By foregrounding we mean the tendency for texts to make some meanings stand out against others. Sometimes we can observe this as a text shifts gears from one phase to the next and certain options get taken up much more often than they were before. By co-articulation we mean systems working together to produce a particular effect. Again these effects of co-articulation shift from one phase to the next. As the significant pattern we found in the text phases above was to-ing and fro-ing in time, we will start our analysis here with co-articulation of systems for managing time.

As introduced above, a recount is a genre which is built up ideationally around activity sequences. The events of the inauguration day begin with day-break and end with the fly-over by the Impala jets:

10 May dawn<u>ed</u> bright and clear.
      ^

On the podium, Mr de Klerk <u>was</u> **first** swor<u>n</u> in as second deputy president.
      ^

Then Thabo Mbeki <u>was</u> <u>sworn</u> in as first deputy president.

When it was my turn, I pled<u>ged</u> to obey and uphold the constitution…

To the assembled guests and the watching world, I sa<u>id</u>: '[…]'

A few moments **later** we all li<u>fted</u> our eyes in awe **as** South African jets… roar<u>ed</u>…

Only moments **before**, the highest generals…salut<u>ed</u> me and pled<u>ged</u> their loyalty.

Finally a chevron of Impala jets le<u>ft</u> a smoke trail…

The main resources used to co-articulate these sequences of events are conjunction (*first, then, when, as, before, finally*), circumstances of time (*a few moments later, only moments before*) and tense (simple past). Basically the text unfolds chronologically, except for the generals' salute, which preceded the fly-over on the day, but follows in the text (*only moments before…*).

In the context of the recount genre, given the explicit temporal markers, and the congruent mapping of field time (event sequence) onto text time (message sequence), we might reasonably predict that the singing of the anthems followed the military display in the course of events, despite a lack of temporal markers. We saw with Helena's story in Chapter 4 that story genres strongly predict temporal sequencing, without necessarily requiring explicit markers. On the other hand, Mandela may have put this episode last to foreground its significance for him as macroNew. In a sense its timing doesn't matter, because the sequence of events is not all that's going on.

In addition to the activities of the day Mandela makes mention of several things that took place before the inauguration – visiting dignitaries, the election, military honours, and attitudes in the apartheid era:

For the **past** few days I **had been** pleasantly besieg**ed** by dignitaries and world leaders who were coming to pay their respects **before the inauguration**
For decades this **had been** the seat of white supremacy
a new government that **had been** freely and fairly elect**ed**.
their chests bedecked with ribbons and medals from days **gone by**
the fact that not so many years **before** they **would** not **have** saluted but arrest**ed** me.
the lyrics of the anthem they **once** despis**ed**,

And he twice looks ahead to things that follow – from before Inauguration Day to the day itself, and from the singing of the anthems to the day when South Africans would know the words by heart:

> The inauguration **would be** the largest gathering ever... on South African soil.
> they **would soon** know the words by heart.

A range of resources is used to manage this hopping back and forth through time:

> tense (secondary past for things that happened previously, *had been besieged, had been, had been elected; would not **have** saluted but arrested*)
> circumstances of extent in time (*for the past few days, for decades*)
> temporal mood adjuncts (***once** despised, would **soon** know*)
> modification of temporal nouns (***past** few days, days **gone by**, not so many years **before***)

And the general drift of these resources is to construct a past that impinges on the inauguration (e.g. *for the past few days...had been besieged*) – which in turn impinges on the future (*would soon know*). This is also the pattern in the projected speech:

> **Today**, all of us do, by our presence here ... confer glory and hope to newborn liberty.
>
> We, who were outlaws **not so long ago**, have **today** been given the rare privilege to be host to the nations of the world on our own soil.
>
> We have, **at last**, achieved our political emancipation.
>
> **Never, never, and never again** shall it be that this beautiful land will **again** experience the oppression of one by another.

In our experience this kind of time travel is unusual in recounts; so we need to ask why Mandela moves in and out of time so frequently as he relates a simple sequence of events.

Genre and tenor: evaluating time

The reasons for moving in and out of time are to be found in the prosody of evaluation which is interpersonally critical to the meaning of any recount, and particularly so in this one. As the time shifts occur within each episode, so the evaluation is also managed by the text phases, as follows.

In the first setting, flashing back a few days allows Mandela to make a point about the respect paid by international leaders from around the world:

marked Theme	Subject/Theme	New
	10 May	**bright and clear** [+appreciation]
← For the past few days	I	**dignitaries and world leaders** who were coming to **pay their respects** before the inauguration [+judgement]
→	the inauguration	the **largest gathering ever** of international leaders on South African soil [+appreciation]

In the second setting, a flashback of decades allows him to comment on the transformation that has taken place, from the impropriety of the white supremacist regime to the non-racial government:

marked Theme	Subject/Theme	New
	the ceremonies	in the **lovely sandstone amphitheatre** formed by the Union Buildings in Pretoria [+ appreciation]
← For decades	this (amphitheatre)	the seat of **white supremacy** [-judgement]
now	it (amphitheatre)	the site of a **rainbow gathering of different colours and nations** for the installation of South Africa's **first democratic, non-racial government** [+judgement]

What is perhaps most critical here is that change is evaluated as a transformation from one kind of society into another, not as black power replacing white (i.e. 'evolution' not 'revolution'). The seat of white supremacy becomes the site for a *rainbow gathering*. Technically speaking the text repeatedly recontextualizes negative judgement (impropriety) as positive judgement (propriety) and appreciation (reaction and composition), a similar pattern to that discussed in Chapter 2, in connection with Tutu's conception of *ubuntu*. The texture of resources woven together here triumphs over racism. The swearing in episode is then relatively neutral in appraisal:

marked Theme	Subject/Theme	New
on the podium	Mr de Klerk	as second deputy president
	Thabo Mbeki	as first deputy president
When it was		
my turn	I	the constitution
	[I]	to the **well-being** of the republic and its people [+judgement]
To the assembled guests and the watching world	I	said

But this neutrality is only to provide a background for the projected speech, in which negative judgement of the past is repeatedly recontextualized by positive judgement and appreciation in both Themes and News. The speech's macroTheme opens with the present context of *newborn liberty*, then condemns the past with a marked Theme, and appeals to the future as New:

| Today | all of us | **glory and hope to newborn liberty** [+ appreciation] |
| ← Out of the experience of **an extraordinary human disaster that lasted too long** [–judgement] | **[we]** | **a society of which all humanity will be proud** [+ judgement] |

The 'thanks' and 'pledge' phases then open with the past judgement of Mandela and his comrades as *outlaws*, which is recontextualized with *nations of the world* as witnesses and participants in the *common victory* as News. But the final New is a strong condemnation of injustice that continues in the present:

←We, who were **outlaws** not so long ago [-judgement]	**host to the nations of the world on our own soil** [+ appreciation]
We	**a common victory for justice, for peace, for human dignity** [+ judgement]
We	**political emancipation** [+ appreciation]
We	**continuing bondage of poverty, deprivation, suffering, gender and other discrimination** [– judgement]

This condemnation forms the context for the speech's macroNew in which Mandela prophesies the end of oppression, invokes freedom, and calls on God's blessing:

→ **Never, never, and never again** [amplified engagement]	this beautiful land	**the oppression of one by another** [– judgement]
	The sun	**so glorious a human achievement** [+ judgement]
		freedom reign [+ appreciation]
	God	**bless** Africa! [+ judgement]

The 'miltary display' episode then recontextualizes *awe* at the display as positive judgement of the generals, which is countered by their behaviour *not so many years before*, but recontextualized again as positive appreciation of the smoke trail symbolism.

| a few moments later | we | **in awe** [+ affect] |
| | a spectacular array of South African jets, helicopters and troop carriers | over the Union Buildings |

	it	a display of **pinpoint precision** and **military force** [+appreciation], but a demonstration of the military's **loyalty to democracy** [+judgement], to a new government that had been **freely and fairly elected** [+judgement]
← only moments before	the highest generals of the South African Defence Force and police, **their chests bedecked with ribbons and medals** [+judgement] ← from days gone by	**saluted** [+judgement]
← not so many years before	[the generals] they	**their loyalty** [+judgement] **not have saluted but arrested me** [–judgement]
	a chevron of Impala jets	**a smoke trail of the black, red, green, blue and gold of the new South African flag** [+appreciation]

It is interesting to note that the one event that is out of chronological time here is one that foreshadows the generals' change in behaviour. How many of the ribbons and medals bedecking their chests were awarded as part of their struggle against the ANC and their allies?

The transforming rainbow texture is reworked ideationally in the recount's macroNew. Here, as in the macroTheme, time is construed as a participant and unmarked Theme (*May 10... The day...*). As a participant, *Inauguration Day* (i.e. the meaning of the day) can enter into symbolic relationships and is symbolized for Mandela by converse relations between participants – whites singing a black anthem and blacks singing a white anthem. The complementarity is further resolved through Mandela's vision of a time when each group would know by heart the words of the anthem they once despised – with balance winning through, recontextualizing negative affect (hate):

The day		our two national anthems, and the vision of whites singing 'Nkosi Sikelel' iAfrika' and blacks singing 'Die Stem', the old anthem of the republic.
Although on that day	neither group they	the lyrics of the anthem they ← **once despised** [–judgement] → would soon **know the words by heart** [+judgement]

As we can see, Mandela has singled out the anthems from the other events of the day in order to consolidate the point of his recount – the resolution of the struggle in his rainbow republic.

Still more could be said about time shifts, evaluation and the resolution of difference in this recount. Participant identification, for example, is intriguing – South African and international leaders, Mandela and Zenani (not Winnie), de Klerk, Mbeki and Mandela (past, present and future presidents), the military and the government, whites and blacks. But perhaps we can leave these oppositions, their textures and the meanings they co-articulate for the reader to unravel.

8.3 *The Cost of Courage*: from domination to freedom

If the dominant semantic motif in the *Inauguration Day* recount is time travel and the resolution of difference, then the main trend in the *Cost of Courage* report is contrast and the personal cost of the struggle which Mandela was unable to resolve. We noted earlier that reports are a genre used for making generalized descriptions. Ideationally, whereas recounts are focused on activities, reports are focused on entities. In the *Cost of Courage* report, the entities under focus are people who were comrades in the struggle, and abstract things: the old and new societies, the meaning of courage, the goodness in people's hearts, the price of commitment, and irreconcilable obligations.

The macroTheme of a report typically classifies the entity or entities to be described. In this case Mandela names the entity as *a sense of history* that overwhelms him, and characterizes it by the contrast between *a system of racial domination* and *one that recognized the rights and freedoms of all peoples*. The next two paragraphs describe and evaluate *all those African patriots that have gone before him*. The next describes what he has learnt about *the meaning of courage*. In the next he reflects on *the mercy and generosity* in *every human heart*. Then he introduces the price that he and his comrades paid for their commitment, and he elaborates on this in the following paragraph, in personal terms of the conflict between his *twin obligations* to his family and to his people. If the report has a macroNew, it is the final recontextualization of this conflict as a mini-exemplum, about *the terrible words* he was forced to tell his children.

The rhetorical movement through these phases is thus from the historical context of political conflict, to the freedom fighters who fought it, to the courage that they displayed. This positive judgement then expands to embrace the humanity of all peoples, even his jailers, before personalizing the conflict as the terrible choice Mandela himself was forced to make between the nation that he loved and his children who loved him.

Foregrounding contrasts

How then are these movements achieved by discourse systems? Whereas co-articulation of resources for managing time was the outstanding pattern in the *Inauguration Day* recount, here it is **foregrounding** of resources for drawing **contrasts**. We have already pointed out the lexical contrast in the classifying macroTheme between *a system of racial domination* and *one that recognized the rights and freedoms of all peoples*. This lexical contrast is presented as News, but it is signalled with contrasting temporal Themes:

> <u>In the first decade of the twentieth century, a few years after the bitter Anglo-Boer war and before my own birth</u>, the white-skinned peoples of South Africa patched up their differences and erected a system of racial domination against the dark-skinned peoples of their own land. The structure they created formed the basis of one of the harshest, most inhumane, societies the world has ever known. [**implicit contrast**] <u>Now, in the last decade of the twentieth century, and my own eighth decade as a man</u>, this system has been overturned forever and replaced by one that recognized the rights and freedoms of all peoples regardless of the colour of their skin.

In each case, time is thematized not once but twice or three times, powerfully flagging the contrast to come. Later on, contrasting spatial Themes are reinforced conjunctively with the **contrastive *but***:

> <u>In a civil and humane society</u>, each man is able to fulfil those obligations according to his own inclinations and abilities. [**explicit contrast**] **But** <u>in a country like South Africa</u>, it was almost impossible for a man of my birth and colour to fulfil both of those obligations.

And *but* is used to explicitly signal contrast throughout the report:

> The policy of apartheid created a deep and lasting wound in my country and my people. All of us will spend many years, if not generations, recovering from that profound hurt. [**expl contr**] **But** the decades of oppression and brutality had another, unintended, effect, [**expl add**] **and that was** that it produced the Oliver Tambos, the Walter Sisulus, the Chief Luthulis, the Yusuf Dadoos, the Bram Fischers, the Robert Sobukwes of our time – men of such extraordinary courage, wisdom and generosity that their like may never be known again.

> I learned that courage was not the absence of fear, [**expl contr**] **but** the triumph over it.

> The brave man is not he who does not feel afraid, [**expl contr**] **but** he who conquers that fear.

> For myself, I have never regretted my commitment to the struggle, and I was always prepared to face the hardships that affected me personally. [**expl contr**] **But** my family paid a terrible price, perhaps too dear a price, for my commitment.

Another conjunctive relation that extends this contrast motif is **concessive *but*** since it opposes expectations with propositions:

> My country is rich in the minerals and gems that lie beneath its soil, [**explicit concession**] **but** I have always known that its greatest wealth is its people, finer and truer than the purest diamonds.

Here concessive *but* counters what is predicted with what is in fact proposed (cf. 'although my country is rich in mineral and gems they aren't its greatest wealth; its greatest wealth is its people'):

> My country is rich in the minerals and gems that lie beneath its soil
> **predicting:**
> they are its greatest wealth
> **countered by:**
> its greatest wealth is its people, finer and truer than the purest diamonds.

There are several more instances of this pattern:

> I felt fear myself more times than I can remember, [**expl conc**] **but** I hid it behind a mask of boldness.
>
> Not only because of the great heroes I have already cited, [**expl conc**] **but** because of the courage of the ordinary men and women of my country.
>
> Even in the grimmest times in prison, when my colleagues and I were pushed to our limits, I would see a glimmer of humanity in one of the guards, perhaps just for a second, [**expl conc**] **but** it was enough to reassure me and keep me going.
>
> I did not in the beginning choose to place my people above my family, [**expl conc**] **but** in attempting to serve my people, I found that I was prevented from fulfilling my obligations as a son, a brother, a father and a husband.
>
> It was as simple [**expl add, conc**] **and yet** as incomprehensible as the moment a small child asks her father

Both **identification** and **ideation** play a critical role in specifying these contrastive conjunctive links and constructing other oppositions as well. Here's a list of oppositions involving identification – one participant or group of participants opposed to another (as signalled by '≠' below):

> the first decade ≠ the last decade
> a system of racial domination ≠ one that recognized the rights and freedoms of all peoples regardless of the colour of their skin
> the white-skinned peoples of South Africa ≠ the dark-skinned peoples of their own land

Thousands of my people/all those African patriots/that long and noble line ≠ me
(produced) a deep and lasting wound ≠ another, unintended, effect
the absence of fear ≠ the triumph over it
The great heroes ≠ the ordinary men and women
love ≠ its opposite
my colleagues and I ≠ one of the guards
I ≠ my comrades
I ≠ my family
his family... his parents... his wife and children ≠ his people, his community, his
country
a civil and humane society ≠ a country like South Africa
my people ≠ my family
the millions of South Africans I would never know or meet ≠ the people I knew best
a small child ≠ her father
other children... a great many of them ≠ you

Typically, ideation specifies the grounds on which the opposition is formed:

white-skinned ≠ dark-skinned
depths ≠ height
great heroes ≠ ordinary men and women

and supports additional oppositions, beyond the realm of participant identification:

ended ≠ began
eyes wide open ≠ illusion

As with the *Inauguration Day* recount, **transformation** is foregrounded – both for
changes in the world outside (*patched up their differences, overturned, replaced,
recovering, resilience, transformation*), and for changes within ('learning' by
'seeing'):

It is from these comrades in the struggle that I have **learned** the meaning of courage.
Time and again, I have **seen** men and women risk and give their lives for an idea. I have
seen men stand up to attacks and torture without breaking, showing a strength and
resilience that defies the imagination. I **learned** that courage was not the absence of
fear, but the triumph over it.

I always **knew** that deep down in every human heart, there was mercy and generosity.
No one is born hating another person because of the colour of his skin, or his
background, or his religion. People must **learn** to hate, and if they can **learn** to hate,
they can be **taught** to love, for **love** comes more naturally to the human heart than its
opposite. Even in the grimmest times in prison, when my colleagues and I were pushed
to our limits, I would **see** a glimmer of humanity in one of the guards, perhaps just for
a second, but it was enough to reassure me and keep me going.

Evaluating contrasts

These notions of contrast and transformation are also important for evaluation. The macroTheme contrasts the impropriety of the apartheid regime with the propriety of its opposition:

> harshest, most inhumane ≠ recognized the rights and freedoms of all peoples regardless of the colour of their skin

The following 'African patriots' phase makes similar contrasting judgements:

> oppression and brutality = depths of oppression ≠ extraordinary courage, wisdom and generosity = heights of character

And Mandela takes pains to argue within the clause that impropriety in fact produced its opposite. Cause is realized nominally (*effect*) and verbally (*produced, requires*) as negative evaluations generate positive ones:

> But the decades of oppression and brutality had another, unintended, **effect**, and that was that it **produced** the Oliver Tambos, the Walter Sisulus, the Chief Luthulis, the Yusuf Dadoos, the Bram Fischers, the Robert Sobukwes of our time – men of such extraordinary courage, wisdom and generosity that their like may never be known again. Perhaps it **requires** such depths of oppression to acquire such heights of character.

In the 'meaning of courage' phase, what seems most important is the interplay of affect and judgement. Mandela is particularly concerned with the privileging of character and principle in relation to emotion. He deals first with the triumph of courage over fear, bridging from his extraordinary colleagues to the meaning of courage (from foregrounding them as Theme – *It is from these colleagues in the struggle...*):

> It is from these comrades in the struggle that I have learned the meaning of **courage**. Time and again, I have seen men and women risk and give their lives for an idea. I have seen men stand up to attacks and torture without breaking, showing a **strength** and **resilience** that defies the imagination.
> I learned that **courage** was not the absence of **fear**, but the triumph over **it**.
> I felt **fear** myself more times than I can remember, but I hid **it** behind a mask of **boldness**.
> The **brave** man is not he who does not feel **afraid**, but he who conquers that **fear**.

Here each clause elaborates Mandela's point that he and his colleagues did not always feel secure and confident; they did indeed feel afraid. But they learned to manage fear with courage – with strength of character in relation to their principles (technically speaking, to manage affect with judgement).

Similarly in the 'every human heart' phase, mercy, generosity, humanity and goodness triumph over hate:

> I always knew that deep down in every human heart, there was **mercy** and **generosity**.
>
> No one is born **hating** another person because of the colour of his skin, or his background, or his religion. People must learn to **hate**, and if they can learn to **hate**, they can be taught to **love**, for **love** comes more naturally to the human heart than **its opposite**. Even in the **grimmest** times in prison, when my colleagues and I were pushed to our limits, I would see a glimmer of **humanity** in one of the guards, perhaps just for a second, but it was enough to **reassure** me and keep me going.
>
> Man's **goodness** is a flame that can be hidden but never extinguished.

In this paragraph, judgement is foregrounded in the hyperTheme and hyperNew, and affect in the exemplification of Mandela's faith.

This is inspirational material, to be sure. The stuff heroes are made of. But Mandela had to pay a terrible personal price for his principles. The 'twin obligations' phase foregrounds **obligations, inclinations** and **abilities** several times in every clause.[1] But in <u>trying</u> to fulfil one obligation, Mandela was <u>prevented</u> from fulfilling another. The conflict is presented lexically in the hyperTheme, and its outcome in the hyperNew:

> In life, every man has **twin obligations – obligations to his family, to his parents, to his wife and children**; and he has an **obligation to his people, his community, his country**.
>
> In a civil and humane society, each man is **able** to fulfil those **obligations** according to his own **inclinations** and **abilities**. But in a country like South Africa, it was almost **impossible** for a man of my birth and colour to fulfil both of those **obligations**. In South Africa, a man of colour who <u>attempted to live</u> as a human being was punished and isolated. In South Africa, a man who <u>tried to fulfil</u> his **duty** to his people was inevitably ripped from his family and his home and was **forced** to live a life apart, a twilight existence of secrecy and rebellion.
>
> I did not in the beginning **choose** to place my people above my family, but in <u>attempting</u> to **serve my people**, I found that I was <u>prevented from fulfilling</u> my **obligations as a son, a brother, a father and a husband**.[2]

In this phase, obligation, contrast (*but*) and conation (*attempted, tried, attempting, prevented*) are all foregrounded, and interact to co-articulate Mandela's dilemma. The twin obligations are elaborated twice, with identification connecting the first instance to the second (*twin obligations – both of those obligations*). With respect to ideation, the twin obligations are unpacked three times; the third time round the point is not elaboration but Mandela's inability to serve both his people and his family:

twin obligations −
    obligations to his family, to his parents, to his wife and children;
    an obligation to his people, his community, his country.

both of those obligations −
    to live as a human being
    to fulfil his duty to his people

place my people above my family −
    to serve my people
    my obligations as a son, a brother, a father and a husband

In the first elaboration, listing is used to add parallel weight to both responsibilities (*family, parents, wife, children; people, community, country*); but third time round it's the personal failings that are repeated, weighing heavily as they do on Mandela's conscience, and male perspective converses of the initial listing are deployed (*son, brother, father, husband*).

Ultimately the report unfolds as if its point is to explain the meaning of courage but ends up as one that underlines its personal cost. The macroNew reviews the competing obligations once more, reiterating their cost:

> In that way, **my commitment to my people, to the millions of South Africans I would never know or meet**, was at the expense of **the people I knew best and loved most**. It was as simple and yet as incomprehensible as the moment a small child asks her father, 'Why can you not be with us?' And the father must utter the terrible words: 'There are other children like you, a great many of them...' and then one's voice trails off.

To generalize the story, as one that happened to many families, Mandela uses generic identification (*a small child – her father – the father*) and present tense. But we can't help imagining it has happened to him; and by the time he chooses the 'generalized reference' item *one* to identify the father's voice impersonally as his own, it is clear that generalization is being used as well to hide his pain. This is presented behind a mask of compassion for others, thereby inviting our compassion for him. Perhaps what ties the *Inauguration* recount to the *Courage* report is humility – not victory but resolution of difference, and not just courage but personal loss.

8.4 *The Meaning of Freedom*: from self to community

So we have a recount dealing with healing (the resolution of the struggle) and a report dealing with conflict (unresolved personal costs); what about the *Meaning of*

Freedom? In this autobiographical recount, Mandela orients the reader to its focus on freedom in the first sentence (*I was not born with a hunger to be free*); and the text then unfolds as a synopsis of his life, with each succeeding episode devoted to a different life stage (*I was born free...*, *as a young man...*, *I joined the African National Congress...*, *those long and lonely years...*, *When I walked out of prison...*). Through each of these five life stages, his conception of freedom expands, from *free in every way that I could know* as a child, to *freedom only for myself* as a young man, to *the greater hunger for the freedom of my people* as a freedom fighter, to *a hunger for the freedom of all people* as a prisoner, and finally to his mission to *liberate the oppressed and the oppressor both*, as a free man. The last two paragraphs then review these developments with respect to their significance for the future of his nation, *the true test of our devotion to freedom is just beginning*, and himself, *...with freedom come responsibilities, and I dare not linger, for my long walk is not yet ended*.

The rhetorical movement in this autobiographical recount is thus an inner growth of social consciousness, from oneself to the world as a whole, within an outer growth in social roles, from a small child to the leader of a nation. In a time-honoured tradition across cultures, Mandela uses the metaphor of a journey to map his inner growth onto his outer life – the extended journey metaphor outlined in section 8.3 above.

Negation and concession

How is this double movement achieved? A significant pattern is foregrounding and co-articulation of negation and concession. Almost half the clauses are negative, whereas the normal English pattern is about 1 in 10, and alongside negation is concessive conjunction:

> Later, as a young man in Johannesburg, I yearned for the basic and honourable freedoms of achieving my potential, of earning my keep, of marrying and having a family – the freedom **not** to be obstructed in a lawful life.

> **But** then I slowly saw that **not only** was I not free, **but** my brothers and sisters were **not** free.

> I saw that it was **not just** my freedom that was curtailed, **but** the freedom of everyone who looked like I did.

> I am **no more** virtuous or self-sacrificing than the next man, **but** I found that I could **not even** enjoy the poor and limited freedoms I was allowed when I knew my people were **not** free.

> Some say that has now been achieved. **But** I know that this is **not** the case.

> We have **not** taken the final step of our journey, **but** the first step on a longer and even more difficult road.

For to be free is **not merely** to cast off one's chains, **but** to live in a way that respects and enhances the freedom of others.

I have tried **not** to falter; I have made missteps along the way. **But** I have discovered the secret that after climbing a great hill, one only finds that there are many more hills to climb.

I have taken a moment here to rest, to steal a view of the glorious vista that surrounds me, to look back on the distance I have come. **But** I can only rest for a moment, for with freedom come responsibilities, and I dare **not** linger, for my long walk is **not yet** ended.

This is a lot of negation and counterexpectation for such a short phase of discourse. If we think for a moment about the meaning of these two engagement systems, negation and concession, we can see the complementarity of their prominence. Unlike positive, negative implicates its opposite;[3] something 'in the air' is being denied. Throughout his story, Mandela makes assumptions about what readers might believe and sets the record straight. At times this involves not just denying mistaken beliefs but replacing them with 'true' ones:

I was **not** born with a hunger to be free.
I was born free...

The truth is that we are **not** yet free;
we have merely achieved the freedom to be free, the right not to be oppressed.

Concession is not so much concerned with mistaken beliefs as with unrealistic expectations. Through concession Mandela makes assumptions about what readers might expect to follow as the text unfolds and steers them down an alternative path – he takes a moment to rest for example, and after all he has been through readers might reasonably expect a long vacation is in order, which is not the path he is about to follow:

I have taken a moment here to rest... **But** I can only rest for a moment,

At three points in the recount, negation and concession interact directly as Mandela aligns his readers:

Some say that has now been achieved.
But I know that this is **not** the case.

We have **not** taken the final step of our journey,
but the first step on a longer and even more difficult road.

For to be free is **not** merely to cast off one's chains,
but to live in a way that respects and enhances the freedom of others.

And to this interaction of negation and concession we can add another system for adjusting expectation – the use of continuatives to re-position readers who might have expected a little more or less than Mandela means:

> When I walked out of prison, that was my mission, to liberate the oppressed and the oppressor both. Some say that has now been achieved. But I know that this is not the case. The truth is that we are not **yet** free; we have **merely** achieved the freedom to be free, the right not to be oppressed. We have not taken the final step of our journey, but the first step on a longer and **even** more difficult road. For to be free is not **merely** to cast off one's chains, but to live in a way that respects and enhances the freedom of others. The true test of our devotion to freedom is **just** beginning.

What is being co-articulated here is Mandela's determination to guide readers – to take them along with him on his journey to enlightenment – not just by making his wisdom available but by predicting their assumptions and expectations and leading them home. He does this gently, without directly attributing mistaken assumptions and expectations to anyone – so projection is not used to source anything to anyone other than himself. But he works relentlessly, through a range of complementary resources, to get us firmly onside.

Abstraction

Alongside the inner and outer fields of the story, construed as a metaphorical journey, another development taking place is in mode; in one sense this is also a kind of journey that parallels that from childhood to maturity, that is from spoken to written ways of meaning. Mandela begins his story using relatively concrete language. Participants (people, places and things) are realized as nouns; qualities (descriptive and attitudinal) are realized as adjectives; processes (doings and happenings) are realized as verbs; assessments of modality are realized as modal verbs; and logical connections are realized as conjunctions. Some examples follow, illustrating the choices Mandela uses to construct his childhood, and symbolizing perhaps in their directness the untroubled nature of his life:

> **participant as noun**
> I, fields, hut, stream, village, mealies, stars, bulls, father. . .
> **quality as adjective**
> free, clear, broad
> **process as verb**
> was born, to run, to swim, to roast, rise, obeyed. . .
> **assessment as modal verb**[4]
> I **could** know
> **logical relation as conjunction**
> as long as

As the recount continues, however, the relation of meaning to wording becomes much more indirect. Alongside participants realized as nouns, we find processes, qualities and modal assessments realized as nouns as well (contrast the direct realizations in small caps alongside each example):

process-as-thing (noun)
this desire	cf. I DESIRED freedom
hatred	cf. They HATED the prisoner

quality-as-thing (noun)
a hunger to be free	cf. I was HUNGRY to be free
dignity	cf. They were DIGNIFIED
narrow-mindedness	cf. They were NARROW-MINDED
humanity	cf. They were HUMANE

assessment-as-thing (noun)
achieving my potential	cf. I achieved what I COULD
truth	cf. It CERTAINLY was
responsibilities	cf. I MUST act

And as part of this pattern of abstraction, causal relations (that might otherwise have been realized as connections between clauses) are realized inside the clause as nominalized Agents which act on other nominalizations and initiate events. Note the agentive role of *this desire for the freedom of my people...* in relation to *my life* and four pivotal transformations below:

logical relation as agency (inside the clause)
It was this desire for the freedom of my people to live their lives with dignity and self-respect
that **animated** my life,
that **transformed** a frightened young man into a bold one,
that **drove** a law-abiding attorney to become a criminal,
that **turned** a family-loving husband into a man without a home,
that **forced** a life-loving man to live like a monk.

Language of this kind is a long way from language in which people act and do things to other people and things. We've entered a world of abstraction, which typifies the writing of uncommon sense discourse across institutions and disciplines and which a trained lawyer and politician like Mandela has learned to control. The advantage of this language for Mandela is the range of meanings it makes available to him to interpret his life, meanings not available in the relatively straightforward language of his Orientation.

Ideationally, as we noted above, the text opens by construing freedom as a quality (grammatically an Attribute realized by an adjective) – the kind of realization we associate with spoken language in informal registers and with child language in our culture:

> *free* **as quality**
> I was not born with a hunger to be **free**.
> I was born **free** – **free** in every way...
> **free** to run...
> **free** to swim...
> **free** to roast mealies...

Subsequently, freedom is generally realized as an entity, and once nominalized it can take on a wide range of participant roles. We have already taken note of freedom as an Agent of change (*It was this desire for freedom...that transformed...*). In addition, in action processes it becomes a commodity that can be exchanged (i.e. given or taken away):

> *freedom* **as a commodity**
> when I discovered... that my **freedom** had already **been taken** from me,
> ...it was not just my **freedom** that was **curtailed**, but the freedom of...
> A man who **takes away** another man's **freedom** is a prisoner of hatred...
> if I am **taking away** someone else's **freedom**
> when my **freedom** is **taken** from me.

In mental processes it functions as an object of desire:

> *freedom* **as a desire**
> that I **began to hunger** for it (freedom).
> At first, as a student, I **wanted** freedom...
> Later, ..., I **yearned** for the basic and honourable freedoms of...
> ...that I **could not even enjoy** the poor and limited freedoms I was allowed

As an entity in processes of being it is subject to classification and transformation.

> *freedom* **as a class**
> It was only when I began to learn that my boyhood **freedom** was **an illusion,**
> **Freedom is indivisible**...
> ...that my hunger for **the freedom of my own people** became a hunger for **the freedom of all people**, white and black.
>
> *freedom* **as an identity**
> ...that is when the hunger for **my own freedom** became the greater hunger for **the freedom of my people**.

Once nominalized it can also function circumstantially, as an abstract destination, and even as an abstract companion along the way:

freedom **as a place**
I have walked that long road **to freedom**.

freedom **as an accompaniment**
But I can only rest for a moment, for **with freedom** come responsibilities. . .

So ideational metaphor puts virtually the entire ideation system of English at Mandela's disposal for talking about freedom. We'll return to the question of just how he marshals this potential across the text below. Note at this point that it is the circumstantial realization (*long road to freedom*) that establishes the extended lexical metaphor of a journey that consolidates Mandela's interpretation of his life:

freedom **as extended lexical metaphor**
When I walked out of prison. . . We have not taken the final step of our journey, but the first step on a longer and even more difficult road. . . I have walked **that long road to freedom**. I have tried not to falter; I have made missteps along the way. But I have discovered the secret that after climbing a great hill, one only finds that there are many more hills to climb. I have taken a moment here to rest, to steal a view of the glorious vista that surrounds me, to look back on the distance I have come. But I can only rest for a moment, for with freedom come responsibilities, and I dare not linger, for my long walk is not yet ended.

This journey metaphor is of course a familiar one in our culture; and Mandela elaborates it in his own terms towards and during the recount's culminative phase. The relevant taxonomic strings, based on class and co-class, are *journey, road, road, way; walked, taken the final step/the first step, tried not to falter, made missteps, climbing, climb, my long walk; to rest, rest, dare not linger*. These strings of meanings develop the semantic motif that provides the title of his book.

Enlightenment

Abstraction gives Mandela the language he needs to produce what we interpret as a double-barrelled recount in which two stories are mapped onto each other: the story of his day-to-day experience as he moves through space and time alongside the story of his political development as his understanding of freedom transforms. His journey, in other words, is more than a physical one; it is a metaphysical journey as well – a spiritual quest, towards enlightenment. How exactly does this unfold?

As the text is a recount, it moves through time. Temporal linearity is managed through linkers (*at first, later, then, when, when, during, when*) and tense (generally past – Orientation *I was not born. . .*, then past in present as the recount joins the present – Reorientation *I have walked...*). This is reinforced through the lexis that names stages in a cycle of life, e.g. *born, boyhood, young man, husband, family*, and the lexis that phases us through the steps along the way, both verbal (*when I <u>began</u> to learn, I <u>began</u> to hunger for it, <u>achieving</u> my potential, has now been <u>achieved</u>, <u>achieved</u> the freedom to be free, is just <u>beginning</u>, is not yet <u>ended</u>*) and nominal (*the <u>final</u> step of our journey, the <u>first</u> step on a longer and even more difficult road*).

But as noted above, this movement through time is reconstrued by Mandela as movement through space. And courtesy of ideational metaphor, the journey is not just a journey through physical space, but a walk to abstraction – to freedom. Through these steps, movement in space/time acquires the possibility of depth; the text develops from two-dimensional to three-dimensional progression.

To construe depth Mandela constructs his walk to freedom as a mental quest (a pattern we glanced at in the *Courage* report). Life is about learning:

> free in every way that I could **know**
> when I began to **learn** that my boyhood freedom was an **illusion**
> when I **discovered** as a young man that my freedom had already been taken from me
> But then I slowly **saw** that not only was I not free
> I **saw** that it was not just my freedom that was curtailed
> but I **found** that I could not even enjoy the poor and limited freedoms I was allowed
> when I **knew** my people were not free
> I **knew** as well as I knew anything that the oppressor must be liberated
> But I **know** that this is not the case
> But I have **discovered** the secret that after climbing a great hill
> one only **finds** that there are many more hills to climb

And life is about change (another parallel with the *Courage* report):

> the hunger for my own freedom **became** the greater hunger for the freedom of my people...
> It was this desire for the freedom of my people to live their lives with dignity and self-respect that animated my life, that **transformed** a frightened young man into a bold one, that drove a law-abiding attorney to **become** a criminal, that **turned** a family-loving husband into a man without a home, that forced a life-loving man to live like a monk.
> It was during those long and lonely years that my hunger for the freedom of my own people **became** a hunger for the freedom of all people, white and black.

What the learning and transformation achieve is a steadily unfolding conception of freedom, throughout the text from beginning to end. Ideationally speaking we can recognise 7 phases of understanding, corresponding to 7 stages of Mandela's life:

(1) 'boyhood freedom'
Free to run... free to swim... free to roast mealies under the stars and ride the broad backs of slow-moving bulls

(2) 'as a student'
the transitory freedoms of being able to stay out at night, read what I pleased and go where I chose

(3) 'as a young man'
the basic and honourable freedoms of achieving my potential, of earning my keep, of marrying and having a family – the freedom not to be obstructed in a lawful life

(4) 'joined the African National Congress'
the hunger for my own freedom became the greater hunger for the freedom of my people... to live their lives with dignity and self-respect

(5) 'during those long and lonely years' [in prison]
my hunger for the freedom of my own people became a hunger for the freedom of all people, white and black

(6) 'When I walked out of prison'
to be free is not merely to cast off one's chains, but to live in a way that respects and enhances the freedom of others

(7) [as President]
...But I can only rest for a moment, for with freedom come responsibilities, and I dare not linger, for my long walk is not yet ended.

In the first three phases Mandela is oriented to himself and family, as he moves through stages of life:

[stages of life...	freedom to]
childhood freedom	'to play'
adolescent freedom	'to be independent'
mature freedom	'to support a family'

In the next two phases Mandela re-orients himself to the needs of his people, and then to the needs of his entire community (including his oppressors). Individual freedom **to** do things transforms into communal freedom **from** oppression:

factional freedom	'for my people'
communal freedom	'for all people'

Finally Mandela develops his more abstract appreciation of freedom as freedom to respect and enhance the freedom of others, and to get on with things that freedom positions him as responsible **to** do:

democratic freedom	'to respect/enhance freedom of others'
institutional freedom	'with freedom come responsibilities'

Overall, Mandela's enlightenment is organized as three waves of recontextualiz-ation. The first wave includes three stages of his life (childhood, adolescence, maturity). Taken together these constitute the first stage of his shifting focus from himself (individual) to the needs of his people (factional) and then to his country as a whole (communal). Taken together these constitute the first stage of his move from personal liberty to the freedom to respect others' freedom (democracy) and finally freedom with responsibilities (democratic institutions). These three waves within waves are summarized as follows:

```
1 personal freedom
  I individual freedom
    i childhood freedom      'to play'
    ii adolescent freedom    'to be independent'
    iii mature freedom       'to support a family'
  II factional freedom       'for my people'
  III communal freedom       'for all people'
2 democratic freedom         'to respect/enhance freedom of others'
3 institutional freedom      'with freedom come responsibilities'
```

The texture of these phases, in terms of global information flow, is also significant. If we take Mandela's paragraphs, we find a consistent pattern with an introductory hyperTheme followed by its elaboration. The first hyperTheme introduces boyhood freedom, the second introduces adolescent and mature freedom, the third freedom for black Africans and the fourth communal freedom for both oppressor and oppressed:

> I was not born with a hunger to be free. I was born free – free in every way that I could know.
>
> . . .
>
> It was only when I began to learn that my boyhood freedom was an illusion, when I discovered as a young man that my freedom had already been taken from me, that I began to hunger for it.
>
> . . .
>
> But then I slowly saw that not only was I not free, but my brothers and sisters were not free.
>
> . . .
>
> It was during those long and lonely years that my hunger for the freedom of my own people became a hunger for the freedom of all people, white and black.
>
> . . .

With the move to abstract freedom in paragraph 5 however, the hyperTheme introduces the paragraph, but does not specify the new phase of understanding:

> When I walked out of prison, that was my mission, to liberate the oppressed and the oppressor both. Some say that has now been achieved. But I know that this is not the case.
>   . . .

That is saved for a later, penultimate sentence in the paragraph (a more newsworthy position):

> For to be free is not merely to cast off one's chains, but to live in a way that respects and enhances the freedom of others.

Similarly in the final paragraph of the recount, the hyperTheme introduces its elaborating clauses:

> I have walked that long road to freedom.
>   . . .

But the final phase of freedom, institutional freedom, is reserved for the concluding sentence of the book:

> for with freedom come responsibilities. . .

Globally then, Mandela's understanding of personal freedom as liberty (freedom to act and freedom from oppression) is treated as a kind of retrospective – his angle on his life, as given by the volume as a whole. But once we move to the implications for the present in the last two paragraphs, Mandela's ultimate conception of freedom (freedom to respect freedom, freedom with responsibilities) is positioned late in the paragraphs as News, prefaced in each case with the conclusive conjunction *for*, consummating our journey:

> . . . We have not taken the final step of our journey, but the first step on a longer and even more difficult road. **For** to be free is not merely to cast off one's chains, but to live in a way that respects and enhances the freedom of others. The true test of our devotion to freedom is just beginning.
>
> . . .I can only rest for a moment, **for** with freedom come responsibilities, and I dare not linger, **for** my long walk is not yet ended.

The newsworthiness of Mandela's ultimate conception of freedom is further enhanced by the final paragraph's summarizing of the recount, and of the recount itself as a synopsis of the autobiography as a whole. Thus final position in the clause, the phase, the genre (our text), the chapter and the book harmonizes to foreground the responsibility of respecting freedom as the culminative evaluation for this story of Mandela's life.

Engagement

We have already considered the foregrounding of negation and concession in this story, and commented on the way these resources are deployed to position readers. Alongside this pattern of reader alignment, we find a constellation of features which continually clarify and reinforce Mandela's position, lest there be any doubt about what is being asserted. This pattern works at the level of meaning, where propositions are reworded again and again to make their meaning clear. We symbolize these elaborations with an '=' sign below.

elaboration (of meaning):

I was born free
= free in every way that I could know.
= Free to run in the fields near my mother's hut, free to swim in the clear stream that ran through my village, free to roast mealies under the stars and ride the broad backs of slow-moving bulls.
= As long as I obeyed my father and abided by the customs of my tribe, I was not troubled by the laws of man or God.

It was only when I began to learn that my boyhood freedom was an illusion,
= when I discovered as a young man that my freedom had already been taken from me . . .

At first, as a student, I wanted freedom only for myself,
= the transitory freedoms of being able to stay out at night, read what I pleased and go where I chose.

Later, as a young man in Johannesburg, I yearned for the basic and honourable freedoms of achieving my potential, of earning my keep, of marrying and having a family
= the freedom not to be obstructed in a lawful life. . .

Freedom is indivisible;
= the chains on any one of my people were the chains on all of them,
= the chains on all of my people were the chains on me.

A man who takes away another man's freedom is a prisoner of hatred,
= he is locked behind the bars of prejudice and narrow-mindedness.
= I am not truly free if I am taking away someone else's freedom,
= just as surely as I am not free when my freedom is taken from me.
= The oppressed and the oppressor alike are robbed of their humanity.

. . . that was my mission,
= to liberate the oppressed and the oppressor both

The truth is that we are not yet free;
= we have merely achieved the freedom to be free,
= the right not to be oppressed.
= We have not taken the final step of our journey,
= but the first step on a longer and even more difficult road.

For to be free is not merely to cast off one's chains, but to live in a way that respects

and enhances the freedom of others.
= The true test of our devotion to freedom is just beginning.

And at the level of wording, these elaborations are reinforced by recurrent use of parallel grammatical structures in succeeding clauses ('grammatical parallelism'). We saw something of this pattern in the Courage report, but nothing like the frequency we see here and nothing like the same rhetorical impact:

parallelism (in wording):
I was not born with a hunger to be free.
I was born free – free in every way that I could know.
Free to run in the fields near my mother's hut,
free to swim in the clear stream that ran through my village,
free to roast mealies under the stars and ride the broad backs of slow-moving bulls.
It was only when I began to learn that my boyhood freedom was an illusion,
when I discovered as a young man that my freedom had already been taken from me,
the transitory freedoms of being able to stay out at night,
read what I pleased
and go where I chose.
the basic and honourable freedoms of achieving my potential,
of earning my keep,
of marrying and having a family
- the freedom not to be obstructed in a lawful life.
But then I slowly saw that not only was I not free,
but my brothers and sisters were not free.
I saw that it was not just my freedom that was curtailed,
but the freedom of everyone who looked like I did (was curtailed).
That is when I joined the African National Congress,
and that is when the hunger for my own freedom became the greater hunger for the freedom of my people.
It was this desire for the freedom of my people to live their lives with dignity and self-respect that animated my life,
that transformed a frightened young man into a bold one,
that drove a law-abiding attorney to become a criminal,
that turned a family-loving husband into a man without a home,
that forced a life-loving man to live like a monk.
the chains on any one of my people were the chains on all of them,
the chains on all of my people were the chains on me.

We would argue that both patterns, of realignment and reinforcement, reflect a rhetoric more strongly associated with spoken oratory than written exposition (Gee 1990, Olson 1994, Ong 1982). This is hardly surprising since Mandela was groomed, like his father before him, to counsel the rulers of his Thembu people. These skills he learned by observing tribal meetings in which all men were free to voice their opinions, but at which the opinions of councillors carried great weight:

I noticed how some speakers rambled and never seemed to get to the point. I grasped how others came to the matter at hand directly, and who made a set of arguments succinctly and cogently. I observed how some speakers used emotion and dramatic language, and tried to move the audience with such techniques, while others were sober and even, and shunned emotion. (Mandela 1995: 25).

Unfortunately we have no extant record of precisely what Mandela heard. But the influence of the public spoken discourse he studied is more than apparent, if we draw parallels to related orality around the world (Hymes 1995, Whitaker and Sienaert 1986). Consider, for example, the following speech given by Aboriginal elder, Vincent Lingiari, on the occasion of a handover of land to his people by the Australian Prime Minister:[5]

The important White men are giving us this land ceremonially, ceremonially they are giving it to us. It belonged to the Whites, but today it is in the hands of us Aboriginals all around here. Let us live happily together as mates, let us not make it hard for each other. The important White men have come here, and they are giving our country back to us now. They will give us cattle, they will give us horses, then we will be happy. They came from different places away, we do not know them, but they are glad for us. We want to live in a better way together, Aboriginals and White men, let us not fight over anything, let us be mates.

He (the Prime Minister) will give us cattle and horses ceremonially; we have not seen them yet; they will give us bores, axes, wire, all that sort of thing. These important White men have come here to our ceremonial ground and they are welcome, because they have not come for any other reasons, just for this (handover). We will be mates, White and Black, you (Gurindji) must keep this land safe for yourselves, it does not belong to any different 'welfare' man.

They took our country away from us, now they have brought it back ceremonially.

Space precludes a detailed analysis here; but the audience-oriented patterns of realignment and reinforcement are readily apparent, even in translation from the original Gurindji language. Note as well that the text unfolds in cycles (as presented above), returning 4 times to the point the Whites took away Gurindji land but are now giving it back – including a gracious message of reconciliation as far as living together as mates is concerned. Local realignment and reinforcement thus harmonizes with global text structure here, much as it does in Mandela's recount.

The major difference between the texts is that Mandela draws as well on the resources of written language (i.e. grammatical metaphor), to map orality (cycles) onto linearity (temporal unfolding) – a mapping which gives rise to a spiral texture through which our understanding of freedom deepens as we are carried along. Reasoning along these lines, we might suggest that Mandela has reworked the autobiographical recount genre, blending features of western literacy with aspects of Thembu orality – in order to fashion the new meanings that interpreting his life demands.

Before closing this section, it is perhaps worth noting that Mandela's rhetoric of engagement makes us feel included rather than instructed. He doesn't tell us what to think; rather, taking our misconceptions into account, he lets us in on what he's learned. In this respect his rhetoric reflects his understanding of leadership, which once again he learned as a child, in the court of the Thembu regent:

> As a leader, I have always followed the principles I first saw demonstrated by the regent at the Great Palace. I have always endeavoured to listen to what each and every person in a discussion had to say before venturing my own opinion. Oftentimes, my own opinion will simply represent a consensus of what I heard in the discussion. I always remember the regent's axiom: a leader, he said, is like a shepherd. He stays behind the flock, letting the most nimble go on ahead, whereupon the others follow, not realizing that all along they are being directed from behind. (Mandela 1995: 25–6)

8.5 Reprise

Having worked through our text from the perspective of genre and field, and then patterns of discourse (though not exhaustively by any means), we can return for a moment to a global perspective and ask how the *Inauguration Day* recount, *Cost of Courage* report and *Meaning of Freedom* recount are working together as a macro-genre comprising the final chapter of Mandela's autobiography.[6] If we take into account the story of Mandela's life that preceded it, then one clear function of the *Inauguration* recount is to bring things to a close – the inauguration ceremony is the end of things as far as this book is concerned. But the book does not end there; Mandela adds on a report and another recount to bring things to a close. What keeps him going?

As we have seen, Mandela is very concerned in Chapter 115 to evaluate his achievements, and to share his evaluations with readers. This disturbs the time line of the *Inauguration* recount, making room for Mandela to evaluate the present in relation to the past and compose a resolution to the struggle – his rainbow coalition transcending racial divisions. Not a victory, but a resolution.

Mandela then extends this with a report in recognition of the people of the struggle and the ways in which their strength of character and principles sustained them. He writes respectfully, in gratitude, but takes care to deflate adulation – since ordinary people also played a role, and in addition paid a price for the political commitment of family members. Not just great heroes, but great personal cost. Not just the triumph of judgement over affect, but loss.

Mandela then closes with a recount which evaluates the meaning of his life in relation to his changing conception of freedom. Whereas the *Inauguration* recount resolves his political struggles and the *Courage* report flags his personal conflict, this final recount deals with his spiritual quest – to appreciate what it was that he was struggling for. The spiral texture weaves together compelling engagement with a journey of enlightenment. To make us feel it's not just freedom from, but freedom to.

Overall, what ties the chapter together ideationally is a sense of evolution, rather than revolution. Although in one sense the struggle is over, in another sense there is work to do – learning the anthems, recovering from wounds, learning to govern. Freedom for. Interpersonally, what unifies the chapter is humility – it naturalizes our admiration for someone who is gracious in victory, combines admiration for courage with compassion for loss, and modestly assumes responsibilities. Not just achievement, but ongoing political and moral development. Not eulogy or invocation. A pledge. An invitation.

Notes

1   Halliday (1994) groups assessments of obligation, inclination and ability together as types of **modulation**, concerned with proposals for exchanging goods and services (i.e. the obligation, inclination or ability to provide goods or a service).

2   Modulation here is mainly realized as nouns and adjectives (objective forms); we have included *choose* because of its semantic affinity to inclination and *forced* because of the close relation of causation to obligation. But we've stopped short of conation (*prevented; attempted, tried, attempting*), which expands on this semantic drift.

3   This is perhaps more obvious in questions, where 'Aren't you coming?', for example, implies the speaker thought you were; 'Are you coming?' doesn't privilege a positive or a negative response.

4   Modal verbs are the auxiliary verbs in English that carry probability, usuality, inclination, obligation and ability, e.g. **must** be liberated, **could** know.

5   This handover was a lease of 1250 sq. miles, formerly part of Wave Hill Station, by the (then) Prime Minister, Gough Whitlam, and Minister of Aboriginal Affairs, Les Johnson, to the Mura Mulla Gurindji Co. on 16 August 1975 (Lingiari 1986). Translation from Gurindji language by Patrick McConvell.

6   For more on macro-genres see Martin (1995a, 2001).

Connections

In this chapter we explore connections between our approach to discourse semantics and the contexts of social life on the one hand, and of other avenues of discourse analysis on the other. We begin in section 9.1 by outlining the stratified model of social context we are working with, including three dimensions of register – field, tenor and mode, and relations between the contextual strata of register and genre. This is followed in section 9.2 by a discussion of the nature of linguistic data and how to handle it, addressing issues of inertia and change in semiotic systems.

We then make connections with complementary approaches to discourse analysis. In section 9.3 we present a theoretical model of relations between the field of critical discourse analysis (CDA) and our model of genre, register and discourse semantics. In section 9.4 we briefly outline an approach to analysing other social semiotic modes, or multimodal discourse analysis (MDA). In section 9.5 we discuss some connections with other linguistic paradigms that address the systems we explore here, concluding with some prospects for the field of discourse analysis.

As noted in our Introduction, we have had to make some decisions about what regions of the language system to focus on in this book. Language is an immensely complex phenomenon, no less than the contexts of social life that it realizes, and discourse analysis is a very large and growing field of practice, so our focus has been on providing the tools that analysts can use to start exploring these domains. To this end we have focused on systems at the level of discourse semantics rather than the levels of lexicogrammar or social context, although we have touched on these lower and higher level systems at certain points. In particular we have explored discourse semantic resources for enacting social relations through APPRAISAL and NEGOTIATION, for construing fields of experience through IDEATION and CONJUNCTION, and for presenting our enactments and construals as meaningful text-in-context through IDENTIFICATION and PERIODICITY. As far as discourse semantics is concerned, one set of textual resources we have not dealt with here is substitution and ellipsis – in part because we cannot enhance the accounts given in Halliday and Hasan's 1976 *Cohesion in English*, and in part because rehearsing them would involve a lot of additional grammatical description. Martin's 1992 *English Text* also contains discussions of cohesive harmony and modal responsibility that we have not developed here; and it also outlines a model of context, about which we'll now say something further.

9.1 Context: register and genre

Throughout this book the main theoretical construct we have used to get a handle on context is genre. And for the most part we spent time on just five of these – exemplum, exposition, act, recount and report. That's a very small window on culture, even if as linguists we try to model culture as a system of genres. But it's a start, and one that suits functional linguistics and has served it well in its negotiations with social theory over the past twenty years. (For an excellent overview of genre theory and practice, including work informed by SFL and other perspectives, see Hyland (2002). Martin and Rose (2006) shows in detail how the genre analysis introduced here can be developed in various directions.)

Register

Alongside genre, the main construct used by functional linguists to model context is known as register. In SFL, register analysis is organized by metafunction into field, tenor and mode. The dimension concerned with relationships between interactants is known as **tenor**; that concerned with their social activity is known as **field**; and that concerned with the role of language is known as **mode**. Halliday has characterized these three dimensions of a situation as follows:

Field refers to what is happening, to the nature of the social action that is taking place: what it is that the participants are engaged in, in which language figures as some essential component.

Tenor refers to who is taking part, to the nature of the participants, their statuses and roles: what kinds of role relationship obtain, including permanent and temporary relationships of one kind or another, both the types of speech roles they are taking on in the dialogue and the whole cluster of socially significant relationships in which they are involved.

Mode refers to what part language is playing, what it is that the participants are expecting language to do for them in the situation: the symbolic organisation of the text, the status that it has, and its function in the context. (Halliday and Hasan 1985: 12)

As language realizes its social contexts, so each dimension of a social context is realized by a particular metafunction of language, as follows:

METAFUNCTION	CONTEXT	
interpersonal	tenor	'kinds of role relationship'
ideational	field	'the social action that is taking place'
textual	mode	'what part language is playing'

Taken together the tenor, field and mode of a situation constitute the register of a text. As its register varies, so too do the kinds of meanings we find in a text. Because they vary systematically, we will refer to tenor, field and mode as **register variables**. This model of language in social context is illustrated in Figure 9.1. As far as genre is concerned we can think of field, tenor and mode as resources for generalizing across genres from the differentiated perspectives of ideational,

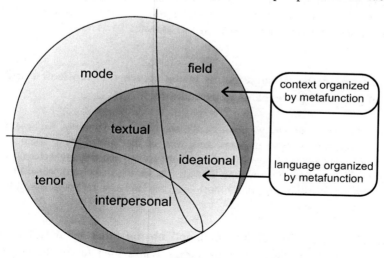

Figure 9.1 Metafunctions and register variables

interpersonal and textual meaning. In other words, taking tenor as an example, we need to take account of recurrent patterns of domination and deference as we move from one genre to another; we don't want to have to stop and describe the same thing over and over again each time. Similarly for mode, the move from more concrete to more abstract metaphorical discourse takes place in explanations, expositions, historical recounts and reports (as we have seen); register allows us to generalize these shifts in abstraction as a resource that can be deployed in many genres.

Mode

Let's explore each of these variables a little here, beginning with mode. One important variable in mode is the amount of work language is doing in relation to what is going on, that is to what degree it simply accompanies a field of activity or constructs its own field. And a complementary dimension of mode is the cline of monologue through dialogue, its orientation to interaction.

Let's start with the orientation to goings on. In Vincent Lingiari's speech (Lingiari 1986), for example, there are several exophoric references to people, places and things which are materially present at the hand-over ceremony: chains initiated by *the important white men* (Whites), *us* (Aboriginals), *this land, today* and arguably *here* (if not taken as anaphoric to *this land*). Texts of this kind can be characterized as context dependent, since we can't process the participant identification without information from the situation (things we see from being there or that we read through images later on):

> **The** important White men are giving **us this** land ceremonially, ceremonially they are giving it to us. It belonged to the Whites, but **today** it is in the hands of us Aboriginals all around **here**. Let us live happily together as mates, let us not make it hard for each other.

It's for this reason that at some points in the speech the translator clarifies the identity of presumed participants in parentheses:

> He (the Prime Minister) will give us cattle and horses ceremonially; we have not seen them yet; they will give us bores, axes, wire, all that sort of thing. These important White men have come here to our ceremonial ground and they are welcome, because they have not come for any other reasons, just for this (handover). We will be mates, White and Black, you (Gurindji) must keep this land safe for yourselves, it does not belong to any different 'welfare' man.

Mandela's construction of his childhood on the other hand is not context dependent in this way. Everything presumed is provided for in the co-text. We know what's going on simply by reading, not by being there:

I was born free – free in every way that I could know. Free to run in **the fields near my mother's hut,** free to swim in **the clear stream that ran through my village,** free to roast mealies under **the stars** and ride **the broad backs of slow-moving bulls.** As long as I obeyed **my father** and abided by **the customs of my tribe,** I was not troubled by **the laws of man or God.**

Beyond this we have texts which free themselves from situations by generalizing across them, as with Mandela's generalized exemplum about the experiences of an indefinite number of South African families:

It was as simple and yet as incomprehensible as the moment **a small child** asks her father, 'Why can you not be with us?' And **the father** must utter the terrible words: 'There are other children like you, a great many of them . . .' and then **one's voice** trails off.

Taking this a step further, the key resource which unties texts from situations is grammatical metaphor because of its power to reconstrue activities as things and thus break the iconic connections between linguistic and material activity.[1] This transforms social action into another realm of discourse in which abstractions enter into relations of various kinds with one another. Note for example how Mandela reconstrues aircraft roaring over the Union buildings as symbols (*a display* and *a demonstration*) of precision, force and loyalty; in doing so he reworks evaluation of the event through affect and appreciation (*in awe as a spectacular array ... in perfect formation ...*), into evaluation through judgement (capacity, tenacity and propriety: *pinpoint precision and military force, loyalty to democracy ... freely and fairly elected ...*). The transformation enables the evaluation he wants for this event of the day:

A few moments later we all lifted our eyes in awe as a spectacular array of South African jets, helicopters and troop carriers roared in perfect formation over the Union Buildings. It was not only a display of **pinpoint precision and military force,** but a demonstration of the military's **loyalty to democracy, to a new government that had been freely and fairly elected.**

Once this step into ideational metaphor is taken then the entire world of uncommon sense discourse is opened up including all of humanities, social science and science and their applications as bureaucracy and technology. The power of this discourse is not simply to generalize across experience, but to organize it and reflect on it at a high level of abstraction which can be instantiated in variable ways, sometimes with a view to enabling behaviours:

ACT – To provide for the **investigation** and the **establishment** of as complete a picture as possible of the **nature, causes** and **extent** of gross **violations** of human **rights**

> committed during the **period** from 1 March 1960 to the cut-off date contemplated in the **Constitution**, within or outside the **Republic**, emanating from the **conflicts** of the past, and the **fate** or **whereabouts** of the victims of such **violations**

– and sometimes to evaluate a myriad of acts:

> The **policy** of apartheid created a deep and lasting wound in my country and my people. All of us will spend many years, if not generations, recovering from that profound **hurt**. But the decades of **oppression** and **brutality** had another, unintended, **effect**, and that was that it produced the Oliver Tambos, the Walter Sisulus, the Chief Luthulis, the Yusuf Dadoos, the Bram Fischers, the Robert Sobukwes of our time – men of such extraordinary **courage**, **wisdom** and **generosity** that their like may never be known again. Perhaps it requires such **depths** of **oppression** to acquire such **heights** of **character**.

This range of mode variation is sometimes discussed as a cline from language in action to language as reflection. We've been able to illustrate the middle and reflective end of this continuum here, since our written genres ranged along this part of the scale. For texts in which language plays a smaller role in what is going on we'd need to look at spoken language accompanying activity, for example running commentary on a sporting event or parade, or pushing further, the things people manage to say when most of their directed consciousness is taken up with intense physical activity (playing sport, hard physical labour, rock climbing, dancing and so on). Here, for example, is an exchange in which a teacher directs a learner without naming any of the things or places he is acting on, so that the activity is not interpretable without being there (see Rose 2001a and b, 2006a for this exchange in the original Pitjantjatjara):

Learner:	Here?
Teacher:	– No, this is no good. It's over there. Dig on the far side.
Learner:	– Here?
Teacher:	– Yes, there.
Teacher:	– See there?
Learner:	– Aha!

The other dimension of mode analysis we need to consider here is the complementary monologue through dialogue cline. This scale is sensitive to the effects of various technologies of communication on the kind of interactivity that is facilitated in spoken vs written discourse, and across a range of electronic channels such as short wave radio, intercom, telephone, fax, e-mail, chat rooms, websites, radio, audio tape, CD/MD, television, DVD/VCD, video and film. The key material factors here have to do with whether interlocutors can hear and see one another (aural and visual feedback) and the imminence of a response (immediate or delayed).

Obviously our written data is not ideal for illustrating this cline here. But technologies facilitate textures; they don't absolutely determine them. And in any case a technology such as writing affords various degrees of interactivity along the continuum. There's the possibility of writing dialogue for one thing (scripts of various kinds) and projection can always be used to import dialogue, as it was in Mandela's exemplum for the imagined repartee:

| Child | 'Why can you not be with us?' |
| Father | – 'There are other children like you, a great many of them ...' |

Even where a response is not expected, as in prayers and various forms of public address, an interlocutor may be invoked as in Helena's quoted prayer for example:

| Helena | 'God, what's happening? What's wrong with him? Could he have changed so much? Is he going mad? I can't handle the man anymore! But, I can't get out. He's going to haunt me for the rest of my life if I leave him. Why, God?' |

And both Mandela and Lingiari exhort an audience in their speeches, without giving up the floor:

| Lingiari | Let **us** live happily together as mates, let **us** not make it hard for each other. |
| Mandela | Today, all of **us** do, by our presence here ... confer glory and hope to newborn liberty. Out of the experience of an extraordinary human disaster that lasted too long, must be born a society of which all humanity will be proud ... **We** thank all of our distinguished international guests ... **We** pledge ourselves to liberate all our people ... Never, never, and never again shall it be that this beautiful land will again experience the oppression of one by another ... Let freedom reign. God bless Africa! |

Written discourse can also imitate dialogue, for rhetorical effect, as when Tutu asks a question, then answers it himself; or when Mandela replaces a mistaken proposition with its contradiction:

So is amnesty being given at the cost of justice being done?
This is not a frivolous question, but a very serious issue, one which challenges the integrity of the entire Truth and Reconciliation process

Some say that has now been achieved.
But **I know that** this is not the case.

For something virtually monologic we probably need to turn to the Act, where propositions and proposals are enacted as performed. There is no right of reply:

> It is hereby notified that the President has assented to the following Act which is hereby published for general information ... **Be it therefore enacted** by the Parliament of the Republic of South Africa, as follows

It is tempting to move at this point from a consideration of turn taking resources to engagement, and consider the effect of mode on dialogism in something closer to the Bakhtinian sense of the term. We won't pursue this here (see Martin and White 2005 for discussion), preferring to treat engagement at this stage as a resource for construing tenor, solidarity in particular. But in doing so we don't wish to foreclose exploration of engagement in relation to mode.

So cutting across genres then, we have the question of the role language is playing, i.e. mode. And we can explore the effect of technologies of communication on texture with respect to two clines: degrees of abstraction (action/reflection) and degrees of interactivity (monologue/dialogue). This is an area that needs a lot more research, but there are hints of progress in Halliday and Martin (1993), Martin and Veel (1998), Martin (2001a) and Christie (2002).

Tenor

The key variables in tenor are power and solidarity, the vertical and horizontal dimensions of interpersonal relations. The power variable is used to generalize across genres as far as equalities and inequalities of status are concerned.

There are five main dimensions of inequality in post-colonial societies, by which we are all positioned, very early in life in the home: generation, gender, ethnicity, incapacity and class. By generation we refer to inequalities associated with maturation; gender covers sex and sexuality-based difference; ethnicity is concerned with racial, religious and other 'cultural' divisions; incapacity refers to disabilities of various kinds; class is based on the distribution of material resources and arguably the most fundamental dimension since it is the inequality on which our post-colonial economic order ultimately depends. We should stress that we understand all of these as social semiotic coding orientations, which are thus materialized through both physical embodiments and semantic styles. The ways in which they operate is of course culturally specific, and far beyond the scope of this book to consider further here. The main influence on our thinking in this area is the sociologist Bernstein, as has perhaps become apparent to readers familiar with his work. For some of our dialogue with him, see Christie (1999). All five dimensions condition access to the hierarchies we encounter outside the home in education, religion, recreation and the workplace and so for most texts we have to consider power carefully in relation to field.

Poynton (1985) outlines important realization principles for both power and solidarity. For power, she considers reciprocity of choice to be the critical variable. Thus social subjects of equal status construe equality by having access to and taking up the same kinds of choices, whereas subjects of unequal status take up choices of different kinds. Terms of address are the most obvious exemplar in this area. It is easy to imagine Helena addressing Tutu as Bishop Tutu and him addressing her as Helena, just as it is easy to imagine her calling her husband by his first name and him calling her Helena; but for Helena to address Tutu as Desmond would be a surprise. From this we can see that it is not just a question of reciprocity, but also of the different kinds of choices that might be available for interlocutors in dominant and deferential positions. An example from Chapter 7 above contrasts Llewelyn greeting Sannie, as his peer:

Llewelyn:	Hello.
Sannie:	– Hello.

with greeting Sannie's parents as his elders, who respond to him as a junior:

Llewelyn:	Mrs Grootboom. Mr Grootboom.
Magda:	– Llewelyn.

This is a huge research area; but one point we can make is that writing is not an option available to everyone in South African or Australian society since it depends on some form of institutionalized learning, and illiteracy is found in both societies. Beyond this, the modes of writing Tutu and Mandela control depend on a tertiary education and apprenticeship into one or more professions. And only a minority of South Africans or Australians can read discourse of this kind, let alone compose it as eloquently as we have witnessed here. So we have dealt mainly with discourses of power in our analyses. There are lesser voices too, of course. But Helena speaks courtesy of those more powerful than her (the SABC and Bishop Tutu) and Lingiari's Indigenous Australian voice has always been projected to the wider world through the transcriptions of non-Indigenous academic scribes and political activists. If you have read this far in our book then you are reciprocating in ways to which certainly Lingiari, and probably Helena did not have access – whether you actually ever get around to responding directly to David and Jim or not. And note that by first-naming ourselves we are attempting to construe a sliver of equality that might make responding possible.

The horizontal dimension of tenor, solidarity, is used to generalize across genres with respect to the alignment of social subjects into communities of all orders: networks of kith and kin, and collegial relations associated with more and less institutionalized activity (leisure and recreation, religion, citizenship and work).

There are degrees of integration into these communities related to the range and frequency of activities undertaken together and also to shared feelings about the value of what is going on. For example, a hardcore fan of Stevie Ray Vaughan will listen to more of his recordings more often and with more pleasure than 'softcore' SRV fans, and will have more books and memorabilia, will spend more time on his websites, may even have made a pilgrimage to his grave and so on. The rave reviews of his recordings and videos on Amazon's website suggest a finely tuned sense of membership which, quoting from his fans, we might scale from nucleus to periphery along the following lines:

a **hardcore Stevie fan**   nucleus
any SRV fan! or SRV lover
into the mainstream **blues guitar** scene
any fan of . . . **pure blues**
any blues fan's collection
If you're even a **part-time blues** fan
just plain music fan's collection
If you . . . just like **a good show**   periphery

For solidarity Poynton suggests the realization principles of 'proliferation' and 'contraction'. Proliferation refers to the idea that the closer you are to someone the more meanings you have available to exchange. One way of thinking about this is to imagine the process of getting to know someone and what you can talk about when you don't know them (the weather) and what you can talk about when you know them very well (almost anything). Or to return to the Stevie Ray Vaughan appreciation society, Amazon's in-house editors are mindful of outsiders and tend to refer to him with his full name in their reviews; fans on the other hand use this and several other names (*Stevie, Stevie Ray* and *SRV*) and Leigh (1993: 3) quotes Stevie's older brother Jimmie addressing him as *little bro*' and Stevie calling Jimmie *man*:[2]

> 'Way to go, **little bro**'!' Jimmie yelled, slapping him on the back. 'You hear that? Listen! They're going nuts! Stevie, I've never heard you play like that! You're great!'
> Maybe it was the first time he heard Jimmie say it, maybe it was the first time he believed it, but Stevie's eyes watered up and he hugged Jimmie tight, saying, 'Thanks, **man**. You know how much that means to me.'

Proliferation of attitude is especially powerful, since sharing feelings is such a critical resource for bonding. The intimate moment documented by Leigh is packed with appraisal, including verbal and non-verbal (back slapping, hugging, crying) realizations. Similarly the exempla Helena and Mandela share with us naturalize a personal relationship with readers; just as Lingiari's affect supports his invitation to be mates.

Contraction refers to the amount of work it takes to exchange meanings, and the idea that the better you know someone the less explicitness it takes. Poynton exemplifies this in part through naming, pointing out that knowing someone very well involves short names, knowing them less well longer ones. For outsiders, Stevie might be introduced as *Texas bluesman Stevie Ray Vaughan* for example, whereas for hardcore fans just his initials will do:

> Texas bluesman Stevie Ray Vaughan
> Stevie Ray Vaughan
> Stevie Ray
> Stevie
> SRV

Technically speaking, the less information a homophoric reference contains, the tighter the community it constructs and the more people it excludes. Acronyms in general are incisive membership signals in this respect, as are all of the resources noted in Martin 2000a under the heading of involvement (e.g. swearing, slang, anti-language, specialized and technical lexis).

Where cultural difference comes into play, contracted realization can be particularly excluding. We can take a moment to resolve the exophoric reference in Lingiari's speech:

> **The important White men** are giving **us this** land ceremonially, ceremonially they are giving it to us. It belonged to the Whites, but **today** it is in the hands of us Aboriginals all around **here**. Let us live happily together as mates, let us not make it hard for each other.

the important white men	Gough Whitlam, Len Johnson and others
us	Vincent Lingiari and Gurindji people
this land	Wave Hill Station (later Daguragu Station)
today	16 August 1975
here	Wattie Creek

But this simply introduces a pulse of homophoric reference that many (but not all) Australians and few others can resolve. Beyond this of course Lingiari assumes, quite rightly, that everyone present knows what the handover is all about. Australian songwriter Paul Kelly expands on this as follows, by way of introducing the song *From Little Things Big Things Grow* which he and Aboriginal musician Kev Carmody wrote about this landmark struggle:

> 'From Little Things Big Things Grow' is dedicated to Vincent Lingiari, the Gurindji stockmen and their families who walked off Lord Vestey's cattle station in 1966 thus initiating a land claim that lasted eight years. The Whitlam government handed back

much of the Gurindji country in 1974, Gough Whitlam himself pouring dirt into Vincent Lingiari's cupped hands in a ceremony symbolizing the legal restoration of their lands. From this simple action of walking off in 1966 many consequences flowed. (Paul Kelly and the Messengers 1991)

And Lingiari's editors, Hercus and Sutton, expand on this by way of prefacing his speech as follows:

This is the speech made by Vincent Lingiari (Plate 40), leader of the Gurindji people, on the occasion of the hand-over of a lease to 1250 sq. miles, formerly part of Wave Hill Station, by the (then) Prime Minister, Gough Whitlam, and the Minister of Aboriginal Affairs, Les Johnson, to the Mura mulla Gurindji Co. on 16 August 1975.

By 1977, the Gurindji were running over 5000 head of cattle on Daguragu Station, had put down several new bores and fenced new paddocks. Although they had won their long battle for their land, they still held only pastoral, not freehold lease, and were still engaged in helping other groups seeking land rights.

Vincent Lingiari, now a frail man in his seventies, remains the acknowledged and widely respected leader of some 500–600 Gurindji at Daguragu, Libanangu settlement, and the neighbouring stations. He was awarded membership of the Order of Australia in 1976.

Each step in this expansion process extends the community of readers that can follow what is going on. For insiders mere mention of Gough Whitlam pouring dirt into Vincent's hands, or a glance at its well-known image, is more than enough.

Field

This brings us to the final register variable, field, which is concerned with generalizing across genres according to the domestic or institutional activity that is going on. By definition a field is a set of activity sequences that are oriented to some global purpose within the institutions of family, local community or society as a whole. The activity sequences, the figures in each step of a sequence, and their taxonomies of participants create expectations for the unfolding field of a discourse. On this basis, when identifying fields we need to consider expectations about what is going on, for example, finishing a concert as opposed to starting a strike:

Shortly after the last note rang out at 11:20, the five exhilarated musicians left the stage through a rear exit, exchanging hugs and kind words. They posed for pictures together, signed autographs, compared calluses on their fingertips, and chided each other, saying 'Check this one out, man' and 'No, look at this. Mine's bigger than yours!' It was all punctuated with uproarious laughter. (Leigh 1993: 3)

On 23 August 1966 Vincent Lingiari, a Gurindji elder, led his people off the cattle station operated by the giant Vesteys pastoral organisation in protest against their wages and conditions. Their calls for Commonwealth involvement also strongly argued the case for land to establish their own cattle station. They subsequently sent a petition to the Governor-General, with no immediate result. Their stand against injustice, however, attracted national publicity for Aboriginal land rights grievances. The strike developed into a seven-year campaign by the Gurindji for the return of their traditional lands and became a *cause célèbre* across Australia. The campaign was strongly supported by the trade union movement and sparked a campaign for human rights, including land rights, by many Aboriginal people. It was a cry for Commonwealth leadership that would not be acted upon until the election of the Whitlam government. (Tickner 2001: 8)

Distinctive sequences implicate distinctive events, linked by expectations derived from participation in a field:

> They posed for pictures together
> signed autographs
> compared callouses on their fingertips
>
> Vincent Lingiari, a Gurindji elder, led his people off the cattle station
> They subsequently sent a petition to the Governor-General

And events implicate distinct participants, arranged in relation to one another according to the classifications and compositions of a given field, for example, blues guitarists and their songs ...

> **blues guitarists**
> Eric Clapton, Robert Cray, Buddy Guy, Stevie Ray Vaughan, Jimmie Vaughan
>
> **SRV set list (partial)**
> Texas Flood, Pride and Joy, Riviera Paradise, Crossfire, Couldn't Stand the Weather, Goin' Down, Voodoo Chile, Sweet Home Chicago

... vs prospective mates bearing gifts:

> **mates**
> the prime minister Gough Whitlam/Vincent Lingiari
> important White men/us Aboriginals
> White men, White/Aboriginals, Black
>
> **gifts**
> land, country; cattle, horses, bores, axes, wire

By working along these parameters of activities and participants, and their realization across the range of relevant genres, we can explore different domains of life, particularly the differences between everyday, technical and institutional domains, and the kinds of apprenticeship required for participation in them. This is critical to understanding cultural difference in relation to communication. What, for example, did Lingiari understand by 'giving land back ceremonially' compared with non-Indigenous Australians, and within the latter community, just who is it that appreciates the legal niceties of land ownership (the difference between a pastoral lease and inalienable freehold title for example):

> ... **giving us this land ceremonially**, ceremonially they are giving it to us, it is in the hands of us Aboriginals all around here, giving our country back to us. These important White men have come here to our ceremonial ground ... for this (handover), it [the land] does not belong to any different 'welfare' man, brought it [the land] back ceremonially. (Lingiari 1986)
>
> the **legal restoration** of their lands (Paul Kelly and the Messengers 1991)
>
> Although they had won their long battle for their land, they still held only **pastoral, not freehold lease** ... (Hercus and Sutton 1986)[3]

Misunderstandings in this arena have been ruthlessly exploited in Australia by right-wing populist politicians in relation to land rights issues and provide a useful forum for exploring common and uncommon sense readings of land ownership and custodial care (Gratton 2000).

For immediately relevant work and related references on everyday language, technicality and abstraction, on technology and bureaucracy, and on the discourses of humanities, social science and science see Halliday and Martin (1993), Hasan and Williams (1996), Christie and Martin (1997), Martin and Veel (1998), Christie (1999), Unsworth (2000), Hyland (2000), Martin and Wodak (2003); Christie and Martin (2007) explores fields in relation to work on the sociology of knowledge by Bernstein and his collaborators.

Genre and register

Register analysis then gives us another way of thinking about context, alongside genre. The main difference is that register analysis is metafunctionally organized into field, tenor and mode perspectives whereas genre analysis is not. For us the relationship between the register and genre perspectives is treated as an inter-stratal one, with register realizing genre (as in Figure 9.2). The relationship between register and genre in other words is treated as similar to that between language and context, and among levels of language (as outlined in Chapter 1). Following Lemke (1995), the relationship between levels in diagrams of this kind can be thought of as 'metaredundancy', the idea of patterns at one level redounding with patterns at the next level. Thus genre is a pattern of register patterns, just as register variables are a pattern of linguistic ones. Note however that the relation between levels is realizational, not a hierarchy of control; genre does not determine

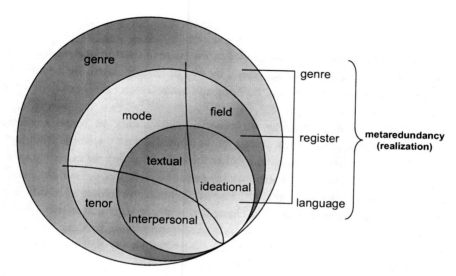

Figure 9.2 Genre, register and language

register variables, any more than register determines linguistic choices. Rather a genre is construed, enacted, presented as a dynamic configuration of field, tenor and mode; which are in turn construed, enacted, presented as unfolding discourse semantic patterns. Relations among genre, register, discourse and grammar are to some extent predictable for members of a culture, but at the same time they are independently variable; these complementary characteristics give language and culture the capacity for both stability and change.

Another perspective on the relationship between register and generic structure is proposed by Hasan and her colleagues, who model it on the 'axial' relationship between system and structure. In this model, obligatory elements of genre structure appear to be determined by field, and the presence of optional ones by tenor and mode. The question of relationships among genres is thus a question of the field, tenor and mode selections that genres do and do not share. This contrasts with the model developed by Martin (1992), where choices among genres form a system above and beyond field, tenor and mode networks at the level of register. Because field, tenor and mode remain relatively underspecified theoretical constructs in SFL, it is difficult to evaluate the relative strengths and weaknesses of these modelling strategies (inter-stratal vs axial realization) at this stage. Martin's model has certainly been influenced by our work in educational linguistics where mapping relationships among genres across disciplines has been a central concern (Martin 2001a, 2002a, b; Martin and Plum 1997). For further discussion see Mattheissen (1993), Martin (1999c, 2001d), Hasan (1995, 1999), Martin and Rose (2005, 2007).

9.2 Data

By way of opening this chapter we looked at the issue of what to analyse from the perspectives of genre and ideology. Here, by way of closing down, we'll return to the problem with reference to what Halliday and Matthiessen (1999) refer to as the 'cline of instantiation'.

Instantiation involves the way we observe metastability in social semiotic systems as apparent flux or as inertia or as something in between. Halliday's analogy here is weather and climate; weather the capricious flux we experience day to day, climate the comforting inertia we try to use to plan. But as Halliday points out, weather and climate are actually the same phenomenon looked at in different ways. And we can argue that weather changes climate, in ways that matter (global warming) and ways that don't (like today's temperature being two degrees above average) or that climate determines weather (like when we say it always rains in a rival city because the climate is terrible there).

Halliday's point is that text interacts with system as weather interacts with climate. His cline of instantiation includes system (the generalized meaning potential of a language), register (sub-potentials of meaning characterized as registers and genres), text type[4] (generalized instances, a set of texts that actualize the potential of the system), and finally text (the meanings actually afforded by an instance). And we could add at the end of the cline reading (the meaning taken from a text according to the subjectivity of the reader):

system	(generalized meaning potential)
register	(semantic sub-potential)
text type	(generalized actual)
text	(affording instance)
reading	(subjectified meaning)

We've added reading to the cline to take into account the fact that texts invariably afford a range of interpretations, which we can generalize provisionally under the three headings of 'tactical', 'resistant' and 'compliant' (pace de Certeau 1984). Compliant readings take up the reading position which is naturalized by the overall trajectory of meanings in a text. We've worked very hard in this book to show how the co-articulation of meanings in a text naturalizes a reading position: how Tutu works hard at getting us to agree with him, Helena works to get our sympathy for her man, and Mandela strives to guide us on side. Resistant readings work against the grain of this naturalization process; we might want to argue that amnesty was a bad idea, for example, or that freedom with responsibilities is not really freedom at all. Resistant reading positions are generally associated on a culture-specific basis with non-mainstream readings. (In the west, these may include readings that don't enact the discursive power of white, Anglo, middle class, mature, capable, social subjects.) Tactical readings are readings that take up some aspect of the meaning a text affords, and rework it obliquely in the direction of specific interests. For example, if we as linguists had taken Helena's story out of context and analysed it simply as an exemplar of one or another linguistic system, then we would have been responding to both Tutu and Helena tactically; we would be neither complying with nor resisting their discourse but simply using it to further our own professional interests.

A more typical example of a tactical response would be the way in which fans use the Amazon.com website for their own purposes to construct community. In order to exemplify appreciation in Chapter 2 we used one of the in-house editorial reviews provided by Amazon for Stevie Ray Vaughan's record *Texas Flood*. But following their 'Editorial Reviews' Amazon makes space for 'Customer Reviews of the Day', a continually updated flow-through corpus of responses from fans who take advantage of the site to rave on about their favourite star. Here's a couple of these rave reviews:

> Stevie Ray Vaughan – Texas Flood, March 18, 2000
> If you can't appreciate the music on this cd, then you aren't a fan of true, god-blessed American music. Stevie Ray Vaughan absolutely RIPS on this cd! When you listen to it, you'll notice two of the songs sound exactly alike, referring to 'Pride and Joy' and 'Tell Me.' When Stevie's wife first heard 'Pride and Joy', she became jealous thinking he had written it for another woman. So, the poor guy went and rewrote it with different lyrics. (A little trivia for ya . . .) Anyway, this cd is a must! The title cut is the blues anthem of the eighties AND nineties.

> How do you spell 'blues'?, February 18, 2000
> S-T-E-V-I-E R-A-Y, that's how. I gotta tell you, I never knew I was a blues fan til I found this guy. This CD showcases the master 'in the beginning', and I defy you to listen to him and tell me you don't feel the same. He's got everything from the 'suitable for car-dancing' Love Struck Baby and Tell Me, to the gut-wrenching, this-is-what-blues-are-all-about title cut Texas Flood, to the full-steam-ahead Rude Mood that, by god, makes MY fingers bleed! And, of course, the inimitable Pride and Joy, Stevie's signature song. Gotta love it.

Obviously Amazon is trying to sell CDs. There is a clear logic of consumption operating here: 'if a fan (or even if not), you will like it, so buy it'. At the same time, the fans pursue another interest, namely that of expanding their community. Alongside the logic of consumption there's a rhetoric of belonging: 'if you buy it, you will like it, and so become a fan'. As Jay Lemke has pointed out to Jim, this is an exemplary tactical response to the global power of a post-Fordist 'e-tail corporation'.

Introducing readings as a final step in the instantiation cline of course begs the question of how we determine what those readings are. And there is no doubt in our mind that we need to explore compliant, resistant and tactical responses on the basis of how those readings are materialized in texts, whatever the modalities involved. And this means looking at the readings the texts themselves afford, shunting back and forth between 'texts' and 'readings', until we feel we've said enough about the negotiation of meanings among them, as diverse social subjectivities engage. This produces in effect a kind of recursive loop at the end of the instantiation cline; but that is just what we want here: readings feeding back into texts, texts feeding back into text types, text types into registers and so on.

What this all means is that we have to be very clear how we position ourselves on the instantiation cline when collecting data and analysing it. In contrast to some views on analysing discourse, we do believe it is important to analyse instances in individual texts. What is unique about a specific text may be just what matters; we don't want to lose what's special by only valuing generalizations across a text corpus. Beyond this, as discourse analysts generalize, the tendency at this stage of our work is to lose sight of how texture is construed as a text unfolds, through its particular logogenetic contingencies. We can tend to lose sight in other words of the very kinds of analysis we've been promoting in this book. So the text and reading end of the instantiation cline is an important one, however reluctant journal editors may be about publishing analyses of a single text, as if they believe climate is all that matters and weather doesn't count.

That being said, of course we want to know things about text types, registers and systems as well. As far as discourse semantics is concerned the main problem here is technological. It takes a long time to analyse texts by hand even where we have some idea of what to look for, i.e. which systems are foregrounded and are co-articulating what matters to us. This limits the number of texts we can generalize across. One tool that could potentially save us time is automated analysis. Unfortunately, automatic parsing at present remains pretty much limited to the analysis of grammatical forms; but what we want are the meanings, and meanings beyond the clause for that matter. Automatic analysis of discourse is still a good deal of time and money away. In the short term we'll have to make do with interactive workbenches involving a mix of automatic, semi-automatic and manual analysis. And this will slow us down. The main thing we'd like to argue for here is not to mistake a lot of clause analysis for discourse analysis. It doesn't matter how many clauses we analyse, it's only once we analyse meaning beyond the clause that we'll be analysing discourse. And we need to analyse discourse right along the instantiation cline if we want to make sense of the semiotic weather we experience in the ecosocial climate of our times.

To make all this a little more concrete, at the level of instance we've read the mix of spoken and written discourse in Mandela's *Meaning of Freedom* recount as a novel pattern, a kind of fusion of written discourse like Tutu's exposition, with spoken discourse like Lingiari's hand-over speech. This fusion was designed especially by Mandela in his autobiography to drive his message home. At the level of text type we'd be looking for this kind of pattern to recur across a set of recounts (or other genres) and it might be worth exploring spoken texts as well as written ones, especially those written to be spoken aloud on public occasions. At the level of register, after a lot more analysis of a lot more discourse, we might be tempted to propose a new mode, blending features we've traditionally associated with either spoken and written text (cf. Halliday 1985). This may be something that's been evolving all along in the rhetoric of certain kinds of religious and political discourse. Eventually, along this imaginary evolutionary journey, we might discover that the system itself had changed, that the systemic probabilities associated with negation, concession and elaboration for example just weren't the same anymore. We'd be living in a different world, where speaking and writing weren't just complementary fashions of meaning, where there was something in the seam, engendered through expanding electronic modalities of communication perhaps. Who knows? Our point here is only to illustrate a range of vantage points on data, the way in which instances can impact on systemic change and the monumental cost of doing as much discourse analysis as we'd like.

Focusing on a single text, or just a few, is sometimes referred to as 'qualitative' analysis and contrasted with 'quantitative' research where counting and statistical analysis come into play. We've relied on a great deal of qualitative analysis in our own applied work, since we've never had the money, technology and time to actively pursue quantitative discourse analysis. The success of this work depends on the quality of the exemplars chosen for analysis: typical scientific procedures, typical historical recounts, typical book reviews and so on. This in turn depends on good ethnography, drawing on the expertise of core members of a given field and whatever insider knowledge outsiders can acquire. Such transdisciplinary work is ideal for exchanging the relevant expertise, as in our language education work where educational linguists took charge of collecting relevant data and trialing their analyses in teaching materials and practice. In our experience trying to intervene in social issues is a good way of 'testing' the quality of qualitative analysis, since the better the theory the more progress can be made. In the short term, one of the ways we'd like to see the ideas in this book used is in the kind of dialectic of theory and practice we're referring to here. For more quantitative work to bear fruit in social practice we may have to wait some time.

9.3 Critical Discourse Analysis (CDA)

Critical discourse analysis (hereafter CDA) has always had close links with SFL, reaching back to its foundation in the work of Fowler et al. (e.g. 1979) on critical linguistics at East Anglia in the 1970s. Halliday's conception of linguistics as an ideologically committed form of social action has been one important factor in this dialogue; and SFL's relatively rich semantic orientation to text in context across languages and modalities has meant that CDA has regularly visited the theory in search of tools for analysis where close systematic readings of texts are required. Martin (2000b) reviews various connections from the perspective of SFL; and Chouliariki and Fairclough (1999) look back from CDA; Young and Harrison (2004) bring together work across the two traditions.

Where CDA has tended to focus on semiosis in the service of power, and even to define its concern with language and ideology in such terms (e.g. Fairclough 1995), SFL has tended to take a wider view which takes ideology as permeating linguistic and other semiotic systems (as we suggested in Chapter 1). On the one hand this is suggesting that every choice for meaning is ideologically motivated; on the other it focuses attention on the distribution of meaning in a culture. Which meanings are shared across the community and which are not, how is access to meaning distributed, and what kinds of principles are there for distributing access? In our discussion of tenor above we considered the principle of social status in relation to generation, gender, ethnicity, incapacity and class, and this is critical to making generalizations about reciprocity of choice across genres. But beyond this, generation, gender, ethnicity, incapacity and class are major parameters along which all meaning is distributed and every social subject is positioned. In Bernstein's terms these parameters predispose our generalized orientations to meaning, or 'coding orientations', which distinguish one social subjectivity from another. This makes every text an interested one (acting on someone's interests); from this perspective there is no meaning outside of power.

In SFL the major work on coding orientation and subjectivity has been undertaken by Hasan and her colleagues at Macquarie University, many aspects of which are introduced in Christie (1999). This research is informed from the perspective of social theory by Bernstein's sociology, and has focused on class and gender in relation to the transition from home to school. Another pulse of ideologically oriented work in SFL has been in the field of language education, where Jim, David and many colleagues have attempted to design literacy programmes which redistribute access to written discourse across social classes and ethnicities. The initial research strategy used in this work has been to identify and deconstruct the genres of power for a particular field. The pedagogic approach used is to deconstruct these genres together with learners, so that their organization can be brought to consciousness and shared. This provides access to privileged genres for all social subjects, without assuming that such genres can be accessed 'subconsciously' through semiotic osmosis. This pedagogy is based on SFL research into language development in the home (Painter 1984, 1998), and features carefully designed scaffolding that moves subjects along a spiral curriculum, from their everyday experience to the technical realms of 'uncommon sense'. Following Bernstein (1996), applied work of this kind needs to deal with what he calls 'realization and recognition rules'. Realization rules are concerned with how to produce a genre and recognition rules with how and when to use it. For introductions to these initiatives see Cope and Kalantzis (1993), Halliday and Martin (1993), Hasan and Williams (1996), Christie and Martin (1997), Martin and Veel (1998), Christie (1999), Martin (2000c, Whittaker et al. (2006)); Johns (2001) and Hyland (2001) relate this work to comparable projects around the world.

Research which concentrates on describing coding orientations is of course complementary to action research projects which aim to redistribute access to meaning. You can't redistribute what you don't understand, and intervention is what motivates a research interest in language and ideology in the first place. Where CDA has tended to concentrate on the analysis of discourse which sustains inequalities, SFL is equally concerned with redressing inequality.[5] And we think this means looking at the texts through which people make the world a better place alongside those which naturalize power relations we don't accept. It's partly for this reason that we were drawn to the writing of leaders such as Tutu and Mandela who enact reconciliation – who make peace not war. One way of putting this would be to argue that we need to balance critique with Positive Discourse Analysis (or 'PDA'), so that our interventions have good news to learn from as well as bad news to overthrow (Martin 2002, 2003, 2004a, b, 2006; Martin and Stenglin 2006).

Pushing this a step further, we are suggesting that the main focus of CDA work has been on hegemony, on exposing power as it naturalizes itself in discourse, and thus feeling in some sense part of the struggle against it. (We might characterize this as a trajectory of analysis flowing through Marx, Gramsci and Althusser.) Janks and Ivanic's (1992) salutary work on emancipatory discourse strikes us as the exceptional in its orientation to texts that make the world a better place, confirming this trend. We are arguing that we need a complementary focus on community, taking into account how people get together and make room for themselves in the world in ways that redistribute power without necessarily struggling against it. (Gore's (1993) discussion of Foucault in relation to notions of empowerment in critical and feminist pedagogy are relevant here, especially in relation to the de-demonization of power.) Figure 9.3 outlines the complementary research foci on hegemony and community we have in mind, which could facilitate work on deconstructive **alongside** productive activity.

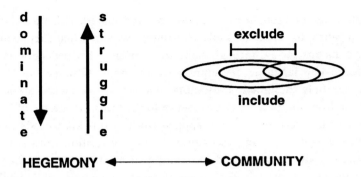

HEGEMONY ◄————————► **COMMUNITY**

Figure 9.3 Research foci on hegemony and community

We'll leave a detailed ideological analysis of the texts we've been considering to people better positioned than we are to take up the challenge. There are just too many South African intertexts we don't share for us to pronounce on what exactly is going on, especially in such a volatile site of political change. Martin (1985) suggests a model for exploring political change involving two dimensions: left/ right and protagonist/antagonist. On the left are people with power to gain, and on the right are people with power to lose. Protagonists are people attempting to resolve issues, while antagonists are people attempting to create issues. On the basis of these oppositions we can establish a power profile for players and their texts around various issues, as outlined in Figure 9.4.

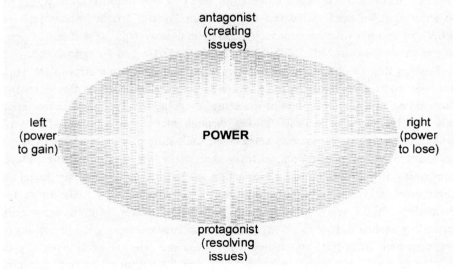

Figure 9.4 Profiling social change

To fill in this profile around an issue such as the struggle against apartheid we need to position players such as the broadly-based ANC, the Bantu-based Inkatha Freedom Party, the Afrikaner-based National Party in government, the Liberal Party opposition, and others, and take into account different phases of the struggle as we do so. From our perspective as outsiders it appeared that the ANC functioned as left antagonists (to gain power they needed to create issues) until the time of Mandela's rehabilitation as someone the National Party would negotiate with. The ANC then assumed the role of left *protagonist* (to gain power they worked with the leadership of the National Party towards a peaceful resolution of the struggle). During these negotiations, the Inkatha Freedom Party appeared to assume the role of right antagonist, stirring up trouble because of their fears about the power they would lose under an elected ANC regime. The ensuing violence helped the National Party government to pretend neutrality in an apparently black-on-black conflict. These changes and relations are summed up in Figure 9.5.

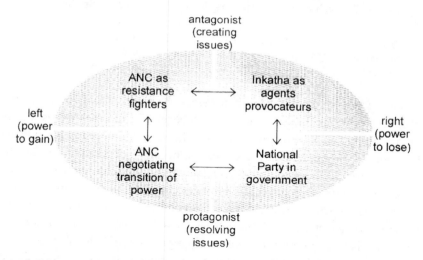

Figure 9.5 Players and power in the struggle against apartheid

This kind of framework encourages us to look at both peacemakers and warriors, the genres they take up and the interested ways they might rework them to promote their position in the struggle. It also allows for change, as interests and power relations shift. And it foregrounds the question of dialogism (in Bakhtin's sense (1981)): the multiplicity of voices resonating through a text (as we discussed in relation to Tutu's interrogators and his arguments, and Mandela's intense engagement with his readership). But as we apologized above, there are better analysts than us to flesh out these concerns.

The play of genres and their recontextualizations around issues draws attention to the crucial role of change in ideological analysis. For the distribution of power in a culture is never more than metastable; in order for power relations to remain stable over time, they must continually adapt to change: there has to be both inertia and change for life to carry on. Halliday and Matthiessen (Halliday 1992, 1993; Halliday and Matthiessen 1999) have developed a comprehensive outline of social semiotic change which is highly relevant here. For relatively short time frames such as that involved in the unfolding of a text, they suggest the term 'logogenesis' (the perspective we've been foregrounding in this book); for the longer time frame of the development of language in the individual, they use the term 'ontogenesis' (Painter 1984, 1998); and for maximum time depth, 'phylogenesis' (as in Halliday's reading of the history of scientific English in Halliday and Martin (1993)). A good example is Mandela's *Meaning of Freedom* recount, which unfolds in a spiral texture that maps out his development as a political leader (ontogenesis) in the context of major cultural shifts in post-colonial history (phylogenesis). This trinocular framework is summarized as follows.

logogenesis	'instantiation of the text'[6]	**unfolding**
ontogenesis	'development of the individual'	**growth**
phylogenesis	'expansion of the culture'	**evolution**

In a model of this kind, phylogenesis provides the environment for ontogenesis which in turn provides the environment for logogenesis. In other words, where a culture has arrived in its evolution provides the social context for the linguistic development of the individual, and the point an individual is at in their development provides resources for the instantiation of unfolding texts, illustrated in Figure 9.6. Conversely, logogenesis provides the material (i.e. semiotic goods) for ontogenesis, which in turn provides the material for phylogenesis; in other words, texts provide the means through which individuals interact to learn the system. And it is through the heteroglossic aggregation of individual systems (that are always already social systems), through the changing voices of us all, that the semiotic trajectory of a culture evolves. Language change in this model is read in terms of an expanding meaning potential, a key feature of semiotic systems as they adapt to new discursive and material environments.

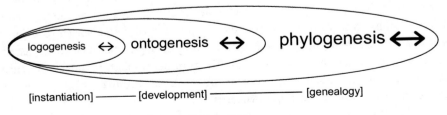

Figure 9.6 Time frames and semogenesis

Read from the perspective of critical theory, phylogenesis might be glossed in terms of a concern with the evolution of discourse formations (as explored in Fairclough (1995)), ontogenesis with the development of social subjectivities (e.g. Walkerdine and Lucey (1989)) and logogenesis with the de/naturalization of reading positions (e.g. Cranny-Francis (1996)). Glossing with respect to Bernstein (1996), phylogenesis is concerned with changes in a culture's reservoir of meanings, ontogenesis with the development of individual repertoires (i.e. coding orientations); logogenesis is concerned with what in SFL is referred to as the instantiation of system in text (or 'process' for a more dynamic perspective). These perspectives are illustrated in Figure 9.7.

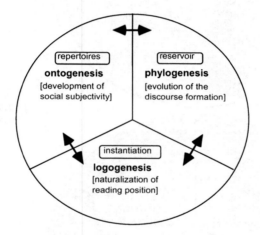

Figure 9.7 Semogenesis in relation to critical theory

In Chapters 2 and 3 we described how processes of saying and sensing can project locutions (what is said) or ideas (what is sensed), and also attribute the source of saying or sensing, as well as locating it in time. So if we say *Bakhtin argued that creativity depends on mastery of the genre*, then the projecting clause *Bakhtin argued*:

- projects the locution *that creativity depends on mastery of the genre*, through the process *argue*
- places the saying in the past (*argued*) with respect to *if we say*
- sources the locution to Bakhtin.

The projecting clause in other words provides a frame for interpreting its projection. By analogy, we can argue that genesis projects language, register and genre by conditioning the semantic oppositions that hold sway at one or another

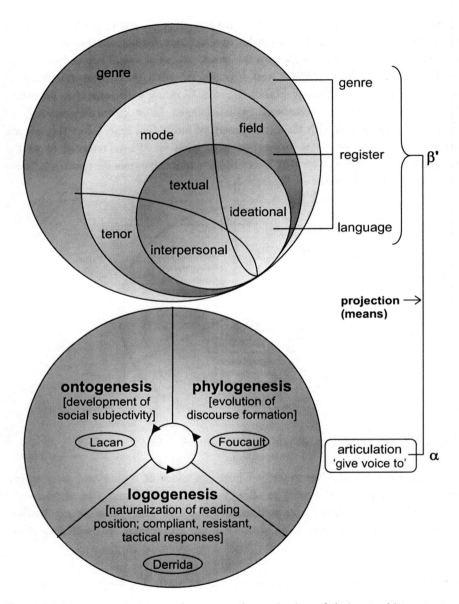

Figure 9.8 Language, register and genre as the projection of their semohistory across time frames

point of time, with respect to the unfolding of a text, with respect to interlocutors' subjectivities and with respect to the meanings at risk in the relevant discourse formations. Along these lines, configuring language, register and genre as system amounts to mapping the reservoir of meanings available to interlocutors within discourse formations. Systems of language, register and genre are immanent as a result of the meanings that have been or could have been made by interlocutors in the past and are still relevant. Of these meanings, repertoires are distributed across subjects according to their socialization. And of these meanings, arrays of choices are negotiated through unfolding text. This notion of time giving value to meaning is outlined in Figure 9.8. To this diagram we have appended the names of the French 'masters' who have inspired a great deal of the more relevant critical analysis: logogenesis (Derrida), ontogenesis (Lacan) and phylogenesis (Foucault). Halliday's (1994) α 'β notation for the projecting relation between clauses has been borrowed to represent the idea of time giving value to meaning. This represents one of the senses in which history (i.e. semogenesis) gives meaning to synchronic (albeit always changing) semiosis, since where we are in all three kinds of time is what sets the relevant valeur – the ways in which meanings are opposed to one another and thus have value in the system.

One of our main concerns in pursuing questions of language and ideology over the years has been to open up dialogue with theorists who are trained to read texts (and so can interpret meaning beyond the clause) and who are trained to read critically (and so can deconstruct) – to lure social theorists in as we linguists struggle to break out. Giblett and O'Carroll (1990), Christie (1991) and Christie *et al.* (1991) document some very productive negotiations. Our current reckoning is that looking at meaning from the perspective of social change, as Figure 9.8 is intended to suggest, will facilitate further dialogue, certainly in relation to Critical Discourse Analysis (Fairclough (1995), Chouliarki and Fairclough (1999)) as it develops around the world.

9.4 Multimodal Discourse Analysis (MDA)

In our discussion of mode above we talked about the way in which the exophoric references in Vincent Lingiari's speech made it 'context dependent' – dependent on our being there or on reading images of what was going on. Another way of putting this would be to say that more than one modality was involved, using the term modality here in the sense of a modality of communication such as language, music, image or action. To understand Lingiari, in other words, we need to process language in relation to image, or language in relation to action. There are two modalities co-articulating what is going on. In register terms what this suggests is that we need to expand our conception of mode to embrace multimodal discourse analysis (hereafter MDA). This entails moving beyond linguistics into social semiotics and taking into account as many modalities of communication as we can systematically describe. In SFL we now have productive accounts of image (O'Toole

1994, Kress and van Leeuwen 1996/2006; see Goodman 1996, Jewitt and Oyama 2001, Stenglin and Iedema 2001 for useful introductions), music and sound (van Leeuwen 1999), space (Martin and Stenglin 2006) and action (Martinec 1998, 2000a, b), alongside language (Halliday and Matthiessen 2004, Caffarel *et al.* 2004). As a result MDA has become a very exciting research frontier in functional linguistics (Kress and van Leeuwen 2001, Martinec 2005), both inspired and enabled by the new electronic modalities of communication enabled by personal computing technologies (Baldry 1999, Baldry and Thibault 2006, O'Halloran 2004).

There is only space here for a glance at the significance of MDA, which we'll relate to our work on the final chapter of Mandela's book. We'll use four sets of tools for analysis. The first analyses ideational patterns in images, developed from general categories of IDEATION described in Chapter 3 above. The second analyses interpersonal patterns, developed from general types of APPRAISAL in Chapter 2. The third concerns textual organization within images and layouts, building on a model first developed by Kress and van Leeuwen (1996). And the fourth analyses relations between images and accompanying texts, using logicosemantic relations of expansion and projection (cf. Martinec and Salway 2006). Whereas previous work on MDA has often taken a bottom-up path from functional grammar, reapplying grammatical categories to visual patterns, our perspective is from discourse semantics, asking how semantic patterns at the level of discourse are realized as visual patterns at the level of image. Our goal is to briefly suggest what may be possible with these kinds of tools, as the field is in its infancy and is wide open for innovative research.

We will illustrate these possibilities with just one analysis, of the final double page spread in the 1996 'coffee table sized' edition of Mandela's autobiography, *The Illustrated Long Walk to Freedom*. In this edition, words are accompanied by one or more glossy black and white or colour photographs on every two-page spread – a radical contrast with the 1995 edition which is mainly writing (except for the few black-and-white photos grouped together in the middle of the book). To make room for the images the 1995 text has been abridged. In the new 'illustrated' edition verbiage and image are mediated by marginalia which refers to images.

On the final two pages of the book (202–3) is a horizontal triptych composed of an abridged version of the *Meaning of Freedom* recount, with a photo of a young boy with raised fist to the left of the text, and to the right a bigger photo of the crowd at Mandela's presidential inauguration, featuring a prominent South African flag. This photo takes up all of page 203 and spreads over a fifth of page 202. These images are presented in colour as the front and back covers of our book. The full layout is presented and labelled in Figure 9.9.

Down the left-hand margin is another triptych, with the image of the young boy in the centre, and above and below him the following marginalia from the *Cost of*

Figure 9.9 Layout of images and text in Mandela 1996: pp. 202–3

Courage report, that we have labelled 'regimes' and 'effects' (this is all that remains of that report in the 1996 coffee-table edition):

'regimes' above photo of young boy
On the day of the inauguration I was overwhelmed with a sense of history. In the first decade of the twentieth century, a few years after the bitter Anglo-Boer war and before my own birth, the white-skinned peoples of South Africa patched up their differences and erected a system of racial domination against the dark-skinned peoples of their own land.

'effects' below photo of young boy
The structure they created formed the basis of one of the harshest, most inhumane, societies the world has ever known. Now, in the last decade of the twentieth century, and my own eighth decade as a man, that system has been overturned forever and replaced by one that recognised the rights and freedoms of all peoples regardless of the colour of their skin. (Mandela 1996: 202)

In place of a verbal macro-genre then, what the illustrated edition gives us is a multimodal genre in which images co-articulate meaning with verbiage. In effect, the *Inauguration* recount and *Courage* report have been reworked as images with attendant marginalia; and these verbiage/image texts co-operate with the abridged *Freedom* recount to construe a recontextualized culminative meaning for Mandela's book. What's the message this time round? To try and answer this question we will interpret the page from the metafunctional perspective of ideational, interpersonal and textual meanings, within and between its images and texts.

Ideational meanings construed by visual images

In ideational terms developed in Chapter 3 above, the primary focus of a visual image is either on entities or on activities. Entity-focused images either classify them or compose their parts; activity-focused images construe either a single activity (simple) or an activity sequence (complex). As we discussed for genres in Chapter 8, images may also have secondary foci realized by their elements.

In this framework, the photo of the young boy is a classifying image. In nuclear terms, we have a young black boy (central), with his hand raised in a fist (nuclear), in front of a crowd (peripheral). But from the perspective of field, each of these elements has at least two possible referents. The boy at once represents the past roles of black youth in the anti-apartheid resistance, and their future lives in a free South Africa. His 'black power' salute evokes both the schoolchildren's historical protests against the regime, and the celebration of Inauguration Day. In his 1995 edition, Mandela refers to this gesture as the *Afrika* salute (in photos between pp 402–3), underlining its function in indigenous solidarity. And the boy can be construed both as a member of the crowd, and as its embodiment – a leader in other words, implying a connection with Mandela. The potential ambiguity of visual images is part of their power: their interpretation is left relatively open to the viewer, widening their appeal, and their multiple interpretations can map onto each other in the manner of metaphors, to evoke more general or abstract categories than the simple images they depict (cf. the discussion of grammatical metaphor and mode, in section 9.1 above).

The inauguration photo construes a simple activity, in which the crowd is looking up to the stage and across to the left, underneath a huge flag. Within this activity however, the image could also be interpreted as implicitly classifying the ordinary people in the lower foreground, separate from the dignitaries above them on the stage. The central flag can then be interpreted as mediating these categories, representing the superordinate category of the nation. The flag itself is a compositional image, in which the categories of South African peoples and histories that it symbolizes are implicit. That is, the red, white and blue refer to the pre-apartheid era British flag, and black, green and yellow to the flag of the African National Congress, all converging from the past towards the future.

In sum, these photos illustrate the four ideational categories we have suggested for images: classifying or compositional entities, and simple or complex activities. Beyond this is the manner in which they are construed. Photos and realistic drawings can depict entities and activities iconically; there is a direct visual relation between the image and the category it construes. In contrast, images such as flags or diagrams construe their categories symbolically; the viewer must know the symbol to recognize its meaning. In between are images that are neither iconic nor symbolic, but indicate categories by one or more criteria; an example is the relation between the crowd, the dignitaries on the stage, and the flag, which indicate the categories of the people, their leaders and the nation by their relative positions – bottom, top and middle. In Peirce's 1955 terms, this kind of visual construal is indexical.[7] (Categories in an image may be either explicitly labelled in a caption, or implicit for the reader to infer – from assumed knowledge of the field, or from the accompanying verbal text.) A very general outline of options for ideational meanings in images is given in Figure 9.10.

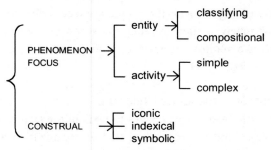

Figure 9.10 Some general options for ideational meanings in images

Interpersonal meanings enacted by visual images

In terms of APPRAISAL developed in Chapter 2, images can inscribe feelings, for example with an image of a person crying or smiling, or invoke them with images that we respond to emotionally; they can invoke appreciation of things by the relative attractiveness of the object or scene presented; and they can invoke judgements of people, by means such as their activity, stance or facial expression. Engagement with the viewer can also be varied in images, for example by the gaze of depicted people looking directly at the viewer, obliquely to one side, or directly away from the viewer into the image. And of course feelings, appreciation and judgement can also be amplified and diminished.

In APPRAISAL terms, the photo of the boy invokes a positive judgement of tenacity that must be read in relation to the texts that surround him. The protest against the regime construed by his raised fist reflects the tenacious resistance of Mandela and his comrades as recounted in the adjacent *Freedom* text. The fist can then be read as amplifying his tenacity to the level of defiance (more so than if he had waved or saluted with an open hand). This is a *retrospective* reading of his tenacity as defiance against the old regime; on the other hand his tenacity can also be read *prospectively* as youthful determination in the nation's hopes for the future. These are complementary readings as protest against the regime vs celebration of its overthrow, that are expanded by the texts above and below the photo – image-text relations that are discussed in the following section. As the boy directly faces the viewer, his defiance/celebration engages us directly, but at the same time his oblique gaze averts a potentially confronting challenge to the viewer. The message is not that I'm defying you, but is rather an invitation to join us in the victory over injustice.

On the other hand the inauguration–flag photo invokes positive appreciation, including aspects of reaction, composition and valuation. With respect to terms exemplified in Table 2.10, the inauguration crowd appears *imposing, exciting* and *dramatic*, as does the huge flag, whose composition is both *complex* and *unified*, and which carries values that are at once *profound, innovative* and *enduring*. These values are amplified by the size and centrality of the flag, and the intensity of its colours. With respect to engagement, the people are facing directly away from the viewer, so we are obliquely invited to enter the scene in the direction they are facing. In sum, the two photos illustrate options in attitude, engagement and graduation, set out in Figure 9.11.

Textual organization and image–text relations

To interpret the semantic relations of images to texts in the layout of pages 202–3, we need to introduce several dimensions of textual organization and image–text relations. Kress and van Leeuwen (1996) suggest two forms of textual organization

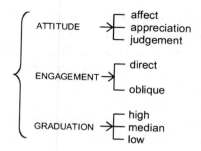

Figure 9.11 Some general options for interpersonal meanings in images

for images, 'polarized' and 'centred'. On the one hand there is polarization along horizontal and/or vertical axes. For images that are horizontally polarized, the left-hand side is glossed as Given and the right as New – organization comparable to that outlined by Halliday for the English clause, as introduced in Chapter 6 above. For vertically polarized images Kress and van Leeuwen suggest the terms Ideal and Real, where Ideal may be characterizsed as a more general or abstract category, and Real as more specific or concrete. Alternatively, images may be organized around a Centre and Margin principle, with Centre the nucleus of information on which marginal elements depend. These axes are schematized in Figure 9.12.

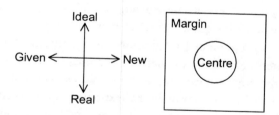

Figure 9.12 Values in 'polarized' and 'centred' structures of images

A further textual dimension is the relative salience of elements in an image or page layout that draws readers' attention to one element before another. Salience may be indicated by a number of factors, including size, colour intensity or the strength of vectors, as well as centre–margin, left–right, top–down positions.

Image–text relations include their logical relations, the boundaries between text and image, and identification. Logical relationships can be mapped in terms of expansion or projection, as we described for texts in macrogenres in Chapter 8. For example, images and texts can restate, specify or summarize each other (elaborating), they can be added to each other (extending), or explain or follow each other in time (enhancing). Images can also project wordings as thought or speech bubbles, and the reverse is also possible. Boundaries between image and text may be weak or strong: images may intrude into text, and text may overlap images, or there may be strong demarcation. And finally elements of images may be identified explicitly in accompanying texts (e.g. in captions), and elements of text or other images may be referred to in accompanying images, for example by vectors that point to them.[8]

In the horizontal triptych on pages 202–3, the photo of the boy is Given and that of the inauguration is New. The photos are more salient than the texts by virtue of their colour intensity and Given–New positions, with the inauguration image by far most salient. Our eye is attracted first to this large picture, then back to the photo of the boy, and then to the texts to explain the images for us. Within the left-hand vertical triptych, the image of the boy is more salient than the marginal texts above and below him, due to its size, colour and centrality. As a result we expect these texts to expand on the meaning of the photograph, and indeed they do, with enhancement. The semantic contrast between the top and bottom texts is between the historical origins of apartheid (*Ideal*) and their outcomes in the recent past and present (*Real*); the text above deals with both the inauguration of a new republic and erection of the former apartheid regime; the text below notes the effects on people, first of the old regime (*harsh and inhumane*), and then of the new (*respect for the rights and freedoms of all peoples*). The photo of the boy mediates this temporal succession: the top-bottom layout construes the apartheid regime as preceding the boy's protest, and its overturning as following his protest. The relatively high salience of the image has the effect of emphasizing the causative role of the people's defiance, represented by the boy, in overturning the inhumane regime. This is a reading of the texts enhancing the image, but as we discussed above for appraisal, the boy's tenacity can also be read as determination for the future, which is elaborated by the words in the text below (*overturned forever*).

In the horizontal triptych, image-text relations are both elaborating and enhancing. The image of the boy restates the words that begin Mandela's story, *I was not born with a hunger to be free ... It was only when I began to learn that my boyhood freedom was an illusion ... that I began to hunger for it.* The analogy with the text is signalled by the weak image-text boundary, with the photo intruding into the text. In contrast, the image of the inauguration is more strongly bounded from Mandela's story, and Mandela himself is noticeably absent from the photo, replaced by the people of South Africa under the flag of their new nation. So this image is clearly marked off from the text as distinct new information. The left-right axis of the page, the vectors in the inauguration-flag image, and its relations with preceding text, combine to construct an indexical temporal sequence. The gaze of people in the crowd is up to the stage and across to the left. Implicit in these gazes is the inauguration ceremony they are watching, and its central protagonist, Mandela. And their gaze is also towards Mandela's life story that lies to the left of the image. These vectors realize implicit identification, all pointing anaphorically to 'him', Mandela. But Mandela himself is not in the picture. Counterbalancing this up and leftward gaze is the powerful vector in the flag, which points down and right towards the people who surround it, cataphorically identifying 'them'. In sum, the layout and images indexically construe a complex activity sequence, in which not only apartheid belongs to the past, but also the struggle against it, and Mandela's own life story. In contrast the future belongs to the people.

In sum, images and layouts are organized by their left–right, top-down and centre–margin axes, and by the relative salience of their elements. Image–text relations include expansion or projection, boundary strength and identification. These options in textual organization are set out in Figure 9.13, and options in image-text relations in Figure 9.14.[9]

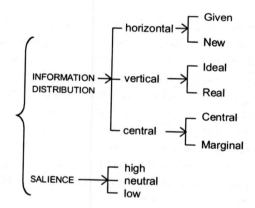

Figure 9.13 Some general options for textual organization of images

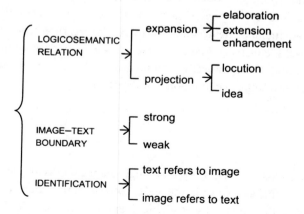

Figure 9.14 Some general relations between images and texts

It seems to us that Mandela might have had a hand in choosing the layout of images in pages 202–3, as it reflects the humble view of his role that he displays throughout his book. This conclusion is reinforced by the apparent analogy between the symbolism of the flag and the people flying it, and the last episodes in Mandela's recount of his *Inauguration Day*, that point to the future with undeterrable tenacity:

> Finally a chevron of Impala jets left a smoke trail of the black, red, green, blue and gold of the new South African flag.
> The day was symbolised for me by the playing of our two national anthems, and the vision of whites singing 'Nkosi Sikelel' iAfrika' and blacks singing 'Die Stem', the old anthem of the republic. Although that day neither group knew the lyrics of the anthem they once despised, they would soon know the words by heart.

The interaction of verbiage and image in multimodal texts creates new meanings that may not be available to either mode alone (multiplying meaning as Jay Lemke (1998) refers to it). The multimodal text foregrounds change – the replacement of a white supremacist regime with a non-racial democratic one. The images and marginalia which foreground this political transformation surround the *Freedom* recount which as we have seen foregrounds changes in understanding – Mandela's spiritual quest for the meaning of freedom. So in this multimodal text we have political change recontextualizing spiritual development. And if political change is what is dominating, where is Mandela? What is his role? In the *Meaning of Freedom* recount he embraces freedom with responsibilities; he sets off to govern. But in the multimodal text he is missing – present only by implication, as *Given* – the object of the crowd's gaze to the previous page, or perhaps reborn, through his reincarnation as the young boy born with a hunger to be free.

We suspect that the new meaning here has to do with regeneration. As the marginalia declares, the apartheid system has been 'overturned forever'; and the interlocking triptychs construct Mandela's legacy – one nation, united, underpinned by a generation of empowered youth for whom the freedom to respect and enhance the freedom of others is the point of departure.

9.5 Voices

To this point we have taken a relatively monologic stance on discourse analysis, so it is time to re-frame this as a voice in the wider conversation in our field. Our goal has been to make a set of tools more available than they have been in the past, and this has meant concentrating on just one tool-kit informed by just one point of view. By contrast Martin's 1992 *English Text* spends more time motivating analyses in relation to alternatives, and includes discussion of the relationships between several of the analyses presented here and other work – for example, conjunction in relation to Rhetorical Structure Theory (RST), exchange and speech function in relation to conversation analysis (CA). Some of the most obvious connections to our work are with west-coast functionalism, referenced in Table 9.1 (see also Matthiessen 2002). The table compares the systems we have discussed here in *Working with Discourse* (WWD) and in *English Text* (ET) with other functionalist analyses and work in SFL.

Table 9.1 Connections between WWD, ET and other work

WWD and ET	other approaches	SFL connections
IDENTIFICATION	identity (Du Bois 1980)	reference
CONJUNCTION	RST (Mann and Thompson 1992)	conjunction
PERIODICITY	New flow (Chafe 1994)	Theme, information
IDEATION	cognitive grammar (Langacker 1987)	ideational semantics
APPRAISAL	hedging (Hyland 1998)	modality, projection
NEGOTIATION	CA (Ochs *et al.* 1996)	exchange, speech function

Perhaps the most relevant west-coast functionalist study for comparison with our work is Fox (1987), since it brings several discourse semantic regions (CA, RST and participant identification) to bear on the 'grammar' of text development. Hyland's (2005) introduction to what is referred to in the pragmatics literature as 'metadiscourse' explicitly addresses its relationship to our more Hallidayan perspective. Beyond this of course there are many connections to be made. We'll leave this phase of intertextual excursions to readers, who will have their own resistant and tactical highways and byways to explore.

From our own vantage point, there have been some interesting shifts of focus in discourse analysis over the four decades of Jim's involvement and two decades of David's. In the 1970s, cohesion was the favoured episteme, as grammarians cast their gaze outwards beyond the clause. In the 1980s it was genre that came to the fore, fostered in important respects by work on literacy development in the Sydney School, English for Academic Purposes and New Rhetoric traditions (Hyon 1996). The 1990s saw the emergence of evaluation as a major theme, as analysts developed models of attitude in functional and corpus linguistics (Hunston and Thompson 2000, Martin and Macken-Horarik 2003). Currently we are in the midst of a surge of interest in multimodal discourse analysis, inspired by the ground-breaking work of Kress and van Leeuwen (1996/2006, 2001) on images. Looking ahead, we can probably expect an emerging rapprochement between qualitative and quantitative approaches to text analysis, depending on the kinds of technology that can be brought to bear in large-scale studies of many and longer texts. Just how this will tend to focus discourse analysis epistemes is harder to predict. Our own approach, in this book and beyond, contrasts strikingly with current trends, which for operational reasons (or worse) tend to elide discourse semantics in favour of word counts, collocations and colligations – as if texts where random sequences of words, phases or clauses. As analysis technologies develop, we need to ensure these trends do not become entrenched in the field in the long term.

Our experience is that the most influential factor shaping the direction of research is what we are developing our linguistics for. For us, as participants in the Sydney School, the development of discourse semantics out of cohesion, the emergence of genre theory and appraisal analysis, and the current interest in intermodality, have all been very much tied up with our concern with redistributing the literacy resources of western culture to the peoples who have historically been subjugated by them. Our aim has never been to promote a particular ideology, but simply to offer what we know about these language resources, so that people could redeploy them as they choose. This remains a central concern of our work and a major application in educational contexts, that continues to grow internationally, as we illustrated with David's South African lesson in Chapter 7.

But as far as we can see these peoples, be they working class, indigenous minorities, or third world nations, will have increasingly limited opportunities for such redeployment given current projections for global warming. This creates a new and pressing agenda for socially responsible linguistics. To this point in time we have been primarily concerned, like the authors we have studied in this book, with subverting what Halliday (1993) has called the 'lordism' of the Eurasian culture bloc. We are now all confronted with the urgency of tackling head-on the 'growthist' ideology of global capitalism that is fuelling the greenhouse effect. We can't be sure how interventions of this order will focus functional linguistics – but as the comrades of our youth once took Bob Dylan's words to heart, you don't need a weatherman to know which way the wind blows. As culpable weather-makers, it is time to re-imagine the possibilities of our craft, and to realize them as social action.

Notes

1. By iconic we mean matching relations between the world as we perceive it and ideation, i.e. between people and things as nouns, actions as verbs and so on.
2. Two paragraphs later Leigh, valuing in no small part through Stevie's eyes, refers to Eric Clapton as *God*, in a chapter entitled 'Prelude: and the Gods

made love', referring to Stevie, Jimmie, Eric, Buddy Guy and Robert Cray on stage, as well as to the title of a Jimi Hendrix tune *And the Gods Made Love* (cf. the headline on the back cover of Leigh's book 'They called him Guitar Hurricane').

3. Although the walk-off was in 1966, the Gurindji did not attain inalienable freehold title for their land until 1986.

4. Halliday and Matthiessen in fact discuss registers as sub-potentials in relation to system, and text types as super-potentials in relation to text, at the same level of generality along the cline; we've taken the liberty of adding a rung here by making text type more specific than register.

5. Bernstein (1996) also points out the focus of CDA on the ideological 'content' of the 'pedagogic relay', at the expense of investigating, and so acting on, how it is 'relayed'.

6. The term 'instantiation' refers to texts as instances of the semiotic system of a culture, i.e. the language system is instantiated in texts.

7. Previous efforts to interpret ideational and interpersonal meanings in visual images have been based on analogies with grammatical categories of process types, mood and modality (e.g. Kress and van Leeuwen 1996, O'Toole 1994, Unsworth 2001) rather than discourse semantics. In keeping with the discourse oriented approach here, and to keep labels manageable, we have used the same terms as for verbal texts wherever possible. For example, where Kress and van Leeuwen use the cryptic terms 'overt/covert', we use 'explicit/implicit'; and where they use polysemous terms 'concrete/abstract', we have found the semiotic terms 'iconic/indexical/symbolic' less ambiguous.

8. Kress and van Leeuwen draw attention to vectors, which can be constructed through the gaze of participants or lines formed by the position of people and things. Whereas they interpret vectors in ideational terms, its seems to us that vectors are realizational strategies for ideational or textual functions.

9. Kress and van Leeuwen's terms *Given* and *New* derive from Halliday's description of the linguistic system of INFORMATION (Halliday and Matthiessen 2004). We have generalized their *Given–New*, *Ideal–Real* and *Centre–Margin* contrasts as options in INFORMATION DISTRIBUTION. The term 'salience' is used by Kress and van Leeuwen, but the SALIENCE values of high/neutral/low are our own. We have used the term IMAGE-TEXT BOUNDARY whereas Kress and van Leeuwen (1996) use the term 'framing' for boundary strength, which conflicts with Bernstein's (1971, 1996) use of 'framing' for control within a context.

Appendix 1: Promotion of National Unity and Reconciliation Act

OFFICE OF THE PRESIDENT

No. 1111.

26 July 1995

NO. 34 OF 1995: PROMOTION OF NATIONAL UNITY AND RECONCILIATION ACT, 1995.

It is hereby notified that the President has assented to the following Act which is hereby published for general information:

ACT

To provide for the investigation and the establishment of as complete a picture as possible of the nature, causes and extent of gross violations of human Rights committed during the period from 1 March 1960 to the cut-off date contemplated in the Constitution, within or outside the Republic, emanating from the conflicts of the past, and the fate or whereabouts of the victims of such violations;

the granting of amnesty to persons who make full disclosure of all the relevant facts relating to acts associated with a political objective committed in the course of the conflicts of the past during the said period;

affording victims an opportunity to relate the violations they suffered;

the taking of measures aimed at the granting of reparation to, and the rehabilitation and the restoration of the human and civil dignity of, victims of violations of human rights;

reporting to the Nation about such violations and victims;

the making of recommendations aimed at the prevention of the commission of gross violations of human rights;

and for the said purposes to provide for the establishment of a Truth and Reconciliation Commission, a Committee on Human Rights Violations, a Committee on Amnesty and a Committee on Reparation and Rehabilitation;

and to confer certain powers on, assign certain functions to and impose certain duties upon that Commission and those Committees;

and to provide for matters connected therewith.

SINCE the Constitution of the Republic of South Africa, 1993 (Act No. 200 of 1993), provides a historic bridge between the past of a deeply divided society characterized by strife, conflict, untold suffering and injustice, and a future founded on the recognition of human rights, democracy and peaceful co-existence for all South Africans, irrespective of colour, race, class, belief or sex;

AND SINCE it is deemed necessary to establish the truth in relation to past events as well as the motives for and circumstances in which gross violations of human rights have occurred, and to make the findings known in order to prevent a repetition of such acts in future;

AND SINCE the Constitution states that the pursuit of national unity, the well-being of all South African citizens and peace require reconciliation between the people of South Africa and the reconstruction of society;

AND SINCE the Constitution states that there is a need for understanding but not for vengeance, a need for reparation but not for retaliation, a need for ubuntu but not for victimization;

AND SINCE the Constitution states that in order to advance such reconciliation and reconstruction amnesty shall be granted in respect of acts, omissions and offences associated with political objectives committed in the course of the conflicts of the past;

AND SINCE the Constitution provides that Parliament shall under the Constitution adopt a law which determines a firm cut-off date, which shall be a date after 8 October 1990 and before the cut-off date envisaged in the Constitution, and providing for the mechanisms, criteria and procedures, including tribunals, if any, through which such amnesty shall be dealt with;

(English text signed by the President.)

(Assented to 19 July 1995.)

BE IT THEREFORE ENACTED by the Parliament of the Republic of South Africa, as follows:

CHAPTER 1

Interpretation and application

Definitions

1. (1) In this Act, unless the context otherwise indicates:

(i)   'act associated with a political objective' has the meaning ascribed thereto in section 20(2) and (3); (ii)

(ii)   'article' includes any evidence, book, document, file, object, writing, recording or transcribed computer printout produced by any mechanical or electronic device or any device by means of which information is recorded, stored or transcribed; (xix) (iii)　'Commission' means the Truth and Reconciliation Commission established by section 2; (ix)

(iv)　'commissioner' means a member of the Commission appointed in terms of section 7(2)(a); (viii)

(v)　'committee' means the Committee on Human Rights Violations, the Committee on Amnesty or the Committee on Reparation and Rehabilitation, as the case may be; (vii)

(vi)　'Constitution' means the Constitution of the Republic of South Africa, 1993 (Act No. 200 of 1993); (iv)

(vii)　'cut-off date' means the latest date allowed as the cut-off date in terms of the Constitution as set out under the heading 'National Unity and Reconciliation'; (i)

(viii)　'former state' means any state or territory which was established by an Act of Parliament or by proclamation in terms of such an Act prior to the commencement of the Constitution and the territory of which now forms part of the Republic; (xvii)

(ix)　'gross violation of human rights' means the violation of human rights through:

　(a)　the killing, abduction, torture or severe ill-treatment of any person; or

　(b)　any attempt, conspiracy, incitement, instigation, command or procurement to commit an act referred to in paragraph (a), which emanated from conflicts of the past and which was committed during the period 1 March 1960 to the cut-off date within or outside the Republic, and the commission of which was advised, planned, directed, commanded or ordered, by any person acting with a political motive; (v)

(x)　'joint committee' means a joint committee of the Houses of Parliament appointed in accordance with the Standing Orders of Parliament for the purpose of considering matters referred to it in terms of this Act; (iii)

(xi)　'Minister' means the Minister of Justice; (x)

(xii)　'prescribe' means prescribe by regulation made under section 40; (xviii)

(xiii)　'President' means the President of the Republic; (xi)

(xiv)　'reparation' includes any form of compensation, ex gratia payment, restitution, rehabilitation or recognition; (vi)

(xv)　'Republic' means the Republic of South Africa referred to in section 1(2) of the Constitution; (xii)

(xvi)　'security forces' includes any full-time or part-time:

　(a)　member or agent of the South African Defence Force, the South African Police, the National Intelligence Service, the Bureau of State Security, the Department of Correctional Services, or any of their organs;

　(b)　member or agent of a defence force, police force, intelligence agency or prison service of any former state, or any of their organs; (xvi)

(xvii)　'State' means the State of the Republic; (xiv)

(xviii)　'subcommittee' means any subcommittee established by the Commission in terms of section 5(c); (xv)

(xix)　'victims' includes:

　(a)　persons who, individually or together with one or more persons, suffered harm in the form of physical or mental injury, emotional suffering, pecuniary loss or a substantial impairment of human rights:

(i)   as a result of a gross violation of human rights; or

(ii)   as a result of an act associated with a political objective for which amnesty has been granted;

(b)   persons who, individually or together with one or more persons, suffered harm in the form of physical or mental injury, emotional suffering, pecuniary loss or a substantial impairment of human rights, as a result of such persons intervening to assist persons contemplated in paragraph (a) who were in distress or to prevent victimization of such persons; and

(c)   such relatives or dependants of victims as may be prescribed. (xiii)

(2) 'Commission' shall be construed as including a reference to 'committee' or subcommittee', as the case may be, and 'Chairperson', 'Vice-Chairperson' or commissioner' shall be construed as including a reference to the chairperson, vice-chairperson or a member of a committee or subcommittee, as the case may be.

CHAPTER 2

Truth and Reconciliation Commission

Establishment and seat of Truth and Reconciliation Commission

2. (1) There is for the purposes of sections 10(1), (2) and (3) and II and Chapters 6 and 7 hereby established a juristic person to be known as the Truth and Reconciliation Commission.

(2) The seat of the Commission shall be determined by the President.

Objectives of Commission

3. (1) The objectives of the Commission shall be to promote national unity and reconciliation in a spirit of understanding which transcends the conflicts and divisions of the past by:

(a)   establishing as complete a picture as possible of the causes, nature and extent of the gross violations of human rights which were committed during the period from I March 1960 to the cut-off date, including the antecedents, circumstances, factors and context of such violations, as well as the perspectives of the victims and the motives and perspectives of the persons responsible for the commission of the violations, by conducting investigations and holding hearings;

(b)   facilitating the granting of amnesty to persons who make full disclosure of all the relevant facts relating to acts associated with a political objective and comply with the requirements of this Act;

(c)   establishing and making known the fate or whereabouts of victims and by restoring the human and civil dignity of such victims by granting them an opportunity to relate their own accounts of the violations of which they are the victims, and by recommending reparation measures in respect of them;

(d)   compiling a report providing as comprehensive an account as possible of the activities and findings of the Commission contemplated in paragraphs (a), (b) and (c), and which contains recommendations of measures to prevent the future violations of human rights.

(2) The provisions of subsection (1) shall not be interpreted as limiting the power of the Commission to investigate or make recommendation concerning any matter with a view to promoting or achieving national unity and reconciliation within the context of this Act.

(3) In order to achieve the objectives of the Commission:

(a) the Committee on Human Rights Violations, as contemplated in Chapter 3, shall deal, among other things, with matters pertaining to investigations of gross violations of human rights;

(b) the Committee on Amnesty, as contemplated in Chapter 4, shall deal with matters relating to amnesty;

(c) the Committee on Reparation and Rehabilitation, as contemplated in Chapter 5, shall deal with matters referred to it relating to reparations;

(d) the investigating unit referred to in section 5(d) shall perform the investigations contemplated in section 28(4)(a); and

(e) the subcommittees shall exercise, perform and carry out the powers, functions and duties conferred upon, assigned to or imposed upon them by the Commission.

Functions of Commission

4. The functions of the Commission shall be to achieve its objectives, and to that end the Commission shall:

(a) facilitate, and where necessary initiate or coordinate, inquiries into-

(i) gross violations of human rights, including violations which were part of a systematic pattern of abuse;

(ii) the nature, causes and extent of gross violations of human rights, including the antecedents, circumstances, factors, context, motives and perspectives which led to such violations;

(iii) the identity of all persons, authorities, institutions and organisations involved in such violations;

(iv) the question whether such violations were the result of deliberate planning on the part of the State or a former state or any of their organs, or of any political organisation, liberation movement or other group or individual; and

(v) accountability, political or otherwise, for any such violation;

(b) facilitate, and initiate or coordinate, the gathering of information and the receiving of evidence from any person, including persons claiming to be victims of such violations or the representatives of such victims, which establish the identity of victims of such violations, their fate or present whereabouts and the nature and extent of the harm suffered by such victims;

(c) facilitate and promote the granting of amnesty in respect of acts associated with political objectives, by receiving from persons desiring to make a full disclosure of all the relevant facts relating to such acts, applications for the granting of amnesty in respect of such acts, and transmitting such applications to the

Committee on Amnesty for its decision, and by publishing decisions granting amnesty, in the Gazette;

(d) determine what articles have been destroyed by any person in order to conceal violations of human rights or acts associated with a political objective;

(e) prepare a comprehensive report which sets out its activities and findings, based on factual and objective information and evidence collected or received by it or placed at its disposal;

(f) make recommendations to the President with regard to-

    (i) the policy which should be followed or measures which should be taken with regard to the granting of reparation to victims or the taking of other measures aimed at rehabilitating and restoring the human and civil dignity of victims;

    (ii) measures which should be taken to grant urgent interim reparation to victims;

(g) make recommendations to the Minister with regard to the development of a limited witness protection programme for the purposes of this Act;

(h) make recommendations to the President with regard to the creation of institutions conducive to a stable and fair society and the institutional, administrative and legislative measures which should be taken or introduced in order to prevent the commission of violations of human rights.

Powers of Commission

5. In order to achieve its objectives and to perform its functions the

Commission shall have the power to:

(a) determine the seat, if any, of every committee;

(b) establish such offices as it may deem necessary for the performance of its functions;

(c) establish subcommittees to exercise, carry out or perform any of the powers, duties and functions assigned to them by the Commission;

(d) conduct any investigation or hold any hearing it may deem necessary and establish the investigating unit referred to in section 28;

(e) refer specific or general matters to, give guidance and instructions to, or review the decisions of, any committee or subcommittee or the investigating unit with regard to the exercise of its powers, the performance of its functions and the carrying out of its duties, the working procedures which should be followed and the divisions which should be set up by any committee in order to deal effectively with the work of the committee: Provided that no decision, or the process of arriving at such a decision, of the Committee on Amnesty regarding any application for amnesty shall be reviewed by the Commission; direct any committee or subcommittee to make information which it has in its possession available to any other committee or subcommittee;

(g) direct the submission of and receive reports or interim reports from any committee or subcommittee;

(h)   have the administrative and incidental work connected with the exercise of its powers, the execution of its duties or the performance of its functions carried out by persons-

(i)   employed or appointed by it;

(ii)   seconded to its service by any department of State at the request of the Commission and after consultation with the Public Service Commission;

(iii)   appointed by it for the performance of specified tasks;

(i)   in consultation with the Minister and through diplomatic channels, obtain permission from the relevant authority of a foreign country to receive evidence or gather information in that country;

(j)   enter into an agreement with any person, including any department of State, in terms of which the Commission will be authorized to make use of any of the facilities, equipment or personnel belonging to or under the control or in the employment of such person or department;

(k)   recommend to the President that steps be taken to obtain an order declaring a person to be dead;

(l)   hold meetings at any place within or outside the Republic;

(m)   on its own initiative or at the request of any interested person inquire or investigate into any matter, including the disappearance of any person or group of persons. Certain powers shall be exercised in consultation with Minister

6. Subject to the provisions of section 45, any power referred to in section 5(a), (b) and (c), and, if it is to be exercised outside the Republic, any power referred to in sections 5(d) and (1), 10(1) and 29(1), shall be exercised in consultation with the Minister.

Constitution of Commission

7. (1) The Commission shall consist of not fewer than 11 and not more than 17 commissioners, as may be determined by the President in consultation with the Cabinet.

(2)   (a) The President shall appoint the commissioners in consultation with the Cabinet.

(b) The commissioners shall be fit and proper persons who are impartial and who do not have a high political profile: Provided that not more than two persons who are not South African citizens may be appointed as commissioners.

(3) The President shall make the appointment of the commissioners known by proclamation in the Gazette.

(4) The President shall designate one of the commissioners as the Chairperson, and another as the Vice-Chairperson, of the Commission.

(5) A commissioner appointed in terms of subsection (2)(a) shall, subject to the provisions of subsections (6) and (7), hold office for the duration of the Commission.

(6) A commissioner may at any time resign as commissioner by tendering his or her resignation in writing to the President.

(7) The President may remove a commissioner from office on the grounds of misbehaviour,

incapacity or incompetence, as determined by the joint committee and upon receipt of an address from the National Assembly and an address from the Senate.

(8) If any commissioner tenders his or her resignation under subsection (6), or is removed from office under subsection (7), or dies, the President in consultation with the Cabinet, may fill the vacancy by appointing a person for the unexpired portion of the term of office of his or her predecessor or may allow the seat vacated as a result of a resignation, removal from office or death to remain vacant.

Acting Chairperson of Commission

8. If both the Chairperson and Vice-Chairperson are absent or unable to perform their duties, the other commissioners shall from among their number nominate an Acting Chairperson for the duration of such absence or incapacity.

Conditions of service, remuneration, allowances and other benefits of staff of Commission

9. (1) The persons appointed or employed by the Commission who are not officials of the State, shall receive such remuneration, allowances and other employment benefits and shall be appointed or employed on such terms and conditions and for such periods as the Commission with the approval of the Minister, granted in concurrence with the Minister of Finance, may determine.

(2) (a) A document setting out the remuneration, allowances and other conditions of employment determined by the Commission in terms of subsection (1), shall be tabled in Parliament within 14 days after each such determination.

(b) If Parliament disapproves of any determination, such determination shall cease to be of force to the extent to which it is so disapproved.

(c) If a determination ceases to be of force as contemplated in paragraph (b):

(i) anything done in terms of such determination up to the date on which such determination ceases to be of force shall be deemed to have been validly done; and

(ii) any right, privilege, obligation or liability acquired, accrued or incurred up to the said date under and by virtue of such determination, shall lapse upon the said date.

Meetings, procedure at and quorum for meetings of Commission and recording of proceedings

10. (1) A meeting of the Commission shall be held at a time and place determined by the Chairperson of the Commission or, in the absence or inability of such Chairperson, by the Vice-Chairperson of the Commission or, in the absence or inability of both such Chairperson and Vice-Chairperson, by the Acting Chairperson of the Commission.

(2) Subject to section 40, the Commission shall have the power to determine the procedure for its meetings, including the manner in which decisions shall be taken.

(3) The Commission shall cause a record to be kept of its proceedings.

(4) The quorum for the first meeting of the Commission shall be two less than the total number of the Commission.

Principles to govern actions of Commission when dealing with victims

11. When dealing with victims the actions of the Commission shall be guided by the following principles:

(a)   Victims shall be treated with compassion and respect for their dignity;

(b)   victims shall be treated equally and without discrimination of any kind, including race, colour, gender, sex, sexual orientation, age, language, religion, nationality, political or other opinion, cultural beliefs or practices, property, birth or family status, ethnic or social origin or disability;

(c)   procedures for dealing with applications by victims shall be expeditious, fair, inexpensive and accessible;

(d)   victims shall be informed through the press and any other medium of their rights in seeking redress through the Commission, including information of-
(i) the role of the Commission and the scope of its activities;
(ii) the right of victims to have their views and submissions presented and considered at appropriate stages of the inquiry;

(e)   appropriate measures shall be taken in order to minimize inconvenience to victims and, when necessary, to protect their privacy, to ensure their safety as well as that of their families and of witnesses testifying on their behalf, and to protect them from intimidation;

(f)   appropriate measures shall be taken to allow victims to communicate in the language of their choice;

(g)   informal mechanisms for the resolution of disputes, including mediation, arbitration and any procedure provided for by customary law and practice shall be applied, where appropriate, to facilitate reconciliation and redress for victims.

[Chapter 3-7 continue]

Appendix 2: A synopsis of common genres, their purposes and stages

	genre	purpose	stages
Stories	recount	recounting events	Orientation Record of events
Stories	narrative	resolving a complication in a story	Orientation Complication Evaluation Resolution
Stories	exemplum	judging character or behaviour in a story	Orientation Incident Interpretation
Text responses	personal response	reacting emotionally to a text	Evaluation Reaction
Text responses	review	evaluating a literary, visual or musical text	Context Description of text Judgement
Text responses	interpretation	interpreting the message of a text	Evaluation Synopsis of text Reaffirmation
Text responses	critical response	challenging the message of a text	Evaluation Deconstruction Challenge
Arguments	exposition	arguing for a point of view	Thesis Arguments Reiteration
Arguments	discussion	discussing two or more points of view	Issue Sides Resolution
Factual stories	autobiographical recount	recounting life events	Orientation Record of stages
Factual stories	biographical recount	recounting life stages	Orientation Record of stages
Factual stories	historical recount	recounting historical events	Background Record of stages
Explanations	sequential explanation	explaining a sequence	Phenomenon Explanation
Explanations	factorial explanation	explaining multiple causes	Phenomenon Explanation
Explanations	consequential explanation	explaining multiple effects	Phenomenon Explanation
Reports	descriptive report	classifying & describing a phenomenon	Classification Description
Reports	classifying report	classifying & describing types of phenomena	Classification Description
Reports	compositional report	describing parts of wholes	Classification Description
Procedures	procedure	how to do experiments & observations	Purpose Equipment Steps
Procedures	procedural recount	recounting experiments & observations	Purpose Method Results

References

Bakhtin, M. M. (1981) *The Dialogic Imagination*, translated by C. Emerson and M. Holquist. Austin: University of Texas Press.

Baldry, A. [ed.] (1999) *Multimodality and Multimediality in the Distance Learning Age*. Campo Basso: Lampo.

Baldry, A. and P. Thibault (2006) *Multimodal Transcription and Text Analysis: a multimedia toolkit and coursebook with associated on-line course*. London: Equinox.

Bernstein, B. (1996) *Pedagogy, Symbolic Control and Identity: Theory, Research, Critique*. London: Taylor & Francis.

Biber, D. (1988) *Variation across Speech and Writing*. Cambridge: Cambridge University.

Biber, D. and E. Finnegan (1988) Adverbial stance types in English. *Discourse Processes* 11(1): 1–34.

Biber, D. and E. Finnegan (1989) Styles of stance in English: lexical and grammatical marking of evidentiality and affect. *Text* 9(1) (special issue on the pragmatics of affect): 93–124.

Biber, D. and E. Finnegan (1994) *Sociolinguistic Perspectives on Register*. Oxford: Oxford University Press.

Caffarel, A., J. R. Martin and C. M. I. M. Matthiessen [eds] (2004) *Language Typology: A Functional Perspective*. Amsterdam: Benjamins.

Carter, R. A. (1987) *Vocabulary: An Applied Linguistic Guide*. London: Allen and Unwin.

Chafe, W. (1994) *Discourse, Consciousness and Time*. Chicago: University of Chicago Press.

Channel, J. (1994) *Vague Language*. Oxford: Oxford University Press.

Chouliariki, L. and N. Fairclough (1999) *Discourse in Late Modernity: Rethinking Critical Discourse Analysis*. Edinburgh: University of Edinburgh Press.

Christie, F. [ed.] (1991) *Literacy in Social Processes: Papers from the Inaugural Australian Systemic Functional Linguistics Conference, held at Deakin University, January 1990*. Darwin: Centre for Studies of Language in Education, Northern Territory University.

Christie, F. [ed.] (1999) *Pedagogy and the Shaping of Consciousness: Linguistic and Social Processes*. London: Cassell.

Christie, F. (2002) *Classroom Discourse Analysis*. London: Continuum.

Christie, F., B. Devlin, P. Freebody, A. Luke, J. R. Martin, T. Threadgold and C. Walton (1991). *Teaching English Literacy: A Project of National Significance on the Preservice Preparation of Teachers for Teaching English Literacy*, Vols 1, 2 & 3. Canberra: Department of Employment, Education and Training.

Christie, F. and J. R. Martin (1997) *Genre and Institutions: Social Processes in the Workplace and School*. London: Cassell.

Christie, F. and J. R. Martin [eds] (2006) *Knowledge Structure: functional linguistic and sociological perspectives* London: Continuum.

Collins Cobuild Grammar Patterns 2: Nouns and Adjectives. 1998. London: HarperCollins.

Cope, W. and M. Kalantzis [eds] (1993) *The Powers of Literacy: A Genre Approach to Teaching Literacy*. London: Falmer.

Cope, B. and M. Kalantzis (1999) *Multiliteracies: Literacy Learning and the Design of Social Futures*. London: Routledge.

Corrigan, C. (1991) *Changes and contrasts: VCE geography units 1 and 2*. Milton, Qld: Jacaranda Press.

Cranny-Francis, A. (1996) Technology and/or weapon: the disciplines of reading in the secondary English classroom. In Hasan and Williams, 172–90.

Cumming, S. and T. Ono (1997) Discourse and grammar. In T. A. van Dijk [ed.] *Discourse as Structure and Process*. London: Sage, 112–37.

de Certeau, M. (1984) *The Practice of Everyday Life*. Berkeley: University of California Press.

Drozdowski, T. (2000) Editorial Reviews (*Texas Flood*). Amazon.com.

Du Bois, J. W. (1980) Beyond definiteness: the trace of identity in discourse. In W. L. Chafe [ed.] *The Pear Stories: Cognitive, Cultural and Linguistic Aspects of Narrative Production*. Norwood: Ablex, 203–74.

Eggins, S. and D. Slade (1997) *Analysing Casual Conversation*. London: Cassell.

Fairclough, N. [ed.] (1992) *Critical Language Awareness*. London: Longman.

Fairclough, N. (1995) *Critical Discourse Analysis: The Critical Study of Language*. London: Longman.

Fowler, R., B. Hodge, G. Kress and T. Trew (1979) *Language and Control*. London: Routledge and Kegan Paul.

Fox, B. (1987) *Discourse Structure and Anaphora: Written and Conversational English*. Cambridge: Cambridge University Press.

Fries, P. H. (1981) On the status of theme in English: arguments from discourse. *Forum Linguisticum* 6(1): 1–38. Republished in J. S. Petofi and E. Sozer [eds] *Micro and Macro Connexity of Texts*. Hamburg: Helmut Buske Verlag, 116–52.

Fries, P. and M. Gregory [eds] (1995) *Discourse in Society: Systemic Functional Perspectives*. Norwood: Ablex.

Fuller, G. (1998) Cultivating science: negotiating discourse in the popular texts of Stephen Jay Gould. In Martin and Veel, 35–62.

Gee, J. (1990) *Social Linguistics and Literacies: Ideology in Discourses*. London: Falmer.

Giblett, R. and J. O'Carroll [eds] (1990) *Discipline – Dialogue – Difference: Proceedings of the Language in Education Conference, Murdoch University, December 1989*. Perth: 4D Duration Publications, School of Humanities, Murdoch University.

Goodman, S. (1996) Visual English. In S. Goodman and D. Graddol [eds] *Redesigning English: New Texts, New Identities*. London: Routledge, 38–105.

Gore, J. (1993) *The Struggle for Pedagogies: Critical and Feminist Discourses as Regimes of Truth*. London: Routledge.

Gregory, M. (1995) *Before and Towards Communication Linguistics: Essays by Michael Gregory and Associates* (edited by Jin Soon Cha) Seoul: Sookmyng Women's University.

Gratton, M. [ed.] (2000) *Reconciliation: Essays on Australian Reconciliation*. Melbourne: Black Inc.

Halliday, M. A. K. (1976) Anti-languages. *American Anthropologist* 78(3): 570–84. Reprinted in Halliday (1978), 164–82.

Halliday, M. A. K. (1978) *Language as a Social Semiotic: The Social Interpretation of Language and Meaning*. London: Edward Arnold.

Halliday, M. A. K. (1985) *Spoken and Written Language*. Geelong: Deakin University Press. Republished London: Oxford University Press 1989.

Halliday, M. A. K. (1992) Language as system and language as instance: the corpus as a theoretical construct. In J. Svartvik [ed.] *Directions in Corpus Linguistics: Proceedings of Nobel Symposium 82, Stockholm, 4–8 August 1991*. Berlin: De Gruyter, 61–77.

Halliday, M. A. K. (1993) *Language in a Changing World*. Canberra: Applied Linguistics Association of Australia.

Halliday, M. A. K. (1994) *An Introduction to Functional Grammar*. London: Edward Arnold.

Halliday M. A. K. and R. Hasan (1976) *Cohesion in English*. London: Longman.

Halliday, M. A. K. and R. Hasan (1985) *Language, Context, and Text: Aspects of Language in a Social-semiotic Perspective*. Geelong: Deakin University Press.

Halliday, M. A. K. and Z. James (1993) A quantitative study of polarity and primary tense in the English finite clause. In J. M. Sinclair, G. Fox and M. Hoey [eds] *Techniques of Description: Spoken and Written Discourse*. London: Routledge, 32–66.

Halliday, M. A. K. and J. R. Martin (1993) *Writing Science: Literacy and Discursive Power*. London: Falmer.

Halliday, M. A. K. and C. M. I. M. Matthiessen (1999) *Construing Experience through Meaning: A Language-based Approach to Cognition.* London: Cassell.

Hasan, R. (1977) Text in the systemic-functional model. In W. Dressler [ed.] *Current Trends in Textlinguistics.* Berlin: Walter de Gruyter, 228–46.

Hasan, R. (1984) The nursery tale as a genre. *Nottingham Linguistic Circular* 13 (Special Issue on Systemic Linguistics): 71–102.

Hasan, R. (1985) The structure of a text. In M. A. K. Halliday and R. Hasan *Language, Context and Text.* Geelong, Vic.: Deakin University Press, 52–69 [republished by Oxford University Press 1989].

Hasan, R. (1990) Semantic variation and sociolinguistics. *Australian Journal of Linguistics* 9(2): 221–76.

Hasan, R. (1995) The conception of context in text. In Fries and Gregory, 183–283.

Hasan, R. (1996) *Ways of Saying, Ways of Meaning: Selected Papers of Ruqaiya Hasan* (edited by C. Cloran, D. Butt and G. Williams). London: Cassell.

Hasan, R. (1999) Speaking with reference to context. In M. Ghadessy (ed.) *Text and Context in Functional Linguistics.* Amsterdam: Benjamins, 219–328.

Hasan, R. and G. Williams [eds] (1996) *Literacy in Society.* London: Longman.

Hercus, L. A. and P. Sutton [eds] *This Is What Happened.* Canberra: Australian Institute of Aboriginal Studies.

HREOC (1997) *Bringing Them Home: The 'Stolen Children' report.* Canberra: Human Rights and Equal Opportunity Commission, http://www.hreoc.gov.au/social_justice/stolen_children/

Hunston, S. (1994) Evaluation and organisation in a sample of written academic discourse. In M. Coulthard [ed.] *Advances in Written Text Analysis.* London: Routledge, 191–218.

Hunston, S. and G. Thompson [eds] (2000) *Evaluation in Text: Authorial Stance and the Construction of Discourse.* Oxford: Oxford University Press.

Hyland, K. (1998) *Hedging in Scientific Research Articles.* Amsterdam: Benjamins.

Hyland, K. (2000) *Disciplinary Discourses: Social Interactions in Academic Writing.* London: Longman.

Hyland, K. (2002) Genre: language, context and literacy. *Annual Review of Applied Linguistics* 22: 113–35.

Hyland, K. (2005) *Metadiscourse.* London: Continuum (Continuum Discourse Series).

Hymes, D. (1995) Bernstein and poetics. In P. Atkinson, B. Davies and S. Delamont [eds.] *Discourse and Reproduction: Essays in Honor of Basil Bernstein.* Cresskill: Hampton Press, 1–24.

Hyon, S. (1996) Genre in three traditions: implications for ESL. *TESOL Quarterly* 30(4): 693–722.

Iedema, R., S. Feez and P. White (1994) *Media Literacy (Write It Right Literacy in*

Industry Project: Stage Two). Sydney: Metropolitan East Region's Disadvantaged Schools Program.

Janks, H. and R. Ivanič (1992) CLA and emancipatory discourse. In Fairclough 1992, 305–31.

Jewitt, C. and R. Oyama (2001) Visual meaning: a social semiotic approach. In van Leeuwen and Jewitt, 134–56.

Johns, A. (2001) *Genre in the Classroom.* Mahwah: Erlbaum.

Kelly, P. (1999) *Don't Start Me Talking: Lyrics 1984–1999.* Sydney: Allen & Unwin.

Kinnear, J. and M. Martin (2004) Biology 1: preliminary course. Milton, Qld: Jacaranda.

Kress, G. and T. van Leeuwen (1996) *Reading Images: The Grammar of Visual Design.* London: Routledge.

Kress, G. and T. van Leeuwen (2001) *Multimodal Discourse: The Modes and Media of Contemporary Communication.* London: Arnold.

Krog, A. (1999) *Country of my Skull.* London: Vintage.

Langacker, R. (1987) *Foundations of Cognitive Grammar.* Stanford: Stanford University Press.

Leigh, K. (1993) *Stevie Ray: Soul to Soul.* Dallas: Taylor.

Lemke, J. L. (1995) *Textual Politics: Discourse and Social Dynamics.* London: Taylor & Francis.

Lemke, J. (1998) Multiplying meaning: visual and verbal semiotics in scientific text. In Martin & Veel, 87–113.

Lingiari, V. (1986) Vincent Lingiari's speech, translated by P. McConvell. In Hercus and Sutton, 312–5.

Mandela, N. (1995) *Long Walk to Freedom: The Autobiography of Nelson Mandela.* London: Abacus.

Mandela, N. (1996) *The Illustrated Long Walk to Freedom: The Autobiography of Nelson Mandela.* London: Little, Brown and Company.

Mann, W. C. and S. Thompson [eds] (1992) *Discourse Description: Diverse Analyses of a Fund Raising Text.* Amsterdam: Benjamins.

Manne, R. (1998) The stolen generations. Quadrant 343(42) (1–2): 53–63.

Martin, J. R. (1985) *Factual Writing: Exploring and Challenging Social Reality.* Geelong: Deakin University Press. Republished London: Oxford University Press 1989.

Martin, J. R. (1992) *English Text: System and Structure.* Amsterdam: Benjamins.

Martin, J. R. (1993) Life as a noun. In Halliday and Martin, 221–67.

Martin, J. R. (1995a) Text and clause: fractal resonance. *Text* 15(1): 5–42.

Martin, J. R. (1995b) More than what the message is about: English Theme. In M. Ghadessy [ed.] *Thematic Development in English Texts.* London: Pinter, 223–58.

Martin, J. R. (1996) Evaluating disruption: symbolising theme in junior secondary narrative. In R. Hasan and G. Williams [eds] *Literacy in Society*. London: Longman, 124–71.

Martin, J. R. (1999a) Grace: the logogenesis of freedom. *Discourse Studies* 1(1): 31–58.

Martin, J. R. (1999b) Modelling context: a crooked path of progress in contextual linguistics (Sydney SFL). In M. Ghadessy [ed.] *Text and Context in Functional Linguistics*. Amsterdam: Benjamins, 25–61.

Martin, J. R. (2000a) Beyond exchange: appraisal systems in English. In Hunston and Thompson, 142–75.

Martin, J. R. (2000b) Close reading: functional linguistics as a tool for critical analysis. In Unsworth, 275–303.

Martin, J. R. (2000c) Design and practice: enacting functional linguistics in Australia. *Annual Review of Applied Linguistics* 20 (20th anniversary volume: *Applied Linguistics as an Emerging Discipline*): 116–26.

Martin, J. R. (2000d) Factoring out exchange: types of structure. M. Coulthard, J. Cotterill and F. Rock [eds] *Working with Dialogue*. Tubingen: Niemeyer, 19–40.

Martin, J. R. (2001a) Giving the game away: explicitness, diversity and genre-based literacy in Australia. In R. Wodak *et al.* [eds] *Functional Il/literacy*. Vienna: Verlag der Österreichischen Akademie der Wissenschaften, 155–74.

Martin, J. R. (2001b) A context for genre: modelling social processes in functional linguistics. In R. Stainton and J. Devilliers [eds] *Communication in Linguistics*. Toronto: GREF, 1–41.

Martin, J. R. (2002a) From little things big things grow: ecogenesis in school geography. In R. Coe, L. Lingard and T. Teslenko [eds] *The Rhetoric and Ideology of Genre: Strategies for Stability and Change*. Cresskill: Hampton Press, 243–71.

Martin, J. R. (2002b) Writing history: construing time and value in discourses of the past. In C. Colombi and M. Schleppergrell [eds] *Developing Advanced Literacy in First and Second Languages*. Mahwah: Erlbaum, 87–118.

Martin, J. R. (2002c) Blessed are the peacemakers: reconciliation and evaluation. In C. Candlin [ed.] *Research and Practice in Professional Discourse*. Hong Kong: City University of Hong Kong Press, 187–227.

Martin, J. R. (2003) Voicing the 'other': reading and writing Indigenous Australians. In G. Weiss and R. Wodak [eds] *Critical Discourse Analysis: theory and interdisciplinarity*. London. Palgrave, 199–219.

Martin, J. R. (2004a) Positive discourse analysis: power, solidarity and change. *Revista Canaria de Estudios Ingleses*, 49, 179–200.

Martin, J. R. (2004b) Negotiating difference: ideology and reconciliation. In M. Pütz, J. N. van Aertselaer and T. A. van Dijk (eds) *Communicating Ideologies: Language, Discourse and Social Practice*. Frankfurt: Peter Lang (Duisburg Papers on Research in Language and Culture), 85–177.

Martin, J. R. (2006) Vernacular deconstruction: undermining spin. *DELTA - Documentação de Estudos em Linguistica Teorica e Aplicada* 22.1, 177–203.

Martin, J. R. and G. Plum (1997) Construing experience: some story genres. *Journal of Narrative and Life History* 7(1–4) (Special Issue, 'Oral Versions of Personal Experience: Three Decades of Narrative Analysis', guest-edited by M. Bamberg): 299–308.

Martin, J. R. and D. Rose (2005) Designing Literacy Pedagogy: Scaffolding democracy in the classroom. In R. Hasan, C. M. I. M. Matthiessen, and J. Webster, (eds.) *Continuing Discourse on Language*. London: Equinox. (Spanish translation *Revista Signos*, 2005), 251–80.

Martin, J. R. and D. Rose (2006) *Genre Relations: mapping culture*. London: Equinox.

Martin, J. R. and M. Stenglin (2006) Materialising reconciliation: negotiating difference in a post-colonial exhibition. In T. Royce and W. Bowcher [eds] *New Directions in the Analysis of Multimodal Discourse*. Mahwah, New Jersey: Lawrence Erlbaum Associates, 215–38.

Martin, J. R. and R. Veel [eds] (1998) *Reading Science: Critical and Functional Perspectives on Discourses of Science*. London: Routledge.

Martin, J. R. and R. Wodak [eds] (2003) *Re/reading the Past: Critical and Functional Perspectives on Discourses of History*. Amsterdam: Benjamins.

Martineč, R. (1998) Cohesion in action. *Semiotica* 120 (1/2): 161–80.

Martineč, R. (2000a) Types of process in action. *Semiotica* 130(3/4): 243–68.

Martineč, R. (2000b) Rhythm in multimodal texts. *Leonardo* 33 (4): 289–97.

Martineč, R. and A. Salway (2005) A system for image-text relations in new (and old) media. *Visual Communication* 4.3, 337–71.

Matthiessen, C. M. I. M. (1993) Register in the round: diversity in a unified theory of register analysis. In M. Ghadessy [ed.] *Register Analysis: Theory and Practice*. London: Pinter, 221–92.

Matthiessen, C. M. I. M. (1995) *Lexicogrammatical Cartography: English Systems*. Tokyo: International Language Sciences Publishers.

Matthiessen, C. M. I. M. (in press) Combining clauses into clause complexes: a multi-faceted view. In J. Biber and M. Noonan [eds] *Complex Sentences in Grammar and Discourse: Essays in Honor of Sandra A. Thompson*. Amsterdam: Benjamins, 237–322.

Milton, G. (1999) *Nathaniel's Nutmeg: How One Man's Courage Changed the Course of History*. London: Hodder & Stoughton, 206–7.

Myers, G. (1989) The pragmatics of politeness in scientific articles. *Applied Linguistics* 10: 1–35.

Nesbitt, C. and G. Plum (1988) Probabilities in a systemic-functional grammar: the clause complex in English. In R. P. Fawcett and D. Young [eds] *New Developments in Systemic Linguistics. Vol. 2: Theory and Application*. London: Pinter, 6–38.

Ochs, E., E. A. Schegloff and S. A. Thompson [eds] (1996) *Interaction and Grammar*. Cambridge: Cambridge University Press.

Office of the President of South Africa (1995) *Promotion of National Unity and Reconciliation Act*, No. 1111. *http:/www.truth.org.za/*

O'Halloran, K. (2004) *Multimodal Discourse Analysis: systemic-functional perspectives*. London: Continuum.

Olson, D. (1994) *The World on Paper*. Cambridge: Cambridge University Press.

Ong, W. (1982) *Orality and Literacy: The Technologizing of the Word*. London: Methuen.

O'Toole, M. (1994) *The Language of Displayed Art*. London: Leicester University Press.

Painter, C. (1984) *Into the Mother Tongue: A Case Study of Early Language Development*. London: Pinter.

Painter, C. (1998) *Learning through Language in Early Childhood*. London: Cassell.

Paul Kelly and the Messengers (1991) *Comedy*. Sydney: Mushroom Records.

Peirce, C. (1955) *Philosophical Writings of Peirce*. Dover Publications: New York.

Pike, K. L. (1982) *Linguistic Concepts: An Introduction to Tagmemics*. Lincoln: University of Nebraska Press.

Poynton, C. (1985) *Language and Gender: Making the Difference*. Geelong: Deakin University Press. Republished London: Oxford University Press. 1989.

Quirk, R., S. Greenbaum, G. Leech and J. Svartvik (1985) *A Comprehensive Grammar of the English Language*. London: Longman.

Rafael, V. (1988) *Contracting Colonialism: Translation and Christian Conversion in Tagalog Society under Early Spanish Rule*. Manila: Ateneo de Manila University Press.

Rose, D. (1993) On Becoming: the grammar of causality in English and Pitjantjatjara. *Cultural Dynamics*, VI, 1–2, 42–83.

Rose, D. (1996) Pitjantjatjara Processes: an Australian grammar of experience. In R. Hasan, D. Butt and C. Cloran [eds] *Functional Descriptions: Language Form and Linguistic Theory*. Amsterdam: Benjamins, 287–322.

Rose, D. (1997) Science, technology and technical literacies. In Christie and Martin [eds] 40–72.

Rose, D. (1998) Science discourse and industrial hierarchy. In J. R. Martin and R. Veel [eds] 236–65.

Rose, D. (1999) Culture, Competence and Schooling: approaches to literacy teaching in Indigenous school education. In F. Christie [ed.], 217–45.

Rose, D. (2001a) *The Western Desert Code: an Australian cryptogrammar*. Canberra: Pacific Linguistics.

Rose, D. (2001b) Some variations in Theme across languages. *Functions of Language* 8.1, 109–45.

Rose, D. (2004a) The Structuring of Experience in the Grammar of Pitjantjatjara and English. In K. Davidse and L. Heyvaert [eds], *Functional Linguistics and Contrastive Description: Special issue of Languages in Contrast* 4:1, 45–74.

Rose, D. (2004b) Sequencing and Pacing of the Hidden Curriculum: how Indigenous children are left out of the chain. In J. Muller, A. Morais and B. Davies [eds] *Reading Bernstein, Researching Bernstein*. London: RoutledgeFalmer, 91–107.

Rose, D. (2004c) Pitjantjatjara: a metafunctional profile. In A. Caffarel, J. R. Martin and C. M. I. M. Matthiessen [eds] *Language Typology: a functional perspective*. Amsterdam: Benjamins, 479–537.

Rose, D. (2005a) Narrative and the Origins of Discourse: patterns of discourse semantics in stories around the world. *Australian Review of Applied Linguistics Series* S19, 151–73.

Rose, D. (2005b) Grammatical Metaphor. *Encyclopaedia of Language and Linguistics* 2nd Edition. Oxford: Elsevier, 15pp.

Rose, D. (2005c) Democratising the Classroom: a literacy pedagogy for the new generation. *Journal of Education*, Vol 37 (Durban: University of KwaZulu Natal), 127–64.

Rose, D. (2006a) A systemic functional model of language evolution. *Cambridge Archaeological Journal* 16:1, 73–96.

Rose, D. (2006b) Reading Genre: a new wave of analysis. *Linguistics and the Human Sciences*, 2:1, 25pp.

Rose, D. (2006c) *Scaffolding the English curriculum for Indigenous secondary students: Final Report for NSW 7–10 English Syllabus, Aboriginal Support Pilot Project*. Sydney: Office of the Board of Studies.

Rose, D. (in press a) Negotiating Kinship: interpersonal prosodies in Pitjantjatjara. *Word*, 20pp.

Rose, D. (in press b) Literacy and equality. Plenary for *Future Directions in Literacy* public lecture series. Faculty of Education and Social Work, University of Sydney.

Rose, D. (in press c) Towards a reading based theory of teaching. Plenary for the *33rd International Systemic Functional Linguistics Conference*, Sao Paulo 2006.

Rose, D. (to appear) History, Science and Dreams: Genres in Australian and European cultures. *Journal of Intercultural Communication*, 22p.

Rose, D. and C. Acevedo (2006) Closing the gap and accelerating learning in the Middle Years of Schooling *Australian Journal of Language and Literacy*, 14.2.

Rose, D. and C. Acevedo (in press) Designing literacy inservicing: Learning to Read: Reading to Learn. *Proceedings of the Australian Systemic Functional Linguistics Conference 2006*, University of New England.

Rose, D., D. McInnes and H. Korner (1992) Scientific Literacy (Literacy in Industry Research Project – Stage 1). Sydney: Metropolitan East Disadvantaged Schools Program (Equity Division, NSW Department of Education and Training).

Rose, D., L. Lui-Chivizhe, A. McKnight, and A. Smith (2004) Scaffolding Academic Reading and Writing at the Koori Centre. *Australian Journal of Indigenous Education*, 30th Anniversary edition, www.atsis.uq.edu.au/ajie, 41–9.

Rothery, J. and M. Stenglin (1997) Entertaining and instructing: exploring experience through story. In Christie and Martin, 231–63.

Rothery, J. and M. Stenglin (2000) Interpreting literature: the role of appraisal. In Unsworth, 222–44.

Silkstone, B. (1994) *Australian Reptiles: Lizards.* Sydney: Longman Cheshire.

Stenglin, M. and R. Iedema (2001) How to analyse visual images: a guide for TESOL teachers. In A. Burns and C. Coffin [eds] *Analysing English in a Global Context: A Reader.* London: Routledge, 194–208.

Thibault, P. (1987) An interview with Michael Halliday. In R. Steele and T. Threadgold [eds] *Language Topics: Essays in Honour of Michael Halliday. Vol. 2.* Amsterdam: Benjamins, 599–627.

Tickner, R. (2001) *Taking a Stand: Land Rights to Reconciliation.* Sydney: Allen & Unwin.

Tsavdaridis, N. (2001) TURNED AWAY 'We have a lot of sick people on board. These people are in really bad shape'. *The Daily Telegraph* 28-08-2001, 1.

Tutu, D. (1999) *No Future without Forgiveness.* London: Rider.

Unsworth, L. [ed.] (2000) *Researching Language in Schools and Communities: Functional Linguistic Perspectives.* London: Cassell.

van Leeuwen, T. (1999) *Speech, Music, Sound.* London: Macmillan.

van Leeuwen, T. and C. Jewitt (2001) *Handbook of Visual Analysis.* London: Sage.

Veenendal, L. (1996) Testimony of Leonard Veenendal: Truth and Reconciliation Commission (Case No. MR/146).

Ventola, E. (1987) *The Structure of Social Interaction: A Systemic Approach to the Semiotics of Service Encounters.* London: Pinter.

Walkerdine, V. and H. Lucey (1989) *Democracy in the Kitchen: Regulating Mothers and Socialising Daughters.* London: Virago.

Whittaker, R., M. O'Donnell & A. McCabe (eds) 2006 *Language and Literacy: Functional Approaches.* London: Continuum.

Whitaker, R. and E. Sienaert [eds] (1986) *Oral Tradition and Literacy: Changing Visions of the World.* Durban: Natal University Oral Documentation and Research Centre.

Wodak, R. (1996) *Disorders of Discourse.* London: Longman.

Young, L. and C. Harrison [eds] (2004) *Systemic functional linguistics and critical discourse analysis: studies in social change.* London; New York: Continuum.

Index

Lightning Source UK Ltd.
Milton Keynes UK
UKOW01f1417090915

258336UK00006B/191/P